Effective Small Group Communication in Theory and Practice

Effective Small Group Communication in Theory and Practice

Mary Ann Renz
Central Michigan University

John B. Greg
St. John's University

Allyn and Bacon

Boston • London • Toronto • Sydney • Tokyo • Singapore

Vice president: *Paul A. Smith*
Series Editor: *Karen Bowers*
Series Editorial Assistant: *Scout Reilly*
Marketing manager: *Jackie Aaron*
Composition and prepress buyer: *Linda Cox*
Manufacturing buyer: *Megan Cochran*
Cover Administrator: *Linda Knowles*
Editorial-Production Service: *Shepherd, Inc.*
Electronic Composition: *Shepherd, Inc.*

Copyright © 2000 by Allyn & Bacon
A Pearson Education Company
Needham Heights, Massachusetts 02494

Internet: www.abacon.com

Library of Congress Cataloging–in–Publication Data
Renz, Mary Ann.
    Effective small group communication in theory and practice / by
Mary Ann Renz, and John B. Greg.
        p.   cm.
    Includes bibliographical references.
    ISBN 0–205–28201–6
    1. Small groups. 2.   Communcation in small groups.
    I. Greg, John B, 1940–   II. Title.
HM736.R45   1999
302.3'4—dc21

                                                                99–26149
                                                                    CIP

Printed in the United States of America.

10 9 8 7 6 5 4 3 2 1   04 03 02 01 00 99

TABLE OF CONTENTS

PREFACE

An Introduction to Your Book

You are beginning the study of small group communication. Throughout your study, you will work in one or more small groups to do brief exercises and to complete other, larger projects. You might consider this experience to be an internship in small group communication because, like any internship, it provides a chance to put into practice the information you learn.

Perhaps you are approaching your work in small groups eagerly. If so, you may already know that working with others in a group can allow you to accomplish more than you could by yourself as each of you contributes resources of time, knowledge, and contacts in addressing an issue of joint concern. You may have noticed that the quality of your work increases when others challenge your suggestions and then you work out the best possible solution together. Moreover, you may have found that others in a group motivate you, either with direct encouragement or just by making working together enjoyable.

On the other hand, some people approach work in a small group with concern. Maybe you are one of them. If so, you may have had experiences with groups in which other members took advantage of you, leaving you responsible for more than your share of the work. Your groups may have had trouble reaching agreements. You may have been frustrated by the amount of time your group took to complete its tasks. These are some of the problems that groups frequently face, and your groups now are not immune to them. However, as you develop

- an ability to discriminate between those situations in which group members should work together or independently,
- an understanding of the forces at work within a small group,
- skill in the behaviors most helpful to groups,
- and knowledge of the strategies groups can use and the circumstances under which each is most helpful,

then you will be better able to influence the outcome of your group's activity in a positive way. This book is designed to help you in that venture.

Several features of this book were conceived to help you learn important concepts about small group communication and increase your ability to apply them. First, each chapter begins with one or more **narratives** about real individuals in actual groups. You will share their troubles and triumphs. Some of them are students who were in college classes. Others are groups and group members at work in varied jobs. Some are members of groups they joined for pleasure; others became involved when an important issue presented itself to them, calling forth their involvement. The variety of examples is purposeful because, whatever your career goals and life plans, you are likely to be working in groups some of the time. You will hear the story of these groups and group members because each one has learned something from experience that can benefit you. Talking to the individuals has been important to us, too. For example, we had not planned to discuss parliamentary procedure in this book, feeling that it is a topic more relevant to large groups than to small. Yet, when preparing Chapter 8, we talked to Al Lewis about managing effective group meetings; he mentioned how important a knowledge of parliamentary procedure was to him in leading meetings. Talking to others afterward reinforced the idea that individuals can contribute more effectively even to small groups if they have some understanding of procedural rules. Therefore we added information that comes from the basic concepts of parliamentary procedure to that chapter. When we interviewed people who talked about negative experiences in groups or negative attitudes toward groups, we included that information. As a result, the information you find in the following pages is not sugarcoated; it will be more useful to you, we believe, because it is realistic. The most important point to be made about the narratives, however, is that we have used them to illustrate the concepts developed in the chapter that follows. By reading the narratives, you will have a shared foundation that can be built upon in the rest of the chapter.

Second, each chapter integrates information that members of contemporary groups need to know: results of recent research on small group behavior, including information about the impacts of technology and culturally diverse members, and information that is less recent but still current about the critical thinking skills necessary in groups. Technology represents an opportunity for group members, but it is an opportunity that can also alter the group in some significant ways. Throughout the book, you will encounter sections identified as **Technology Notes.** They make particular application of the concepts being discussed at that point in the chapter to groups that use E-mail, fax, teleconferences, or computer-assisted programs in their work.

Just as increased use of technology has an important impact on groups, so does the increasingly diverse membership within groups. Diverse group members enhance the group experience at the same time that they increase the potential for misunderstandings to occur. References to the impact of culture on group members are integrated throughout the chapters, because those influences affect every aspect of the group process. The information this book includes should make you more conscious of the impact of these contemporary forces on small group activity.

Both of us were introduced to small group communication as a tool to improve critical thinking. Some communication scholars believe that because small groups are not always effective deliberative bodies, it would make more sense to tell you just how groups *do* behave, rather than how they *ought* to behave. We reject that position. You can perform as ineffective members of small groups without any further learning. We assume, instead, that you are embarking on a study of small group communication so that you can learn how to be as effective a small group member as you can be. Therefore, throughout the chapters of this book, we encourage you to adopt the behaviors of thorough, thoughtful decision makers, for effective deliberation is of critical importance to members of contemporary small groups.

Although most of the information in this book is based on very recent research, not all that we know about groups has been discovered in the past decade. This book also incorporates results from some of the significant research done in the early years of studying small group communication. We believe that your understanding of groups will be deeper if you know about both the foundations of research in small group communication and its more recent directions.

Besides the use of narratives and the inclusion of key concepts relevant to contemporary groups, a third feature of this book is that each chapter asks you to consider the ethical impact of group members' behaviors. Too often we do not stop to think about how our behaviors affect our group's ability to function in a moral manner. We ask you to stop periodically for some **Ethical Considerations.** In later chapters, the Ethical Considerations often raise questions for you to consider; but many of the Ethical Considerations, particularly those in earlier chapters, take a pretty firm position, despite the fact that ethical issues are not always clear-cut. You may want to disagree with the positions taken in the text; in fact, we encourage you to debate these positions. But you should know that three broad principles underlie the ethical positions we have taken:

1. Because groups are composed of individuals in relationships with one another, we take the position that ethical behaviors are those that respect the dignity of each individual as a human being and that thereby allow group members to continue to trust one another. Behaviors designed to hurt another group member violate the dignity of that person and destroy trust.
2. Because groups function within the "real world," we take the position that ethical behaviors are those that encourage the discovery and reasonable interpretation of relevant data. Behaviors designed to frustrate this "search for the truth" distort group members' understanding of others and the worlds they share.
3. Because groups are involved in making decisions, we take the position that ethical behaviors are those that allow group members to make informed decisions freely. Behaviors that limit the freedom of group members to speak and decide among alternatives interfere with this basic tenet of a democratic society.

As you consider whether you agree with our positions, and as you answer the questions we have posed for you, we encourage you to keep these principles in mind.

A fourth feature of this book is that a discussion of **relevant communication theory** is integrated into most chapters to help explain how groups function or why they function as they do. You may be a student who is taking a small group communication class as part of a major or minor in communication. If so, you may also be required to take a class in communication theory. It should please you to know that there is a relationship between the two classes, because communication theory applies to the small group context, just as it does to interpersonal relationships, organizational behavior, and public communication. If you are not (yet) planning to major or minor in communication, then this may be your only chance to explore the interesting (and useful) theories that explain the communication processes we use every day. We do not often stop to consider them in a thoughtful way, but now is your chance to do so. If this book focused only on communication theory, then you would read here about the challenges theorists have directed toward some of the theories. You might want to look elsewhere to discover some of those challenges if a particular theory catches your interest, because in this book only the basic concepts of the theories are introduced. Our assumption is that the perspective offered by the theory is useful in providing insight into some element of small group functioning. You should be able to look at small group communication in a new way with each theoretical discussion you read.

The chapters in the book do not need to be read in the order they are printed, but the book is designed to consider the issues groups normally face. Because groups develop along many levels at the same time, there may be developments in your group that you will understand better by reading some material in this book out of sequence. Our hope is that this book, along with your own experiences in groups, will serve to make your internship in small group communication a success.

You are most likely to experience success if you keep a journal of your group experiences. Keep a thorough record of what is happening in your group and evaluate the developments. Are they positive? Or, is there room for improvement? Do not stop at this point. Take the time to explain what is happening in your group by applying the concepts developed in this book to your own experiences. Then try to figure out how to improve your group experiences. If a problem crops up in your group, you permit it to grow by doing nothing to change the circumstances. Read the book—sometimes looking ahead for relevant material you might not have expected to read until later—so that you can identify some strategies that could be used to resolve the problems your group faces. Make some prescriptions, and then keep track of what outcomes developed from following your prescriptions. Only then will you be able to determine what works for you in a small group and what you will need to do to transfer your learning from this group to the other groups you will be in throughout your life. It is not easy to observe your own behaviors in a small group at the same time that you participate in the group's activities. Nonetheless, if you are able to be introspective about your group while being active within it, then your internship in small group communication will be a success.

If that is the outcome of your use of this book, then it is because of a large group of people who deserve our thanks. We owe a personal debt to mentors like George Bohman, who taught us how rich the field of speech communication is; to George Ziegelmueller, who models the role of an extraordinary communication professional: committed, probing, and humane; and to David Ling for engaging dialogues about ideas.

We want to acknowledge those who affected the development of the book itself: the students at Central Michigan University, who used the book as it was being developed; our own colleagues such as Janet Yerby, whose reading of early chapters provided suggestions for improvement and the encouragement to continue; a former student, Mary Rae Bonato, whose experiences as a visual learner enhanced the visual elements of this book; the editorial staff at Allyn and Bacon and the reviewers—Ruth M. Guzley, California State University-Chico; Nan Peck, Northern Virginia Community College; Barbara J. Holmes, University of Colorado at Denver; Charles Griffin, Kansas State University; Janie Harden Fritz, Duquesne University; Joseph M. Mazza, Central Missouri State University—whose reading of the text was careful and whose comments led us to strengthen the book; and colleagues at other universities—Ernest Bormann, Marshall Scott Poole, Carolyn

Anderson, and Randy Hirokawa—who responded willingly when asked for information about their work, for clarification of their ideas, or permission to include in the Appendix scales they developed. Our debt is especially great to the people who made themselves available to be interviewed for the narratives in these chapters. Among them are family members, friends, friends of friends, present and former students and colleagues, and individuals we had read about in national publications. Not only did each contribute time to this project, but the stories they have told of their experiences are central to the spirit of this book. To all of these people, we extend our gratitude.

Effective Small Group Communication in Theory and Practice

1 The Nature and Uses of Small Groups

CHAPTER OBJECTIVES

After reading this chapter, you should be able to

- Define a "small group"
- Apply the characteristics of systems to small groups
- Recognize the factors that account for variations among groups
- Explain why individuals join groups
- Identify the functions served by groups
- Distinguish tasks most appropriate for groups from those appropriate for individuals

The Narratives

Melissa Scram, 19, is a sophomore at New York University, majoring in journalism. She describes the role groups played during her first year at college:

> *Even before I got my letter of admission to NYU, I got a letter inviting me to join a Scholars Group. The top 5% of students in the College of Arts and Sciences are placed in one of the three Scholars Groups, each headed by a dean. We had to take an honors seminar as freshmen and do community service. We got free tickets to plays and were invited to a Scholars lecture series. We could also go on trips for a small fee—$200 to go to Spain last year. I'm still in the Scholars Group. I've met a few people through the group, but not that many, which surprises me. We've gone on trips together, but everyone still seems to be kind of separated.*
>
> *Last year, as a freshman, I went to the annual club fair. They had blocked off the street between the library and the student center. All the clubs had tables, and members were handing out literature, trying to get people to sign up. I signed up for two or three clubs. The Philosophy Club sounded interesting. I thought I probably wouldn't have time to take classes in philosophy, but the club would be an opportunity to get a little knowledge, have fun, and meet people. I tried to go to the first meeting. I went to find the room, and it didn't exist. That ended that. I did join the orchestra. I found out about that because I was interested in it. I went to the Center for Music Performance and said, "I'm a violinist, and I want to audition."*

Then, second semester, I started writing for the newspaper. I only wrote four times that semester. This year I'm an assistant in the news department for the independent student paper, the Washington Square News. *There's a hierarchical structure, so we know exactly what we're supposed to be doing. Having a clear purpose is important. We work on many tasks individually, but for a group cause, which seems to be working pretty well. It's been a lot of work, but I'm really enjoying it. It's made me firmer about my decision to go into newspaper journalism, because now I know what's involved.*

Last year I had two classes that included assignments to work on projects in groups. The first was my freshman honors seminar, called The University and the Community. *We were setting up a hypothetical settlement house. There were four groups in the class. One had to put together programs; one had to deal with finances; another group dealt with bureaucratic issues. My group was responsible for the mission and goals of the settlement house. There were about four people in that group, and we met during class and tried to meet outside of class. But we would meet for the group, and people would forget the times. I didn't really enjoy that project, in part because we didn't have a purpose that was clearly defined. Also, there were two strongly opinionated people in the group who would argue about everything. They ended up in gridlock. Another student and I would say, "What's the point? We're not accomplishing anything."*

In the other class, Media in America, *we had to write a paper, and we could do it in a group with two or three people. So I did it with my suitemate. We each wrote ten pages independently. We wrote the introduction and conclusion together, and we'd get together to discuss our hypothesis. I think smaller groups work better. At least, that group worked smoothly. First, since we were suitemates, meeting together wasn't difficult. We stayed focused on the assignment. It was great to have somebody to bounce ideas off of and to sit there and theorize with about what would happen.*

I also have an informal group of friends. There is a core of about six or seven people. It varies. A lot of us live near each other. Our activities usually start with somebody dropping in and saying, "What's up for tonight?" Sometimes deciding what to do takes a while. We all want to do something, but I don't want to spend a lot of money. So we do a lot of wandering around the city, because it's entertaining. There is some interdependence among the friends, not as much for the group as a whole as for individual relationships. In high school, I was always the cynic in the corner of the classroom. My friends here seem to be sort of the same. We're all sort of wacky and weird. They're all like me, in a way, but they're all very different, too—all very diverse. But I guess that's New York!

David Sebastianelli, 37, is Vice President of Sales and Marketing for the Cooper Instrument Corporation, based in Connecticut. He has worked there for eight years. During that time, the company's use of teams has grown. He describes the way work teams function in his job:

Our company is very team oriented. For nearly every situation, whether it's an opportunity or a problem, a team will be assigned to work on it. At times, there may be four or five teams working at once. We're using teams a lot more than we used to, an evolution that comes directly from our president. Part of her management initiative is to empower the workforce, using a reverse pyramid method that literally turns the organizational chart upside down. This ensures that everyone has a part in finding solutions and in improving efficiency.

On the sales and marketing team, I'm typically the leader of the group. I take the leader's role because, as head of the departments, I'm ultimately responsible for the decision and accountable for the outcome. In sales and marketing, we have to be extremely proactive. The market is in a constant state of change, and we have to react to it quickly. Our sales and marketing teams are comprised of members who all have a vested interest in the results and also expertise in marketing and sales plans and programs. Our team meetings are often informal. Our focus is on quick, effective results.

Our company also uses cross-functional teams, usually with six or seven members. Right now, I'm on a team that's made up of people from engineering and from maintenance, operators from the floor, someone from shipping, and me. We're tackling a degreasing problem. Many of our component parts have to be thoroughly cleaned before assembly can take place. The EPA has already restricted many of the solvents used in the degreasing process, due to the long-term negative health effects associated with overexposure to the solvents. There are other methods available, such as aqueous systems (using soap and water), but the effectiveness of these systems isn't yet clear. The team is investigating the subject from many different angles, including environmental and community issues, potential future liability, and alternatives to our present system.

Groups are important in problem solving, because people take ownership of a solution, especially when it has come from their participation in the group. A successful result gives those team members a sense of pride and worth.

I do have some reservations about the use of independent work groups. Sometimes the group process becomes very convoluted. A problem that could be solved quickly with a focused effort by the people trained to deal with it can drag on for months if a team approach is used, since that requires choosing the work team, establishing consistent meeting periods, electing a facilitator and a scribe, and rehearsing a presentation. Those are all time-consuming activities that do not draw the group closer to a solution. The group can slow down the results. For someone like me, who is action oriented, that can be frustrating. Also, if a team has responsibility for making every decision, including some that are no-brainers, then people are being pulled away from their jobs unnecessarily. In a manufacturing environment, this translates into decreases in efficiency and productivity and increases in costs. There will be additional costs if the workers need to work overtime to accomplish their primary tasks.

Another possible problem is that the results of teamwork can be watered down by the management. Then the attitudes of the people on the team will sour, and the effort will be viewed as another empty initiative. One thing is certain: if the decision is made to employ problem-solving and improvement teams, management must be ready to support the decisions of the teams.

Everett Grambort, 84, moved to Bella Vista, Arkansas, after retiring from his job as a school diagnostician. He had begun work in that career when he retired from the Army. He describes his membership in small groups in his retirement community:

There are four small groups I have joined in Bella Vista. The first is a tennis group of eight retirees ranging in age from 65 to 84. We play tennis doubles. I joined the tennis group because I am athletically inclined. As a boy and young man, I enjoyed basketball and baseball, but I was never exposed to tennis. Now I find that tennis has the benefits of exercise, companionship, and sportsmanship.

I belong to a mixed (two men and two women) bowling team. We bowl twice each week, September through March. As a teenager I established a lifelong interest in bowling. I enjoy the fellowship with other bowlers, the exercise, and the maintenance of physical skill that depends on timing and coordination.

I belong to a social duplicate contract bridge group, which meets once each week, and also a three-table bridge group that meets once a month. I learned a little about contract bridge from my older sisters when I was 18. I didn't play for the next ten years, but then I played endlessly during my travels on troop transports throughout my military service, mostly during World War II. I've always recognized that bridge is the world's best card game. It's challenging and mentally stimulating. Generally, during the auction and play of the hand, players may not communicate with their partners by words, gestures, or even by changes in facial expression. Here, in Bella Vista, I had some instruction, and I began to develop greater skill. Then I was able to teach bridge to other retirees. Through teaching others, I became a better player and a more skillful analyst of the game. I've been a member of a small informal social duplicate bridge group for about 15 years.

Finally, I am a lifetime member of The Retired Officers Association (TROA). I joined because the national organization protects the interests of its members and supports the military establishment and the national defense. I am a charter member of the local chapter of TROA, formed about 16 years ago. I was asked to be an officer of the chapter, and I agreed to be a member of the nine-member board of directors. Later, I was asked to chair the activities committee. After conducting a survey of schools and organized groups to determine what activity would be desirable and feasible, I organized a group of speakers from our membership. The speakers made presentations in their areas of expertise before elementary and secondary school classes throughout the county. The group gained national notice. Later I became chairman of the legislative committee of the chapter. Our committee successfully lobbied the governor (Governor Clinton) and the state legislature for a change in state law to restore tax exemptions that had been lost by military retirees after our arrival in Arkansas. I am no longer a member of the board, but I served as a member for several years.

There are some groups I have chosen not to join, such as service clubs that raise money to support their charitable efforts and secret fraternal organizations. I have known just a few of their members and have not been favorably impressed. I haven't joined the Eighteen Holers Men's Golf Association. They all ride in golf carts, and golf is intended to be a walking game.

If I hadn't joined any groups in Bella Vista, I would not have fulfilled my potential as a contributing member of the community. Perhaps 2,000 people in Bella Vista recognize me, call me by name, and are friendly with me and with my wife. Most of them took bridge lessons from me, but many know me from tennis, from bowling, from TROA, and from playing bridge. Had I not joined in any of the group activities, my life would have been less interesting.

Small Groups: What Are They?

You have just met three individuals at very different points in their lives. Yet each is a member of several small groups. A **small group** is *a small number of humans, drawn together through interaction, whose interdependent relationships allow them to achieve a mutual goal.* If you consider the definition more carefully, you will notice four key concepts: the size of the group, the interaction between members, the mutual goal, and the members' interdependence.

Size

The exact limits on the size of a small group have been the subject of some disagreement. Although there are writers who set the lower end of the limit at two members, most communication scholars agree that communication between two people (a dyad) is quite different from communication among three or more people.

If you have ever looked forward to dinnertime conversation with one close friend and then had to adjust as a third person (even another close friend) joined you, you understand the difference from experience. Your communication probably became less personal or intimate. It became more difficult to manage the rules for turn taking in the conversation and less likely that all of you could participate equally. It is no wonder that Melissa described her experience working on a project with her suitemate as much easier than working with a larger group. However, by our definition, Melissa and her suitemate would not be considered a "group," even though their cooperative action on the project was very similar to the activities a group would have undertaken.

The presence of a third person (or a small group) is not automatically frustrating or disappointing. In fact, it is possible that the conversation of a small group becomes livelier and less stressful than the conversation of a dyad. The point is only that because the qualities of the interaction change when communication is no longer dyadic, the two situations constitute two distinct communication contexts; therefore, to be considered a small group, there must be at least three members.

Setting the upper limit on group size is difficult, even though there is general agreement that five to seven members is an ideal size for a group. Some writers use the general standard that if a group gets too large, it will subdivide into subgroups. However, that standard runs into problems, because groups as small as four to six members may divide into two subgroups to accomplish some tasks. Those who offer a specific number as an upper limit mention between 12 and 20 (Rothwell, 1992); from 12 to 15 (Cathcart, Samovar, & Henman, 1996); and 11, 12, 14, or 25 (Brilhart & Galanes, 1995).

The trouble with setting a specific upper limit on the size of a small group is that other factors (particularly task, time, and amount of interaction) influence the limit. With some tasks, it seems as if group interaction is too strained by having as "many" as 7 members for a group of that size to be deemed ideal, whereas other groups may struggle to accomplish their task with "only" 15 members. In addition to task, time can interact with size. A class of 20 students can, over the course of a semester, meld itself into a small group. Early on, however, even classes of much smaller size would not designate themselves a group. And for some classes, or other collections of people, a sense of being a small group will never occur if they are constrained in their abilities to communicate with one another.

Rather than setting a hard-and-fast number, a more useful way of thinking about the upper size limit is the standard that Brilhart and Galanes (1995) use: "a group small enough that each member is aware of and able to recall each other member" (p. 7). As long as each member has an impression of the other members, then the communication of any member can be adapted to the others.

Interaction

Imagine walking into an elevator car and glancing at the four other passengers. Quickly you gather an impression of your fellow passengers. You move into a corner, turn to face the door, and lift your eyes to watch as the number of the floor

Technology Note: Must Interaction Be Face-to-Face?

Earlier writers have stipulated that group members must communicate in face-to-face interaction. However, contemporary technology makes it possible for individuals at some distance from each other to communicate quickly and to provide feedback to others' messages. In fact, Lipnack and Stamps (1997) claim that "we are experiencing the most dramatic change in the nature of the small group since humans acquired the capacity to talk to one another" (p. 40).

Other writers have studied the impact of electronic media on group communication. Farmer and Hyatt (1994) found that the groups they studied who used audio conferencing had more difficulty with decision making than face-to-face groups, but those groups that shared computer screens in the decision-making tasks fared as well as face-to-face groups did. Straus (1996) found that small groups completing a problem-solving task using computer conferences had patterns of interaction or performance that did not differ substantially from those of groups completing the task through face-to-face interaction. Valacich, George, Nunamaker, and Vogel (1994) found that in the group they studied, computer assistance allowed a distributed group to work effectively. And so, apparently, individuals linked by E-mail, Internet connections, or video lines can communicate fully and with the ease previously thought to exist only in face-to-face interaction.

changes. Although the five of you fit the size requirements for a small group, you qualify only as a collection of people. A small group requires communication among its members. Even though the contract bridge groups to which Everett belongs limit their interaction during some parts of play, members talk about a hand after it has been played and socialize before, between, and after games, so they do communicate and qualify as small groups.

Mutual Goal

The force that brings many groups into existence is a goal shared by the group's members. The desire to do well on an upcoming exam motivates the formation of a study group. Safety needs motivate the formation of a neighborhood watch group. An interest in keeping mentally or physically active led Everett to his membership in bridge clubs, bowling leagues, and tennis groups. Sharing a mutual goal is important in giving a small group a sense of direction. In fact, Melissa mentioned that the absence of a clear goal was a problem for one of the classroom groups she described.

It is possible for members of a group to have additional goals that differ from member to member. Suppose Everett had had the personal goal of meeting then-Governor Clinton when he worked on changing Arkansas tax laws on retirement income. It would not have been necessary for everyone in the group to have that same goal; as long as the group shared the goal of trying to get the tax laws changed, they shared a mutual goal.

A small group is drawn together through interaction. (Photo compliments of the Isabella County Commission on Aging.)

Ethical Consideration

Individuals joining a group must be honest with themselves and with the other group members about their commitment to the group goal. If you have no interest in the goal of a group, but join anyway because the group helps you achieve your personal goal, then you are using the group's resources unfairly.

Interdependence

When a cross-functional work team is formed, employees who work in different areas of the company come together to resolve a problem that affects all of them. They rely on each other, because each member has different knowledge and experience. The degreaser team that David mentioned needs to have information on mechanical issues, equipment operation, marketing, engineering, and shipping. Because their task requires them to depend on each other, they work together as a group. Even the news group Melissa mentioned, which does quite a bit of its work independently, pulls together to plan and publish the paper.

It is possible for individuals to have parallel goals that can be achieved without interdependent behaviors. For instance, students in a class might each have the goal of passing the class. If they can achieve their goals independently, they will not be bound in a group. Sharing a mutual goal requires group members to depend on others, whether for their support, their insight, or their hard work.

Ethical Consideration

As a member of a group, you will depend on others, but they must also be able to depend on you. If you cannot or will not fulfill your responsibilities to a group, then you should not join it. If you are required to be a member of a group, then you automatically must accept the corollary requirement to contribute to the group's effort.

Small Groups as Systems: A Theoretical Perspective

As interdependent and goal-oriented bodies, small groups are considered, by definition, to be systems. We define a **system** as *a body composed of interdependent members, which adapts to changes in the environment while working to achieve a goal.* A systems approach to small group communication represents the application of a theory that originated in another field entirely.

Systems theory has been traced to 1928, when a book titled *Modern Theories of Development (Kritische Theorie der Formbildung)* was published. The author, Ludwig von Bertalanffy, was a young biologist who had received his doctorate from the University of Vienna two years earlier. Von Bertalanffy argued that biologists should not just study organs in isolation, but instead should attempt to discover the laws of biological systems at all levels.

The field of biology benefited from von Bertalanffy's systems approach. It led to the development of equations on animal growth used in fisheries throughout the world and of a means for early detection of cancer. However, von Bertalanffy did not focus only on biology. He also studied psychology, philosophy, and the origin of Italy's postal service in the fifteenth century (Lazlo, 1972). Integrating his observations from all these areas, von Bertalanffy proposed a theory of interdisciplinary systems in his 1968 book, *General Systems Theory.*

Three years later, scholars from the fields of biology, physiology, economics, psychiatry, psychology, education, philosophy, and communication met at a symposium in Geneseo, New York, to honor von Bertalanffy on the occasion of his seventieth birthday and to recognize the contributions of systems theory to their disciplines (Lazlo, 1972). For over two decades, small group communication scholars have recognized the relevance of systems theory to their field. The definitional overlap between small groups and systems is clear: both are goal oriented, and the members of both are interdependent. The goal orientation of a small group system is similar to that of the human respiratory system, which accomplishes the goal of supplying oxygen to human cells and removing carbon dioxide from them. Because systems work to achieve a goal (for which the Greek word is *telos*), they are said to be **teleological** or *goal oriented.* Small group members are interdependent much as the parts of the respiratory system are: all must work together if the system is to achieve its goal. We can better understand the way groups function if we understand some additional characteristics of systems: the complementary principles of nonsummativity and wholeness, the structure of systems, and the nature of change within systems.

Two Complementary Principles: Nonsummativity and Wholeness

The inherent interdependence of system components is the basis of two complementary principles of systems: nonsummativity and wholeness. The first, **nonsummativity,** is a principle that reminds us that *a system is different from the sum of its parts.* It might be tempting to think that a group composed of skilled members will naturally be successful while one composed of previously less successful members will automatically struggle. However, according to the principle of nonsummativity, we cannot simply add (or sum) the parts of a system to understand its whole. We know that an individual in isolation behaves differently than he or she does as a member of a given group. Then, when the individual joins a different group, his or her behavior will change again. The interdependence of the group members affects the interactions among them, and it is their interactions that are important in a system. When the parts of a system interact to create a product that could not have been produced by the individual members acting alone, it is described as the result of **synergy** (Salazar, 1995).

Sports teams have come to understand the principle of nonsummativity. A team may pay exorbitant salaries to buy star players, but if the star players do not interact well with each other, then (despite the tremendous investment) the end product may be something "less" than the sum of its parts, which is sometimes described as **negative synergy.** In contrast, a team of less talented players can perform better than anyone could have expected if something clicks for the team. Then the team is something "more" than the sum of its parts, demonstrating **positive synergy.** In both cases, though, the team is *different from the sum of its parts.* Thus, in both cases, the systems are characterized by nonsummativity. Due to the system quality of nonsummativity, if we want to understand how a particular group functions, we will not focus on the individual members of the group. Instead, we will pay attention to the interactions among the group members.

The second principle that is directly derived from member interdependence is the principle of **wholeness,** which states that *"every part of the system is so related to every other part that a change in a particular part causes a change in all the other parts and in the total system"* (Hall & Fagen, 1975, p. 59). To understand the nature of wholeness, suppose that one of the members of Everett's bridge group becomes ill. In that situation, the group would not be able to continue to play as it had. The group would either need to suspend its normal rules of play or have another person fill in. Even if a substitute could be found, the play of the group would be affected. Perhaps the substitute would be more (or less) skilled than the member who was ill. Perhaps the substitute would balance the competitive elements against the social elements differently than the absent member had. As they adjusted to the substitute, the behaviors of the other players would change. In short, the illness of one group member would affect all of the other members.

Consider also Melissa Scram's report of her classroom group in which two members were regularly deadlocked. Imagine what would happen if one of them took a more moderate position. The likelihood is that the other opinionated group member

Ethical Consideration

Because your own concerns will have an impact on the group, you do the group a disservice if you have a personal agenda that you conceal from the group.

---

would feel comfortable backing down a bit, too. Then, if the other members now gained hope about the possibility of reaching an agreement, they would both begin to increase their involvement. Because groups are characterized by wholeness, a change in one member of the group brings change to every member. The principle of wholeness should lead you to expect that the attitudes and concerns you bring to a group meeting will have an impact on others in the group, just as you will be impacted by the behaviors of other group members.

The Structure of Systems

A system has a boundary around it that makes it possible to identify what is part of the system and what is not. Identifying the boundary is difficult for those teams that communicate primarily by electronic means, since membership in the team (those people who are communicating with one another) may change as the task needs change (Lipnack & Stamps, 1997). Even for groups that meet face-to-face, however, the task is complicated by the fact that there are differences in the permeability of systems' boundaries. No system is free from outside influences. Instead, each system interacts with its environment. Because of its relationship with the environment, each system may actually be a subsystem of another, more encompassing system. Consider the degreaser team at Cooper Instrument Corporation that David Sebastianelli described in the opening narrative. David's work as a member of the team would be influenced by his other assignments in the sales and marketing division. The outside environment for the team—what can be called the **suprasystem**—would include the company as a whole and other groups of workers at the company, other companies that have an interest in the product, the Environmental Protection Agency (which has an interest in the degreasing option the team selects), and even the public as a whole. Groups will vary in the amount of interaction between the system and the environment, along a continuum of openness from a closed group to an open group.

In some groups, efforts are made to limit the amount of influence the outside environment has on the group. Those groups are relatively **closed** systems. If you are in a group that does not seek information from sources outside the group, but relies instead on the information members of the group had when the group first formed, and that does not seek evaluation of its work from outsiders, then you are in a group that is relatively closed. The problem is that there is some natural decay within any system, but in a closed system, with no corrective for that natural process, the system deteriorates.

An **open** system, on the other hand, encourages interaction between the system and the environment, in the process correcting the system's tendency toward decay. The degreaser team at Cooper Instruments fits at the open end of the continuum. By seeking information from outsiders on the environmental, political, and legal impacts of their possible choices, the team will utilize the connections between the system and the outside environment. There are still boundaries around the system. Team members know who is a member of the team and who is outside the team, so the system is not entirely open. There are unlikely to be any systems that are pure examples of openness or closedness; groups will vary in their placement along the openness continuum. Moreover, a group's position on that continuum can change over time as its interaction with the outside environment varies.

The structure of a system does not end at its boundary. A system may also have within it subsystems. For instance, Melissa Scram mentioned in the opening narrative that the staff of the *Washington Square News* is composed of subsystems organized hierarchically. A portion of the structure could be visualized as shown in Figure 1.1. A hierarchical structure of a system depicts the distribution of power from the top of the hierarchy to the bottom. Figure 1.1 suggests that the greatest power is in the hands of the news editor, moderate power in the hands of the news associates and assistants, and least power in the hands of the staff writers and contributing writers. Figure 1.1 suggests that subsystem divisions may be quite rigid (so that some staff writers are responsible to only one of the news assistants), but within some organizations there are no such rigid separations. A writer might be given assignments by two different individuals, creating a situation in which the writer would be pulled in two directions at once.

In fact, even if group members do not overlap the subsystems within a given hierarchical structure, they are seldom members of only a single system. McGrath (1991) described this as the "partial nesting" of group members: "partial nesting means that a given individual is ordinarily not a member of one and only one group but, rather, is a member of multiple groups at any one time" (p. 152). Therefore, each member of any group can be torn between the goals of different systems to which the member belongs at the same time. Rosen (1989) described workers caught at a point of conflicting group goals, including a man who was a member of both a conservation group and a work group in a factory that was polluting a local stream. He valued both his job and a clean water supply, but chose to report his factory for its pollution. Because each of us is only partially nested in any group to which we belong, we are subject to similar conflicts whenever the values or behaviors of groups to which we are loyal begin to clash.

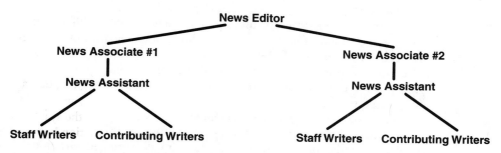

FIGURE 1.1 The Structure of the Newspaper Staff Is a Hierarchy.

Not only is David Sebastianelli (right) "partially nested" in work groups, but he is also a member of a family group. At times, the demands of the two groups may be in conflict.

Ethical Consideration

When you are a member of two groups with conflicting values, you must acknowledge that conflict. You will have to decide which values should be given priority. Determining which value is consistent with the greater good might be a helpful strategy.

Some groups do not envision their structure as a hierarchy, but rather as subsystems more equal in power. For instance, in Chapter 2 of this text, you will meet the Warranty Information Network System (WINS) team at General Motors Headquarters. Their goal is to systematize warranty claims for the automobile company. They depict their team structure as a segmented circle, with six component parts, each dependent on the others, as shown in Figure 1.2.

Team "coaches" are shown as a part of the team, but not of the subsystems. They have a responsibility for the team as a whole, but they are not members of specific divisions within the team. Within a subsystem, some individuals have greater power or responsibility than others (and are identified by bold type), but the image of the system's structure suggests more shared power within the system than a typical hierarchy suggests.

By recognizing the structural elements of systems, you can anticipate something of the nature of interaction within them. You may be able to tell where communication is likely to be more frequent and where it will be tinged with power issues. Also,

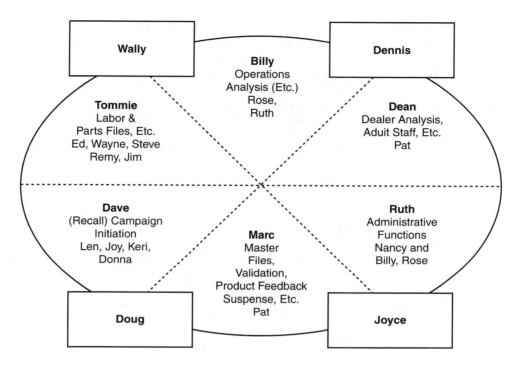

FIGURE 1.2   The WINS Team Structure Distributes Power More Equally.

recognizing that there will be an internal structure within a system modifies somewhat the message of wholeness: it *is* possible to examine a portion of a system (a subsystem) to see how a system works.

Change within Systems

It is a mistake to think of a system as a static unit. Because a system is goal directed, it is constantly in pursuit of change—movement toward accomplishing its goal. In addition, the environment external to the system causes fluctuations in the system. The system must adapt to those changes. Three concepts will help clarify the nature of change in a system: (1) the system's effort to maintain homeostasis, (2) the presence of positive and negative system feedback, and (3) the principle of equifinality.

Effort to Maintain Homeostasis.   If a system simply followed the direction of every external influence with no correctives, chaos would ensue. But systems, from those that are mechanical or biological to those that are social, make efforts to avoid chaos by maintaining **homeostasis,** *an internal equilibrium or stability achieved by making changes within the system.* You are probably familiar with the efforts some systems make to maintain homeostasis. A car operating with cruise control maintains a stable speed by regulating the gas flow and braking operations as the environment changes (uphill giving way to downhill). A thermostat in a house maintains a stable temperature by adjusting furnace activity when the temperatures outside change. A human body also makes adjustments to maintain a stable internal body temperature. Similarly, a small group system will alter its behaviors in an attempt to maintain some stability while it adapts to changes in the environment. So, for instance, if a newspaper staff is faced with increases in workload from an important breaking story, in order to avoid chaos, it might adopt measures designed to increase staff efficiency. Not making some changes within the system would result in a system operating without any level of stability, a state that systems—by their very nature—avoid. Rapoport (1975) explained that a system "reacts to changes in the environment in whatever way is required to maintain its identity" (pp. 46–47).

Positive and Negative System Feedback.   In Chapter 4, you will read about feedback, the communication from one member of a group to another. That kind of feedback provides reinforcement for a member to continue positively evaluated behaviors or encouragement to cease negatively evaluated behaviors. The feedback we are describing here is somewhat different from that. Here we are talking about the communication of the system with itself. The positive or negative quality of the feedback is related to the direction of the change encouraged by the feedback, not to its tone and only indirectly to the evaluation of the behavior to which it is responding.

A system that experiences change can either continue with the change or introduce a counteraction, to move in an opposite direction from the first change. If a system tells itself *to continue in the direction of the change*, it is sending itself **positive system feedback.** For instance, if a group has introduced changes to improve the quality of its work, members may send themselves the message to continue those changes. That constitutes positive system feedback—not because the changes are positive ones (although they are), but rather because the system has been told to continue to change in the same direction. As a further example, a car placed in neutral at the top of a hill will gather speed as it moves downhill. With no counter-action, the car will send itself positive feedback ("continue this kind of change") and will continue to gather speed, even though the outcome might be disastrous.

Negative system feedback is *a message from the system to itself to introduce a counteraction.* When a car operating with cruise control reaches the top of a hill and begins its descent, the car is sent negative feedback, for instead of continuing to increase the gas flow, the braking system begins to act. Negative feedback is directly related to a system's effort to maintain homeostasis. If the system sent itself only positive feedback, the changes in the system would continue to spiral, perhaps out of control. It is by countering the direction of the change, a process initiated by negative feedback, that homeostasis is maintained.

Bavelas and Segal (1982) illustrate the function of positive and negative system feedback in a family group. As a child becomes an adolescent and makes moves to become independent, the rest of the family system may encourage those moves (positive system feedback) or they may respond with counteracting moves (negative system feedback) to squelch the efforts toward independence so that the family continues to function as it had. If you can imagine the problems that would occur both if an adolescent were given too much independence too quickly and if the adolescent were given no independence, then you can understand the importance of finding the appropriate balance between change-supporting feedback and change-controlling feedback in a system. Systems need to change to remain vital, but loss of stability can destroy a group.

Equifinality.   You can anticipate that every group you are a member of or will observe will experience change. However, because the interactions of a system unite its members in a way that is unique to that system, we cannot predict how one system will operate by observing other systems. Systems follow the principle of **equifinality,** which states that *the initial state of the system is independent from the final state of the system.* What this means is that, regardless of the initial components of the system, a system may choose from among multiple routes to reach the same final goal and may also choose from among multiple goals. For instance, if a team David Sebastianelli served on was trying to improve its efficiency, it might do that by decreasing its staff (improving efficiency by producing the same output with fewer people); by increasing its staff (increasing efficiency by eliminating overloads); by dividing the staff into subteams (thus streamlining organizational structure); by restructuring the work day (to allow workers to choose their most productive times to work); or by reducing distractions (such as celebrations of workers' birthdays). These (and countless other) strategies are all possible ways for the group to achieve the goal of improving efficiency. Clearly, the system has multiple routes available to achieve the same final goal.

Moreover, a system has multiple goals available to it. In this case, a work team could decide that increasing efficiency is not as much a priority as increasing productivity, and they may recognize that some strategies that would increase efficiency could diminish productivity. For instance, efficiency could increase if the team no longer celebrates employee birthdays. But when the team members begin to feel as if they are not acknowledged as people (no one even remembers their birthdays), then their performance at work may slip. Because systems are characterized by equifinality, an outsider studying the group may not be able to predict which of the possible goals the group will select, let alone which of the routes to the goal it will choose. In fact, the principle of equifinality cautions us that we cannot predict how a group will interact even if we have previously observed each of its members interacting in other groups or other settings. Quite simply, the systems quality of equifinality means that the final outcome will be determined by the system's processes, not just by its components.

Small groups operate as systems. Therefore, as you analyze small group behavior and as you experience it, you can anticipate observing some qualities characteristic of all systems: the influence of each member's behaviors on the others, the influence of the outside environment on the group, the struggle to balance change with stability, and the central role of group processes in determining group outcome. Although groups will share the characteristics of systems, each group will be unique. Among the factors that help explain differences among groups are variations in their type.

Varied Types of Small Groups

No two groups are exactly alike. Even two groups with exactly the same purpose and size will differ, as the members create a dynamic unique to that group. However, three factors can be used to distinguish among the types of groups: their purpose, their life expectancy, and the internal or external origin and control of the group. These factors are visualized in Figure 1.3.

Purpose

Based on differences in purpose, four types of groups can be identified: social groups, learning groups, personal growth groups, and task accomplishment groups. The primary purpose of a **social group** is for its members to enjoy the company of each other. Frequently, the group meets to engage in an activity (such as bowling, bridge, or excursions around the city). It is possible to do some of those activities as separate individuals, but the group forms because it is more enjoyable to share the activity with companions. Groups of family and friends are the most important social groups we have, because they meet our needs to be secure, included, and loved.

Learning groups recognize the utility of more than one mind in understanding new ideas. The group might be formed by a teacher (who could require a group to compose a group report, perform an experiment, or complete a group exam) or by the members of the group themselves, as is typically the case when a study group forms. Learning groups are not limited to an educational setting. A family group functions as a learning group, too, for it is the primary means by which a child is socialized.

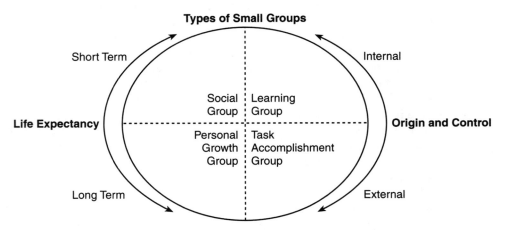

FIGURE 1.3   If this book had moving parts, the center shape in this diagram would rotate. Groups of each purpose vary on the continuum from long to short life expectancy and from internal to external origin and control.

People who want to change some aspect of their lives might join a **personal growth group.** Parents might seek support for their feelings of despair at the death of a child and join a grief support group. Someone trying to cope with and conquer an addiction might join Gamblers Anonymous, Alcoholics Anonymous, or Overeaters Anonymous. A person seeking help with a transition in lifestyle might join a group such as Parents Without Partners. Personal growth groups encourage expression of feelings, sharing of strategies for coping with difficulties, and reinforcement of efforts to change behavior.

Groups that have **task accomplishment** as their goal may occur in a variety of contexts. A surgical team forms to accomplish a task. In business, the task to be accomplished may range from producing a new car to creating an ad campaign. In the community, it might involve solving the problem of safety at a busy intersection or selecting a new county supervisor. The task can involve problem solving, decision making, and/or implementing a procedure.

Although distinct purposes can exist for groups, a single group can have multiple purposes, with one dominant at any particular time. For instance, imagine a group of college students assigned to work on a class project together. They originate as a learning group. If one of the group members is having trouble adjusting to the demands of school, the group may take on dimensions of a personal growth group. While working together for a semester, the students may become friends and function more as a social group. If they decide to host a party, they must function as a task group. Even though some groups may move easily from one purpose to another, other groups successful in achieving one purpose may have difficulty making such an adjustment.

Life Expectancy of the Group

A second factor that can distinguish one group from another is the length of its existence. Some groups are expected to last for a long time. A **standing committee,** for instance, is expected to continue over a long period of time, because the charge of the committee is to deal with a recurring issue. In contrast, an **ad hoc committee** is formed for a short time to deal with an issue of immediate concern that should be resolved when the committee's work is done. Another type of group created to have a short life is a **focus group,** which meets to discuss an issue of immediate concern to the individual who created the group, such as someone who might want the group's reactions to a political or product campaign. Groups with a long life expectancy can change their members and still persist, whereas some other groups will not survive the loss of even a single member.

Internal or External Origin and Control

A third distinguishing factor involves the relationship of the group to forces outside the group. Some groups may be formed by the members themselves, as study groups usually are. Such a group would have total autonomy, with its own authority to determine procedures and objectives. Other groups may be formed by a "superior"—such as a teacher or boss. Control of a formed group can also be located either within or outside the group. Even if someone with authority over group members has formed the group, the group itself may be given internal control, as is the case for a **self-directed work group.** Other groups remain under the control of the individual who created them, perhaps meeting only with the group's creator as the leader of each meeting. Droge, Arntson, and Norton (1986) distinguish between a self-help group and a therapy group on the basis of internal versus external control. The self-help group, controlled internally, has a looser connection with its environment than does the therapy group, which is led by a nonmember of the group.

Since these three factors (purpose of the group, life expectancy, and internal or external origin and control) will interact with one another, significant differences in the patterns followed by groups can result. A short-lived externally created learning group will differ from a long-term externally created learning group, perhaps in the types of goals they set and in the amount of difficulty members are willing to overlook. Both will differ from internally formed learning groups—probably in the members' commitment to each other—as well as from groups with other purposes. It can be helpful, however, to understand the type of group one is studying or joining, since the type is likely to affect the functioning of the group.

A Group or a Team

A combination of the factors just described may distinguish a group from a team. Although the term "team" is used with inconsistent meanings by others, we take a **team** to be *a task-oriented group, typically with long-term goals, whose members differ in their areas of expertise but share at least some degree of internal control.* A **cross-functional team** *is one in which members come from diverse functional divisions of the organization in which they work.* The degreasing team described by David Sebastianelli is a cross-functional team.

Team members have a level of interdependence that exceeds that of a normal group, because their task requires specialized, cooperative behavior from each member. For example, the chart of the WINS team at General Motors you saw earlier in Figure 1.2 reveals that its size exceeds the size usually associated with a small group, although it is still small enough that members have impressions of each other. Team-building activities were used in that team's early stages, because it was hoped that the group would have a long and successful life. Weekly meetings occur to coordinate

Technology Note: New Kinds of Teams

Given today's technological capacities, there are also some **cross-organizational teams** whose members belong to and represent distinct companies, but who come together to accomplish a task of importance to all of the organizations from which they have come. When they communicate primarily by electronic means and seldom, if ever, meet in person, they may be called **virtual teams** (Lipnack & Stamps, 1997).

action; team members all have specialized roles to play, but share the common goal of maintaining records of warranty claims for General Motors products. The team "coaches" have responsibilities that parallel those of managers in other businesses, but unlike managers in some organizations who seek to protect their authority, the coaches attempt to empower other group members. For instance, team members rotate the job of leading group meetings.

Not all groups are teams (if the members are able to function primarily independently, if members aren't specialized in their expertise, and if control is primarily external, for instance), nor are all teams small groups (if their size prohibits a sense of "groupness"). However, because many groups are also teams, we will talk about both groups and teams throughout this book. In describing an actual group or team, we will typically use the term its members use to describe themselves.

Reasons for Joining a Group: A Theoretical Perspective

Joining a group is an event that is repeated multiple times since, every year, thousands of groups are joined by thousands of individuals. Recurring events stimulate the interests of communication theorists who want to know why they happen as they do. Sometimes the reason seems obvious: you might join a group because membership would look good on a resume or because the group's activities sound enjoyable. Or perhaps a new friend has made a point of inviting you to a meeting. But at least two theorists have provided psychological explanations that may be less immediately obvious for individuals' decisions to join groups.

Schutz's Interpersonal Needs Theory

One explanation is an interpersonal needs theory, developed by William Schutz. Schutz (1966) began with the assumption that people need people. In fact, he identified three specific needs: the need for inclusion, the need for control, and the need for affection. Schutz explained that each need has two dimensions: an expressive and a receptive (or wanted) dimension. Therefore, there is a need to include others and to be included, to control others and to be controlled, to show affection and to be shown affection.

Each need may exist in different degrees. If an individual does not attempt to have the need fulfilled, then it exists at a deficient level. For example, if David Sebastianelli made no effort to influence the work teams he belongs to, we would say that he had a deficient control need. If Melissa Scram had made no effort to be included in activities by the members of the groups to which she belonged, then we would say that she had a deficient inclusion need. However, if the fulfillment of those needs becomes the focus of too much attention, then it exists at an excessive level (or, if even more extreme, at a pathological level). A need can also exist at an ideal level. At that level, an individual makes an effort to satisfy the need, but will be able to focus on other activities besides those which satisfy the need.

Ethical Consideration

Although it is reasonable for us to expect a group to help meet our interpersonal needs, if those needs exist at an excessive or pathological level, then we are expecting too much of an ordinary task group to expect the group to satisfy our needs. It may be necessary for us to seek help in another setting so that our needs more closely approach the ideal level as we join a task group.

Just as a biological need motivates a human to take action that can meet the need, so these psychological needs should motivate human action. According to Schutz, individuals will seek to join groups that best satisfy their needs and in which there is the best matching of needs among members. Everett Grambort, for instance, joined the board of directors of the Retired Officers Association, a group in which he could influence the members. He may have felt that he would have had a limited ability to influence members of the secret fraternal associations that he did not join.

Schutz argued that groups meet the needs of their members in a pattern, with inclusion needs satisfied first, then control, and finally affection. He also believed that if members' needs for inclusion are ill-matched, the group will experience greatest difficulties during the initial stages of interaction; if control needs are ill-matched, the difficulties will occur later, but not as late as if the members' affection needs are not well matched.

Festinger's Social Comparison Theory

The second theorist, Leon Festinger (1954), also believed that we join groups to satisfy a need, but he identified quite a different need from those mentioned by Schutz. Festinger claimed that a basic need of humans is to evaluate their own opinions and abilities. Some abilities can be evaluated against an objective measure (for instance, we can use a tape measure to judge how far we can jump or a stopwatch to judge how fast we can run), but other abilities and all opinions are too subjective to be measured against such a standard. They must be evaluated in a social manner, by comparing ourselves to others. According to Festinger, we affiliate with others whose opinions and abilities are fairly similar to our own in order to have a meaningful standard against which to measure ourselves. In the opening narrative, Melissa mentioned that the members of her social group are all quite similar to herself (cynical, somewhat weird and wacky, and interested in exploring New York City). You might have chosen a very different set of groups to join than those she joined, especially if you see yourself as very different from her.

If a group is too divergent from us, we will avoid joining it, because it will not give us information we can trust. In the opening narrative, Everett's explanation of his decision to avoid joining the Eighteen Holers Golf Association suggests that he saw the members of the golf group as having an attitude toward golf that differed from his own ("Golf is intended to be a walking game"). They would not have been suitable

Melissa Scram (left) and her friends have found that exploring New York City, even underground, is more fun with a group than alone. (Photo by Kerry Cavanaugh.)

measures against which to evaluate himself. This search for "others like us" may pose problems for groups formed in organizations whose workers represent the full diversity of the American workforce. Even if the workers interact with those "different" from themselves on tasks, they are likely to seek out others of their own ethnic group for social contacts at work, which may be perceived negatively by their coworkers (Morrison, Ruderman, & Hughes-James, 1993).

Our search for similar others can explain whether we join a group; once in a group, if we find our opinions discrepant from those of other members, then we will strive to reduce the discrepancy in one of three ways. (1) We might change our own opinions if we find ourselves quite out of line with other members. (2) We might bring pressure to bear on other members if we find ourselves close to their opinions, but slightly off the mark. (3) Or we might ignore some members of the group as we make comparisons, narrowing the range of members we use in evaluating our own selves. If a group no longer serves to meet our needs for comparison, Festinger (1954) said, we will leave the group—as long as we are free to do so and it does not meet other needs of ours. (Thus, Festinger suggested that our membership in groups is not motivated solely by the need for social comparison.) In sum, Festinger claimed that "to the extent that self-evaluation can only be accomplished by means of comparison with other persons, the drive for self-evaluation is a force acting on persons to belong to groups, to associate with others" (p. 135).

Functions Served by Small Groups

The theories just described explain an individual's decision to join a group as a means of meeting a psychological need. But what explains the initial formation of a group? Groups are formed because they serve four functions. They (1) create connections that counter isolation, (2) foster learning, (3) improve worker productivity, and (4) facilitate democratic action in contemporary society. As you read about group functions, you will probably notice considerable overlap between the purposes of groups and the functions they serve. After all, social groups form because groups serve the function of creating connections. Both personal growth groups and learning groups form because groups function to foster learning. Task purposes can be accomplished because groups both improve worker productivity and increase citizen participation. It is important to realize that groups are not only designed in the hopes that they will achieve a specific purpose, but there is clear evidence that they serve several functions.

Creating Connections

As we have become a more mobile society and as family members separate from their extended families, we have increased our experience with isolation. Welcomed in small doses, perhaps, isolation is painful for most of us if it extends for a long time. After all, isolation is reserved as a severe punishment for prisoners. Yet many of us come face-to-face with the fear of isolation or alienation. Students beginning school at a new college wonder how they will fit in with their roommates and classmates. Family members moving to a new community wonder how they will replace the ties they are breaking as they leave their former home. A new job raises similar concerns for an employee.

Through communication, small groups work to build and maintain the connections we seek. And, whereas interpersonal, dyadic communication builds relationships with one person at a time, within a small group we can multiply the links to build a sense of community. On rare occasions, those links can last a lifetime. Foster (1996), for instance, reports that in 1946, a group of high-school girls gathered in a home in the Upper Peninsula of Michigan where they experimented with coloring their hair. They decided to form a club. Fifty years later, their story was reported in the *Detroit Free Press*, because the group of women had met every month for fifty years—600 months. As members moved away from and then returned to their hometown, married, were divorced or widowed, raised children, faced the death of loved ones and the birth of grandchildren, the club continued to meet. The community they created eased the members' way through the changes in their lives.

Researchers have confirmed the importance of group memberships as a means of creating connections. Dansky (1996) studied workers' affiliations with professional associations and found that group membership provided psychological and social support for their members and created links to social and professional networks. Professional group memberships provided a means by which new workers could reduce their uncertainty about the job without having to bother the boss with questions. Although professional organizations may be large groups, the same value can be attained by membership in a small professional group, or even by a group of coworkers on the job who stop after work for dinner and talk.

Rugel (1991) directed his attention to therapeutic groups that aided in the recovery process of their addicted members. He argued that members experiencing group acceptance would be affected positively throughout the recovery process. Initially, acceptance by group members will increase the new members' self-esteem, reduce the members' defensiveness about the problem behavior, and allow "them to accept unpleasant realities regarding their addiction" (p. 481). In the negative state of isolation, denial of addiction may be a strategy used to control the degree of negativity an individual experiences. Against the positive background of an accepting group, facing up to personal failings becomes more possible. In any group, when we feel that the members have accepted us as humans, we are more open to their feedback, which can allow us to grow as individuals.

Researchers who have studied focus groups (Swenson, Griswold, & Kleiber, 1992) and support groups (Chesney & Chesler, 1993) have found that through participation in a group, members discover that the issues they themselves believe to be significant are perceived by others to be important, too. As one group member remarked, "With a group you learn you aren't alone[;] that helps in convincing you that you are not paranoid or obsessed" (Swenson, et al., p. 467). Such validation of self-perceptions binds the group members together. Particularly when one's problems are so overwhelming as to create a sense of isolation, the impact of the group in creating a shared concern is significant. People who have lost a loved one to suicide, who are caretakers for Alzheimer's patients, or who have been diagnosed with a bipolar disorder are among those who can find consoling connections through small group membership.

Fostering Learning

Group participation is effective in encouraging learning, both about ourselves and about the ideas and skills discussed and practiced within the group. We can enhance our self-understanding because we use our group memberships as a tool of self-definition, identifying the ways we are similar to other members of groups we have joined and the ways in which we are distinct from the groups we have chosen not to join (McGarty, Haslam, Hutchinson, & Turner, 1994). We also learn about ourselves when we are forced by the group setting to articulate our thoughts. There is something about saying aloud what we believe that helps us to discover what we truly believe.

We learn, too, about the ideas of others. Freeman (1996) explained that, within a group, a member "is exposed to divergent opinions and ideas that may serve to develop and clarify his or her own perspectives and an appreciation for alternative viewpoints" (p. 268). Such an effect does occur for individuals who have participated in focus group discussions. Swenson et al. (1992) did a follow-up study of participants in a focus group on the role of journalism in rural development. Four to six months after the discussion had occurred, participants reported that they continued to think about the issues discussed, had discussed the issues with others, and had found it helpful to discover others' ideas and opinions.

The role of groups in facilitating learning has led classroom teachers to increase their use of group learning projects. As students share information in a group, two things happen: (1) those who speak clarify their ideas in their own minds, and (2) those who listen benefit from the shared resources. Eeds and Wells (1991) reported the effects of group discussions about books read in an elementary school classroom. They found that through discussion, students (and teacher) jointly constructed an interpretation of the story. Students were supported in their search for understanding, teachers were exposed to legitimate meanings they had not thought of, and the collaborative atmosphere encouraged risk taking by students. Aspy, Aspy, and Quinby (1993) found that when medical schools integrated small-group discussion in their classrooms, students' comfort levels rose, as did the students' ability to learn independently. Freeman (1996) examined the impact of study groups on the academic performance of students in a masters of business administration program. She discovered that both positive attitudes toward work in the group and the time spent within the group were related to higher grade point averages for the students. Students in groups that had performed well said that study groups added significantly to their learning process. The amount of time spent in the study groups was the best predictor of the students' academic success.

New modes of behavior, as well as new ideas, can be taught and reinforced by group activity. This point was learned during World War II when the country encouraged citizens to alter some basic behaviors in support of the war effort. Families were asked to save nylon stockings to be transformed into parachute silk and to grow victory gardens and use variety meats (kidneys, beef hearts, and sweetbreads) so that other food was available for transport to the troops. This last effort became the focus of one of the earliest examples of applied small group research. Kurt Lewin (1947) reported the results of a study of housewives who were members of Red Cross groups, volunteers organized for home nursing during the war. Six groups ranging from thirteen to seventeen members were involved in the study. Three of them heard effective lectures on the nutritious and economic benefits of variety meats, ways to avoid the obstacles to serving variety meats, and recipes that the lecturer had successfully served to her own family. The other three groups used a group discussion procedure to identify the obstacles to serving variety meats, followed by a nutrition expert's solution to the group-generated problems. Two weeks later, only 3% of those hearing the lecture had served variety meats to their families, while 32% of those in the discussion groups had done so. Similar results were found in changing behaviors on milk use, even with groups whose members did not meet regularly, as the Red Cross groups did. Lewin explained that the active participation of the discussion method increases one's involvement in learning. Group members also become more willing to adopt a requested behavior change when their decision to do so is made in an atmosphere of group support, rather than in the psychologically isolated atmosphere they are in while listening to a lecture or a mass media presentation. He added that group activity has the advantage of unfreezing old beliefs (as a group member hears contrary ideas from a person with whom there is a personal connection), learning fully the new behavior through participation in a group activity, and reinforcing the new behavior through support from other group members.

Improving Worker Productivity

The benefits of group work carry over into the workforce, so much so that the use of self-managed work teams is growing rapidly. An estimated 5% of U.S. employers used self-directed work groups in the early 1980s, but Freeman (1996) predicted that by the beginning of the twenty-first century, nearly half of the country's employees would work in such groups. This trend cannot be explained as a mere experiment, for companies are too interested in making their workforce lean and competitive to invest in a faddish experiment. In fact, it is likely that when businesses and industries began to experience economic difficulty, management began to look to the practices used in the then-thriving Japanese economy. They found that groups played a central role. (The role of groups in Japan is discussed in Zander, 1983.)

In practice, work groups have a number of advantages (Seibold, 1995). They improve company flexibility (by training workers to perform multiple jobs within a team). Because workers solve problems together, they can share expertise, increasing product quality. Worker involvement leads to a more motivated and committed workforce. That, in turn, reduces the need for supervision. Turnover rates and the accompanying high costs for retraining are reduced, which further enhances the company's success. Hanlon and Taylor (1991) argued that the low growth expected for the U.S. workforce in the coming years mandates increases in employee involvement and empowerment. Group activity is one means to those ends.

Facilitating Citizen Participation

In addition to the social, educational, and economic value of groups to our society, there is a political benefit as well. Participation within small groups facilitates social change, an outcome of particular importance now when citizen involvement in politics appears to be declining. One explanation for this decline, suggested by Pilisuk, McAllister, and Rothman (1996), is that there are forces in contemporary society that discourage our involvement in the democratic process. These authors identify forces that inhibit citizen involvement, including a decrease in tightly knit families and communities (which has reduced social dialogue); the trend toward globalization (so that a problem's cause may be distant from the individuals affected by it); concentration of wealth, power, and information in the hands of a fewer people; and the view that the role of media is to activate purchasers rather than to inform an active citizenry. Together these forces suggest that we live in a world in which, as individual citizens, we are becoming more isolated, more powerless, more passive, and less able to effect change in our lives. Involvement in small groups, according to this explanation, counteracts the forces that limit our power.

A different explanation of the decline in political involvement begins by acknowledging that lifestyle changes have occurred in American society. Putnam (1995) argues that factors such as increased mobility of family members, the increased influx of women into the workforce, and a more isolated, private use of leisure time have combined to reduce Americans' involvement with their neighbors and in civic organizations. As a result, there has been a decline in "social capital," a term that Putnam says "refers to features of social organization such as networks, norms, and social trust that facilitate coordination and cooperation for mutual benefit" (p. 67). Just as economic capital is necessary for the health of economic institutions, social capital is necessary for the health of social institutions. Putnam notes that individuals who are involved in civic organizations report more trust in others and more involvement in political activity. According to this explanation, involvement in small groups is a prerequisite for political involvement.

Both explanations, however, see a critical role for small groups in relation to political activity. As Pilisuk, McAllister, and Rothman (1996) note, a local citizen action group can define the problems it faces, rather than delegating that role to an outsider who misses the true nature of their pain. One member benefits from the agreement of other members about how the problem should be solved, increasing confidence in the decision and willingness to take risks. (The role of groups in decisions involving risk is considered by Hartman and Nelson, 1996.) Working together in a group, members can develop a network of individuals concerned about the issue and able to act on it. They can divide labor to accomplish more, and they can unify their numbers to create a greater pressure for change. They can share their successes, thus empowering themselves to succeed in the future.

In a narrative in Chapter 3, you will meet Lillian Robinson, the leader of a citizens group, United for Action. That group demonstrates how this process works. The group members have identified as unacceptable the placement of environmental hazards in their neighborhood, despite outsiders' views that the neighborhood had nothing to lose (and perhaps jobs to gain) with an additional hazardous waste incinerator in their neighborhood. They have met city and state leaders and used legal resources to thwart action by more powerful, wealthier opponents.

Even groups that do not form for the purpose of creating change can have that effect. When Chesney and Chesler (1993) studied parents of children with cancer and compared parents who had joined a support group with those who had not, they found that those who had joined a support group became more secure about their own capacity to make changes in the medical system that treated their children and more willing to work with others to create change. Whether in fighting the medical establishment, creating safe play areas within a community, stopping the placement of a pollution source near the neighborhood school, creating a means to feed and house the area's impoverished citizens, or sharing pieces of art with school children and nursing home residents, citizens whose actions individually might be stymied can have an impact when they join with others as members of a small group.

Group Versus Individual Efforts

Does the significance of groups mean that they should always be turned to in preference to individual action? No. There are situations in which individual action is more likely to be effective than group effort. For instance, Vandervoort and Fuhrman (1991) found that individual rather than group therapy is more effective in treating more severe forms of depression. Stasson and Bradshaw (1995), in testing whether groups were better than individuals, found mixed results. The average group score on the tasks their subjects performed was lower than the best combination of individual efforts. If only one member had selected the correct answer before the group met to make a unified decision, the group seldom chose the correct answer. And on individual items, individual members were better than the group. However, even if no member had selected the correct answer, the group sometimes did. And on the total effort, groups scored better than individuals. Stasson and Bradshaw found an "assembly effect bonus" (a benefit coming from the assembling of the group). It could be explained by the facts that group members with non-overlapping knowledge filled in the missing information for individuals and that, through interaction, the group sometimes came to correct answers even when no member had had the information individually.

In general, groups are more advantageous when the issue they are facing requires a diversity of information unlikely to be in the hands of a single person. In the opening narrative, Melissa Scram mentioned that, as long as the focus of the assignment is clear, group work in classes can benefit students as ideas are "bounced off one another." However, groups achieve the advantage of diversity of information only if their membership is diversified (with backgrounds that are not entirely overlapping) and only if each member can be encouraged to participate. That has been something of a problem to date because, as Kirchmeyer (1993) found, in multicultural task groups, the minority members typically had low levels of contribution. McLeod, Lobel, and Cox (1966) found that "diverse teams that actually utilized the variety of perspectives present outperformed the homogeneous teams, whereas diverse teams that did not utilize their diversity performed worse than the homogeneous teams" (pp. 260–261). Therefore, they cautioned that it is the proper management of diversity, not simply the presence of diversity, that improves the quality of the group's product. It is important, therefore, to find ways of increasing the comfort level for all group members to contribute. The strategies described in Chapter 4 for creating a positive climate are useful in this regard.

Because group members feel that they can share responsibility for a decision, they are more willing to take risks when making decisions than are individuals. The danger, of course, is that they will accept ill-advised courses of action because they can share the blame. The decision to launch the Challenger missile in weather too cold to allow sealant to work effectively is one decision in which risks were poorly evaluated, with devastating results (Renz & Greg, 1988).

Groups have an advantage over individuals when the task can be subdivided, so that each group member can be involved in acting on the group's behalf. However, for simple, single-task activities, the member best able to perform the task should be assigned it, assuming that the best-qualified member can be identified. If the task does not involve all group members, use of a group may encourage some members to leave the work to others, a practice called "social loafing" (Pratkanis & Turner, 1996).

If a decision needs to be made quickly, group involvement may be impossible. A single individual can almost always act more quickly than a group can. Moreover, the time involved in group decision making is multiplied by the number of members involved in the process. Anyone who has sat through a meeting in which a group tries to write a paper knows how inefficient such a meeting can be. In the opening narrative, David Sebastianelli cautioned that not every problem is a group problem and that using a group for simple problems can waste time. For such tasks, an individual with a high level of competence and a strong need for achievement would prefer to work alone on a task and should be given the opportunity to do so. However, it should not be assumed that group activity is always inefficient. If a decision affects the group, then the members' involvement in making the decision will be more likely to ensure a fit between the solution and the needs of the group. Group responsibility for the decision will also bring with it a commitment of the group members to the solution. David Sebastianelli mentioned this and the pride the group develops in its solution as advantages of the group process.

Even in situations in which a group would normally function more advantageously than an individual would, groups can lose their natural advantage if there are problems with their processes: if an expert exerts influence outside the realm of expertise, if members conform to the group in an effort to gain social approval, if the group decides quickly without sufficient evaluation, or if members begin to depend on others to evaluate ideas rather than performing that responsibility themselves (Freeman, 1996). In any situation in which an individual opinion is sought, then, of course, the individual should be asked to respond. For instance, if you are asked at the end of a course you are taking to evaluate the faculty member teaching it, your individual opinion is what is wanted. The potential of group processes to alter your individual opinion is too great to give that task to a group.

Because groups are not always better than individuals and because group work may even create some undesirable situations, anyone in a position to assign tasks (whether in a classroom or a workplace) should consider carefully the nature of the task and the effect of a group upon the outcome before deciding whether to assign the task to a group or an individual. Following is a summary of the factors that give the preference to groups or individuals.

Groups Are Preferred If	*Individuals Are Preferred If*
The task requires resources no single group member possesses; group membership is diverse; all members contribute comfortably.	An individual group member has all the resources necessary to complete the task.
There is a need for increased risk taking.	There is a need for a more cautious approach to risks.
The task is complicated and can be divided so all members have a role.	The task is simple, and the best qualified member is available to complete it.
Time for group interaction is available.	A decision must be made without adequate time for interaction.
The decision affects the group so that a fit between the solution and group needs is important, and group commitment to the decision is desired.	The information desired is an individual opinion, free from group influence; or the group process is such that poor decision making would result.

Ethical Consideration

The increasing tendency to use groups in the classroom and on the job may encourage frequent assignment of projects to groups even when the group will have no real power. If you are in the position to assign a task to a group or an individual, be sure that you give group members the responsibility for making a decision only if you are also willing to give them the power to do so.

Summary

A small group is a small number of humans drawn together through interaction, whose interdependent relationships allow them to achieve a mutual goal. Because groups are goal oriented and interdependent, they are systems, characterized by the complementary principles of wholeness and nonsummativity. Their structure will include a boundary (which distinguishes the group from the environment, but allows each to influence the other) and a substructure, which divides the group into subsystems. They will experience change, which is balanced by the desire to maintain stability (homeostasis), controlled by the mixture of positive and negative system feedback, and which is determined more by the processes than the components of the system (as explained by the principle of equifinality).

The nature of small groups will vary with their type, which depends on their purpose, life expectancy, and the source of their origin and control. Included among the reasons we may join small groups are two psychological reasons: to meet our interpersonal needs and to judge ourselves using the group as a social measurement tool. The groups themselves have formed because of the important functions served by groups: creating connections with others, fostering learning, improving worker productivity, and facilitating citizen participation. However, groups are not always the best options for meeting task demands. In some cases, it is more desirable for an individual to take on an assignment than it is for a group, so learning which conditions warrant which approach is important.

In all cases, because the effectiveness of a group is undermined by poor understanding of group processes and poor performance within the group by its members, it will be important to learn more about the nature of groups and how to operate effectively within them. The chapters that follow will aid you in understanding group processes and in developing the skills necessary to perform as an effective group member.

QUESTIONS FOR DISCUSSION

1. Which of the following would you consider to be a small group?
   a. The people you live with
   b. A religious congregation trying to raise money for a new building
   c. The students in a class in small group communication
   d. The Chicago Bulls basketball team
   e. The Scholars Group described by Melissa Scram in the opening narrative

2. Which of the following tasks would you give to a group and which would you give to an individual?
   a. Deciding who the starting quarterback should be
   b. Selecting the textbook for a college course
   c. Determining whether school should be cancelled for bad weather
   d. Deciding whether to launch a nuclear warhead
   e. Writing the end-of-the-year report for a department

3. How do Internet chat rooms differ from face-to-face groups? Consider their purposes, their functions, and the reasons people join them.

4. Earlier definitions of small groups specified that members must interact face-to-face. This book recognizes that people who are electronically connected may be in small groups. Are the interactions between people who are electronically connected fundamentally different from face-to-face interactions?

5. Based on the narratives and your own personal experiences, does it seem to you that what motivates someone to join a group will change over time?

6. Consider a group (such as a school sports team or extracurricular organization) that regularly has a sizable turnover of membership. How can and should such a group maintain the group as a system?

SUGGESTED ACTIVITIES

1. List five groups to which you belong (or have belonged). Describe the groups by type. Identify your reason for joining each group.

2. Identify a group on your campus or in your community that accepts new members. Talk to a current member of the group. Describe the qualities of the group that would appeal to you and those you would not find appealing. How would the group change if you were to join it? How would you change?

3. Form a group that will stay together for an extended period. In later chapters, this will be referred to as your "Project Group." Begin to keep a journal about your group activities. In your journal, identify
   a. The type of group it is
   b. Your reason for joining the group
   c. Some tasks your group will need to complete, distinguishing those you should work on together from those that should be assigned to individuals

4. In your journal, explain how your group will be influenced by (and will influence) the outside environment.

SOURCES CITED

Aspy, D. N., Aspy, C. B., & Quinby, P. M. (1993). What doctors teach teachers about problem-based learning. *Educational Leadership, 50*(7), 22–24.

Bavelas, J. B., & Segal, L. (1982). Family systems theory: Background and implications. *Journal of Communication, 32*(3), 99–107.

Brilhart, J. K., & Galanes, G. J. (1995). *Effective group discussion* (8th ed.). Madison, WI: Brown & Benchmark.

Cathcart, R. S., Samovar, L. A., & Henman, L. D. (1996). *Small group communication: Theory and practice* (7th ed.). Madison, WI: Brown & Benchmark.

Chesney, B. K., & Chesler, M. A. (1993). Activism through self-help group membership: Reported life changes of parents of children with cancer. *Small Group Research, 24*, 258–273.

Dansky, K. H. (1996). The effect of group mentoring on career outcomes. *Group & Organization Management, 21*, 5–21.

Droge, D., Arntson, P., & Norton, R. (1986). The social support function in epilepsy self-help groups. *Small Group Behavior, 17*, 139–163.

Eeds, M., & Wells, D. (1991). Talking, thinking, and cooperative learning: Lessons learned from listening to children talk about books. *Social Education, 55,* 134–137.

Farmer, S. M., & Hyatt, C. W. (1994). Effects of task language demands and task complexity on computer-mediated work groups. *Small Group Research, 25,* 331–366.

Festinger, L. (1954). Theory of social comparison processes. *Human Relations, 7,* 117–140.

Foster, V. (1996, September 29). Friends for life. *Detroit Free Press,* pp. G1–G2.

Freeman, K. A. (1996). Attitudes toward work in project groups as predictors of academic performance. *Small Group Research, 27,* 265–282.

Hall, A. D., & Fagen, R. E. (1975). Definition of system. In B. D. Ruben & J. Y. Kim (Eds.), *General systems theory and human communication* (pp. 52–65). Rochelle Park, NJ: Hayden Book Company.

Hanlon, S. C., & Taylor, R. R. (1991). An examination of changes in work group communication behaviors following installation of a gainsharing plan. *Group & Organization Studies, 16,* 238–267.

Hartman, S. J., & Nelson, B. H. (1996). Group decision making in the negative domain. *Group & Organization Management, 21,* 146–162.

Kirchmeyer, C. (1993). Multicultural task groups: An account of the low contribution level of minorities. *Small Group Research, 24,* 127–148.

Lazlo, E. (1972). Introduction: the origins of general systems theory in the work of von Bertalanffy. In E. Lazlo (Ed.), *The relevance of general systems theory: Papers presented to Ludwig von Bertalanffy on his seventieth birthday* (pp. 3–11). New York: George Braziller.

Lewin, K. (1947). Group decision and social change. In T. M. Newcomb & E. L. Hartley (Eds.), *Readings in social psychology* (pp. 330–344). New York: Henry Holt.

Lipnack, J., & Stamps, J. (1997). *Virtual teams: Reaching across space, time, and organizations with technology.* New York: John Wiley & Sons.

McGarty, C., Haslam, S. A., Hutchinson, K. J., & Turner, J. C. (1994). The effects of salient group memberships on persuasion. *Small Group Research, 25,* 267–293.

McGrath, J. E. (1991). Time, interactions, and performance (TIP): A theory of groups. *Small Group Research, 22,* 147–174.

McLeod, P. L., Lobel, S. A., & Cox, T. H., Jr. (1996). Ethnic diversity and creativity in small groups. *Small Group Research, 27,* 248–264.

Morrison, A. M., Ruderman, M. N., & Hughes-James, M. (1993). *Making diversity happen: Controversies and solutions.* Greensboro, NC: Center for Creative Leadership.

Pilisuk, M., McAllister, J., & Rothman, J. (1996). Coming together for action: The challenge of contemporary grassroots community organizing. *Journal of Social Issues, 52,* 15–17.

Pratkanis, A. R., & Turner, M. E. (1996). Persuasion and democracy: Strategies for increasing deliberative participation and enacting social change. *Journal of Social Issues, 52,* 197–205.

Putnam, R. D. (1995). Bowling alone: America's declining social capital. *Journal of Democracy, 6* 65–78.

Rapoport, A. (1975). Modern systems theory—An outlook for coping with change. In B. D. Ruben & J. Y. Kim (Eds.), *General systems theory and human communication* (pp. 33–51). Rochelle Park, NJ: Hayden Book Company.

Renz, M. A., & Greg, J. B. (1988). Flaws in the decision-making process: Assessment of risk in the decision to launch flight F1-L. *Central States Speech Journal, 39,* 67–75.

Rosen, N. (1989). *Teamwork and the bottom line: Groups make a difference.* Hillsdale, NJ: Lawrence Erlbaum Associates.

Rothwell, J. D. (1992). *In mixed company: Small group communication.* Fort Worth, TX: Harcourt Brace Jovanovich College Publishers.

Rugel, R. P. (1991). Addictions treatment in groups: A review of therapeutic factors. *Small Group Research, 22,* 475–491.

Salazar, A. J. (1995). Understanding the synergistic effects of communication in small groups: Making the most out of group member abilities. *Small Group Research, 26,* 169–199.

Schutz, W. C. (1966). *The interpersonal underworld; FIRO: A three-dimensional theory of interpersonal behavior* (Reprint ed.). Palo Alto, CA: Science & Behavior Books.

Seibold, D. R. (1995). Developing the "team" in a team managed organization: Group facilitation in a new-design plant. In L. R. Frey (Ed.), *Innovations in group facilitation: Applications in natural settings* (pp. 282–298). Cresskill, NJ: Hampton Press.

Stasson, M. F., & Bradshaw, S. D. (1995). Explanations of individual–group performance differences: What sort of "bonus" can be gained through group interaction? *Small Group Research, 26,* 296–308.

Straus, S. G. (1996). Getting a clue: The effects of communication media and information distribution on participation and performance in computer-mediated and face-to-face groups. *Small Group Research, 27,* 115–142.

Swenson, J. D., Griswold, W. F., & Kleiber, P. B. (1992). Focus groups: Method of inquiry/intervention. *Small Group Research, 23,* 459–474.

Valacich, J. S., George, J. F., Nunamaker, J. F., Jr., & Vogel, D. R. (1994). Physical proximity effects on computer-mediated group idea generation. *Small Group Research, 25,* 83–104.

Vandervoort, D. J., & Furhman, A. (1991). The efficacy of group therapy for depression: A review of the literature. *Small Group Research, 22,* 320–338.

Zander, A. (1983). The value of belonging to a group in Japan. *Small Group Behavior, 14,* 3–14.

2 The Process of Group Formation

CHAPTER OBJECTIVES

After reading this chapter, you should be able to

- Identify member characteristics likely to affect group interaction
- Describe the effects of group size and membership change on interaction
- Define norms, roles, and cohesiveness
- Distinguish between task-related, group maintenance, and process-hindering behaviors
- Identify the process through which roles and norms develop and can be changed
- Identify strategies that help develop cohesiveness
- List the stages in the group formation process, and, for each stage, describe the issues a group resolves and the nature of the group's communication

The Narrative

The Warranty Information Network System (WINS) team works at the General Motors Tech Center in the Detroit metropolitan area. It is responsible for systematizing warranty claims and product recall campaigns for General Motors in this country and abroad. The group has weekly meetings. Eleven of the team members were present at a recent meeting.

There is considerable diversity within the team. Of the members present at the meeting, five are male and six female; ages range from 28 to the mid-fifties; and experience with the company varies from 10 to 35 years. Team members also represent different racial and ethnic groups, so the group discussed having an ethnic potluck prior to the holidays to celebrate their diverse heritage. A round-table discussion allowed each team member to raise any issue the member chose to bring to the attention of the team.

When it was Joy's turn to speak, she said she had nothing to say except that she was frustrated. Team members knew that much of the previous day Joy had been coping with a computer virus. Ruth commented that the virus problem concerned all of the members. Other team members described their recent problems with viruses. Tommie offered to get someone responsible for the computer system to come to the meeting; within a few minutes, she returned with a computer specialist who made suggestions about how to get the problem solved.

When Marc's time to address the group came, he described his visit to a local car dealership to see a new system for reporting warranty claims. Marc discussed the upcoming birthday celebrations for the month of November. That led one of the team members to check on plans to collect money and gifts for the needy at Christmas. Then Marc asked whether the team's meeting day could be changed now that two members had a conflicting meeting on Tuesday mornings. After a quick poll, members agreed to switch team meeting days to Wednesdays.

After meeting for nearly two hours, team members seemed to lose their concentration on the issues. As one team member described a procedure each of them was being required to follow, a side conversation developed at the other end of the table, and three members started to laugh. The person who had the floor reacted with annoyance.

Enough time had passed that the team had to table a significant item on the agenda for the day's meeting: team rejuvenation. Several team members had expressed concern that the energy motivating the team during its first year of operation was no longer present. To insure that the issue received attention, a special meeting was called for the following week with team improvement as the single agenda item.

Patricia Litwiller, 43, has been a member of the WINS team since its inception. Here she describes her experience as a member of the team:

Before I worked for the WINS team, I had worked for Oldsmobile. My actual job responsibilities weren't that much different from what they are now, but I didn't have as much interaction with other people within the department. We could go to our cubicles and, through our phone and computer terminals, get pretty much all of our work done for the day. Now there's much more interaction.

People were actually hired on to the WINS team early in 1993, but for about a year before that, representatives from each division were meeting about three times a week. The management team brought us all together and asked us if being on a team was something we would like to try and how we thought we should set it up. Our team is structured like a wheel. And the management actually gave us the opportunity to pick what part of the wheel in the organization we wanted to be in.

Denny is our director, and Wally, Doug, and Joyce are managers under Denny. There is some division in their responsibilities, but they're all involved in a lot of other projects. So when any one of us has a problem that we need to talk to a coach about, we can talk to any one of them, based on our personal preference or whoever is available.

When we first formed the team, some concerns were expressed, such as how it would affect our upward mobility, and how the team leaders were going to be selected—that sort of thing. At first, as with any new relationship, we were always on our best behavior. We didn't want to let the others see our ugly side. I think the biggest change in our behavior is that we feel much more comfortable now bringing up a controversial issue and discussing it. As we worked more with each other, everybody started feeling more at ease. There was more joking around and sharing of more personal stuff, rather than just job-related stuff. So everybody has gotten to know each other as people, not just as coworkers. When new members have joined our team, they have marveled at the fact that we all seem to like each other, get along, and do things together. We're very open, sharing, and supportive of each other. New people almost always comment that it's just so different from where they came from.

In the beginning, we went to several team-building exercises. We might have gone off-site once a week over a six-week period. We spent a whole day and a half at the Saturn facility in Tennessee, doing exercises to build teamwork. One involved a wall about 40 feet tall. It's pretty vertical and has some hand grips. We had to scale the wall. But the trick is that you don't climb the wall by yourself. You're tethered to two other people. You're all going up this wall together. Well, obviously, one of you is not going to make it to the top of the wall without the other two. And some people are better at that sort of thing than others. So you help the person that needs the help to scale the wall. Our meeting norm for "S'port" came out of that. It means that we will support each other in our efforts to reach a common goal, even if we have differences of opinion on other issues.

We have some other written meeting norms, including "no zingers"—negative comments directed at the others. We're pretty bad at that. In fact, somebody spoke up yesterday and reread the norms to us because we weren't following them too well. And we are all pretty guilty of zingers, but all in good humor, and most everybody takes it pretty well. We all kid around together and joke. But I would have to say that we probably don't really do a real good job of following our written norms. If somebody wants to take issue, they can go back to the norms and say, "You guys aren't doing that." Also, we have a different facilitator for each meeting. It's the job of the facilitator to enforce the norms, or at least not let it get completely out of hand. If it does, then usually the facilitator speaks up and reminds everybody of the norms. Then everybody falls into line. Our group is pretty open, and I don't think anybody has a problem telling anybody else in the group if they think they're out of line or if a comment was unnecessary. I can't think of any unwritten norms, offhand.

I ask a lot of questions of other team members to understand what is happening in their work. Especially lately, I've really been trying to champion the team effort. And so I think that the team almost expects me to speak up. They also expect me to be a volunteer. I volunteer my help, my opinion, my support, and my expertise to all members of the team—sometimes to the point of being a little pushy. Because of my job responsibilities, I'm involved in a lot of the pieces of what our whole team does. Some other members have jobs where they don't have as much interaction with everyone else. So maybe they don't have as much a feeling of being a vital member of the whole team.

If I could make one change in the team, I guess it would be that I would like full participation from everybody. I don't think that, at this point, we're getting that. Some people still want to be directed rather than self-directed. They want somebody to tell them what to do and when to do it. I know it takes time and work and more effort to be self-directed, make decisions, and admit mistakes rather than to be able to blame your manager for it. But that's what I would change. If we did change it, we could really improve the process.

Our team has undergone some structural changes, adding another group to the team. In our team meeting this week, we talked about that to quite an extent, because we have had some concern that our team wasn't working as effectively as it had in the past. We realized that new people are coming into our group without having had the advantage of working together right from the beginning and building the same kind of bonds. They didn't feel as much a part of the team as some of the rest of us. I guess the rest of the team didn't tell them how this department works. We've had some incidents where, rather than working through an issue with a team member or a team leader, the new members went straight to management. That's not really the way we like to operate. We like to solve things ourselves—bubble it up from the bottom. Instead of going straight to the top, you start at the lowest level and keep moving up until you get it resolved. So we talked about that and how our group is changing and will continue to change, because we're going to continue to bring more groups into our area. We decided that to make a team work, it takes a lot of effort and a lot of time. We haven't done any team-building exercises in a long time. Probably half of our members have never gone through those team-building exercises. And we thought that maybe it's a good time to do that again—to reinforce it for the old team members and maybe get the newer team members indoctrinated.

There are a lot of changes going on within the team right now. Denny is moving on, and we're getting a new director. At this point, I would prefer to stay with this team. I drive a long way—over an hour each way—to come to work. There are a lot of GM facilities closer to my home that I could probably transfer to. Right now it's fun to come to work and work with these people. And part of that is because we have the opportunity to make a lot of our decisions and to do a lot of things that other people in our position can't do because of the way their departments are structured and organized. If we didn't utilize that and take advantage of that, then I would definitely move. But I would definitely choose to be on a team again.

Pat Litwiller and the other members of the WINS team are joined together by their common mission, which is posted on the walls of the team meeting room: "Implement and operate a consolidated international claims processing system with common business practices worldwide." The WINS team operates as a system to achieve its goal. It possesses the characteristics of a system described in Chapter 1.

A systems perspective prepares you to treat each group as a unique entity. That does not mean, however, that there will be no similar patterns from group to group. In fact, Rentsch, Heffner, and Duffy (1994) found that individuals who had limited experience with teams described the teams in very specific, concrete terms. As their experience with teams increased, their descriptions became more abstract and complex. The experienced team members were able to conceptualize the common elements of their experience, developing a teamwork schema that then aided them in adapting to new situations they faced. Increasing your experience with groups increases your ability to generalize about them, which allows you to adapt to new group experiences with greater ease.

The way groups form can be likened to the process of piecing a quilt. In creating a quilt, attention must first be given to individual fabric pieces. Then, when the pieces are grouped together, patterns are created that can be expected throughout the quilt. The pieces are sewn together, more tightly in some quilts than in others. Then, layer by layer, the whole quilt is formed. Our attention to the group formation process in this chapter will be similar to the attention we might pay to quilt making. We will consider the individual components of groups: first, the members; second, the patterns (of behavior) that come to be expected of members; third, how tightly connected the members of the group become; and fourth, the series of stages groups follow in developing themselves into a fully functioning system. Finally, we will consider the role of communication in the group development process.

The Individual Components: Group Members

Even before the WINS team formed, the individual employees worked at GM in other capacities. But those employees became essential components of the team. No

This quilting group has gone through a process of formation that can be likened to the quilt they are creating. From individual pieces (or members) that are tied together more or less closely, patterns of expected behaviors begin to appear. Like a quilt that is formed from layers, a group develops in a series of stages. (Photo by Craig Johnson.)

group could exist without members. Although in a system the interactions among members receive more attention than the actual individuals themselves, three factors affect the members' interactions: the nature of the members, the number of members, and change in a group's membership.

The Nature of the Members

In many ways, the WINS team membership is ideal for encouraging effective interaction. First, it is diverse. If a group is to gain the full advantages of interaction, then diversity in membership is desirable. Rogelberg and Rumery (1996) clarify the fact that homogeneity and heterogeneity are never absolute: group members are always similar in some qualities and different in others. Often it is useful, though, for group members to be somewhat homogeneous in task-irrelevant qualities (so that conflict over irrelevancies does not develop) and heterogeneous in task-relevant qualities (so that the group members can bring different perspectives and skills to analyzing issues and implementing solutions). In the case of the WINS team, there are both task-relevant and task-irrelevant differences among group members. However, as their consideration of an ethnic potluck reveals, the team members make an effort to celebrate all types of diversity within the group.

Each member comes to a group with some personality and communication traits that will affect the nature of group interaction. Among the traits relevant to a member's communication in a group are the member's level of dogmatism, willingness to communicate, argumentativeness, and willingness to collaborate.

Dogmatism refers to an individual's closed-mindedness. A dogmatic group member will enter the group discussion with a rigid belief structure, including a clear separation between ideas believed (those supported by a central, accepted source) and those rejected. If you have seen syndicated episodes of the old television series, *All in the Family*, you may recognize Archie Bunker as a typical dogmatic. He had strong ideas about what and who was right, and he rejected everyone outside of that circle. Groups are more likely to function smoothly if their members fall at the opposite end of the continuum, because individuals low in dogmatism are more open-minded. They will evaluate ideas within the group discussion on the merits of the ideas themselves.

Willingness to communicate is a second trait relevant to small group members. Group members who are less willing to communicate may feel a general sense of social alienation, be introverts (rather than extroverts), feel less skillful as communicators, or have low self-esteem. Or they may feel different enough from the rest of the group that they are unsure of their reception within the group. Whatever the specific cause, an apprehension about communication makes it unlikely for some people to volunteer comments in a discussion. If you find yourself in a group with members who seem unwilling to communicate, it will be important for you to discover the comfort range of those group members. By making it more comfortable for them to communicate, without pressuring them to do so, you could add valuable perspectives to the group—and, in the process, increase the members' willingness to communicate in the future.

If you, yourself, are a group member who experiences discomfort when you communicate, then increasing your training in small group communication can be especially helpful to you. As you build your skill within a group and experience success as a part of a group, you should discover your value to your group and the value that groups can have for you. That realization should increase your willingness to communicate in the future. At the other extreme, of course, there may be some who are overly willing to communicate, and they will need to learn to be sensitive to the signals from the group that regulate the flow of communication so that all members of the group can participate.

A third trait of group members is their **argumentativeness.** Despite the fact that many people regard argument as negative, argumentativeness is a positive quality (Infante, Rancer, & Womack, 1993). It relates to an individual's tendency to develop a position, to present reasons for the position being taken, and to analyze the arguments made by other members of the group. A group member high in argumentativeness can assist the group in making good, well-reasoned decisions and avoiding bad decisions. In contrast to someone who is argumentative, the member who is verbally aggressive attacks not the arguments of another, but the other person's self-concept. A group member high in verbal aggressiveness will only add to the discomfort of the group, because the group will not feel safe for the other members. Often an individual resorts to verbal aggressiveness out of a feeling of inadequacy—not knowing any more sophisticated ways of expressing disagreement. Knowledge of the tools of analysis discussed in Chapter 6 can combat such feelings of inadequacy.

It should be obvious that interaction would be affected by a fourth trait of group members: their **collaborativeness.** Anderson, Martin, and Infante (1999) defined decision-making collaborativeness as a trait reflecting a member's willingness to be actively involved with others in the negotiation required during decision making. They have developed a scale to measure decision-making collaborativeness; it is included in the Appendix of this book. The scale correlates strongly with measures of argumentativeness and willingness to communicate. Someone willing to collaborate is likely to seek reasons for positions others have taken, suggest and explore alternate solutions, and speak freely and directly to other group members, even when there is conflict. Having group members with this trait will make it easier to reach good decisions.

Group Size

The number of members included within a group has a major impact on interaction. If the group is too small, there may be insufficient resources to stimulate interaction among the members. There may also be more conflict—and conflict that is less easily resolved—because each member is so fully involved in the interaction that it is difficult for any one of them to get the distance from the issue necessary to resolve it. Groups of three might reduce the difficulties associated with coordinating meeting times, but could still end up being too small for the comfort of the members in the long run.

On the other hand, as group size increases, each member's involvement in the group decreases. As involvement declines, so does the satisfaction of group members. Leadership of a large, participating group becomes more difficult. As a result, the leader of a large group is more likely to use an authoritarian style, which also decreases group member satisfaction (Carron & Spink, 1995).

A range of sizes may be acceptable, depending on the group's task or history. The general prescription is that the ideal size for a group is five to seven members. It would not be surprising to find that in classroom groups, a group of five seems ideal. Perhaps the best rule of thumb to follow is provided by Brilhart and Galanes (1995), who recommend the creation of a **least-sized group**—one with the fewest possible members needed to get the job done. Someone who is part of the group but is not needed to complete the task will add to the problems of the group. In the case of the WINS team, group size has increased as additional tasks have been assigned to the team. However, the ability to communicate freely at meetings is constrained by the size of the team.

Change in Membership

Few groups maintain constant membership throughout their lives. Not only are changes in membership common, but they can be desirable. Change reduces routinization within the group. Conflict can be lower (while the group "behaves" in the presence of the newcomer), and the focus on the task can increase. If group members choose the change themselves, then cohesiveness can increase. Also, when the membership changes, the group often becomes more attuned to its own processes, which has advantages for the group and its members. In the WINS team, the addition of new members brought the group's attention to its processes.

Some changes can be costly to groups, as work groups quickly discover. In fact, Dawn Cross, who serves Corning as a director of diversity, reported that Corning became involved in diversity efforts when they realized how costly it was to lose workers (in their company, frequently women and African American workers) who felt uncomfortable in an environment that did not seem to welcome them. The company estimated that it was spending close to two million dollars a year in training new workers to replace the lost skilled workers (Morrison, Ruderman, & Hughes-James, 1993). The cost of change in groups is more than financial. Whenever the membership of the group changes, disruption within the group is inevitable, because the established patterns of interaction no longer hold. In the opening narrative, Pat Litwiller mentioned that the WINS team has realized that not all of the team members have been indoctrinated into the philosophy of the group. When changes have come from one or more new members being added to the group, then nearly normal patterns of interaction can be resumed once new members have been socialized into the group. Jones and Crandall (1985) recommend that both the original group and the new members should be prepared for changes about to occur in group membership. Then the new member is more likely to know how to behave in ways acceptable to the group. The old members are more likely to be accepting, too, both because they are prepared to remember what is was like to join the group themselves and because they see a member performing in ways consistent with the group's norms.

In addition to the amount of preparation before the change, other factors can affect the impact that membership change has on the group. Arrow and McGrath (1993) list several relevant factors:

- The arithmetic of change matters (whether members are added, substracted, or substituted and the size of the change, both in absolute and proportional terms).
- The impetus for change matters (whether it is initiated by one member of the group, by the group as a whole, or by an individual outside the group).
- Temporal aspects associated with the change matter (how frequent, regular, and predictable the change is, what its duration is, and how the timing of the change interacts with other factors in the group's development).
- Who changes matters (the centrality of the role played by a departing member, or the skills brought to the group by a new member).

A single highly skilled member, asked to join a group by its members who have identified a need for additional help, will add to the success of the group. On the other hand, a group can be undermined if individuals on whom the group is dependent are regularly transferred to other work teams just as the group is about to begin functioning in predictable ways.

Change in group membership may occur by chance as members change jobs or classes. However, it can also be initiated into the group purposefully. In that case, the changes introduced should be made with enough attention to the factors that matter to allow the group to succeed and even improve. When excessive change is unavoidable, then groups cannot expect to forge ahead, nor be expected to be immediately productive. They need time to redesign themselves, for the changes made in group membership are changes felt throughout the entire system. The nature and number of members, along with changes in membership, all affect the interaction within a group. Considering group membership is the first step toward understanding the group formation process, because members are the initial components of the group.

Ethical Consideration

If you are responsible for forming groups, then you should give them a chance to succeed. Frequent, large, or unpredictable changes in groups leave them unable to experience success.

Expected Patterns of Behavior

Just as the initial components of a quilt (the fabric pieces) are joined together to create patterns reappearing throughout the quilt, so the group members are joined together in such a way that we expect to see recurring patterns of behavior within the group. Some of those behaviors, the roles, are expected of individual group members. Others, the norms, are behaviors expected of all group members. Both develop through interaction once group members have been brought together.

Roles

A **role** can be defined as *the patterns of behavior performed by and expected of a given group member.* A role, then, is a composite of behaviors that come to be associated with a specific individual within a group.

Types of Role-Related Behaviors. There are any number of behaviors that are fundamentally communicative that groups need someone to perform. They fall within two categories, representing the two distinct areas of concern for the group members: behaviors related to task accomplishment and behaviors related to group maintenance (Benne & Sheats, 1948). Actually, this distinction may be oversimplified. Any given message conveys two types of information: (1) some related to the content of the message (the content dimension) and (2) some related to the relationship between the communicators (the relationship dimension). A message that says, "Let's meet at noon in my office," has content about a future meeting, its time, and its place. The same message may convey dominance over the other group members (my office, not theirs) and (depending on its tone and other nonverbal behaviors) could communicate levels of trust and liking of the others. Because of the presence of both content and relationship dimensions within each message, one comment can enhance the group relationship at the same time it advances task accomplishment. Nonetheless, some behaviors are intended to address task needs primarily, while others are intended primarily to advance group maintenance needs. The following list identifies the behaviors by name and, as a means of defining each, illustrates the kinds of comments that serve each identified function.

Task-Related Behaviors

1. Initiate discussion.

   "I guess it is time for us to start. We have a lot to decide about setting up volunteers for the community soup kitchen."

2. Orient and energize the group.

   "It is five o'clock, and we have only fifteen minutes left before we have to leave, so we had better get back to the topic at hand." Or, "I think our ideas are great. Now we all need to agree to complete our part of the project by our next meeting."

3. Seek information and/or opinions.

   "If we are going to figure out a system for getting volunteers for the soup kitchen, then we need to know how many volunteers we need. Were you able to get that information, Ned?" or "We need to evaluate these ideas we have come up with. This is a good time to give your opinions, whatever they are. Anita, what are your opinions about these ideas?"

4. Supply information and/or opinions.

   "Yesterday I interviewed the director of the soup kitchen. She said that in addition to the regular cooks, each day three volunteers are needed to help serve the meal and clean up afterward." Or, "I like the first idea better than the second."

5. Expand on another's contribution (by elaborating or clarifying).

   "Ned said that we need to find three volunteers, minimum, for each day. Because the soup kitchen is open five days a week, then I guess we would need to find fifteen people a week." Or, "Brenda, do you mean that we need to find the people ourselves or that we need to devise a system with which someone else could find fifteen people a week?"

6. Evaluate.

   "I have been thinking about the information Ned got from the director of the soup kitchen. She has been a bit disorganized, and I am not sure that we can rely on her estimates. For instance, she said we would need about three people a day to serve lunch and then stay to clean up. We might want to consider getting more volunteers, so that each of them would have a more limited job. If they did not feel overworked, they would be willing to come back again, so we might not need to have a different set of people each day of the week."

7. Summarize.

   "Okay, we have had two different ideas presented—one that we need to get a commitment from campus groups to staff the soup kitchen, with each group committing itself to two weeks throughout the school year. The other idea is that, because we have developed an interest in this project, we stay involved and seek volunteers, whether from campus groups or from individual students, even if they are not members of other groups."

8. Coordinate ideas—and test for consensus.

   "From the comments I have heard so far, it seems as if most of us think that the best approach would be to commit campus groups. Is that what all of you are thinking at this point, or are there other ideas I have overlooked?"

9. Coordinate procedure.

"Let me read what we have said we need: First, someone to get us a list of all campus groups, and a phone number and address where each can be reached. Second, a couple of people to write a letter to all of the campus groups, explaining the program, and send it to them. Third, someone to call them all to be sure they got the letter and see what they have decided. A couple people, at least, will need to go to any groups who ask us to come to speak to them about the program. If I am not forgetting anything, then I guess we should all pick something from this list that we are willing and able to do."

10. Record.

"I took notes from the last meeting, and Jan said she would get the list of organization names, addresses, and phone numbers."

Group-Maintenance Behaviors

1. Manage the conversational flow (serve as "gatekeeper").

"Tom, you have not had a chance to talk yet. What do you think about this?"

2. Observe and report on group process.

"I noticed that when Chris missed the last meeting, no one said anything about it. Now today, Chris is missing again."

3. Set and maintain standards for group process.

"Attendance should be expected of each of us. If we are letting one person miss meetings without making it clear that it is a problem, then we are really encouraging everyone to miss meetings. We need to make it clear to Chris that attendance is required—and we should attach some penalty to the absences."

4. Harmonize or compromise.

"Even though we ended up choosing a different idea than the one you first suggested, I think that having such a good alternative as a possibility made us look more carefully at our ideas. Without you, I do not think we would have succeeded in doing the critical evaluation we are expected to do."

5. Encourage members.

"Chris, your contributions have really been good—and they have made up for the times you had to miss. I know it has been hard for you to devote so much time to the group, but you have really made a difference to us."

6. Relieve tension.

   a. Directly—by joking

   "Okay, so Chris thought that an appendectomy was a legitimate excuse. What a pain that was!"

   b. Indirectly—by dramatizing

   "Did you hear about the time the mayor of San Francisco made a nasty comment about a 49er football player who did not play well? Well, the player's son was undergoing surgery . . . The mayor did not know about that and later had to apologize. It is funny how what we do not know can affect our impressions."

7. Express solidarity.

   "You know, our whole group has done some really great work so far. I think if we keep this up, we will surprise everyone with what we have been able to accomplish. I do not think there is another team that will do as well as we will."

In addition to the behaviors that facilitate effective group action in either the task or group maintenance areas, there are behaviors that are excessive or that focus on the individual rather than the group and therefore interfere with the group's ability to function well. These **process-hindering behaviors** (Salazar, 1996) include an individual's move to

1. Block (an evaluation behavior carried to the extreme, so that every idea proposed by the group is found faulty, but usually in such vague ways that the group has no idea how to succeed in finding a satisfactory proposal).
2. Withdraw (internalizing the tension of the group and deciding not to communicate any further with the group).
3. Seek recognition (a behavior that demands attention from other group members for one's own behaviors).
4. Dominate (a behavior that assumes that small group discussion is competitive rather than cooperative and therefore involves an effort to occupy as much of the group's time as possible).
5. Plead for a special interest (a behavior that directs attention to an issue on the personal agenda of a group member even though it is in conflict with the agenda of the group).

A group member who chooses an anti-group, process-hindering behavior becomes associated with that single behavior. Group members who select from the behaviors that facilitate task accomplishment and group maintenance will almost always perform several of the behaviors, although one or another of the behaviors may be predominant.

An individual's role in the group is normally described by the *patterns of behavior*, not by a single behavior. For instance, Pat Litwiller might be viewed as a team unifier. In addition to expressing solidarity, she expresses her opinion on issues relevant to the team, provides information to other team members, offers procedural assistance, and asks for information from other members. Thus, a role is the total constellation of behaviors that an individual performs and that the group comes to expect of that member.

Development of a Role. A group member's role is developed through a process of interaction within the group. The process is initiated when an individual selects from among the possible behaviors those that feel most comfortable to perform. As we select our roles within a group, we rely first on those behaviors our personalities have prepared us best to perform. Multiple roles are possible, but some are more comfortable than others. Perhaps we decide to experiment with a new role, intriguing to us, but somewhat unfamiliar. More frequently, we will have performed a particular role before and be familiar with the script required to perform it. At times, experience with a role can be overly limiting; a group member might fall into a rut, demanding the same role at all times, regardless of the needs of the group. Benne and Sheats (1948) cautioned that it is important to have the flexibility to adopt new behaviors needed by a group at a particular time in its development.

Our formal position may require us to perform a particular role. For instance, the individual who leads a support group is, by virtue of that position, thrust into the role of a leader required to initiate discussion, seek information and opinions, summarize, manage the conversational flow, maintain standards for group process, and encourage members. In a work group, the member who has just joined the group will be more likely to seek information and to record the group's process than to orient the group. In a work group in which members have an overlap of backgrounds in some areas and gaps in others, the member of management who composed the team may need to engage the group in a discussion of formal roles so that role conflict does not occur (Colantuono & Schnidman, 1988). When more than one member is qualified for a role, members might negotiate among themselves for roles. They will also need to determine who will work to gain expertise in the areas in which no one is currently qualified. In some groups, such as a surgical team, it is critical that group members have clearly defined roles with no role ambiguity before the work of the group begins (Hare, 1994).

It is not uncommon for more than one member to have experience with the same role, such as task leader. When another group member begins to perform a role you might have selected for yourself, then it is likely that one of you will withdraw from the role. Someone who withdraws from one role will select another role instead. The behavior of other group members is a factor in determining role selection within a group. Not only will we avoid a role another member can perform as well as—or perhaps better than—we can, but we may also select a role that no other group member has selected. That is particularly true when the demands of the group require a particular set of behaviors to be performed but no group member has stepped up to perform those behaviors.

The specific demands on a group can be such a powerful determinant of our role selection that Kuypers and Alers (1996) refer to roles as being "sucked out" of a group member. They argue that during the group development process, a group struggles

Ethical Consideration

The needs of the group may require you to move beyond a narrow comfort zone of performing roles familiar to you. Expanding the roles you play in a group has an advantage of developing your own skills within the small group context, but we believe that it is also one's responsibility to perform behaviors that meet a group's needs.

with resolving a set of issues. At each stage of development, a pair of opposite choices confronts the group. The group vacillates between two polarities, neither of which is a comfortable solution for the group. The issue will be resolved only when a group member assumes a role (or is sucked into a role) that allows the group to moderate its original position. Therefore, Kuypers and Alers say that an individual's role within the group is determined by that person's own personality, the behaviors of others, and the demands of the situation.

Working together, these factors identify the role that a group member is likely to assume. The process of assuming a role occurs through interaction. Suppose you enjoy leading a group. Perhaps you have a bit of a perfectionist streak, so your personality encourages you to be in charge of a task to be sure it is done well. In early meetings, you are likely to be less silent than some of the other members. You may also act less tentatively than other group members do. In later meetings, you continue to speak up frequently and you make moves to help the group resolve the issues that it faces. But your actions are not the only ones that are relevant. Suppose that another member of your group, a woman, has been performing much as you have been. You realize that the two of you are in competition for the same role. You begin to evaluate her behaviors and to notice the responses of the rest of the group to both of you. If you begin to feel that she does a fine job of leading the group, or that your leadership is not really necessary in this group and that it would be pleasant not to have the responsibility of being leader for once, or that the rest of the group seems to prefer her style to yours, then you may withdraw from the competition. In that case, perhaps you will begin to perform some other behaviors. You might begin to increase your evaluation of others' ideas, and seek the role of devil's advocate for your group. The needs of the group will lead you to select another role, which you begin to assume. Initially, you would probably perform the required behaviors tentatively; then you will adjust your behavior as you receive feedback from the group.

Role Expectations.   Once a role has been selected by an individual, other group members develop clear expectations that the individual will perform in a role-consistent manner. To illustrate that point, consider the case of George Clooney, who (although he has since become a successful actor) was a student in a small group communication

Technology Note: Importance of Role Clarity

The process of role assignment increases in difficulty for groups that interact at a distance rather than face-to-face. The subtleties of the interaction process make communicating about roles over E-mail more difficult. Moreover, in technologically linked groups, members are likely to play a larger number of roles and to change the roles they play more frequently as team membership and task change. Therefore, Lipnack and Stamps (1997) contend that the need for role clarification is greater for such teams than it is for groups that meet in a single location.

classroom at Northern Kentucky University in the late 1970s. With a personality that enjoyed attention and avoided much that was serious, George assumed the role of tension reliever with ease. He continually cracked jokes and frequently seemed to avoid the task. For an in-class exercise, George was assigned to a group that had to share information to resolve a problem. Each group member had been given a minimal amount of information, so all needed the information of other group members—except George. George had been given all of the information necessary to make a sound decision on his own. However, the task required him to share his information with the rest of the group. He acted the role he was assigned perfectly; he offered the others the pieces of information they needed—and did so seriously. But every time George contributed a piece of information to the group, the other members discounted it. It was not the behaviors George performed during that particular class meeting that led the rest of the group to ignore everything he said. Rather, his previous behavior in the group had created such a clear role for him that the group's expectations affected perceptions of his behavior during the exercise. The roles each of us assumes within a group will affect the expectations others have of us and, ultimately, their perceptions of our behaviors.

Norms

During the same time that a group is determining what roles individual members will play, the group is also establishing its **norms,** *the expectations for behavior of all members while working within the group.* Norms relate to the behavior of members only while they function within the group. For instance, a group may agree that no one will smoke during meetings, but will not regulate that behavior for members when they are away from the group.

Explicit and Implicit Norms. Some norms will be developed *explicitly;* that is, the group will talk directly about its preferred behavior and may even write it down. The WINS group has made explicit its preferred behaviors for group meetings in this list:

> Start on time.
> No zingers.
> Listen to each other.
> One person speaks at a time.
> Encourage total participation (raise your hand if necessary).
> All ideas are good ideas.
> It is OK to disagree.
> Strive for consensus (show of hands, s'port).
> No hidden agendas.
> Set a time limit for topics (controlled by facilitator).

Most of a group's norms remain *implicit*—or understood by group members although no one has ever talked directly about them, let alone written them out. For instance, many groups develop the norm that members always sit in the same places during meetings—but seldom (if ever) because they have talked about it and agreed to

The WINS team learned the norm of "S'port" when they participated in team-building exercises like this one at the Saturn facility. (Photo compliments of the Saturn Corporation.)

do so. The norm is arrived at implicitly. Additional implicit norms may include these: new group members should be quieter in meetings than continuing group members; the way members dress for group meetings at which only group members are present is less formal than the way they dress when those outside the group will be present; if food is brought to a group meeting, it will be shared with anyone who wants some. In the opening narrative, Pat Litwiller said that she could not think of any informal, implicit norms offhand. That is not an uncommon response, because implicit norms seem so natural that it is often difficult to identify them. Nonetheless, Pat mentioned several implicit norms: to laugh and joke with each other, to share personal information, and to solve problems within the team without taking the issues to management.

Development of Norms.   Several factors affect the initial preferences for norms within a particular group; what is personally preferred, what is legal, and what is culturally comfortable will all be relevant. One classroom group chose to sit on the floor during each of its meetings, even when comfortable chairs were available. They were following their personal preferences for a seating arrangement in which each member could spread out and would be "equal" to every other member. Even a group willing to allow members to smoke at meetings would not do so if the group meets in a building which is, by law, smoke free. Cultural norms will also be reflected in the norms groups choose for themselves. Groups of U.S. workers usually share a norm allowing them to challenge each other during group meetings, whereas in groups of Japanese workers, disagreements will be identified and resolved in private conversations between members prior to a meeting. These differences in norms can be traced to differences in cultural rules about avoiding the loss of face for members.

When individuals from different cultures are joined in a group, they may bring with them norm preferences that clash. A worker whose culture places family at the center of the value system would find it more comfortable to work in a group that involves families in recognition ceremonies, but more difficult to work in a group with a norm of scheduling meetings that conflict with family time. Someone from a culture that encourages open expression of emotion may find it difficult to work with others whose cultural norms encourage keeping feelings private. Morrison, Ruderman, and Hughes-James (1993) report a case of a hospital work group in which Filipino workers were performing below standard because they did not want to admit that they had not understood the supervisor's instructions. According to their cultural background, such an admission would have amounted to an unacceptable criticism of the supervisor for having been unclear.

As a group interacts, the initially preferred norms will be supported or rejected through a process that parallels that used to establish roles for group members: behaviors will be performed, initially with some tentativeness; then the responses of the group members will encourage or discourage repetitions of the behavior. Suppose Byron shows up a little late for one of his group's first meetings. If no one says anything about his tardy arrival, his subsequent arrivals may be even later. But if someone in the group jokes that Byron apparently has more important things to do and places to be, the joke serves as a transparent reminder that being on time is expected of all members. Perhaps Byron misinterprets the point of the joke and assumes that the group members were accepting of lateness. Then the group can expect him to repeat his late arrival behavior. If nothing further is said to him, the group can anticipate that other members will also begin to be late. If the group does not want late arrivals to become the norm, the members must then respond more directly to the behavior, clearly indicating that it is unacceptable to be late to meetings. Unless unacceptable behaviors are responded to negatively in a clear and consistent manner, members are likely to continue to perform them.

In the course of a group's interactions, additional norms will develop. If a group decides that it is willing to produce poor quality work, then the additional norms will allow those low standards to be met. The group may agree not to "rock the boat" by challenging another's ideas. They will agree to tolerate absences of group members. They will agree to allow each member to work independently, with no quality check on the parts of the product when individual segments are assembled as a group product. If, instead, a group decides to demand of itself the high quality work of which its members are capable, then the group's norms will encourage testing of ideas, require commitment to the group through attendance at meetings and completion of assigned tasks, and incorporate quality control mechanisms so that mistakes do not slip through. All groups' norms allow them to function in the manner in which they have agreed to perform.

The Value of Norms.   As norms begin to be determined within a group, the members' comfort level increases. Initial uncertainty about what behaviors are expected within the group gives way to clear expectations. Norms carry with them a level of expectation, evaluation, and enforcement. Group members know, once a norm is established, what the expected behavior is. When a group member's behavior is consistent with the group norms, it will be evaluated favorably; negative evaluations will be associated with behavior inconsistent with the norms. Norms also carry with them a level of enforcement. If a norm truly exists for a particular group, then violations of the norm will be punished. No solitary confinement or capital punishment is envisioned here. But some reprimand will make it clear to the offending member that the group cannot tolerate the offending behavior. With clear group norms, the behavior of members is regulated by the group as a whole. No individual member needs to control behavior. Norms, therefore, equalize power among the group members.

Norm Violations.   Not all group members follow all group norms in all circumstances. A new member may unknowingly violate a norm—and suddenly discover what the group's norms are. Violations are likely if someone feels little commitment to the group or sees him- or herself as different from the group. A norm that seems to make little difference in the way the group functions is likely to be violated. So, if a group accomplishes nothing during its meetings, then its members will come to see attendance at meetings as an unimportant, and even useless, expectation. Norms that are violated by other members and norms that are not enforced are likely targets for violation. Once one member misses a meeting, others are likely to feel comfortable doing so unless the group has punished the norm violation in some clear and consistent way. Punishments for norm violations involve a range of responses; their severity usually parallels the severity of the violation. A joke or raised eyebrow may do for minor violations; more severe ones may be met with an assigned extra task, isolation from or rejection by the group, reports to a superior, or even monetary or legal responses. For most situations, quick, descriptive feedback of the violation (such as that described in Chapter 4) will be sufficient as a reprimand.

Groups often grant their leaders **idiosyncrasy credits,** *permission to be different from the group by violating some norms.* In introducing the concept of idiosyncrasy credits, Hollander (1958) explained that a member's early conforming to group norms yields for the member a higher status; with the status come idiosyncrasy credits. Such credits might allow the leader to talk for a longer time than others do or to express displeasure with the group more directly than others can. Estrada, Brown, and Lee (1995) discovered that idiosyncrasy credits were granted to leaders of groups that performed well, but not to leaders of groups that performed poorly.

Changing Norms.   An effective group may occasionally need to consider whether its norms are appropriate. However, groups are not always aware of their norms, since most norms are implicit. It is easiest to identify a norm when it has been violated by a group member; the norm becomes apparent when responses make it clear that a behavior was unacceptable. Comparing one group to another makes other norms clear. For instance, many of us are unaware of some norms within our own families until we spend time with the family of a friend or, even more telling, meet our in-laws—and discover that families do indeed operate in different ways!

Once norms are discovered, their appropriateness can be determined by evaluating their utility in accomplishing the task well and in creating a comfortable setting for all members. Often groups develop a norm "not to rock the boat," thinking it will increase comfort for group members. However, that norm interferes with task excellence, for it prohibits members from raising challenges to weak ideas. Moreover, prohibiting the expression of negativity even interferes with developing cohesiveness (Stokes, 1983), because group members know the group does not trust them enough to allow them to express their thoughts.

Groups will also change with the influx of new members, and especially as they increase in diversity. As they do so, additional attention needs to be given to norms that limit the comfort of all members. Miller (1988) suggests that with the addition of team members with backgrounds outside of traditional white, male corporate

Technology Note: Changing Norms for Technology Use

Groups that are situated within organizations may need to change norms as the norms of the organizations change. This is particularly true when the organization is changing the way it is communicating. When work groups are expected to communicate via E-mail rather than by memos or in face-to-face meetings, it may take special efforts to reinforce the expected changes. Lipnack and Stamps (1997) found that two factors were useful in such cases: (1) using familiar technologies to remind group members to use new technologies, and (2) making sure that the new technology could be used for social contacts that were pleasurable. Both increase the chances of the technology being used by the group for work.

America, work teams face the fact that their norms may involve racist and sexist behaviors uncomfortable to the new members. He adds that

> part of the new persons' struggle, therefore, is to recognize they may pay a price for being pioneers. . . . if, after joining the team, this person fails to point out instances of sexism and racism, the team will have a false feeling of comfort regarding these issues. (p. 197)

That responsibility continues for all members, new and old, whatever their background. Pat Litwiller, whom you met in the opening narrative, faced that task when a new worker (her hierarchical equal) was added to the team while she was out of the office. She was startled upon her return when, after they met, he asked her to type his report for him. The team's norms had recognized the equal value and equal responsibility of all members, but it was violated when the new member applied a stereotype to assume that since Pat is a female in a male-dominated field, she must also be a secretary. In this case, the norms needed to be reinforced—probably with a good dose of humor. In other cases, norms must be changed to allow the full integration of all members so they can work in comfort despite their diversity. By mentally adopting the role of other group members, you may be able to recognize norms that demean individuals from other cultural backgrounds and identify them as inappropriate and in need of change.

When norms must be changed, a group reenters the turbulent stage it faced prior to establishing norms in the first place. Despite the initial discomfort that it will create, altering the norms so that they become more appropriate pays dividends in the long run. If you are in a group in which inappropriate norms have developed, prepare to change the norm in the following way.

First, observe the norm and its outcome. In some cases, you might even adopt the norm yourself, despite the fact that on first glance it is unproductive. You may discover that it has values you had not appreciated at the outset. Even if your judgment still is that the norm is undesirable in the long run, at least you will have a full appreciation of what else will change in the group when the norm is changed.

Second, describe the norm and its outcome to your group members. You might say, for instance, "I have been keeping track of how prompt we are at the beginning of meetings. At the last four meetings, we have not had a quorum when the meeting was scheduled to begin. The people who were here on time were pretty restless—and even angry—by the time the meeting actually started. Last week, we had to go back over the first agenda item three times as group members trickled in. Because it makes us inefficient and because it creates negative attitudes, I think that we need to stop accepting tardiness for scheduled meetings."

Third, involve the rest of the group in a discussion of the norm to determine what other behaviors are preferable and possible and to identify a new preferred norm. Finally, along with other members, continue the change process by reinforcing the desired behavior and punishing the undesired behavior.

The issue of late arrivals at meetings was one that the Interpersonal and Public Communication faculty at Central Michigan University dealt with at one point. The group considered scheduling meetings later to match the arrival time that had become the norm, but decided to keep the earlier start time. Then the faculty member who

Ethical Consideration

If a current group norm discourages excellence, don't lower your own personal standard to accept the group norms. Instead, initiate the process required to change norms and raise the standards of the group to a higher level.

took minutes implemented a "punishment" for late arrivals: on the list of faculty present, those who arrived late were listed after a semicolon. The minutes were sent to the department chair and to the dean, neither of whom was aware of the meaning of the semicolon. The group members, however, were aware and began to hurry to meetings so that they would arrive "before the semicolon." If a conflict required them to be late, they mentioned it to the leader, asking her to tell the secretary why they would be arriving "after the semicolon." As minor as the "punishment" was, it helped to reinforce the norm the group desired.

Until a group has resolved decisions about the roles members will play and the norms they will follow, the group operates with a sense of uncertainty. Once these issues are resolved, the group can develop a solid sense of itself, with clear expectations about behavior patterns.

Cohesiveness

The patterns we expect to see in a quilt are all sewn together. But how closely together they are sewn will vary. Similarly, groups will vary in how close their members are, or in their level of cohesiveness. **Cohesiveness** is a dynamic, multidimensional property of groups that can be defined as the *shared perception of and attachment to the group by its members*. The members share a perception of the group because they have reached consensus about the goals and values of the group (so they see the group as integrated at the task level) and about the roles and norms for group members (so they see the group as integrated at the social level). The perceptions of the group by its members are not just similar; they are also positive (Keyton, 1992); thus, group members feel attached to the group. They are attracted to both the task and the social components of the group and are committed enough to resist disruption of the group (Cota, Evans, Dion, Kilik, & Longman, 1995). In the opening narrative, Pat discussed the WINS team in such a way that we can identify it as a group working to maintain a high level of cohesiveness. Pat puts up with her long daily commute because it is fun to go to work; the group is clearly attractive to her, and she is committed to it. Cohesive groups would describe their members as being friendly and willing to stick up for one another, help each other out, and work well together.

The number of components involved in cohesiveness explains why it is regarded as multidimensional. It is considered to be dynamic because members' feelings about a group change over time. One factor that can strain cohesiveness is an increase in work pressure, unless the leader of the group is able to absorb some of the pressure (Klein, 1996).

Factors Influencing Cohesiveness.   Central to high cohesiveness within groups is the satisfaction of the members. In trying to understand the nature of satisfaction, Keyton (1991) found that satisfaction is a global element, and dissatisfaction is more situation-specific. In other words, when everything is going right, we will be satisfied with a group. When any one thing goes wrong, we can become dissatisfied. We are more likely to be able to identify why we are dissatisfied with a group than to identify why we are satisfied with it. Nevertheless, we can pinpoint some specific factors that usually interact with member satisfaction to create a cohesive group.

If members have joined the group voluntarily, receive equal treatment, like one another, communicate freely, and are involved in decision making, their group is likely to be cohesive (Balgopal, Ephross, & Vassil, 1986; Widmeyer & Williams, 1991). Groups in which there is clarity about the goal and the members' roles are likely to be cohesive. Groups that achieve early successes become cohesive. Once a group defines itself as cohesive, its cohesiveness increases. Gemmill (1986) cautions that groups that define themselves as cohesive by comparing themselves to a disliked out-group may be fooling themselves. Often they see in the out-group the shadow of their own disliked behaviors. They recognize and hate those behaviors in the other group, but they fail to recognize or to remedy them in their own group.

True cohesiveness will increase when the leader of the group recognizes the importance of cohesiveness and works to develop it, perhaps with a team-building intervention. Carron and Spink (1995) explain that team-building interventions are most effective when they focus on one of the following items at a time: establishing group norms, establishing stability in roles, producing group distinctiveness, facilitating sacrifices from individuals for the group, and enhancing interactions and communication among the group members. In the opening narrative, Pat described one of the team-building exercises the WINS team members had done and indicated that it was one of many activities designed to build the team as it was forming. When changes in the team occur, as they have for the WINS team, then it is reasonable to explore the use of additional interventions to rebuild and maintain group cohesiveness.

Cohesiveness can also develop much less formally, when group members have time and opportunities to exchange personal information. Such exchanges build trust, and trust is a basic ingredient in cohesiveness.

Technology Note: Trust at a Distance

For groups that meet face-to-face, the exchanges that build trust can occur rather easily. A personal story might be shared while members are gathering for a meeting. An exchange of smiles lets one member know that another understands and cares. For groups that connect electronically, similar exchanges may be possible (but are more difficult). Yet trust is an even more important component of groups that cannot check up on each other in person. Even virtual teams, then, may need to meet in person from time to time so that trust can be built more easily.

The Outcomes of Cohesiveness.   Cohesiveness is desired in most groups because it has outcomes that are, primarily, positive. Cohesive groups increase the sense of security for their members, allowing them to disclose even more information about themselves and to express their conflicts (Evans & Jarvis, 1980). Once expressed, the conflicts can be resolved to the benefit of the group. Members of groups that lack cohesiveness are likely to drop out of the groups (Spink & Carron, 1994). Cohesive group members increase their investment in the group, their commitment to resolve issues the group faces, and their desire to be good group members. Therefore, they are more likely to follow group norms and meet role expectations. In fact, it is the members of highly cohesive groups that are most likely to abide by the norms of the group.

One of the questions that has attracted the attention of researchers is the relationship between cohesiveness and group performance. Most of the evidence suggests that cohesiveness improves performance. For instance, Dorn, Papalewis, and Brown (1995) found that doctoral students who felt a high degree of cohesiveness with the cohort of students in their doctoral programs reported that the group's cohesiveness had a profound influence on their persistence in the program. Kidwell, Mossholder, and Bennett (1997), who studied groups in the service sector, discovered that members of highly cohesive groups worked more as "group citizens" than those in less cohesive groups. Although many groups that are cohesive have been found to have improved performance (Evans & Dion, 1991), we can each probably recall groups that enjoyed each other so much (and so much of the time) that they ended up not being productive.

The evidence that some cohesive groups lose productivity has led some small group scholars (Ellis & Fisher, 1994) to describe a curvilinear relationship between cohesiveness and productivity (assuming that moderate cohesiveness helps productivity, but very high or low cohesiveness will hurt productivity). However, recent research challenges that assumption. It reveals that groups with high cohesiveness will be the most productive groups, as long as they also have norms that support productivity. Langfred and Shanley (1997) argued that the "effectiveness of groups with high cohesiveness and strong task-related norms will surpass that of other groups" (p. 363). Subsequently, Langfred (1998) tested that assumption when he studied more than 400 members of the Danish military. He found that "if the norms are task oriented, the highly cohesive groups will outperform others, but if the norms are not, then the high cohesiveness of a group can be detrimental to group performance" (pp. 136, 138). The least productive groups will be those that are highly cohesive and have norms that directly encourage poor performance (and the cohesive group members follow that norm) or norms that indirectly hinder effective performance, such as the norm to avoid expressing conflict. In the latter case, the group will become subject to groupthink, a phenomenon that will be discussed in Chapter 5.

Interestingly, groups with norms that encourage poor performance can be productive if they are not cohesive and if the task does not require work in unison. That is because without cohesiveness members are both less likely to follow group norms and more likely to compete against other members; the end result is more productive members. When cohesive groups begin to perform poorly, they should reconsider their norms, because being productive is usually a greater necessity than being cohesive. As a group's norms are reexamined and redesigned, there will be a temporary disruption in the cohesiveness of the group. But the final product will be a group that performs well on the task and desires continued group maintenance.

Strategies to Develop Cohesiveness.   Because cohesiveness is desirable under most circumstances, you may want to increase the cohesiveness of a group to which you belong. There are some specific strategies groups can use to increase their cohesiveness.

Your first step may be to **set a goal that the group can achieve early in its life.** Too often, groups put off what they can accomplish early. As a result, members begin to question the value of the group and of its task. By setting a subgoal that a group can achieve early in its life, the group establishes a perception among its members that the group is effective. Then **celebrate the group's accomplishments.**

Allow all group members to participate in discussions and decisions. Group members can then see themselves as an important part of the group, which increases their commitment to the group. To accomplish this, it may be necessary to limit group size.

Treat members equally and as individuals, not just as cogs in the machine. By removing distinctions among group members that highlight differences in status, group members all feel more involved in the group. When group members are recognized as individuals, they feel valued. The time spent sharing personal information is not wasted time, for it allows group members to begin to trust one another, a necessary prerequisite for performing successfully any task that requires interdependence among group members.

Devote some time to discussion of the group, not just discussion of its task, so that the group can express its perceptions of its cohesiveness or resolve issues that are impeding the development of cohesiveness. This is not to suggest that the group should substitute a self-focus for a task-focus. It simply recognizes that the task is only one focus to which a group must direct its attention; some attention to the group itself is necessary if the task is to be performed well by a group that does not disintegrate. Each of these strategies can improve members' attraction and commitment to the group. It is also useful to realize that cohesiveness is a natural outgrowth of the successful resolution of group development issues.

Stages in the Transformation from Individuals to Groups

A group does not operate as a fully functioning system from the moment of its first meeting. Instead, it proceeds through several stages as a collection of individuals is transformed into a cohesive group. Although there are variations from group to group, researchers have found similar patterns of development in groups of all types. For instance, Verdi and Wheelan (1992) discovered that developmental stages were the same regardless of whether groups had all male members, all female members, or were mixed-sex groups. Few writers describe the process in precisely the same way. What follows is a synthesis of the patterns of small group development described by several different authors (Anderson, 1985; Burnand, 1990; Kuypers & Alers, 1996; McGrath, 1991; Mennecke, Hoffer & Wynne, 1992; and Worchel, 1994). It recognizes that at each stage of group development, an issue—or concern—is addressed by members of the group and, if the group is to progress beyond that stage, is resolved. It also recognizes that the communication at any one point is likely to be somewhat different from the communication that occurs in a different stage. The stages are summarized in Figure 2.1 and then are described in detail.

Pre-Group Formation

In the opening narrative, Pat Litwiller mentioned that she had worked for General Motors, doing the same basic job she now does, before the WINS team formed. Prior to the initiation of a small group, there will be individuals who have not yet been drawn together into a single group. Or there may be a group already formed but in a state of disarray, its members sensing little purpose in group involvement. However, a precipitating event occurs that leads one individual or several to call for the formation of a group to tackle a task of some sort. Perhaps (as was the case for General Motors) management in an organization decides to adopt a team approach in an effort to increase competitiveness. Perhaps a crime increase in a neighborhood leads to a call for a neighborhood watch meeting. The neighbors may have previously been active as a social group, but for one reason or another have lost contact. Perhaps individuals who endured their own silent, isolated suffering are called together by a therapist to

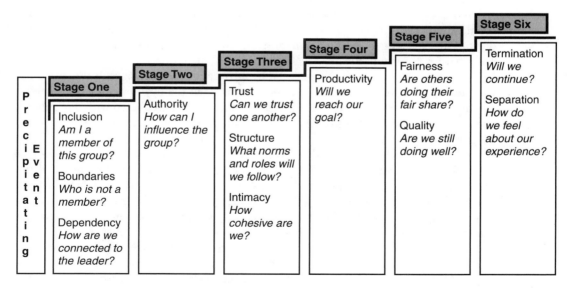

FIGURE 2.1   The Six Stages in Group Formation.

tackle the task of supporting one another and working through their common problems. Or perhaps in a small group communication course, you are required by your instructor to complete a group assignment. The precipitating event initiates the process of group formation, which is described here as involving six stages.

Stage One: Concerns with Inclusion, Dependency, and Boundaries

As members enter the meeting space for their first meeting, few of them feel comfortable. Actually, their level of anxiety is high, because they are concerned about the issue of inclusion, wondering how they will fit into the group. Ernest Bormann (1975) described the feelings group members are experiencing at this point as the first of two kinds of social tension. Likening the feelings at this point to stage fright, he called it **primary tension,** the "social unease and stiffness that accompanies getting acquainted" (p. 181). They are the first—primary—feelings members experience. The tension relates to the question of how the group will work as a group, the most basic—primary—issue the group faces. Thus, there are two different reasons for this tension to be called "primary." However, a casual observer of a group might not recognize the tension within the group, for it sounds very different from the behaviors we usually recognize as tension-related behaviors. Primary tension is quite quiet. Because members are not yet comfortable with one another, there may be long periods of silence at this stage. Because group members hope to be included within the group, they avoid behaviors that might isolate them or divide them from other group members. You may remember that Pat Litwiller mentioned that when the WINS team first formed, all members were on their best behavior and no one was willing to discuss controversial issues. Because efforts at working on the task may invite disagreements, early communication usually avoids much focus on the task. Also, comments made by members during the early stage of group formation are tentative and polite, further limiting the potential for confrontation.

Dependency is a second issue faced by a group in its early stages. If the group has been formed by a leader, as the WINS team was, then the new members are likely to feel highly dependent on the leader. Members have not yet interacted with one another enough to feel secure about relying on each other, so they are more likely to assume that the leader is competent and support the leader's authority by relying on him or her. Even if there is no leader, individual group members will try to identify the position of the majority and mirror that position to avoid appearing deviant. The goals of the group may not be clear yet, but individuals are likely to accept the goals nonetheless. They will probably assume that other group members accept the goals, too.

During this first stage of group formation, the group is struggling to define its boundaries. Conformity among group members helps to create a sense of unity within the group, superficial though it may be. A second factor that helps to define the group's boundaries is a distinction between the group and an "out-group," often perceived as an enemy of the newly forming group. While conflict within the group is low, there may be noticeable conflict between groups.

Stage Two: Concern with Authority

At the end of the first stage, a group has formed that has boundaries around it, but not many distinctions within it. That situation becomes an uncomfortable one in which to continue to function. Individual members want to be recognized as distinct from the others. Moreover, the original source of authority for the group may be perceived more clearly; perhaps the leader first assumed to be competent has been found not to be so. And even if competent, a leader may be challenged by group members who now feel comfortable enough within the group to want some authority for themselves. Therefore, the dominant issue during the second stage of formation is the authority issue.

In the second stage, group members participate more actively in the group. Individuals begin to speak out against the early structure of the group. Their comments include statements that assert their independence from the leader or from the perceived majority; their comments reflect their disagreement and avoid intimacy. They will find support from some members, who join a coalition with them. Other members will disagree and unite in opposition to the first coalition. Conflict is the result.

The members are continuing to feel social tension but expressing it quite differently from the way they had in stage one. Rather than being expressed quietly, this form of social tension, which Bormann (1975) called **secondary tension,** is loud and noisy. It erupts suddenly and disrupts the group. At high levels, it makes the group an uncomfortable place to be; observers would have no difficulty noticing it.

It may seem as if this stage should be avoided by effective groups. However, the conflict in this stage is regarded as a prerequisite for effective group functioning in the later stages. Despite expressions of disagreement over the goals of the group, members begin to clarify the group's goals, leaving the group with a clearer sense of direction. The opposition to the original leader allows the group to bond as a unit, freed from the leader's dominance. Independent of the leader, the group becomes accountable for its own actions. The experience of working through disagreements in this early stage allows members to learn that they can express disagreement without being excluded from the group. Bonds of intimacy can follow.

Stage Three: Concerns with Trust, Structure, and Intimacy

In the previous stage, the group developed a sense of accountability, but it now has to determine whether the group as a whole is accountable for its actions or whether each

Ethical Consideration

Conflict is inevitable in groups and essential to the complete development of the group. Therefore, you interfere with the group process if you try to avoid or smooth over every conflict. This should not be interpreted as an encouragement to aggravate conflict, however.

member can be depended on. Group members in stage three deal with the question of trust. The group divides the labor among its members. To make that possible, individual group members begin at this point to assume specific roles within the group. To be sure that group members live up to their responsibilities and behave in acceptable ways, this is the time that the group develops norms. Some groups may make a point to talk openly about the roles each member will take and the norms the group should follow, as the WINS team did when it wrote a list of norms. But for all groups, it is likely that much of this process occurs more subtly, with implicit norms and roles being developed.

Following the previous stage of conflict, the pressure on group members to conform increases. There is still conflict and some degree of social tension, but it eases and is managed more effectively now than it was earlier. Comments made by group members in this stage convey friendship and support for other group members. They are characterized by warmth and intimacy, so the group develops a sense of cohesiveness. For teams that do not meet face-to-face often (or at all), this stage presents difficulty. If team members attempt to focus only on the task and function with great efficiency, they will not be able to move through this stage. Only if they recognize the importance of having an opportunity to chat, even if only through E-mail, will they be able to share the personal information that is the basis of trust and, consequently, cohesiveness (Lipnack & Stamps, 1997). Once norms, roles, and cohesiveness have been established, the individual members are united in a system. By the end of stage three, the group has designed itself and is ready for work.

Stage Four: Concern with Productivity

Groups in the fourth stage of development are clear about their goals and committed to achieving them. They are comfortable interacting with one another. They are ready to deal with issues of productivity.

As they work to solve problems or make decisions, they may openly disagree with one another. But rather than being an outgrowth of tensions about social relations, this disagreement is task related. The sense of social connection that arose in the previous stage gives the group the comfort with each other that they need to cope with task-related disagreements and resolve them.

The early distrust and dislike of out-groups expressed in the first stage are likely to have weakened by now. Group members may have realized that other groups can be helpful partners in accomplishing the group's goals. Comments of group members in the fourth stage do focus on the task. The communication is purposeful and goal directed.

Even in this stage, however, group members will not ignore the well-being of the group as a whole or providing support for the group members. McGrath (1991) argues that at each stage in the development of the group, members deal with production (contributing to the larger system of which the group is a part), member support (contributing to the component parts of the group), and well-being (contributing to the group itself, as a whole). Most authors, however, suggest that the degree of emphasis on each element varies over the life of a group and that it is not until the group has resolved issues related to the nature of the group itself that it can devote the bulk of its efforts to work.

One small group researcher has found that groups seem to follow another predictable pattern in reaching the productivity stage. Gersick's study of groups (cited in Mennecke, Hoffer, & Wynne, 1992) revealed that about halfway through the available time, however long that was, group members became more productive. She argued that after awhile, group members realized that their previous behaviors were not satisfactory to those outside the group (a teacher for a classroom group, a boss for a work group) who demanded productivity from the group. The group then altered its behaviors in response to this perceived pressure.

It may seem frustrating to you, especially if you are a highly goal-directed person, that groups do not simply get down to business and accomplish their tasks from the moment they are first formed. It should help you to realize that, first, the group has to deal with an even more basic task: the business of being a group. Also, if you are in a position to develop work groups or to make changes within them, it is important for you to understand what a group must go through before it becomes fully productive. Knowledge of the initial stages of group development should help you to plan more effectively, to avoid creating unnecessary conflicts, and to make good decisions about a group's receptivity to the kinds of change you might envision imposing upon it (Rosen, 1989). Of course, if a group simply waits until half of the available time has expired before getting down to business, that would be a misuse of group resources.

Stage Five: Concerns with Fairness and Quality

Group members who work effectively as part of a group are still individuals with their own needs. They may desire recognition for their own contributions to the group. They may seek more personal freedom to accomplish goals unrelated to the goals of the group. Once the group has begun to do effective work, therefore, individual members may raise the question of fairness: When will they get the personal recognition the group has shared? When will they accomplish their own personal goals, which the group activity as a whole does not satisfy?

Also, as the group continues to follow its effective work patterns, the issue of quality may be raised. The problem is that the group's behavior has become rather routine. Whereas earlier, group members had communicated thoroughly to work out problems, now communication is quick and infrequent. Group members no longer need to work out ways of coordinating their efforts. Routinization of work increases efficiency, but it decreases the interest the group has for its members. As the quality of the communication within the group declines, the connection between member and group weakens (McGrath, Arrow, Gruenfeld, Hollingshead, & O'Connor, 1993).

At the same time that connections within the group may have weakened, another alternative for group membership may have developed. The out-group, first seen in strongly negative terms, has come to be viewed more favorably. Members may have worked with other groups and feel quite comfortable with them. Worchel (1994) found that in the period after the work stage, those who are growing dissatisfied with their own group may threaten defection as a bargaining tool to improve their own conditions within the group. Such a tactic, however, is unlikely to strengthen their ties to the other group members.

Ethical Consideration

If you are a member of a group that requires revitalization in order to be productive, commit time to that task. Otherwise, you allow the group to respond to the issue of quality by accepting poor quality.

A group that experiences the tensions of the fifth stage may recognize that survival of the group requires revision of its processes. The WINS team raised issues of quality long before a crisis developed by setting aside time to consider ways to revitalize the team. In this case and others like it, the group may cycle back to one of the earlier stages—redefining group norms and roles and generating a new sense of cohesiveness. Or a group may advance to the final stage.

Stage Six: Concerns with Separation and Termination

Some groups are established for a short time only. They must deal with the issue of separation as the group approaches the time for termination. Wheelan and Hochberger (1996) make the point that even continuing groups have ending points at which group members look back at the group, evaluate it, and decide how to proceed.

If a group—or one's membership in a group—must come to an end to the regret of its members, then the termination stage is characterized by communication that increases the expression of positive feelings. If group members welcome the end of the group, or if they need to rationalize the group's ending, then the communication may express increased negativity, with members blaming each other, not an out-group, for the group's failings. Open conflict and competition may be expressed within the group as it deals with an impending termination. In some cases, a member may defect from the group, leaving with feelings of bitterness toward the group and its remaining members.

After the departure of a group member, remaining members sometimes engage in remembrance ceremonies, recalling behaviors of the departed member that are memorable to the rest of the group. The importance of the individual to the group will determine the amount of attention paid to the departed member.

Keyton (1992) has developed a convincing argument that more attention should be devoted to the termination stages of a group. She notes that within an organization, the end of one ad hoc group does not mean the end of members' relationships with one another. They may work together again on other projects; even if not working together, they may continue to see each other at the same workplace. To make continued positive relationships more likely, Keyton recommends that communication in the termination stage should summarize and celebrate the work completed by the group, assess the quality of both the task and the process, and discuss future access of members to each other. A termination ritual is important to group members because it "affects how they will interpret what they have experienced and what expectations they will take to similar situations" (Keyton, 1993, p. 98).

*At the retirement of a team member, Pat Litwiller (second from right) joined
with other members of the original WINS team to remember the event and honor
the departing member.*

Variations in the Patterns

It might seem from this description as if groups move through the transformation
process in a smooth fashion, from one step to the next. Few of the people who have
observed groups believe that to be the case. Gemmill and Wynkoop (1991) believe
that much of the group development process involves "intellectual and emotional
chaos—a whirlpool in which all elements of the social system lose their anchoring,
being powerfully and rapidly drawn into the unknown center of the whirlpool" (p. 6).
They argue that groups may try to avoid the chaos or uncertainty they face by adopting a familiar group structure, which ultimately fails to utilize the unique qualities the
system possesses. The more difficult, but in the long run more satisfactory, approach
involves facing the chaos and creating an entirely new system. This image of group
transformation is one in which a group's activity revolves around each issue in group
development, centers on a solution for that issue, and then moves on.

Other writers support a view of group development involving recurring experiences with the stages in the transformation process. Mennecke, Hoffer, and Wynne
(1992) note that recurring cycle models of the development process are based on the
assumption that the issues presented by each stage are resolved in only a partial and
temporary way, requiring further attention at a later date. They argue that when the
amount of interaction required to complete a task is high and/or when the group is
composed of members who prefer lax procedural rules, then the group will be less
likely to develop in a sequential manner and will be more likely to require a cyclical
developmental pattern. Wheelan and Hochberger (1996) found support for a cyclical
developmental process. When they tested a group development questionnaire, they
found groups oscillating between stages of development.

Some writers, including Cissna (1984) and McGrath (1991), have found that groups omit stages in the development process. If the task of the group can be completed without ever resolving issues of authority and intimacy, then the group will skip the middle stages of development. Many ad hoc groups follow that model. For instance, a group of parents asked by the director of their children's marching band to put the props on the field before a marching band competition can do the physical labor involved, following assigned roles and accepting outside leadership. A group brought together for a brief classroom exercise can tolerate interacting without resolving issues of group structure. Cissna (1984) suggested that ad hoc groups may end without spending time in the termination stage and may skip a conflict stage. He added that groups formed of members who have had prior experience working with each other may skip the first stage (since they have already oriented themselves to working with one another) and that some groups manage to skip the productivity stage.

When the group needs to design itself and hopes to be productive, however, movement through the steps of group development will be necessary. The groups that never reach the point of productivity may be stymied by their inability to resolve the issues raised at an earlier stage of development. Kuypers and Alers (1996) argue that when a group faces an issue at any stage of development, it must decide between a pair of polarities—between one attribute of group structure and its antithesis. For instance, when the group is trying to resolve the authority issue, it may vacillate between choosing a structure in which order is strictly imposed and a structure in which there is little order. When trying to resolve the accountability issue, the group may vacillate between holding the group as a whole accountable and requiring individual members to be accountable. Coalitions within the group are likely to take opposing views of each issue. To move beyond the issue, a group member must emerge who can provide a more moderate approach to each issue. For instance, the authority issue can be resolved by an individual

Technology Note: Integrating Technology into Group Development

A group of researchers from the University of Minnesota developed a software program, Software Aided Meeting Management (SAMM), to provide support for groups as they made decisions. They then studied four different groups that were using SAMM (Poole, DeSanctis, Kirsch, & Jackson, 1994). Their study made it apparent that a group decision support system will be more likely to be adopted and adapted by a group if it is introduced into the group in the early stages of group formation. Concerns about the use of the system may be included in the primary tension of the group. Eventually, however, the system's use becomes part of the norms of the group. The researchers also found that the patterns and problems of the group carried over into the use of the support system. For instance, one group had continually avoided accepting responsibility for their difficulties. This problem was apparent in the group's relationship with SAMM, which became the group's scapegoat. The results of the research suggest, then, that technology is not a separate element layered over the stages of group development; rather, it is an integral part of each stage in development.

who functions as an organizer and provides a moderate structure for the group rather than either of the extremes in organization. This view makes it clear that the roles group members play are intimately connected to the overall development of the group, for they can serve as an impediment to or a catalyst for further group development.

Whether a group follows the six-stage process of development described earlier or one of the variations, a group goes through some process of development that transforms a collection of individuals into a functioning system. Communication behaviors will change from stage to stage, but without communication of some type, no group development will occur.

The Role of Communication in Group Formation: A Theoretical Perspective

Whitney Otto's 1994 *How to Make an American Quilt: A Novel* (later turned into a movie starring Winona Ryder) tells the story of a young woman, Finn, who stays with her grandmother and great-aunt while completing a thesis and deciding whether she is ready for marriage. But the story is not just Finn's story; the older women are part of a quilting circle, and the stories of each of the circle's members are shared. Each story is inherently interesting, but each functions as more than entertainment: it also has a message for Finn about how she is to behave in relation to others. A shared story can play a central role in the development of any group, as Ernest Bormann's (1996) *symbolic convergence theory* explains.

Symbolic convergence theory grew out of the observations of groups carried out by Bormann and other researchers at the University of Minnesota. Using Bales' interaction process analysis scheme (included in the Appendix) to code group interaction, the researchers began to pay particular attention to behaviors categorized as "dramatizes." What they were discovering was that in the midst of a group discussion, perhaps one that seems to be stagnating, members might take a verbal detour. Someone might begin to tell a story about something that happened in the past or might imagine something in the group's future. On occasion, those stories would generate enthusiastic responses from other members who responded to the emotion of the story and added on to it (what Bormann called a "chaining out" of the fantasy).

The apparent diversion was not inconsequential to the group. It often was the means by which expectations for the group members (in the way of either norms or roles) were introduced into the group. For instance, Bormann (1996) described a classroom group working on their assignment to explore a public policy question. Their choice was to investigate gambling, largely at the suggestion of one member who told the group stories of his gambling adventures in Las Vegas. As the project got underway, another group member surpassed the efforts of all the others by doing extensive library work. At a group meeting, when the hardworking group member began to elaborate on his findings, the "gambler" began to challenge their validity by citing his own experiences. The other group members began to add to those stories. Below the surface of this exchange, the group was establishing a norm against hard work. Unwilling to confront the high expectations of the library researcher directly, they did so indirectly by sharing in stories about gambling. Throughout the term, even after the gambler dropped out of school, the other members expanded on their fantasies, which worked for them to support a belief that there was no valid information on the subject of gambling. (Their instructor, not having been a party to the development of the fantasy, continued to regard it as pure fantasy, to the dismay of the students.) This experience of the group itself helps to explain the phenomenon Bormann called **symbolic convergence,** *the unifying of a group through attaching common meaning to symbols or through shared stories.* The example also supports the claim of Wheelan and Krasick (1993) that the themes communicated within the group emerge from conflict among the group, in this case, a conflict about how much work was expected of members in good standing. Each theme revolves around an issue the group faces, and it emerges at a time when the overall system is able to deal with the issue represented by the theme.

The symbols shared in a group need not lead to diminished productivity, but they do help to describe where the symbolic boundaries of the group lie. For instance, in presenting the student address at the University of Michigan's School of Music graduation in May 1998, Adam Glaser told the story of his grandmother Ruth who had avoided being sent to a foster home after her father's death by knocking on the door of a neighbor woman and asking help in learning, at the age of seven, to prepare the family dinner and serve it when her mother returned from work. Obviously Adam had not been alive to see that happen, but the story was alive for him; it was told in his family to share the value of constancy of purpose. In this case, the story supports a norm of productive, purposeful behavior. To be a member of that family group is to understand the story of seven-year-old Ruth and the importance of working to accomplish your purpose. Bormann (1996) explained that such stories relate to developing group boundaries:

People create a common identity by becoming aware that they are involved in an identifiable group and that . . . they are personally somewhat different from others who are not symbolically tied together by the experience of sharing the same fantasies. (pp. 104–105)

Technology Note: Boundary Difficulties

Groups that meet in person infrequently are likely to have increased difficulty with symbolic convergence for two reasons. First, the group's process is less likely to lead to dramatizing. When such a group is experiencing the moments of stagnation common to all groups, they will be unlikely to stay on line. Second, the actual boundaries of the group may be more flexible, with membership changing as tasks change, and the needs for particular skills determining who will be the members of the group at any particular moment. The increased difficulty simply underscores the need for groups operating at a distance to share interactions that help to create a symbolic unity for a group.

Even as members tell inside jokes, they are communicating the boundaries of their group. Insiders understand the joke; those who do not understand are not group members.

In the opening narrative, Pat Litwiller described the wall-climbing exercise used in team building by the WINS team. New members of the group had not shared that activity. They did not realize the expectation for the team to solve problems on their own, rather than to seek solutions first from management. In that group, as in any other, continued actions will create new stories for a group to share as it continues in the development process. Without convergent meaning for the group, it cannot develop as a system.

Summary

If you are in a group that has had smooth sailing from the first day it was formed, then you are in a minority—and perhaps even in denial. The process of forming a group is not a trouble-free one. It begins with disconnected members of a group (some of whom may have characteristics that are not ideal traits for group members). Expected patterns of behavior are determined as the members of each group begin to play roles within the group. They will perform behaviors that help in completing the group's task or in maintaining the group, and (perhaps) some behaviors that hinder the group process. Groups also will develop norms to regulate members' behaviors. As they begin to perceive themselves as a unit, they develop some level of cohesiveness.

Because groups are not fully formed when they are first formed, each group must go through several stages in the struggle to define itself. That requires resolving a series of issues—and not simple ones at that. The group must navigate some rough waters as it decides how it will operate; it moves through a series of six stages as it does so. The group defines its boundaries and who will have authority within the group, what roles each member will play, how it will be productive, whether its work is characterized by quality and fairness, and whether it will continue as a group or terminate. Communication will play a central role in the group development process, because norms, roles, and group boundaries are embedded in the stories members tell themselves.

The WINS team has not found its journey to be trouble free. But it is a cohesive group whose members enjoy their work because they know they are vital parts of a system that values their involvement. It is concerned about maintaining itself as a vigorous, energized unit that faces the challenges from the outside environment and adapts to change. And when it recognizes that the change has surpassed its adaptation, it makes adjustments. Rather than resting on its past successes, it continues to raise issues of improving team effectiveness. Perhaps labeling the WINS team "an ideal group" would be a mistake, for the team demonstrates that it is in continued group development in pursuit of the ideal, not necessarily in reaching some predetermined endpoint, that a group becomes a success.

QUESTIONS FOR DISCUSSION

1. Compare the measures designed to evaluate cohesiveness found at the end of the book. Which of them seems to be the best measure of cohesiveness?

2. An individual may play a different role in one group than in another. Overall, is it likely for one person's roles to be more different than they are similar?

3. What are some common norms in groups that are likely to threaten the success of a group? What are some norms that are likely to lead to group success?

4. Pat Litwiller says that the WINS team does not do a very good job of sticking to its written norms. Would you say, then, that the written statements are not actually norms for the group?

5. If a group that was experiencing difficulty maintaining its membership asked for your advice, what would you recommend to them?

6. Tuckman (1965) developed a listing of the stages in group formation that has been repeated by dozens of other authors. The four steps Tuckman identified are forming (an orientation stage), storming (conflict), norming (development of rules, roles, and cohesiveness), and performing (productivity). In contrast, this book describes a six-stage process. Match your own experiences and observations against the two descriptions. Which better matches your experiences?

7. Think of some of your family stories. What lessons do they have for you as part of your family group?

SUGGESTED ACTIVITIES

1. Watch a movie that centers around a small group. (The possibilities are endless, but include *Stand By Me*, *The Breakfast Club*, the *Mighty Ducks* series, *The Joy Luck Club*, and *Apollo 13*.) Analyze the group's norms, roles, and level of cohesiveness. Observe the stages in group formation evident in the film. Make a presentation to your class about the group in the film.

2. Develop a list of norms you would like a group to adhere to. Compare your list with the lists of others. Compare your list to the actual norms of a group to which you belong.

3. Observe a group you are not a member of during a meeting. Try to identify the roles of the group members and the group's norms. Evaluate the cohesiveness of the group.

4. Take some time (perhaps over a few days or weeks) to write in your journal describing the developments in the formation of your project group. For instance,
   a. Identify the behaviors (roles) you and other members are performing (playing) in your group. Determine which behaviors changed over the life of your group.
   b. How did you come to play the role you are playing in the group?
   c. If there are behaviors that would be useful to your group that no one is performing yet, describe the strategy you will use to make sure those behaviors are performed by someone.

d. Identify any norms that are hindering the effectiveness of your group. Describe the strategy you plan to use to substitute more appropriate norms.

e. Describe the factors that contribute to the current level of cohesiveness within your group. If your group would benefit from increasing the level of cohesiveness, describe the strategies you will use to enhance cohesiveness.

SOURCES CITED

Anderson, C. M., Martin, M. M., & Infante, D. A. (1999). Decision-making collaboration scale: Tests of validity. *Communication Research Reports, 15,* 245–255.

Anderson, J. D. (1985). Working with groups: Little-known facts that challenge well-known myths. *Small Group Behavior, 16,* 267–283.

Arrow, H., & McGrath, J. E. (1993). Membership matters: How member change and continuity affect small group structure, process, and performance. *Small Group Research, 24,* 334–361.

Balgopal, P. R., Ephross, P. H., & Vassil, T. V. (1986). Self-help groups and professional helpers. *Small Group Behavior, 17,* 123–137.

Benne, K. D., & Sheats, P. (1948). Functional roles of group members. *Journal of Social Issues, 4,* 41–49.

Bormann, E. G. (1975). *Discussion and group methods: Theory and practice.* New York: Harper & Row.

Bormann, E. G. (1996). Symbolic convergence theory and communication in group decision making. In R. Y. Hirokawa & M. S. Poole (Eds.), *Communication and group decision making* 2nd ed., (pp. 81-113). Thousand Oaks, CA: Sage.

Brilhart, J. K., & Galanes, G. J. (1995). *Effective group discussion* (8th ed.). Madison, WI: Brown & Benchmark.

Burnand, G. (1990). Group development phases as working through six fundamental human problems. *Small Group Research, 21,* 255–273.

Carron, A. V., & Spink, K. S. (1995). The group size-cohesion relationship in minimal groups. *Small Group Research, 26,* 86–105.

Cissna, K. (1984). Phases in group development: The negative evidence. *Small Group Behavior, 15,* 3–32.

Colantuono, S. L., & Schnidman, A. A. (1988). E pluribus unum: Building multifunctional work teams. In W. B. Reddy & K. Jamison (Eds.), *Team building: Blueprints for productivity and satisfaction* (pp. 187–191). Alexandria, VA: NTL Institute for Applied Behavioral Science.

Cota, A. A., Evans, C. R., Dion, K. L., Kilik, L., & Longman, R. S. (1995). The structure of group cohesion. *Personality and Social Psychology Bulletin, 21,* 572–580.

Dorn, S. M., Papalewis, R., & Brown, R. (1995). Educators earning their doctorates: Doctoral student perceptions regarding cohesiveness and persistence. *Education, 116,* 305–314.

Ellis, D. C., & Fisher, B. A. (1994). *Small group decision making: Communication and the group process* (4th ed.). New York: McGraw-Hill.

Estrada, M., Brown, J., & Lee, F. (1995). Who gets the credit? Perceptions of idiosyncrasy credit in work groups. *Small Group Research, 26,* 56–76.

Evans, C. R., & Dion, K. L. (1991). Group cohesion and performance: A meta-analysis. *Small Group Research, 22,* 175–186.

Evans, N. J., & Jarvis, P. A. (1980). Group cohesion: A review and reevaluation. *Small Group Behavior, 11,* 359–370.

Gemmill, G. (1986). The dynamics of the group shadow in intergroup relations. *Small Group Behavior, 17,* 229–240.

Gemmill, G., & Wynkoop, C. (1991). The psychodynamics of small group transformation. *Small Group Research, 22,* 4–23.

Hare, A. P. (1994). Types of roles in small groups: A bit of history and a current perspective. *Small Group Research, 25*, 433–448.

Hollander, E. P. (1958). Conformity, status, and idiosyncrasy credit. *Psychological Review, 65*, 117–127.

Infante, D. A., Rancer, A. S., & Womack, D. F. (1993). *Building communication theory* (2nd ed.). Prospect Heights, IL: Waveland Press.

Jones, A., & Crandall, R. (1985). Preparing newcomers to enhance assimilation into groups: A group therapy example. *Small Group Behavior, 16*, 31–57.

Keyton, J. (1991). Evaluating individual group member satisfaction as a situational variable. *Small Group Research, 22*, 200–219.

Keyton, J. (1992). Comment on Evans and Dion: Still more on group cohesion. *Small Group Research, 23*, 237–241.

Keyton, J. (1993). Group termination: Completing the study of group development. *Small Group Research, 24*, 84–100.

Kidwell, R. E., Mossholder, K. W., & Bennett, N. (1997). Cohesiveness and organizational citizenship behavior: A multilevel analysis using work groups and individuals. *Journal of Management, 23*, 775–793.

Klein, S. M. (1996). Work pressure as a determinant of work group behavior. *Small Group Research, 27*, 299–315.

Kuypers, B. C., & Alers, M. B. (1996). Mapping the interpersonal underworld: A study on central roles and their scripts in the development of self-analytic groups. *Small Group Research, 27*, 3–32.

Langfred, C. W. (1998). Is group cohesiveness a double-edged sword? An investigation of the effects of cohesiveness on performance. *Small Group Research, 29*, 124–143.

Langfred, C., & Shanley, M. (1997). The importance of organizational context, I: A conceptual model of cohesiveness and effectiveness in work groups. *Public Administration Quarterly, 21*, 349–369.

Lipnack, J., & Stamps, J. (1997). *Virtual teams: Reaching across space, time, and organizations with technology.* New York: Wiley.

McGrath, J. E. (1991). Time, interaction, and performance (TIP): A theory of groups. *Small Group Research, 22*, 147–174.

McGrath, J. E., Arrow, H., Gruenfeld, D. H., Hollingshead, A. B., & O'Connor, K. M. (1993). Groups, tasks, and technology: The effects of experience and change. *Small Group Research, 24*, 406–420.

Mennecke, B. E., Hoffer, J. A., & Wynne, B. E. (1992). The implications of group development and history for group support system theory and practice. *Small Group Research, 23*, 524–572.

Miller, F. A. (1988). Moving a team to multiculturalism. In W. B. Reddy & K. Jamison (Eds.), *Team building: Blueprints for productivity and satisfaction* (pp. 192–197). Alexandria, VA: NTL Institute for Applied Behavioral Science.

Morrison, A. M., Ruderman, M. N., & Hughes-James, M. (1993). *Making diversity happen: controversies and solutions.* Greensboro, NC: Center for Creative Leadership.

Otto, W. (1994). *How to make an American quilt: A novel.* New York: Ballantine.

Poole, M. S., DeSanctis, G., Kirsch, L., & Jackson, M. (1994). Group decision support systems as facilitators of quality team efforts. In L. R. Frey (Ed.), *Innovations in group facilitation: Applications in natural settings* (pp. 299–322). Creskill, NJ: Hampton Press.

Rentsch, J. R., Heffner, T. S., & Duffy, L. T. (1994). What you know is what you get from experiences: Team experience related to teamwork schemas. *Group & Organization Management, 19*, 450–474.

Rogelberg, S. G., & Rumery, S. M. (1996). Gender diversity, team decision quality, time on task, and interpersonal cohesion. *Small Group Research, 27*, 79–90.

Rosen, N. (1989). *Teamwork and the bottom line: Groups make a difference.* Hillsdale, NJ: Erlbaum.

Salazar, A. J. (1996). An analysis of the development and evolution of roles in the small group. *Small Group Research, 27*, 475–503.

Spink, K. S., & Carron, A. V. (1994). Group cohesion effects in exercise classes. *Small Group Research, 25*, 26–42.

Stokes, J. P. (1983). Components of group cohesion: Intermember attraction, instrumental value, and risk taking. *Small Group Behavior, 14,* 163–173.

Tuckman, B. W. (1965). Developmental sequence in small groups. *Psychological Bulletin, 63,* 384–399.

Verdi, A. F., & Wheelan, S. A. (1992). Developmental patterns in same-sex and mixed-sex groups. *Small Group Research, 23,* 356–378.

Wheelan, S. A., & Hochberger, J. M. (1996). Validation studies of the group development questionnaire. *Small Group Research, 27,* 143–170.

Wheelan, S. A., & Krasick, C. L. (1993). The emergence, transmission, and acceptance of themes in a temporary system of interacting groups. *Group & Organization Management, 18,* 237–260.

Widmeyer, W. N., & Williams, J. M. (1991). Predicting cohesion in a coacting sport. *Small Group Research, 22,* 548–570.

Worchel, S. (1994). You can go home again: Returning group research to the group context with an eye on developmental issues. *Small Group Research, 25,* 205–223.

3 Leadership in Small Groups

CHAPTER OBJECTIVES

After reading this chapter, you should be able to

- Define "leadership" and "leader"
- Explain the difficulties involved in identifying the leader of a group
- Identify the communication behaviors associated with leadership
- Explain Fisher's concept of leader as "medium"
- Describe the nature of a leader's influence
- Describe the process of leader emergence
- Distinguish among the styles of leadership
- Identify the situations in which particular leadership behaviors would be appropriate
- Discuss the value of sharing power in a group

The Narratives

Cecily Yee, 47, is a medical technologist at University Hospital in Albuquerque, New Mexico. She talks about her role in groups at the hospital laboratory and in the community:

> I'm on the board of the Chinese-American Citizens' Alliance, involved in the youth group and entertainment committee. I've also been the secretary of the local chapter, which is a leadership position. There are about 60 active members of this organization, but the same people—perhaps 10% of the total group—seem to volunteer as leaders all the time. The more active members have children involved in the group, which makes them more interested. And some members are just generous with their time.
>
> At work, I've been on the Quality Assurance Committee, Quality Improvement Committee, Safety Committee, and on project groups that try to formulate standardized procedures for a specific technique, such as a blood analysis. Often I lead the project groups in my lab. Most

of the groups at work have appointed leaders. My supervisor might ask me to lead the group if I've volunteered my opinions at earlier meetings. Some of the time I volunteer to be the leader.

I volunteer because I want to make things more efficient and easier for people. When the group makes use of diverse ideas and people are open to try new approaches, it always leads to a better product. Some people are resistant to change. Once they get real comfortable with a procedure, they just don't like change, even if they know that it will improve the procedure. I think I'm just more flexible about change than others are. I would take more risks than some of the other group members. If I fail, then I'm going to try again.

When I'm the leader of a group, I try to have an open discussion and bring up points without involving a lot of emotion. A leader is a lot like a guidance counselor. I try to empower the members, so that each of them has part of the responsibility. If I'm the leader and I come into the group saying, "We're all on equal terms here," then that makes the rest of the group feel more comfortable. They won't feel that way if you're always making the decisions, saying "No, this won't work." I think it's better to say, "Why do you think this will work? How do you think it can work? Do you think we should try something else?"

Sometimes there are problems in a group if people don't do their part. Maybe they felt they didn't have anything to offer, or maybe we misjudged how much they knew about the procedure. Sometimes they can be encouraged to do more, just by talking to them directly. As a leader, it's hard—but important—to make that a building process. The leader has to make a few decisions to get the process moving. Sometimes you just have to decide how to motivate the person. At other times, you have to make the decisions for the person. The group member might not be able to participate effectively otherwise. I would vary my approach, depending on how much impact the person has on the group, whether the process is being slowed down a lot.

Some people think that medical technologists just sit at a bench and do benchwork, analyzing blood, for instance. But half of our work is done at the computer now. Our supervisor uses computers to send us notices by E-mail. In my last job, I was in a group of 18. When my supervisor sent us a notice by E-mail, then we all got it. Because only the person who's sent a message can read it, the supervisor could tell who didn't open the mail in the computer to read it. With this technology, a leader can have more efficient access to the rest of the group, and the rest of the group can have more direct access to the leader.

I think that to be a good leader, you have to learn to be assertive. In college, I was president of a sorority and did a lot for my class. So maybe I was always assertive, but I didn't see myself that way until I got back into the workforce after my kids were born. One difference, now, is that most of the people I work with have been trained as I was. They have some differences, and their diversity makes the group better. But everybody also has some common background. Now that I'm working with my peers—people with similar training—leading the group may be easier. Maybe that's why it seems enjoyable for me.

Lillian Robinson, 69, is the president of a citizens group, United for Action, in Flint, Michigan. The group members are working to improve the environment within their neighborhood. They have been fighting a nearby incinerator since before it was built. Although they are still involved in a court case, they have been able to reduce some of the dangers from the incinerator. Lillian Robinson was involved in the group from its beginning. Here she talks about how she came to take a leadership role in the group:

I don't have any diplomas or anything like that. I just have determination and a lot of wisdom and knowledge of things, experiences from working with my mother when I was young. My father died when I was three years old, so my mother raised ten kids by herself. She did a good job, and she is my hero. I never saw her back down. She taught me that I'll be all right if I stand for what's right and stand up for things that I know are true. I'm not afraid of people.

I can tell you when I first started. I was the first woman bus driver in this city. A black woman. The man who hired me told me that people would do all kinds of things to me, but he would hire me if I promised him that I wouldn't let them run me off. And I was determined that I wanted that job. That was one of my first battles.

The next battle was when I got disabled and couldn't work. The city decided to take my property, condemn it, and put me off my property because I didn't have the money to pay the taxes. They did some devious things to me. I told them that I didn't know all my rights, but I was going to search for them and use every one I could find. I started, and 40 years later, I'm still here. People say you can't fight City Hall. Yes, you can. I did, and I'm still here.

The group now called United for Action was formed in 1992, but I started speaking up in the neighborhood long before that. I moved here in 1955. I wanted to live here because of the river nearby. But people pick on areas and people like this. They come with junkyards, cement plants, composting, and everything. They're burning demolition wood in the incinerator that they get from tearing down old houses; they send it here from anywhere in the state. That brings in a lot of toxins—lead and poison. A doctor called and told me he wanted to meet our group, because he was concerned about what lead poisoning would do to the children. It damages their brains, and it is irreversible. If you can't breathe, if you can't have good water and air and good ground to grow your vegetables in, what have you got left? If you're living here and you see all this, you have to be concerned because you know it's going to affect people's health.

Most people in this area are single women heads of the household, either middle class or below middle class. I'm a senior citizen on a fixed income. So I don't feel I have anything to lose defending my neighborhood and the people here. Our group started out with about 27 people. As time goes on, people thin out as far as meetings are concerned. But I'm going to hold out, even if there won't be anybody there but me. It is going to go on. We have the Sierra Club, the American Lung Association, the NAACP, the health department, even Green Peace on our side. People read about us and contact me.

I don't think I'm an important woman. I just think that others aren't used to people being determined to fight for themselves. When I go downtown to City Hall, I think they don't like to see me coming, but I don't care. I was asked once, "Do you get angry?" Yes. It doesn't send me away; it just makes me more determined to go against what they're doing to me and the people in the neighborhood. Once there was a rumor out there that I would go against the neighborhood if they gave me money. I said I didn't want any money. I'm not getting a salary or anything from anybody. It's just the satisfaction of doing something to keep from being bulldozed over by those who say you don't matter because you're who you are. I say I do matter.

I am not afraid to confront things, not afraid to stand up, not afraid to continue on. I don't get tired, and I don't stop. But most people will follow you if they see you will lead. They will come to your aid and work with you in a group, but they don't want you to put them out in front. I don't think I'm the most determined of all the group. I'm just one that's always there. Nobody else has time. I make myself available to help out in whichever way I'm needed in this neighborhood, wherever problems are. I don't know an awful lot about what leadership is, but I know that if you start something, you have to see it through. I think leadership is determination and having the patience enough just to see it through.

Doug Harris, 25, lives in Lansing, Michigan, while he works as a graduate teaching assistant and on his Ph.D. in economics at Michigan State University. As an undergraduate, he was elected captain of his soccer team. Two summers ago he worked as an adult leader of teenage groups who worked on refurbishing a historic church in Detroit. Last summer he was part of a research team at a Washington, D.C., think tank on environmental policy making. Here he talks about his role in these groups and shares his thoughts on leadership:

I believe that leadership is the intentional and continuous facilitation of group-shared goals or vision and/or of the actions aimed toward the achievement of both. The leader is the person who either facilitates the group-shared goals or the actions required to achieve the goals. It is possible that the leader doesn't do any of the hands-on work. The leader might not come up with the goals to begin with, but still motivates the group to achieve them. I think that you gain power by being a leader. Once you've facilitated the group in reaching some goal, they give you respect and are willing to listen to you. That's power by itself. But someone who has only power would be a dictator. There has to be more than power in leadership.

My situation with the soccer team was an interesting one, because in a way I was more a representative of the group than an actual leader for it. When the team members voted me in as a leader, I really wasn't a part of the group. There was a very strong informal aspect to the team. We all played soccer out on the field together, but most of the people on the team did a lot together—a lot of drinking, so that on the field, they were—literally—hung over. I was never a part of the off-the-field activities. So in a sense, I was alienated because I wasn't partying with the rest of the team. But I believe that they elected me captain because I wasn't getting drunk with them. I think they respected me for what I was doing—and who I was. I tried to change the team, but I don't think I got very far with that. I tried to get people who were borderline—not fully involved in the social situation—to follow my example. It's hard to tell what my influence was. Nobody ever said, "I'm doing this because you are, too." The grade point average started to go up in my last couple of years there. But I don't think that most of the team ever shared my vision of what the team could become.

Two summers ago, when I worked with the program called "Detroit Summer," my group met on weekends, which was a break time for most of the participants. We worked on one of the oldest churches in Detroit. The plaster inside the church was peeling, and a huge hole up in the roof was leaking water. I've done repair work before, but never this exact thing. I got some ideas from my brothers who have been involved in carpentry work. I worked side by side with the teenagers, scraping the walls and doing replastering.

My typical leadership style is interactive, facilitative. In the Detroit Summer project, the group members didn't know how to plaster, so I was essentially telling them what needed to be done. But I still tried to encourage their suggestions. I think there were some kids in the group who worked on weekends with me because I tried to bring everybody into the group. I'm interested in public policy and volunteer work, working in areas that affect everybody, especially people who don't have a lot of power themselves. I don't have other resources like money or power to accomplish these things. I have to influence people—to work with people.

There are times when a person shouldn't try to become the leader. Last summer, I worked in Washington, D.C., on a research project on productivity and natural resource extraction. The person in charge had a Ph.D. in economics from the University of Chicago, which is basically this country's top school in the field. He knew what he was doing, and I knew that. I was trying to learn from him. As an economist-in-training, I didn't have the knowledge or skills to be the leader of the project we were doing. So despite the fact that some writers talk about leaders versus followers, as if they are different people, any individual can be a leader and a follower, at different times. The best kind of person to have in a group is a person who knows when to lead and when not to lead. If the people who have the necessary skills or knowledge don't lead, then they're giving up what should be their responsibility.

The Problem of Defining the "Leader"

Each of the individuals you have just met has served small groups in that particular constellation of roles that we call "group leader." Defining the term "leader" has presented problems for small group communication scholars and researchers.

Observer versus Member Identification

Some researchers have defined a group leader as the person an outsider observes performing a set of behaviors identified with leadership—such as orienting the group, evaluating ideas, and coordinating members' behaviors. Other researchers have defined the leader as the person whom group members name as being most influential in the group process. If it seems to you that both means of identifying a leader would be equally effective, then consider the fact that Cronshaw and Ellis (1991) discovered that these two means of identifying the leader of a group frequently end up naming two different people as the leader. Also consider the fact that Fisher (1985) noted that, because leaders and their followers perform parallel behaviors, it is often difficult for an observer to discover which of them is leading and which are following. Group members may not fare any better in identifying the leader. For instance, Ketrow (1991) discovered that group members identified the person who performed analytical behaviors within a group as having the most influence on group decisions— but *not* as the group leader. Also, apparently each of us has an individual view of what a leader is—our "prototype" of a leader (Nye & Forsyth, 1991; Palich & Hom, 1992). This individual prototype is used as a standard against which we measure the behaviors of our group members. Because each of us has a different prototype, we may each identify a different person as the leader, regardless of whether we are an outside observer of the group or one of its members.

Appointed or Emergent Leaders

Part of the difficulty in defining "leader" comes from the fact that there are different kinds of leaders. First, we can distinguish between an *appointed leader* and an *emergent leader.* An appointed leader may be given the title of group leader by someone external to the small group. For instance, in establishing a work group, upper management may name one individual as leader of a work group or team. That individual is given the authority—and the responsibility—to direct the work of the group, often selecting the members of the group, assigning them tasks, and evaluating their performance as a means of determining whether the members will continue as part of the group. In this case, the leader comes to the group with higher status than other group members, due to the leader's position in the organizational hierarchy.

In other cases, a group of peers grants one member added authority and status by appointing the member as the leader. Perhaps the appointment comes after an election (as might be the case when the elected members of a local school board vote to have one of the members serve as president for the year), or perhaps it comes by proclamation when one or more members feel the group needs to have someone named as the official group leader and proclaims one individual as "it." When Doug Harris was elected captain of his soccer team, he was an appointed leader. Sometimes an individual volunteers to serve as the official leader of the group; Cecily Yee mentioned that when she was not appointed as leader by her supervisor, she often volunteered to lead a group. Such leaders might be called *self-appointed leaders*. An individual who is appointed to lead but is not suited to do so can create problems for the group. However, if one person is skilled at leadership in a group with no one else eager to lead, having that person volunteer or be elected to lead may be helpful to the group. Whether appointed by the group members, by someone outside the group, or by themselves, appointed leaders are formal leaders.

Other groups avoid making the role of leader official. They may, nonetheless, have a definite, though informal, leader who comes to that position by *emerging* from the group interaction with that role. Whatever authority an *emergent leader* has is granted by the group as a whole during the process of role negotiation. It is possible for a group to come to think of a member as a leader even when that person does not have a positive influence on the group. For instance, Wheelan and Johnson (1996) studied the behaviors of individuals who were named by their peers as emergent "leaders" in groups that also had formal (appointed), task-oriented leaders. However, these "leaders" did not assist the group in achieving its task—and even expressed frustration that, at times, they were expected to assist the group in accomplishing its task. Nor did they play a constructive role in maintaining social relationships within the group. In fact, it seems that these group members were named as emergent leaders only because they gave voice to the group members' frustration with the formal leaders. Contrary to these findings, a typical emergent leader comes to fill that position after making positive contributions to the group. For instance, even without the title of group president, Lillian Johnson would be considered to be the leader of United for Action because she is always available to group members and to outsiders, because she coordinates members' activities, and is committed to doing everything she can to help the group succeed.

Differences Due to the Nature of the Group

Differences among leaders will reflect the differences in the groups they lead. Social groups will require a different set of behaviors from their leaders than will task groups. And there will be further differences between leaders of traditional work groups and leaders of self-directed work groups. In traditional work groups, the members complete leader-assigned tasks, whereas in a self-directed work group, members manage and monitor their own performance (Seers, Petty, & Cashman, 1995). Leaders of traditional work groups are frequently concerned with protecting their power base, whereas leaders of self-directed groups are concerned with distributing power—and responsibility—among the group members.

Leaders of therapeutic or support groups have a distinct set of responsibilities, usually including deciding to form a group, selecting group members, ensuring the establishment of a cohesive climate by modeling and enforcing appropriate norms for interaction, and interpreting the group process—all without creating dependence of members on the leader.

There are even differences between leaders based on the stage of development that exists within a group. In a group in the earliest stages of formation, the leader needs to provide a kind of guidance different from the type that is required when a group is maintaining itself.

Definition

Despite the difficulty of finding a "one-size-fits-all" definition, there are some commonalities in the role of leader, regardless of the group and the means by which the leader has assumed the role. Therefore, we can define a group **leader** as *the person whose social relationship with other group members allows the individual to influence the other group members in a manner that facilitates achievement of the group's goals*. It is usually possible to identify one group member who meets this definition of a leader more closely than do the rest of the group members. However, in most groups—and in all effective groups—there is *shared leadership*. **Leadership** is *the influence group members have over their members that facilitates achievement of the group's goals*. To better understand the nature of both leadership and of leaders, it is necessary to consider further three elements in the definition of leader: (1) the nature of the social relationship between leader and follower, (2) the nature of the influence involved in leading, and (3) the relevance of the group goals.

Social Relationship.   If a leader has emerged from the group interaction or has been appointed by the group, the social relationship is clear: other group members agree to follow while the leader leads. However, when the leader has been appointed by someone outside the group or has volunteered to act as leader, if group members do not agree to respect the organizational hierarchy and perform the role of "follower" in relation to the leader, then the leader serves in name only. In fact, if the person in the official role of leader is different from the person to whom group members would award their allegiance, then the group is bound to experience conflict over the issue of group leadership.

Not only must a social relationship exist for one individual to become the leader, but also the leader maintains the social relationship that exists among all members. In essence, the group leader functions to enforce a social contract (which concerns the group's boundaries and norms) between group members. In exploring how a leaderless group differs from one that has a leader, Counselman (1991) concluded that without a leader, all group members must share leadership in order to protect the group contract or the group cannot survive; with a leader, there is someone entrusted with the job of protecting the group contract.

Influencing Other Group Members.   It is possible that a leader appointed by other members of an organization has the ability to control group members. That is, a leader may have such control over organizational resources that subordinate group members will submit to whatever the leader requests. A woman in a group who fears that she will lose her job or fail in efforts to be promoted if she does not do what a superior commands is being *forced* to act in the required way; she is not being *led* to do so. To **lead** is to *exert influence over group members in a manner acceptable to the members.* (Later in the chapter, we will return to the question of influence to consider how it develops and its relationship to power.)

Facilitating Achievement of Group Goals. An outside observer who attends to the amount of talk within a group may erroneously identify as leader a group member who actually thwarts—rather than helps— the group's progress. Such a member may be a "central figure" in the group, but is not the leader. To earn the label of "leader," a group member must advance the cause of the group. That does not mean that each leader will perform the same tasks as others, because the cause of the group can be achieved through varied behaviors. Certainly, each of the individuals you met in the narratives functions differently as a leader, because the needs of their groups are different. In some groups, maintenance of the group as a social unit is its primary goal. Individuals whose behaviors focus on the socio-emotional or group maintenance roles described in Chapter 2 will serve as leaders for such a group. In the early stages of a task group's formation, a leader's behavior is likely to focus on procedural suggestions. In later stages, the leader of a decision-making group may emphasize the analytical behaviors involved in evaluating data and ideas. At each stage and in each kind of group, however, a leader who emphasizes a particular behavioral function will not do so to the exclusion of all other behaviors, because the leader's role repertoire is not unidimensional.

The Leader as "Medium": A Theoretical Perspective

When the nature of small group leadership received the attention of small group communication scholar B. Aubrey Fisher (1985), Fisher rejected the notion that a leader is simply an energizer. Instead he adopted a metaphor for the leader that had been suggested earlier by Karl Weick: the leader is a *medium.* You might imagine the medium at a seance, connecting a group to "outside spiritual forces," able to tell the group what the knocking sound heard in the attic means (Barge, 1996). Fisher wrote that the leader is, in a similar manner, a "medium engaged in registering and acting upon information," functioning "as a mediator between events or group actions and the final conclusion or actions by the group in terms of performance outcomes" (p. 182). A leader who is an effective medium must, first, be attuned to the events faced by the group and be able to interpret those events meaningfully and, second, be able to assist the group as it moves through the decision-making process. In both cases, the leader is a mediating force between the group and the forces external to the group, gathering data from the environment and interpreting it for the group, then assisting the group in its decision making and interpreting the decision for those outside the group (Barge, 1996).

As leader of United for Action, Lillian Robinson (right) sometimes needs to face the bright lights of the television camera as she mediates the boundary between her group and outsiders.

Throughout the entire process, the leader's behaviors are complex. Fisher (1985) explained,

> If the leader is a good medium, he or she is enacting a wide variety of functions when performing leadership. The key to leadership is thus not in the specific type of action but in performing a variety of specific types of actions. As a corollary, nonleaders (or poor leaders) would be those members whose actions include a restricted repertoire of actions performed. (pp. 184–185)

Fisher accepted the "principle of requisite variety"—that the more complex the problem a group faces, the more complex the leader's behaviors need to be. For instance, suppose a neighborhood group is interested in improving the local environment. If the problem is that litter blows out of trash receptacles, then the group may only need to organize a trash pickup on a regular basis. The leader's role for such a group may simply involve energizing group members. However, if the problem is similar to that faced by United for Action, where the community is concerned about the pollutants from an incinerator placed in the neighborhood by a private company and the company has local politicians, the state legislature, and (possibly) the court system on its side, then the group faces a much more complicated task. The tasks of the leader would need, also, to be more complex. It is no wonder that Lillian Robinson described her leadership responsibilities to be doing whatever was necessary to help the group, nor that she was the group member frequently called on to represent the group to outsiders.

In addition to noting the leader's performance of a wide variety of functions for the group, Fisher (1985) differentiated a good leader from a person who approached the group with a preconceived notion of what should be done, or with a limited, preimposed perspective. Such an individual simplifies the situation a group faces, imposing a meaning on events before they have transpired. In contrast, a good leader adapts to the situation at hand, acknowledges the complexity of the situation, acts on it, and makes sense of the events retrospectively. In the opening narrative, Cecily Yee made the point that for her to approach a project group with a preconceived idea of the procedure description would be ineffective. She turns to the group for that. Thus, the leader's influence is not in imposing on the group a view of itself, but in engaging in immediate actions and helping the group to interpret itself afterward.

Fisher (1985) identified a final definitional characteristic: the timing of a leader's influence. He argued that a good leader makes no effort to manage the group without having listened to the group members. Of necessity, that means that efforts to influence group members will be made only during the latter stages of the group's decision-making efforts. These efforts will also lead the group forward in short increments, rather than leading the group forward through a grand vision of what the group is to do. Fisher explained that a long-term vision of what the group is to do may lead to formulaic responses, shortcutting a thorough analysis of the actual situation faced by the specific group. Instead, a good leader acknowledges the richness of information available to and about the group, and "richness of knowledge tends to shorten the time horizon" (p. 186).

Support for Fisher's View.   Fisher's view of the leader's role (Fisher, 1985) helps explain why the amount of interaction in a group has often been associated with leadership but is insufficient to explain leadership. The leader *may* talk more than other group members. Also, other group members may talk to the leader more than they talk to other group members. However, a higher level of interaction is not, by itself, sufficient to create a leader. Perhaps you have been in a group in which one member talks frequently and at length, but not in a manner you perceive to be helpful. You may come to dread that person's comments. Often, the comments seem to have a repetitive function. You may come to expect them to divert the group from the task at hand. Or perhaps they regularly attack the ideas of the group, as a blocker's comments might. Other group members may feel a need to direct comments to this group member in an effort to get the group back on task. So, like a group leader, group members who thwart the group's progress may talk more and be talked to more than those who help the group achieve its goals. But that is where the similarity ends. The differences are that the group leader does not have a "restricted repertoire of actions" and that the leader's contributions do not interfere with the group's productivity. In fact, leaders are likely to be associated most strongly with task-relevant communication (Hawkins, 1995).

Connection with Transformational Leadership Views.   Fisher's view of leadership appears to contradict the view of those who see leadership as *transformational*. Transformational leadership is thought to exist when the leader envisions the direction the group is to go and helps the group through the process of alteration to achieve the desired end state. Hackman and Johnson (1996) write that "communicating a vision to followers may well be the most important act of the transformational leader" (p. 82) because the vision sets a direction for others to follow and inspires commitment from others. In the opening narratives, Doug Harris expressed his view that a leader plays a transformational role when he talked about the importance of developing a vision for a group. Fisher, however, assumed that the group leader was concerned with here-and-now activities and had a short-range view of the future. Moreover, Behling and McFillen (1996) report that several papers on transformational leadership suggest that a leader inspires followers to accept an ideological goal. Fisher, in contrast, claimed that an effective small group leader is not committed to an ideological position.

If we accept Fisher's definition of a small group leader, then are we necessarily rejecting the possibility that a leader has a long-term goal toward which he or she leads a group? There are several possibilities for integrating these apparently conflicting ideas. First, we can distinguish among various levels of leaders. Transformational leadership has typically been discussed in relationship to organizations or movements. The leader of an organization or movement (who needs to have a long-range vision of the group's direction in order to be effective) may be distinguished from the leader of most small groups (who often does not need to have such a long-range, independent vision, particularly when the group is part of an organization that already has such a long-range vision).

Second, we can recognize the difficulty of distinguishing the leader's vision from that of other group members. Because the leader of a small group achieves that position through a social agreement with the group members, it is likely that the group members together develop a shared vision of the group's shared goal. Even if the group leader's view is somewhat longer range than that of the other group members, it may not be noticeably so. Behling and McFillen (1996) suggested that the successful leader's vision involves changes from a group's present course, but changes that are acceptable to the followers. When Doug Harris expressed his doubts about the leadership role he played for his college soccer team, some of them revolved around the fact that, while his teammates respected his vision for the team enough to choose him as their captain, they did not share his vision for the team enough to be directed by it. Changes occurred in the direction desired by Doug, but they did not occur to the degree he desired.

Third, Fisher's emphasis on the actions of the leader may cause us to realize that the transformational leader's vision is communicated with action, not just with words. Without noticing how the actions of the leader help to articulate a vision of the group's goal, it would be possible to overlook the existence of any such vision. For instance, Doug Harris mentioned that he attempted to get his soccer team to accept his vision by leading by example. In analyzing his role in leading the group, it would be a mistake to overlook his actions and focus just on speeches he gave to his teammates.

An acceptance of Fisher's view should focus on the most vital element in his definition: the complexity of the leader's role. In so doing, we acknowledge that whatever the vision of the leader, an individual who simplifies the situation of the group and whose actions are unidimensional will not function effectively as a leader of a small group.

Technology Note: Transformational Leadership in Groups Using Computers

In their discussion of transformational leadership, Hackman and Johnson (1996) asked whether transformational leadership applies to small groups, given the fact that most of the research on transformational leadership had been conducted in organizations. Sosik (1997) began to address that question by studying how transformational leadership affects idea generation in groups communicating with computers. In the study, groups with "high transformational leaders" perceived their work to be higher quality and more satisfying; they also developed more original and more embellished ideas, and they focused more on process than did groups with "low transformational leaders." To operationally define transformational leadership, Sosik asked males using computers to type in nine comments characteristic of either a high or low transformational style. The comments of "low transformational leaders" emphasized external rewards available for completing the task. "High transformational leaders" wrote about the importance of the task, of working together, and of careful thinking, and expressed confidence in the group. These behaviors may have been easy to manipulate with computer-mediated interaction, but whether a leader who presents a long-term vision will be successful in small groups—communicating face-to-face or by computers—is still an open question.

The Leadership Emergence Process: A Theoretical Perspective

An individual who is appointed as leader of a group by a supervisor becomes a leader by meeting whatever criteria the supervisor is using to select the leader. However, if the leader is to serve the group effectively, even an appointed leader must earn the same social relationship with followers that an emergent leader earns through role negotiations with other group members.

Parallel with Other Role Selections: Ending the Tension; Beginning with Predispositions

The emergence of leadership parallels the emergence of other roles within a group. When the group first meets, some tension exists about who will lead the group. Behling and McFillen (1996) refer to the anxiety emerging during the birth of a group as "psychic distress." As the group members begin to reduce the distress by answering the question of who will lead the group, they select the behaviors they will perform. Their choices will have some basis in their personality and communication traits but then will be affected by the behaviors of other group members and by the needs of the group.

Although it is true that a given individual may become the leader of some groups and a follower in others, some behaviors increase or decrease the chances of the individual becoming a leader with any frequency. Just as any other role behaviors will be selected in part because of the predispositions of group members to fill the roles, so it is with the leadership role. Anderson and Wanberg (1991) explained that individuals who view power as a resource that the leader has and on which the rest of the group members must depend will be unlikely to emerge as group leaders, because they will spend their time withholding power, rather than sharing it with the rest of the group members. McClane (1991b) found that leaders differed from other group members in that they had higher levels of achievement motivation and were more likely to have an internal locus of control. (Persons with an internal locus of control believe that they are responsible for what happens to them; those with an external locus of control believe that they are at the mercy of others or other forces over which they have no control.) Lillian Robinson revealed herself in the opening narrative as a woman with an internal locus of control, willing to challenge others with power and to take matters into her own hands. Despite some research findings, there is little, if any, evidence that a single personality trait can predict which group members will emerge as leaders.

However, there is some research that connects emergent leadership with specific communication traits of group members. Schultz (1986) found that individuals who were goal directed, information giving, summarizing, and self-assured were likely to emerge as leaders; those who were quarrelsome and sensible were less likely to be perceived as leaders.

Hawkins and Stewart (1991) reported that individuals with high apprehension about communicating seldom emerge as group leaders. Such individuals are least comfortable communicating in unstructured situations (such as the conditions that groups face early in their formation). High communication apprehensives will contribute task-related comments to a discussion, but are less likely than other group members to engage in small talk. Hawkins and Stewart suggest that their "failure to engage in such small talk may have left higher apprehensives out of the relationship building process" (p. 8). As a group continues to meet, higher apprehensives may come to be viewed as influencing the group; however, during the early stages, when issues of leadership typically begin to be resolved, a group member who is apprehensive about communicating will be unlikely to emerge as a leader.

In several studies, Cronshaw and Ellis have explored the relationship between emergent leadership and group members' levels of *self-monitoring*, a trait that describes the ability of individuals to be aware of social cues and to adapt their own behaviors to meet the needs of the social situation. Cronshaw and Ellis have found that either high or low self-monitors can emerge as leaders, but they will do so under different conditions. High self-monitors, who notice social cues and adapt their behavior accordingly, are more likely to emerge as leaders when there are social cues indicating that leadership is needed. Low self-monitors, who perform as they are inclined to perform with little regard for social cues, will emerge as leaders only if they have a positive attitude toward leadership (Cronshaw & Ellis, 1991). The researchers also found, however, that even high self-monitoring women in mixed-sex groups exhibited leadership behaviors less frequently than did men in such groups (Ellis & Cronshaw, 1992). They suggested that the female group members may have been attentive to social cues that implied an expected dominance by the males, leading the female members to adapt by reducing their own leadership behaviors. Cronshaw and Ellis (1991) indicate that the combination of four traits—intelligence, masculinity, dominance, and self-monitoring—may jointly account for most cases of emergent leadership. Together those factors could explain an individual's decision to increase the performance of behaviors typically associated with leading a group.

Once an individual makes an initial selection of behaviors to perform within a group, the process of role negotiation begins. The patterns followed in the process of negotiating leadership have been described by Ernest Bormann of the University of Minnesota and several of his graduate students, one of whom was B. Aubrey Fisher. The research program at the University of Minnesota spanned decades. Classroom groups and groups created from community members for purposes of research were observed and analyzed. Typically, the groups were "zero history" groups (ones whose members had no previous experience working together). They were formed for "leaderless group discussions" occurring over the course of a semester. Without an appointed leader, most groups nonetheless developed leaders through the process of role negotiation. Bormann described the typical process of leader emergence as a two-step process in which a leader is selected through the "method of residue."

The Method of Residue

Bormann's explanation of leadership emergence involves a process in which most members of the group are excluded from consideration for the role of leader. For one reason or another, one member after another is rejected for the leader role. Whoever remains (the residue—like the residue left in a beaker after a chemistry experiment) becomes the leader. The rate at which members are rejected and the reasons for which they are rejected will differ, depending on which of the two stages in the process the group is in.

Stage One. The first stage in the leadership emergence process takes very little time to complete. Bormann (1975) wrote that it could be completed within minutes and seldom took longer than one session to complete. In the first stage, approximately half of the members of a group are excluded from consideration for the role of leader.

To see how the process might occur, consider a hypothetical five-member classroom group. The members are

- Emily, a very bright and hardworking group member. She is friendly, but also a bit shy; she needs to warm up to a group before she is willing to speak openly.
- Don, someone experienced in leading groups. He has a lot of other work to do at the moment, so he voices his desire not to be the leader of this group, which, he says, isn't as important to him as are his other obligations.
- Barb, who is returning to school after a divorce. She is eager to learn about small group communication and is interested in the project her group has undertaken.
- Tom, also interested in the group project and a good student. When the group members introduce themselves to each other, he mentions that he will have to miss some in-class meetings because he is on the football team, and the team leaves for some games before class is over.
- James, who is particularly happy to be a part of this group because he knows a lot about the topic the group is discussing. In fact, he knows exactly how the group should solve the problem they are considering.

In the first few minutes of the meeting, it is likely that group members would eliminate Emily as a possible leader, because she is unlikely to speak up much. In later meetings, once she is comfortable with the group, she may well have a major influence on the decisions of the group. At this point, however, her leadership potential would be overlooked by the group. Don would also be likely to be eliminated. His expression of disinterest in the group and his openness about not wanting to lead the group would encourage the group members to look elsewhere for their leader. Tom is also likely to be eliminated when the group learns that his attendance will not be regular. Group members who are absent have trouble coordinating the activities of the group. The remaining two contenders, Barb and James, both seem eager, committed to the project, and willing to be involved in the discussion. As in real groups, in this hypothetical group the members eliminated in the first stage are those who are quiet, absent, disinterested in the group, and who express a desire not to be the leader. If a group had a member who was totally unfamiliar with the task of the group and seemed to lack understanding of it, then that member would also be eliminated in the early stage.

Stage Two. The second stage of the leadership emergence process is more time-consuming. It also involves more competition. It is possible for the second stage never to end and for the question of who will lead the group to remain an unresolved issue. Individuals are eliminated during the second stage of the process on the basis of information that takes the group longer to discover:

Which members are inflexible?
Whose leadership style is inappropriate for the needs of the group?
Who proves to be less responsible than was first assumed to be the case?

In the early years of the Minnesota studies, Bormann found that women in mixed-sex groups were usually eliminated from consideration for leadership during the second stage of the process. Later studies, however, challenged this finding; the increase of women in leadership positions of all kinds began to be reflected in small group leadership, too.

Typically, the remaining contenders for leadership will compete among themselves for the support of other members. A member who comes to the support of a contender is considered to be a *lieutenant* for that individual. If you are familiar with the structure of the military, you know that an Army lieutenant is a low-ranking officer. As such, a lieutenant has some power, but not enough to be confused with a colonel or a general. So if Tom says, "I like Barb's suggestion," nods support as she speaks, or comes to her defense when others challenge her ideas, then he is Barb's lieutenant. He is not a leader himself, but he has the power to confer his support on another group member. If Emily and Don also give their support to Barb, then James will be eliminated from contention for the leader's role. At that point, the second stage of the process will be complete, and Barb will have been selected as the unofficial, emergent leader. Even though James seems to be well qualified to lead the group, it is quite possible that he would be eliminated in the second stage. Individuals who seem to "know it all" can become abrasive; their desire to shove a solution through the group may make them unacceptable as a leader to the group members.

It is also possible that the group members could ignore Barb as the leader and line up as lieutenants in support of James. If the group feels the need to complete the task quickly and if Barb encourages all of the members to talk through issues thoroughly before making a group decision, then the group may feel that her leadership style is less appropriate for their needs than James's style is.

Another possibility is that the three members no longer in contention for leadership may be divided in their support for the two remaining contenders. Suppose that Barb and James present conflicting ideas and each quickly gains the support of one of the other members: perhaps Emily is a lieutenant for Barb, and Don is a lieutenant for James. Tom will have the deciding "vote." It is possible that he will find the position of neither contender acceptable and will withhold his support until one or the other leader candidates suggests a compromise position. If Tom then joins with the lieutenant for the compromising contender, the leader will finally be determined.

The issue may not be fully resolved, however, if the "loser" harbors resentment about the outcome of this informal role-negotiation process and, especially, if he or she continues to have the support of one or more group members. In order to overcome this situation, it would be helpful for the "winner" to make some repairs—usually by granting the other contender additional status associated with recognition for another role within the group. For instance, if Barb was chosen as leader of the group, she might grant James the role of "task specialist" or "critical evaluator." No official title needs to be given James; just a simple reference from Barb about how important James is to the group can help put to rest the conflict that developed during the second stage of the leadership emergence process.

It is quite possible for a group to have completed the process of leadership emergence and be unaware of that fact. After all, they may never talk directly about making a decision. They may never have any reason to name a member as their leader. However, when the decision about who will lead the group has been completed in this informal way, the group will generally experience an increase in cohesiveness and a decrease in tension—just as it does when any decision about the structure of the group is completed.

Ethical Consideration

Because resolving the leadership issue is important to a group's functioning, you should assist with the process. You are not obligated to take all responsibility for the group's process or decisions on your shoulders. You will not earn all of the blame—nor all of the credit—for the group's outcomes. Serving as a leader of the group may be necessary. If, for some reason, you are not able to serve as leader of a group or if there is a group member better suited to lead the group than you are, then you should be involved in selecting a leader by identifying the person best able to lead your group and supporting that person's leadership efforts.

Alternate Views

While most researchers confirm the occurrence of some leadership emergence, some find that the process is different from that just described. Bormann's explanation does, after all, assume that more than one group member would like to be the leader of the group—which does not always happen to be the case. For instance, Owen (1987) found that women frequently emerged as leaders of mixed-sex classroom groups. He challenged the description of the process as a method of residues, for he found that the women who emerged were not "leftovers." Instead, they had filled a vacuum within groups in which no one else stepped forward to assume the role of leader. They earned the role through performing a variety of actions—through hard work. In the opening narratives, both Cecily Yee and Lillian Robinson appear to have earned their role as leader in the same way. In contrast to them, however, in Owen's research, the women who emerged as leaders often denied that they were leaders. Owen described this as an intriguing strategy for protecting their leadership role, since a role one does not have cannot be challenged by another group member. It would be interesting to discover whether, in the time since Owen's study, women have begun to seek leadership positions more openly and less apologetically.

The behavior Owen observed is consistent with the ambivalence of many group members—whether male or female—about assuming the leader's role. The ambivalence may come from conflicting desires: the desire to help a group achieve success (and be given credit for having done so) on the one hand and, on the other hand, the desire to avoid the responsibility for the outcome of the group (and avoid being blamed if the group should fail). Capable group members may express these conflicting feelings. Shoemaker (1991) includes excerpts from the journal of a group member who described herself as a leader who did not want the role. She felt she had a greater ability than some in the group to grasp information and mentioned her efforts to involve quiet members and to avoid monopolizing the discussion. She also mentioned resisting being the director and not wanting to be responsible. In the end, however, she was pleased that others in the group saw her as an effective leader. When ambivalence about assuming the role of leader exists among the members most capable of assuming the role, then a group will be likely to experience a leadership emergence process that involves filling the vacuum.

A second pattern may occur that is different from the typical pattern of leadership emergence described by Bormann. Groups may develop two (or more) distinct leaders who complement one another rather than compete. At times, the leadership roles are divided between the two areas of group needs, with one person serving as the task leader and another as the socio-emotional leader. Schnake, Dumler, and Cochran (1993) reported that the most effective leadership style includes behaviors that both show consideration (leadership that is friendly, supportive, and concerned) and that initiate structure (leadership that defines members' roles and assists members in performing their tasks). While a single leader may incorporate both approaches, groups can also thrive if two leaders share these behaviors between themselves. In other cases, two leaders may represent divergent positions within the group, both of which the group values. A relevant case is one reported by Wyatt (1984) in her description of the distribution of power within a Weavers' Guild. Within that group, two women who could be called the leaders of the group held no formal positions but were recognized as being the two most powerful group members. One encouraged the group to participate in activities that were traditional for that group; the other encouraged the group to adopt innovative patterns of action. Wyatt said that the women were not antagonists, but rather functioned to maintain an equilibrium within the group between the two opposing goals, both of which received support from group members. The leadership of the group was shared not only between them, but also among other group members as well. In explaining how the group had maintained this mode of operation successfully for ten years, Wyatt wrote:

> This kind of shared leadership closely resembles what some feminist writers have described as typical of women's interactional style. Certainly the women in this group by and large are not career women; they have not been trained to seek and use power as it is used in other male-dominated organizations. The characteristic orientation of the members of the guild toward power seems to be that power is a bad thing in itself, reprehensible to pursue, and ultimately unnecessary for the successful functioning of the group. (p. 84)

Indeed, for all groups, whether they operate with a single group leader or with leadership shared quite equally, questions of power and influence affect their comfort with the leader or leadership within the group.

Power and Influence

Leadership is related to both power and influence, so that distinguishing between the two concepts is not easy. One of the clearest distinctions was made by Bell (1975) in an essay on political linguistics. He wrote that statements involving power take the form, "If you do X, then I will do Y." Examples might include a threat, "If you report my error, then I will have you fired," or a promise, "If you complete the report, then I will see to it that you get a raise." In both cases, one person seeks to alter the behavior of another and to do so through manipulating sanctions. Fisher (1985) concurred with this explanation, saying that power originates in one individual's control of scarce resources.

In contrast to statements of power, statements involving influence take the form, "If you do X, then you will do Y." An example might be, "If you complete the report, then you will be sure that it gets done to your satisfaction." Such statements do not involve sanctions, but they do make clear the effects an individual's actions will have. An individual who responds to a statement of influence does so willingly, but not because there seems to be no alternative. Instead, the response comes from a commitment to the social relationship between two parties.

In 1959, French and Raven published a taxonomy of power that continues to be incorporated in works on leadership, such as Yukl's 1994 book, *Leadership in Organizations*. The taxonomy includes five types of power:

- Reward—One complies in the hope of receiving a reward believed to be controlled by another.
- Coercive—One complies in the hope of avoiding a punishment believed to be controlled by another.
- Legitimate—One complies from a sense of obligation to an individual who is believed to have the right to request compliance.
- Expert—One complies with the request of an individual believed to be especially knowledgeable.
- Referent—One complies in the hope of getting approval from a respected individual.

Using the distinctions between power and influence described by Bell (1975) and supported by Fisher (1985), reward and coercive power would be properly considered to be power, whereas legitimate, expert, and referent power would more properly be considered to be examples of influence.

Obtaining Power or Influence

How does one group member accumulate power or influence? The means by which power is accumulated are often quite straightforward. When the leader is appointed by an outside source, the resources over which the leader has control are given to the leader with the appointment. When Doug Harris was selected as a leader of a Detroit Summer group, he was given control of the materials for repairing the church his group worked on. In other cases, with a team leader's appointment may come the ability to hire or fire team members or to review their performance and make recommendations that affect workers' job security. Thus, these appointed leaders are in control of scarce resources that permit them to apply sanctions to other group members. When a group appoints or, in the case of emergent leadership, supports one of its members as the leader, the group may relinquish control over group resources to the leader; thus power will come as a by-product of influence. However, because the leader in these cases is serving at the will of the group, an abuse of power by the leader will lead members to reclaim the power for themselves.

Ethical Consideration

If you have been given control over the resources of the group, then you are obligated to use it for the benefit of the group, not simply to improve your own position at the expense of the group.

Influence is usually obtained as a result of interaction within the group. The general pattern is described by Lovaglia (1995): social interaction leads group members to develop expectations for further interaction; when favorable expectations exist about a particular group member, others in the group assign that member higher status. Status then translates into influence. In the case of Doug Harris leading a group of teens, his leadership came less from his control over the materials for plastering than from his encouragement of the teens' involvement with the project. His behaviors led the teens to have favorable expectations about him as their leader. Some research on influence has identified specific communicative behaviors that lead group members to award status (and thus influence) to members. For instance, Wyatt (1984) found that in the Weavers' Guild she analyzed, those with greatest influence were those who were able to clearly articulate the goals of the group and who had plans for the group. Scott and Easton (1996) found that the nature of high- and low-influence group members' contributions differed: those with low influence made more statements and suggestions; those with high influence made more justifications and asked more questions (often questions that served a consensus-testing function, such as asking members whether they agreed on a position or proposal).

Not only the nature of interaction, but also the amount of interaction can affect a member's influence. Scott and Easton (1996) found that group size affects the influence ratings of group members; a member's influence is higher in a small group than in a large one, probably due to the increased opportunity each member has to contribute within a smaller group. The length of time a group member has been with the group

As this group of physics students works together on their lab reports, the frequency and nature of the participation by each member will determine which of them will become leader.

Technology Note: Relationship between Technology and Leadership

It should not be surprising to discover that the technology used in communication may affect the influence of a member. Scott and Easton (1996) found that communicating over computers removed some of the perceived influence of high-influence members and added some influence to lower-influence members. Perhaps this finding suggests that some of the influence comes from nonverbal communication patterns as well as verbal ones; the computer communication emphasizes the verbal communication and de-emphasizes nonverbal communication.

In the opening narratives, Cecily Yee commented on a different relationship between influence and technology: those with higher influence in her workplace use computer technology more often, and those who fail to use the technology (that is, those who do not read their E-mail messages from the supervisor) lose influence. Her observation is corroborated by Lipnack and Stamps (1997), who argue that "in virtual teams and networks, each act of sending information is an act of leadership" (p. 111). They also note that in geographically dispersed teams, independent action by members is often necessary. In acting independently, team members distribute leadership throughout the team.

(or the member's seniority) also affects influence. Baker and Eaton (1992) found, both in groups of monkeys and in groups of humans, that seniority within the group increased a member's influence. In the case of monkeys, influence was determined by the member's dominance. That was measured by a "peanut test": when a peanut was dropped between two monkeys, the one that grabbed and held onto the peanut was considered most dominant. (Identifying the leader of a group of monkeys might be easier than making the same determination in a group of humans!) Baker and Eaton said that chronological age may be used as a determinant of status within casual, temporary groups; however, in longer-term groups, ones in which the social system has become more developed, the duration of one's membership in the group is more significant than one's chronological age in determining influence within the group. Hackman and Johnson (1996) claim that age and seniority will be given more weight in determining leadership in some cultures than in others. They indicate that cultures with high discomfort about uncertainty (such as Greece, Portugal, Belgium, and Japan) will seek to resolve the uncertainty by selecting leaders according to seniority rules. Groups or members from cultures with greater comfort with uncertainty (including Singapore, Denmark, and Hong Kong) will be less likely to rely on seniority in designating the leader.

Although interaction within the group is the most likely source of influence, group members may grant influence based on perceptions affected by factors external to their particular group. Glaser (1996) discovered that when a group's process favored those with social or verbal skills, then those with an interest or expertise in the task, those who had access to relevant information, and those who were attractive or had self-confidence were likely to gain influence. In addition, however, she found that patterns of influence within a group might distinguish between paid staff members (higher influence) and volunteers (lower influence). Status differences within the group might reflect a status difference found in relationships outside the group. For instance, if two workers at the same plant are also both members of a community the-

Ethical Consideration

As you interact in a group, consider why you grant higher status to some group members than to others. If the members have earned higher status through their contributions to the group, then it is well deserved. However, if you are granting higher status to members for reasons other than their contributions to the group (or withholding it from others because you expect that "people like *that*" can't be effective leaders), you may be contributing to undesirable conflict within the group.

---

ater group, they might carry their status differences at work into the theater group. Or the group might recreate within itself the patterns of racism, sexism, or classism that originate in the outside system. In the groups Glaser studied, group members felt that discrepancies in influence that had come from the group's process were justified and acceptable. Members who had worked hard or knew the most about the topic were believed to deserve their higher levels of influence. In contrast, influence discrepancies that came from other sources caused tension within the group.

Conflict Resulting from Unequal Distribution of Power

Inequality in power can lead group members to feel discomfort about the group process that may, ultimately, lead to conflict. McClane (1991a) found that when roles were highly differentiated so that some members had significantly more power than others, group members were dissatisfied with the group. Even if the expressions of conflict within the group are minimal, lower-status members may still feel considerable discomfort. A study by Lovaglia (1995) discovered that to be the case. In this experiment, the power of group members was experimentally manipulated. Those who were given little power interacted with their higher-power partners—confederates of the researcher who were told to disagree with the decision of the first partner, thus overruling the low-status partner. Video recordings of the lower-status partner alone in a room with just a computer screen showed the frustrated and angry partner gesturing wildly (and sometimes obscenely) at the computer screen, pounding on the equipment, and swearing so loudly it could be heard through a soundproof wall. Groups whose low-power members defer to those with more power should not assume that similar emotions do not boil beneath the surface of the apparently docile group members. Tensions among group members who are not in leadership positions within a group may vary as the style of leadership exhibited by the group leader changes.

Leadership Styles

The classic study of leadership styles was done by Lewin, Lippitt, and White, reported in 1939 in the *Journal of Social Psychology,* and described in expanded form in White and Lippitt (1960). The researchers examined the effects of three different styles of leaders on four groups of five 11-year-old boys involved in "G-man clubs." The clubs worked on craft projects, including building club benches and a table, painting a mural and club signs, making a plaster-of-Paris mask and plaster footprints, creating wood and soap carvings, and constructing a model airplane and a crime game. The experimenters assigned adults to lead each group, with each group having a different adult leader in each of three six-week-long sessions. Each adult had been trained to employ two of three leadership styles: democratic, autocratic, or laissez-faire. One group, the "Dick Tracy Club," had autocratic leaders for the early and final sessions, with a democratic leader in the middle sessions. The "Secret Agents Club" began and ended with democratic leaders, but had an autocratic leader during the middle sessions. The "Sherlock Holmes Club" and the "Charlie Chan Club" both had one six-week session each of democratic, autocratic, and laissez-faire leadership.

When the groups had **democratic leaders,** then the boys in the group participated in making decisions about the steps necessary to complete the project and the jobs each would complete. The leader participated in the activities of the group, playing the role of another group member. **Autocratic leaders** identified the steps the boys were to take and assigned tasks to each group member. The leader demonstrated some tasks, but otherwise was not involved in the actual group activity. The **laissez-faire** leaders provided the necessary supplies for the project and expressed their availability to answer questions if asked. Otherwise, they did not perform the behaviors typically associated with leadership of a group. In fact, their participation in the group activity was minimal.

The researchers gathered information about the impact of leadership style in a variety of ways, including having the leaders write a brief summary of each day's events, interviewing each boy after each of the six-week sessions, and having two observers keep a stenographic record of group members' comments while a third observer kept a running account of the group activity. Lewin, Lippitt, and White (cited in White & Lippitt, 1960) found that the effectiveness of the groups varied with the style of leadership used in the group. The groups led by laissez-faire leaders performed the worst. They completed less work than other groups did, and the quality of work was poor. The group members lacked direction and often became silly. Even though the leaders had said they would be available to answer questions, the boys may not even have known what questions were reasonable ones to ask the leader. The members' satisfaction with the group was minimal as well. Even during meetings, they expressed their discontent. In older groups in which members are competent in the tasks required of them, group members might be able to lead themselves without help from a leader. In this study, however, when leaders performed no leadership behaviors, the groups were unsuccessful.

Autocratic leaders were more successful. When they were present with the groups, the groups were very productive, more so than either of the other groups. However, the groups' productivity decreased significantly when the autocratic leaders were absent from the group. Moreover, there were other problems in these groups. Group members were hostile, even destroying their own projects. The boys in these groups made more demands for attention, blamed other group members for problems, and were more likely to drop out of the groups than were members of groups with a different style of leader. Boys in groups led by autocratic leaders were submissive and demonstrated less individuality than did members of other groups.

Although groups led by democratic leaders were somewhat less productive than those led by autocratic leaders, the productivity did not decline in the absence of the leader. In other words, group members felt a sufficient commitment to the process and knowledge of how to proceed—since they had been involved in making the decisions about process—that they were able to work productively even before a leader arrived at the meeting or when one left the room. Their work was also more creative. Moreover, the members of democratically led groups expressed the most satisfaction with the group process of any of the groups. During meetings, their comments were friendlier and more group centered. In interviews after the sessions were complete, boys expressed their preference for the democratic leaders over either of the other styles.

Efforts to replicate the study of leadership styles have had conflicting results. That has led some to believe that information on leadership styles is not actually relevant in groups. However, anyone who has observed different leaders of groups in operation can attest to the fact that there are actual differences in leadership styles that impact the success of groups and satisfaction of group members. The inconsistencies found in the research may be explained in part by the way the research has been designed. Gastil (1994) found that democratic leadership is the most productive leadership style, but he acknowledged that other studies may not have the same finding if the researcher imposes a democratic style of leadership on an appointed leader. As Gastil noted, "democratic leadership is most productive when it is a naturally occurring phenomenon, as opposed to a researcher's manipulation during a field or laboratory experiment. . . . fully democratic leadership is implemented democratically rather than by an experimenter's random assignment to leadership conditions" (p. 402).

Situational Leadership

A second explanation for the inconsistent results on leadership styles lies with the fact that different conditions seem to justify different styles of leadership. Those who support a "situational leadership" view recognize the importance of the situation in determining which leadership style is preferable. For instance, Hersey and Blanchard (cited in Norris & Vecchio, 1992) proposed that the optimal leadership style requires finding the optimal balance between relationship-oriented behaviors and task-oriented behaviors to suit the maturity level of the group. Groups that have not worked together on the task they are assigned require a leader with increased task-oriented behaviors. As groups develop some maturity (and, thus, some skill in completing the assigned task), the leader's task-oriented emphasis can be reduced, but the relationship-oriented behaviors should be increased. When the maturity level of a group is high, both task- and relationship-oriented behaviors from the leader can be less frequent. Of course, a single comment can affect both the task and relationship dimensions. A leader's angry demand that a project be completed by the next day may affect the task positively at the same time it damages relationships. It is still possible, however, to distinguish messages in which the content is designed to affect the task primarily from those whose content is designed to affect relationships primarily.

According to Hersey and Blanchard's situational leadership model, by combining different levels of task and relationship behaviors, four different styles of leadership are possible: telling, selling, participating, and delegating. The first is the *telling* style, useful for leading immature groups whose members have such high task needs that they surpass their relationship needs. The telling style is closely related to an authoritarian approach, because the leader focuses on the task and assigns jobs. The second style involves *selling*. It is appropriate for somewhat more mature groups, which still have high task needs but also high relationship needs. In this case, the maturity level of the group has increased so that members perceive themselves to have some task competence. The leader must therefore persuade—or sell—the group on the approach he or she prefers. When the group is still more mature, the task direction can be reduced. Group members still have high relationship needs that can be satisfied if the leader uses a *participating* style. In the case of mature groups, task and relationship needs have been sufficiently satisfied. The leader can adopt a *delegating* style. In this way, the group members function independently to accomplish tasks on which they might earlier have required more direction to complete satisfactorily.

Cultural differences are likely to affect the success of different leadership styles. For instance, Dorfman and Howell (1997) have done a series of studies comparing concepts of ideal leadership in the United States with such concepts in Mexico. Their results suggest that directive leadership (telling) was effective in Mexico but not in the United States; participation was effective in the United States, but not in Mexico. Mexican leaders were expected to treat followers with respect and personal attention, but not necessarily to ask for suggestions or to act on them if given. Moreover, it is likely that a selling approach would be avoided by leaders from some cultures, regardless of the stage their groups are in. To the extent that selling one's ideas inherently involves self-promotion, it would be uncomfortable for someone whose culture values humility (as is true in China) or in a culture that discourages setting oneself apart from the group (as is true in Native American cultures).

Leadership Styles and Power

There are relationships between the style of leadership used within a group and the distribution of power within the group. Zorn and Leichty (1991) provided a link between situational leadership theory and power when they argued that group members' needs for autonomy (self-determination) would increase as the group matured. In fact, Zorn and Leichty found that when messages from the group leaders of mature groups were perceived to have addressed the members' needs for autonomy, the messages were evaluated favorably.

The connection between style of leadership and control was drawn by Harnack, Fest, and Jones (1977). They argued that laissez-faire leadership involves less control in the hands of the leader than is the case for other styles of leadership, but that democratic and autocratic leadership styles are distinguished by the kind of control each involves, not the quantity of control. Democratic leadership involves control over the *process* of decision making. This control might ensure that the group is to be involved in making the decision, that all members will be encouraged to participate, and that decisions reached by consensus are preferred. Autocratic leadership involves control over the *content* of decision making. An autocratic leader might decide that the group will protest in a letter-writing campaign, not a sit-in (without regard to the preference of the majority) and that James has the job of drafting a model letter (without regard to what task James would have chosen for himself).

There are circumstances in which centralizing the power of the group in the hands of a leader benefits the group. In general, the circumstances parallel those in which individuals do a better job than does a group. For instance, in a crisis situation, when the demands on the group are high and the time available is small, an autocratic leader can act decisively. In contrast, in those situations in which groups fare better than individuals, democratic leadership style is more preferable, because it distributes control over the content of the decisions among group members.

Even those groups that begin as democratic groups and face no crisis situations may find themselves facing threats to their democratic functioning. Inequalities in power may emerge as they could in any group. If the group members define their roles as unequal and if they are committed to maintaining the group's democratic structure, then they will view the inequities as problematic. Glaser (1996) explained that "it is the work of a democratic group to contest power differentials; that is what defines a democracy" (p. 556). She argued that it is natural for egalitarian groups to experience temporary power inequities and then to remove them. Once unequal power distribution is recognized, even informally, it can be challenged and roles renegotiated in a fluid process of role negotiation. Glaser concluded that the democracy within a group would be threatened, not by the mere existence of inequality, but by the inequities not being recognized or, once recognized, not being challenged.

Sometimes groups initially grant power to one member in an effort to reduce the discomfort the members have during the early stages of group formation. Making one person the "leader" gives the group someone on whom they rely to provide them with a sense of direction, even though—with time—the group members might have found the sense of direction themselves. Gemmill (1986) wrote that the group is then giving in to a "rescue fantasy," believing that the leader will dispel their fears and lead them to success. In the process, the members avoid self-examination, which might have identified the skills each of them could have contributed to the group process. Members distance themselves from taking personal responsibility for their own future and, in effect, "de-skill" themselves. The leader who was so quickly empowered by the group comes to see him- or herself as the only one capable enough to provide direction for the group; this perception leads to increased displays of directiveness, which lead the other group members to withdraw even further. The power inequities originally accepted by the group come to be resented by the members. Therefore, the cycle described by Gemmill is an unproductive one.

An example of such a group was a three-person classroom group. One group member who was very concerned about the issue the group was discussing was not able to commit herself to leading the group because she had to work a lot of hours and was facing some personal problems during the period of the course. Another group member viewed herself as very shy; she was uncomfortable with leading a group. They were happy enough at the beginning of the semester to count on the leadership of the male

Cecily Yee (second from left) believes that when she leads work groups, she gets better results if the power in the group is distributed.

group member. He became an active and responsible leader. At times he expressed frustration at having to do so much of the work of the group, but he sensed that it was important for him to act because the rest of the group could not be depended upon. Observers described the group leader's behavior as very autocratic. As the semester continued, the other group members began to resent the leader, apparently regretting giving him the power they had yielded early in the group's life.

If leaders view power as a resource to be shared, they are more likely, in the long run, to maintain power than are those leaders who attempt to hoard power, withholding it from other members. An interesting discovery was made by Tjosvold, Andrews, and Struthers (1991) about perceptions of power. They discovered that when managers perceived themselves as powerful, they also perceived their employees to be influential and competent. When the managers saw the group as cooperative (so that the goals of the group leader and members were positively related), they perceived the employees to be influential and competent. When employees perceived their managers to be competitive or independent, so that the goals of the leaders and members were not positively related, then they perceived both the manager and themselves to have little power. Tjosvold, Andrews, and Struthers concluded that "cooperative interdependence may be a key, because it can be expected to help employees and managers recognize and appreciate each other's valuable resources, as well as encourage them to use their resources to promote each other's work" (p. 297).

These findings relate to small groups as well as organizations: when group members battle over power, each member will perceive power as a resource too

Ethical Considerations

As a group member, you should anticipate the discomfort that exists in groups as the group forms, contribute in whatever ways you can to the leadership process, and support individuals as leaders who will help to empower the group as a whole. Rushing to reduce the initial "psychic distress" by naming someone as the leader or absolving yourself of responsibility for shared leadership by yielding control over the group to another member not only runs counter to your responsibility to your group, but will be counterproductive in the long run. Furthermore, if you serve as a leader of a group, you will better meet your obligation to encourage full participation in decision making if you empower the members of the group rather than hoarding your power.

---

scarce for their comfort; when group members share power and cooperate to achieve mutual goals, then power will seem plentiful. In the opening narratives, both Cecily Yee and Doug Harris mentioned that involving group members in decisions was the style of leadership they preferred. It improved their groups when members were empowered.

Sometimes we may think that unless we act powerful, no one will notice that we are the leader of a group. And, in fact, democratic leaders are less likely to be identified as the leader of a group than autocratic leaders are. But the point is not whether we get the recognition that is our due; the point is whether our groups function as effectively as possible. In most cases, that requires sharing power among the group members, both over the long term and within a single meeting of a group.

Summary

A group may identify a single member as its leader, but effective group members will share leadership with the leader. Thus, each member exerts influence over other members in order to facilitate achievement of the group's goals, but the leader is the individual who, by virtue of a social relationship with other group members, exerts the greatest amount of influence over the members of the group.

Whatever the means were by which a person became the leader—whether by emerging as leader, being appointed to the position, or volunteering—and whatever the style of leadership the individual selects, he or she would be well advised to attend to the social relationship between a leader and the rest of the group members. A leader of a small group is not handed a pedestal with the position. By sharing power with other group members, the leader will come to realize that power is a resource that, shared, strengthens the group as a whole.

QUESTIONS FOR DISCUSSION

1. What style of leadership does each of the leaders described in the narratives seem to use?

2. In what ways will an effective political or business leader be similar to an effective group leader? In what ways will they be different?

3. Has leadership in groups you belong to evolved according to the method of residue?

4. If members have no interest (or skill) in leading a particular group, what can they do to assure that the group has adequate leadership?

5. Do groups of women seem to handle leadership differently than groups of men do?

6. Fisher viewed a leader as a medium. Others have said a leader is an energizer. What metaphor would you suggest to best describe a leader?

SUGGESTED ACTIVITIES

1. Observe a meeting of a group to which you do not belong. Describe the behaviors of the leader and the responses of the other group members. Discuss any evidence you see of either power or influence in the group.

2. Answer the following questions about your project group:
   a. Does your group have a leader?
   b. If you had to identify a single member as leader, whose name would you give?
   c. Do you think other members of your group would agree with your answers?
   d. Would you like to be leader of your group?
   Compare your answers with those of the other group members.

3. In your journal, identify the way your project group has dealt with leadership. If there are problems with leadership in your group, identify the strategies you will use to improve the leadership.

SOURCES CITED

Anderson, S. D., & Wanberg, K. W. (1991). A convergent validity model of emergent leadership in groups. *Small Group Research, 22*, 380–397.

Baker, P. M., & Eaton, G. G. (1992). Seniority versus age as causes of dominance in social groups: Macaques and men. *Small Group Research, 23*, 322–343.

Barge, J. K. (1996). Leadership skills and the dialectics of leadership in group decision making. In R. Y. Hirokawa & M. S. Poole (Eds.), *Communication and group decision making* (pp. 301–344). Thousand Oaks, CA: Sage.

Behling, O., & McFillen, J. M. (1996). A syncretical model of charismatic/transformational leadership. *Group & Organization Management, 21*, 163–191.

Bell, D. V. J. (1975). *Power, influence, and authority: An essay in political linguistics.* New York: Oxford University Press.

Bormann, E. G. (1975). *Discussion and group methods: Theory and practice.* New York: Harper & Row.

Counselman, E. F. (1991). Leadership in a long-term leaderless women's group. *Small Group Research*, *22*, 240–257.

Cronshaw, S. F., & Ellis, R. J. (1991). A process investigation of self-monitoring and leader emergence. *Small Group Research*, *22*, 403–420.

Dorfman, P. W., & Howell, J. P. (1997). Managerial leadership in the United States and Mexico: Distant neighbors or close cousins? In C. S. Granrose & S. Oskamp (Eds.), *Cross-cultural work groups* (pp. 234–264). Thousand Oaks, CA: Sage.

Ellis, R. J., & Cronshaw, S. F. (1992). Self-monitoring and leader emergence: A test of moderator effects. *Small Group Research*, *23*, 113–129.

Fisher, B. A. (1985). Leadership as medium: Treating complexity in group communication research. *Small Group Behavior*, *16*, 167–196.

Gastil, J. (1994). A meta-analytic review of the productivity and satisfaction of democratic and autocratic leadership. *Small Group Research*, *25*, 384–410.

Gemmill, G. (1986). The mythology of the leader role in small groups. *Small Group Behavior*, *17*, 41–50.

Glaser, H. F. (1996). Structure and struggle in egalitarian groups: Dimensions of power relations. *Small Group Research*, *27*, 551–571.

Hackman, M. Z., & Johnson, C. E. (1996). *Leadership: A communication perspective*. Prospect Heights, IL: Waveland Press.

Harnack, R. V., Fest, T. B., & Jones, B. S. (1977). *Group discussion: Theory and technique* (2nd ed.). Englewood Cliffs, NJ: Prentice-Hall.

Hawkins, K. W. (1995). Effects of gender and communication content on leadership emergence in small task-oriented groups. *Small Group Research*, *26*, 234–249.

Hawkins, K. W., & Stewart, R. A. (1991). Effects of communication apprehension on perceptions of leadership and intragroup attraction in small task-oriented groups. *Southern Communication Journal*, *57*, 1–10.

Ketrow, S. M. (1991). Communication role specializations and perceptions of leadership. *Small Group Research*, *22*, 492–514.

Lipnack, J., & Stamps, J. (1997). *Virtual teams: Reaching across space, time, and organizations with technology*. New York: Wiley.

Lovaglia, M. J. (1995). Power and status: Exchange, attribution, and expectation states. *Small Group Research*, *26*, 400–426.

McClane, W. E. (1991a). Implications of member role differentiation: Analysis of a key concept in the LMX model of leadership. *Group & Organization Studies*, *16*, 102–113.

McClane, W. E. (1991b). The interaction of leader and member characteristics in the leader-member exchange (LMX) model of leadership. *Small Group Research*, *22*, 283–300.

Norris, W. R., & Vecchio, R. P. (1992). Situational leadership theory: A replication. *Group & Organization Management*, *17*, 331–342.

Nye, J. L., & Forsyth, D. R. (1991). The effects of prototype-based biases on leadership appraisals: A test of leadership categorization theory. *Small Group Research*, *22*, 360–379.

Owen, W. F. (1987). Rhetorical themes of emergent female leaders. *Small Group Behavior*, *17*, 475–486.

Palich, L. E., & Hom, P. W. (1992). The impact of leader power and behavior on leadership perceptions: A LISREL test of an expanded categorization theory of leadership model. *Group & Organization Management*, *17*, 279–296.

Schnake, M., Dumler, M. P., & Cochran, D. S. (1993). The relationship between "traditional" leadership, "super" leadership, and organizational citizenship behavior. *Group & Organization Management*, *18*, 352–365.

Schultz, B. (1986). Communicative correlates of perceived leaders in the small group. *Small Group Behavior*, *17*, 51–65.

Scott, C. R., & Easton, A. C. (1996). Examining equality of influence in group decision support system interaction. *Small Group Research*, *27*, 360–382.

Seers, A., Petty, M. M., & Cashman, J. F. (1995). Team-member exchange under team and traditional management: A naturally occurring quasi-experiment. *Group & Organization Management*, *20*, 18–38.

Shoemaker, H. J. (1991). Self-construction in a small group setting: Journal narratives. *Small Group Research, 22,* 339–359.

Sosik, J. J. (1997). Effects of transformational leadership and anonymity on idea generation in computer-mediated groups. *Group & Organization Management, 22,* 460–487.

Tjosvold, D., Andrews, I. R., & Struthers, J. T. (1991). Power and interdependence in work groups: Views of managers and employees. *Group & Organization Studies, 16,* 285–299.

Wheelan, S. A., & Johnson, F. (1996). The role of informal member leaders in a system containing formal leaders. *Small Group Research, 27,* 33–55.

White, R. K., & Lippitt, R. (1960). *Autocracy and democracy: An experimental inquiry.* New York: Harper & Brothers.

Wyatt, N. (1984). Power and decision making. In G. M. Phillips & J. T. Wood (Eds.), *Emergent issues in human decision making* (pp. 50–60). Carbondale, IL: Southern Illinois University Press.

Yukl, G. (1994). *Leadership in organizations* (3rd ed.). Englewood Cliffs, NJ: Prentice-Hall.

Zorn, T. E., & Leichty, G. B. (1991). Leadership and identity: A reinterpretation of situational leadership theory. *Southern Communication Journal, 57,* 11–24.

4 Communication in the Small Group: Process and Skills

CHAPTER OBJECTIVES

After reading this chapter, you should be able to

- Explain the process of creating (or failing to create) shared meaning
- Distinguish between appropriate and inappropriate questions for generating discussion
- Create appropriate questions for generating discussion
- Distinguish between appropriate and inappropriate responses for group discussion
- Provide appropriate responses in discussion
- Identify the conditions that interfere with effective listening
- Practice good listening behaviors
- Explain the role of nonverbal behaviors in group interaction
- Describe the communication behaviors that can create a positive group climate

The Narratives

One recent summer, seven women worked together on several projects during a three-week intensive small group communication class at Central Michigan University. Four of the women (Helena, Terrie, Letitia, and Kiki) are African Americans; three (Candice, Dawn, and Melissa) are white. They anticipated that their racial diversity would be an advantage as they prepared a training workshop on handling diversity in small groups. The workshop would be presented at the end of the third week of class.

At the end of the second week, the students had to take their second exam. The exam required them to complete five essay questions within a 90-minute period. They were given the choice of working on all (or any part) of the exam as a group or independently. Several of the group members wanted to take the exam as a group; other members had expressed their desire to work independently. Some of the group members perceived the group to be divided along racial lines on this decision.

Although each of the other groups in the class decided to work together on the exam, the members of this group completed the exam independently. The decision about the exam was the source of some conflict among group members. Three months after they finished the course, five of the group members met again to reflect on the problems the group had faced in deciding how to take the test.

Helena: *Originally, I really wanted to take the exam as a group, because I figured we should—it's a group class. When we went to take it, actually I probably would have taken it as a group if everybody else would have said okay. But since there was so much tension, I just thought, "I'll take it by myself. I don't want to sit here and argue over this. Let's take this test. I don't care about anybody." But I really wanted to take it as a group.*

Letitia: *At first, I thought Helena was neutral because she said, "It doesn't matter." But then I thought Helena wanted to take it as a group because she was concerned about our reputation. After all, this was a small groups test, and here we were taking it individually.*

Terrie: *To me, Helena seemed to have divided feelings about the test, but Dawn certainly didn't. Dawn wanted to take the exam as an individual, because Dawn was a one-woman show. She said, "I can handle it. I want to take it by myself. I'll be all right."*

Candice: *In my journal I wrote about Dawn's statement during the first week of class that she wanted to take the second exam independently. It upset me, because I wanted to do it as a group. I went home and talked to one of my really good friends. He said that maybe she'd had a group experience that had hurt her in the past. He told me about a bad group experience that had happened to his friend, and I said, "Oh, if she had an experience like that, it would be a very huge factor." But figuring out what to do was difficult for me. You know, Dawn had said, "We're definitely not taking it as a group, but if you guys still want to, you guys can." I said, "That's not an option for me." I wanted to take it either as a whole group or individually. I wasn't going to separate the group in half. So if the option of taking it as a group was already ruled out, the only other option that I thought I was left with was saying, "Then, I guess I have no choice but to say I want to take it individually."*

Helena: *I think Letitia wanted to take it as a group. She was group oriented.*

Dawn: *But I hadn't seen it that way. I thought, initially, that she wanted to do it by herself. And even when we had a big argument in class, I still thought that. Only when we were in class taking the test that day did I realize, "You know what? She wanted to take it as a group."*

Candice: *For me, it was the day before that. We were working on an exercise, and Letitia was off to the side. She wasn't really into what we were doing. We were finalizing whether we were going to take this test as a group, and she was very distant. Very cold. Just not happy at all.*

Letitia: *I just didn't want to argue about it, because I refused to jump in and take over. As I told you guys, in the old days I would have decided that we would have taken the exam as a group, and there would have been no discussion, no question about it. But I was determined not to do that, and to let the group make the decision. At that point, whatever happened, happened. If we take it together, then we take it together. If we don't, we don't.*

Dawn: *Letitia, I thought you withdrew because we kept arguing about it. That's why I thought you had pulled away.*

Letitia: *As I remember, there was one point when I stopped talking all together.*

Candice: *That's right. And Terrie, you were so silent about it that I wasn't absolutely positive how you felt. I thought that you wanted to take it as a group because I remembered that you had another test going on. I thought your reasoning would be that it would be easier because there would have been less pressure. I remember when you were in class you said your head was just spinning, you had so much going on.*

Terrie: *I know. I was really pitiful then. I never slept. I was so pitiful then. Actually, I thought it would be easier to take the test individually. We would have spent the whole time trying to agree on one answer. So that's why I said it was better to take it individually.*

Dawn: *I'm not going to say all our conflicts were racially based, but I remember that after I said I wanted to take the test alone, Helena was talking about how she had felt and said, "You let me go into your store to buy something. You'll take my money, but you don't want me in your store."*

Helena: *Yeah, right. Something to that effect. We were good enough to work in a group like that, but we weren't good enough to take the test together.*

Dawn: *Because of your race, that's why. I hadn't thought about it like that . . . and I didn't realize that was how you might feel, because that's never happened to me. So sometimes, I had to get into your mindset to see where you'd gotten that idea. I didn't find out until afterward . . . and I felt so bad. I cried. I cried like crazy. I felt so horrible.*

Candice: *We didn't talk about what position each other had . . .*

Helena: *We didn't really even know how they really felt.*

Jim Osgood, 32, came to national attention in 1997 when he served as foreman of the jury for the trial of Timothy McVeigh (who was sentenced to death for his role in bombing the Federal Building in Oklahoma City). At the time, Jim worked for Teledyne Water Pik as the New Business Development Manager. Now he is Director of Global Product Management for Teledyne's Water Treatment division. He talks here about communicating in work teams and on the jury:

At Teledyne Water Pik, project teams are used to develop new products, solve cross-functional problems, and manage major company initiatives. The first step in creating a team is to establish a team charter. The charter usually includes ground rules for communication and each team member's roles and responsibilities within the team, including a commitment to maintaining an open and effective line of communication. In the past, this commitment to maintaining an open and fair mind, and a commitment to reaching consensus on decisions, has played a critical role. It helps avoid the risk of having a team member concerned only with that person's specific function rather than contributing to the greater good of the team's mission. That same commitment to open communication was important when I led the McVeigh jury.

As soon as we elected a foreperson for the jury, we began our work by simply sharing our thoughts about how the deliberations should be handled. We talked about our common goal of ultimately arriving at a consensus amongst the twelve jurors. That, in effect, started the formation of a process in which all twelve of us could have a sense of contribution, or "ownership." I proposed that I facilitate our deliberations in much the same way I would if this were a project team charged with the task of designing a new product. As foreperson and facilitator, it was my job to ensure that everybody's voice was equally heard throughout the process. It was important for us to recognize that we all had an equal vote, though one person's voice may be louder, more dominant, or better articulated than another's voice. Someone who is quiet has just as important an opinion as the next person. To remind all of us that each of us had a responsibility to comment, and a vested interest in hearing each other's comments, I frequently said, "If you're not contributing, don't be surprised if I call on you."

When one person spoke, everyone listened. There was no other conversation. We gave each other the respect and courtesy of attentively listening as thoughts were shared on a given issue. If others wanted to contribute, I would keep track of who would "have the floor" next and indicate the order we would follow. Each of us knew that way that our opportunity to speak was coming, and that allowed us all to focus on the discussion at hand. It was also important that our process continued to evolve and was never cast in stone. I asked for feedback after every break so that our process could be continually improved to meet each juror's expectations. Everybody had a great sense of ownership of the resultant process.

Each of these narratives raises a different issue about successful communication in a small group. The first causes us to explore our assumptions about the nature of the communication process, whereas the second causes us to attend to the specific communication skills important in group communication. This chapter will first consider the nature of the communication process and then identify skills important to effective small group communication.

The Nature of the Communication Process: A Theoretical Perspective

It may seem curious to us that the members of the classroom group all had different understandings of their group members' feelings about taking an exam individually or as a group. When we think about communication, we may imagine it to be a linear process in which

1. One person, a *sender*, has an idea.
2. That person then translates or *encodes* the idea into verbal symbols (words) and nonverbal symbols or signals, including gestures, facial expression, and vocal tone.
3. That person then sends the message across a *channel*—whether sound waves in a room, a radio frequency, or a computer.
4. The message will be received by others *receivers*.
5. The receivers *decode* the message, that is, assign meaning to the sounds and movements, creating understanding between those communicating.

In this view of communication, the message on both ends of the process is assumed to be identical, unless some element in the channel (perhaps static on phone lines or an interruption in the room, but always called *noise*) interferes with accurate reception of the message.

Those who do not envision communication to be linear may imagine the process to be circular. This view adds the concept of *feedback* from the receiver to the sender. Somewhat different from system feedback described in Chapter 1, this type of feedback can be defined as "a perceived message transmitted to indicate the level of understanding and/or agreement between two or more communicators, in response to an initial message" (Barker, 1971, p. 107n). Thus, those who view communication as a circular process say that individuals who have received a message will create a new message to return to the sender. The new message, because it reveals the receivers' level of understanding of the original message, allows the sender to revise the original communication to increase understanding. If feedback reveals that understanding already exists, the sender may move on to an entirely new message.

Both of these views of communication are helpful in providing labels for parts of the communication process. But they are also the source of some problems because they allow us to make two false assumptions. We are likely to assume, first, that the purpose of communication is to transfer information to individuals who were not aware of it beforehand. The seven members of the classroom group had been in the same room at the same time; therefore, according to this assumption, they would have needed little if any communication about a decision to complete the test together or alone, because they would all have been aware of the same information. We often assume, second, that once something is communicated to a group of people, each person should have the same understanding of the message as do the other members of the group. In this case, that assumption would lead us to believe that each group member would have responded similarly to the notification that an upcoming test could be taken individually or as groups, or at least that they would have shared an understanding of what their action (taking the exam individually) meant to the members. Obviously, our assumptions would have been wrong if we applied them to this classroom group. More appropriate assumptions about the nature of communication as a process are provided by symbolic interaction theory and social construction theory.

Symbolic interactionism is closely associated with the teachings of George Herbert Mead, who taught philosophy at the University of Chicago from 1894 until his death in 1931. His ideas fit within an emerging field of social psychology. Mead viewed group life as central to an individual's existence, because the group "always precedes the individual's arrival on the scene, and society always survives his or her departure" (Reynolds, 1993, p. 49). Some of Mead's ideas relevant to communication are in the book, *Mind, Self, and Society*, published after Mead's death and based primarily on notes his students had taken of his lectures (Meltzer, 1972). Social constructionism was developed later; Littlejohn (1996) places its origin in the mid-1960s. Its concepts extend the ideas of symbolic interactionism, and social constructionists acknowledge their debt to Mead (Harré, 1984). Together, the theories develop several assumptions about the way communication functions. Four assumptions will be identified and applied to the classroom group described in the opening narrative.

The **first assumption** is that *human communication is essentially different from communication in societies of lower animals because it involves responses to interpreted stimuli*. The communication behavior of lower animals involves automatic, biologically driven responses to stimuli. Those responses then become stimuli that are, in turn, responded to automatically. In contrast, a human *chooses* a communicative behavior to fulfill some goal. So once a human observes another's communicative behavior and interprets it, then he or she *chooses* a response.

In the classroom group, Letitia chose to respond to the disagreement about the exam by withdrawing. She did not want to dominate the group by dictating that they would take the exam together. Group members, observing her withdrawal from the group, chose a response to it.

The **second assumption** is that *when an individual communicates, others perceive only a portion of the communicative act (the observable behaviors). A complete communicative act, however, includes not just observable behavior, but also the individual's intentions that moti- vated the behavior.* In the classroom group, observable behaviors included an expressed desire from some members to work independently on the exam, and from others an expressed preference to work as a group. Each group member expected the others to understand her, but none had actually expressed her intentions directly to the other members—and some had not even expressed their preferences about how to take the exam. The unexpressed intentions were, nevertheless, part of the communicative act, and the efforts to assume intentions led to some of the group's difficulty. Candice had assumed that Terrie wanted a group test in order to ease the tension of a heavy class load. In fact, Terrie had wanted to work individually in order to eliminate difficulties reaching agreement. Similarly, group members had assumed, when Candice agreed to work independently on the exam, that she preferred to work independently; they did not realize that, for her, working independently was undesirable but seemed to be the only remaining option for not dividing the group into factions.

It is important to realize that there are cultural differences in the degree to which communicative behaviors will reveal an individual's intentions. Lewis (1996) uses an iceberg metaphor to describe this fact, suggesting that submerged below a waterline is the thought (intention) and the tip of the iceberg (the speech) is above a waterline. In Finnish and Japanese cultures, only a tiny tip is perceptible above the waterline (or speech reveals little of the speaker's thought). The iceberg above the surface is greater for those from Britain, Germany, and France. He represents communicators from South America as having considerably more above the surface than below, suggesting that in those cultures, intentions are revealed quite openly in interactions.

The **third assumption** is that *shared meaning occurs when one human imagines the completed communicative act in the same way as the other intended.* It is by *role taking* that this process occurs. By taking the role of another, we can complete the imagined por- tions of the act as the other would complete it, making cooperative action possible.

The classroom group had some difficulty in role taking, leaving its members without shared meaning. Helena assumed that some of the other members did not want to work in a group because they did not want to work with her. She assumed that others were judging her on the basis of her race as academically incapable of helping them on the exam. As Dawn later explained, she had never experienced being excluded because of race, so she had not imagined the situation from Helena's view- point. When the group had difficulty in role taking, then it failed to share meanings.

In contrast, when Candice spoke to a friend outside the group who told a story that explained why Dawn might have been apprehensive about taking a group test, Candice was able to attach that meaning to Dawn's position. The story had allowed Candice to take Dawn's role. It was not necessary, then, for Candice to agree with Dawn's position. Effective communication might then have led to a change of positions, but it would not have needed to; it could not have done so before the other's position had been understood.

The **fourth assumption** *it is through interactions with others that we create our selves and our reality.* Mead believed that there is a part of each self that is based on our per- ceptions of others' expectations and is influenced by our past interactions with others. In applying this concept to the classroom group, we can imagine that the group members were affected by responses others had given them in the past. Helena's past experiences with racism led her to suspect that factor at play in this case. As Dawn said, "Sometimes you had to go really back into a mindset to see where you'd gotten that idea."

Also, although Dawn and Letitia had strongly different reactions to the test issue, they also had positive feelings about each other because of their earlier interactions. Because each saw the other as similar to herself, each assumed that the other shared her position on the exam. Dawn assumed that Letitia wanted to take the exam independently. Letitia had written in her journal that she hoped Dawn would convince the others to take the test as a group, not realizing that Dawn was the member most adamantly opposed to a group exam. Early interactions created images of each other as similar to themselves; that perception then colored their perceptions of the other's later communicative acts.

It is not just our self that is constituted through communication, but also other elements of our reality. Social constructionists believe that the meaning of an object or event is not in its physical properties, but in the associations communicators bring to it. The cartoon in Figure 4.1 makes it clear that different associations can come quickly to mind for different communicators. Through interaction, individuals construct the

By Mike Smith, Las Vegas Sun, United Feature Syndicate

FIGURE 4.1 Group members, like the students in this class, will have quite different interpretations of the same message. Through interaction, they will come to a shared meaning.
MIKE SMITH reprinted by permission of United Feature Syndicate, Inc.

meaning of the object or event. Consider, for example, whether you are an "adult." The answer relies less on your own physical properties than on how we as a society have come to talk about adulthood. How else can we explain that in some cultures you are considered to be an adult as soon as you have reached reproductive age, but in our culture we express concern about "children" having babies? In our culture, you are considered to be an adult in a voting booth if you are 18, although three decades ago, an 18-year-old was not considered an adult at a voting booth. And at the neighborhood bar, your adulthood has been described differently throughout time and, at times, from state to state. The meaning of "adulthood," therefore, is not in the person, but in how the society has come to talk about adulthood. Smaller groups can also construct meaning for events or objects that are unique to that group. The exam taken by the classroom group was given meaning by individuals, and it had different meaning in this group than it had in any of the other classroom groups. It also had a different meaning for some group members than for others. Without sharing interaction, group members will not share a common reality.

When a group talks about events it has encountered, the meaning of those events can change. As Marsh, Rosser, and Harré (cited in Buttny, 1985) have written, "everything we do can be redone by talk. In the course of talk our actions can be redefined and in the process are transformed" (p. 57). For instance, in the classroom group, after the group's initial conflict about the exam (which was created largely because the group had not talked about what their approach to the exam meant to them), the group did discuss their conflict—both on the weekend after taking the exam and in the discussion reported at the beginning of this chapter. The group could have interpreted the event to mean that racial differences will doom a group to failure. Instead, this group offered a different account of the event: it had provided the group members a chance to discover the importance of talking within a group, especially when its membership is diverse; it had given the group the opportunity to strengthen the bonds between its members. The event was not a stopping point for the group, merely a turning point.

Consider, now, how the concepts drawn from symbolic interactionism and social constructionism transform the linear and circular understandings of the communication process. First, rather than labeling some members as *senders* and others as *receivers*, we would be more accurate to label all communicators as just that, *communicators*. That label is more appropriate because at any given time, each communicator is both sending messages (perhaps nonverbally rather than verbally) and receiving others' messages.

These exchanges occur simultaneously as well as sequentially, which is a second difference. One person need not wait to adjust a message until after feedback from a first message has been received. Images of the other person that are in place before a message is sent initiate adjustments of a message; reactions to the message during its transmission can lead to further adjustments.

A third difference has to do with our understanding of the nature of *meaning*. Those who view communication as a linear or a circular process seem to assume that one communicator has possession of meaning and transfers it—more or less intact—to the other communicators, much as we might pass a ball from one to another. However, following symbolic interactionists and social constructionists, we come to see meaning as being constructed through interaction and possessed by those who have interacted. In small group communication, those meanings extend from the self-concepts of individual group members, through understandings of ideas discussed by the group, to the meaning given to experiences the group has shared.

When we change our view of the communication process, we also alter our view of the potential for "successful" communication. No longer is noise in the channel seen as the only cause for misunderstandings. We begin to realize that shared understanding will occur only when communicators are successful at looking beyond the observable communication behavior to discover the intentions of the other; only when the role of the other has been taken is that likely to happen. Clearly, communication is a more complex process than many people first assume!

Complex though the process is, effective communication is possible. When members of the classroom group resolved their conflict and transformed the meaning of their experience from a failure event to an opportunity, they needed to utilize a range of communication behaviors in a skillful manner. When the jury in the Oklahoma City bombing case considered the procedures they would follow in sorting through testimony and evidence, they benefitted from agreeing to use a set of communication skills. Every small group meeting will be different, requiring group members to adapt their behaviors to meet the needs of each meeting. However, by understanding (and developing) the skills involved in communicating effectively in the small group setting, we can increase the chance of a group's success.

Communication Skills in the Small Group

Effective members of small groups use communication behaviors that positively affect the group's process. For some group members, effective communication behaviors seem natural, but probably only if they have grown up in families where the behaviors were modeled and practiced. Many of us need to be made aware of and trained in desirable behaviors before we are able to use them consistently and effectively. A good starting point in identifying the communicative behaviors necessary in small groups is Parker's list (1994) of the positive process skills for use in cross-functional teams:

- Asking questions that bring out ideas and stimulate discussion
- Using paraphrasing and other listening skills to ensure effective communication
- Managing group discussions to encourage quiet members to participate and talkative members to adhere to limits
- Establishing an informal, relaxed climate where members feel free to candidly express their points of view
- Insisting that team members respect each other and that each person's contribution is valued (pp. 57–58).

Each of these behaviors will be considered when we explore appropriate behavior for (1) asking questions, (2) providing responses, (3) listening, (4) attending to nonverbal messages, and (5) creating a comfortable climate.

Asking Questions

Small groups engaged in discussion seek to share information, analyze it, make suggestions, test ideas, and reach agreements. It is possible for each member simply to volunteer information, but others may not know what to do in response to a simple statement from a member. Thus, it is more likely that the discussion will evolve as some members ask questions that lead to responses from others. In fact, groups brought together to consider an issue may simply sit in silence until someone in the group generates discussion by asking a question of the members. We would even say that it is desirable to think of your role in a discussion as gathering answers to questions. If you adopt that perspective, you will help the discussion fulfill its function of drawing information from all participants.

The characteristics of good discussion questions are consistent with the characteristics of good questions in interviews. Textbooks on interviewing, such as *Interviewing: Principles and Practices* by Stewart and Cash (1997), identify two types of questions: primary questions and secondary (or follow-up or probing) questions. A **primary question** is one that *initiates discussion of a particular point* ("What could we gain by taking the exam as a group?" or "What advantages would there be to taking the exam as individuals?"). A **secondary question** is *asked after the group has received a response to the primary question and, for one reason or another, needs to explore the response further* ("*Why* do you think we would save time?"; "*How much* time do you think we would save?"; or "Terrie, you *look* as if you have some ideas about this, but you haven't said anything. *What* do you think?").

Primary Questions.   Primary questions can often be anticipated before a discussion occurs. By understanding the methods of analyzing a topic the group is discussing, members can formulate questions that focus the discussion on appropriate issues. The questions formulated will serve as an agenda for the group's meeting. (Chapter 6 deals with analyzing the topic of a problem-solving discussion. At the end of that chapter, you will find a generic agenda composed of questions a problem-solving group might consider.)

Because the purpose of a primary question is to draw responses from group members, good questions are those that best encourage relevant responses. If you are in a position of leading a focus group, you will need to have thought of the primary questions that will be most effective in generating discussion relevant to the task of the focus group. The questions that will generate the most productive discussion are those that are (1) clearly worded, (2) ask a single question at a time, (3) ask for information accessible to the responding group member, (4) avoid false choices, (5) avoid signaling a desired response, and (6) include a balance of open and closed questions. As we consider these principles one at a time, suppose you belong to a committee composed of teachers, parents, a high school student, and community members. The group is charged with reviewing materials to be used in the local school district's sex education program. At this particular meeting, your task is to devise a plan for the students' visit to an interactive museum display on AIDS prevention in a nearby town.

Good discussion questions are worded clearly.   If group members cannot understand what is being asked of them, they are unlikely to be able to respond well. To see the difference between clear and unclear questions, compare these sets of questions. The ones on the left lack the desired characteristics that the ones on the right have.

<table>
<tr><td>For which chronological cluster is the probability of apprehending the exhibit highest?</td><td>Which age group is most likely to understand the trip?</td></tr>
</table>

or

<table>
<tr><td>Well, do you, like, know who . . . well, you know?</td><td>Which age group is most likely to understand the trip?
(or most nearly anything else)</td></tr>
</table>

Understanding the first question on the left is certainly not impossible, but understanding does not come as quickly as it does for the preferred question. The second question on the left is totally unclear. It seems as if the person asking the question was not yet clear about what to ask. The question can be improved by taking a moment to decide what it is that is necessary to know, and then phrasing a question that omits the verbal fillers that disrupt clarity of expression.

Good discussion questions ask a single question at a time.   When more than one question is asked at a time, group members need to decide whether to answer the first question, the most recent one, the easiest question, or . . . Actually, they are free to answer whichever question they choose, if they can keep any of them in mind. Compare the possible question on the left with the preferred one on the right.

<table>
<tr><td>Would it be rushing your sex education unit to take the students at this time? —because when do you normally teach the unit?—and how long do you normally spend on HIV and AIDS?</td><td>Would the sixth graders be prepared for the trip by the beginning of the month?</td></tr>
</table>

In the first question, the questioner wants to know the answer to three questions at once. A respondent is likely to forget some of the questions and is free to choose whichever question is easiest to remember or to answer. The preferred question asks only one question at a time. It is more likely to elicit useful information.

Good Discussion Questions Ask for Information Accessible to the Respondent.   Social pressures may make some information inaccessible. For instance, asking a group member to disclose highly personal information in a group before the members have come to trust each other would be inappropriate because the social pressure makes the information inaccessible. Emotional pressures can also make information inaccessible. After race riots in the late 1960s, a national commission on violence in the United

States published a book analyzing the riots. Included in the book was a photograph of a woman lying bleeding on the ground, with a microphone held at her mouth by a reporter. It is hard to imagine any question appropriate to ask at that moment. In group settings as well, we should avoid asking for information that is inaccessible to respondents for emotional reasons. Compare this set of questions:

Would you have been at the right age to understand this material 30 years ago, when you were in seventh grade?

From the seventh graders you see in your classes now, do you think they are at the age to understand this material?

In this case, neither social nor emotional pressures would make the information inaccessible, but memory difficulties might affect the responses. Remembering our mental state a week ago is often difficult enough; recalling it accurately 30 years later is impossible. The preferred question asks for information more accessible to the respondent.

A Good Discussion Question Does Not Eliminate Possible Good Responses.   Sometimes group members are asked to select from among certain options. That is fine, unless the question asking for their choices omits some of the possible options. For instance, consider the two questions on the left in contrast with the question on the right:

Should we have the sixth graders go or the ninth graders?

We have four possible grades that might go: sixth, seventh, eighth, or ninth. To which grades should we give top priority?

or

Should we take the sixth graders or are they too immature for the trip?

Of the questions on the left, the first eliminates some of the decision options that were actually available to the group, and its alternative eliminates some of the reasons the group might have for its decision. Group members might feel that seventh graders should be sent on the trip. They might feel that sixth graders are sufficiently mature for the trip, but that scheduling difficulties would make it difficult to send them. The questions on the left eliminate those responses. The preferred question opens up the decision issue to allow the group to freely consider all available options and all reasons for their position.

A Good Discussion Question Does Not Signal a Preferred Response.   Another way of limiting responses is by asking leading questions—ones that identify an answer the questioner hopes to get. Particularly if the person asking the question is perceived as having some power over the responding group members, the responses are likely to rubber-stamp the position taken by the questioner. Compare the difference between these questions:

> *The ninth graders would find this material repetitive, wouldn't they?*

> *What reactions would you expect the ninth graders to have?*

The preferred question does not lead the respondents in one direction or another. In the next chapter, in the discussion of groupthink, we will consider the potential dangers to a group's decision making if a leader of a group signals the acceptable choices others are to support. The use of leading questions is a subtle way of creating such a potentially dangerous form of influence.

Among the Questions Used to Generate Discussion, There Should Be a Balance of Open and Closed Questions. A **closed question** is one that invites a very specific, short response. An **open question** is one that invites elaboration from the respondent. Both kinds of questions play an important role. If a specific piece of information is needed by the group (such as how many sixth grade classes there are), then a closed question is necessary. If the group is interested in getting more complete information about a particular issue, then an open question should be asked. When closed questions are asked, the question asker has greatest control over the discussion. Control is shared more evenly when respondents have the chance to elaborate as they wish in response to an open question. To see the difference, compare the series of questions on the left with those on the right.

> *How many sixth grade classes are there in the district?*
>
> *Can you assure us that all of the teachers would get to the sex education unit before the trip?*
>
> *Can you assure us that you could find enough parent chaperones?*
>
> *Will you be able to control the students' behaviors throughout the trip?*

> *How many sixth grade classes are there in the district?*
>
> *How can we manage the logistical problems involved with preparing so many groups for the trip?*

Ethical Consideration

In an interesting article, "The identity work of questioning in intellectual discussion," Tracy and Naughton (1994) develop the argument that when we ask questions, we present both our self and our image of the person we are questioning. Our questions may, directly or indirectly, communicate our belief that the respondent is unreasonable or ill-informed. Of course, a group should not follow advice that is unreasonable or false. And, perhaps, challenging the respondent in a subtle way allows the person to maintain a positive image or "save face." It is important, however, to keep our focus on content and challenge ideas, rather than attacking (however subtly) the source of the idea.

A series of closed questions, such as the four questions on the left, creates a sense that the group members are being grilled, just as a hostile witness in a courtroom might be grilled. The preferred sequence begins with a closed question but follows that up with an open question. The preferred series of questions creates a sense that all members of the committee are working together to plan the excursion.

If you notice that discussion during your group meetings is seldom productive, a likely starting point in improving your communication is to consider whether effective questions have been devised and used to lead the group through the consideration of relevant issues. If not, then prepare for future meetings by identifying the relevant issues the group will need to consider and formulating effective questions that address those issues.

Secondary Questions. Secondary questions follow a response from a group member. Their specific form cannot be determined prior to the response, because their function is to remedy a difficulty in the response. A vague or confusing response will need to be clarified. A hesitant respondent will need to be encouraged. An irrelevant response will need to be refocused. An apparently inaccurate response will need to be challenged. By considering the following responses that might have been given during a meeting of the group considering the trip to the museum exhibit on AIDS prevention, you can see how the process of formulating a secondary question involves identification of the problem with the initial response and finding an appropriate way to probe further.

Sometimes the Secondary Question Will Be Able to Clarify the Original Question. At times, group members may not understand the question they have been asked. It may be because the vocabulary was unfamiliar or the question was inaudible. For example, consider this exchange:

> *Question: How can we manage the logistical problems involved with taking sixth graders?*
> *Answer: I don't think we'd have any more legal problems with them than with the other grades.*

Here the respondent either did not hear the question correctly or did not understand the term "logistical." A secondary question is needed that will clarify the primary question, but without insulting the respondent. So a possible follow-up question might be:

> *I'm sorry, I did not mean* legal *problems, but* logistical *ones, such as getting approval from parent groups at each elementary school and keeping the students organized while we are there. Can you think of some ways we might manage those problems?*

The follow-up question avoids embarrassing the respondent, but still clarifies the original question. It does so by repeating (with an emphasis) the key terms so they can be heard and then incorporating a definition (through the use of examples) of "logistical" in case the term's meaning was unclear.

A response that is general or incomplete can be probed for specifics and elaboration. If an earlier comment is vague or incomplete, it may be that the group member is not certain how interested the rest of the group is in an answer. Or the group member's thinking may not have gelled yet and needs further consideration. Suppose, for instance, that after asking how to avoid logistical problems, the complete answer now is

> *Well, there are lots of things we can do.*

Here the respondent is both vague and incomplete in answering the question. A secondary question will need to probe for specifics. For instance, an appropriate question might be

> *Such as . . . ?* or *Can you tell us more?*

Either question, simple though it is, lets the speaker know that the rest of the group wants his or her opinion. With a second chance, the answer can be extended and clarified. A respondent willing to talk might not be sure whether the group is interested in listening. A good follow-up question lets the respondent know the group is interested. Even saying, *"mm-hmmm"* to recognize the early portion of a contribution can encourage further elaboration of a response.

The Reasons for Silence Can Be Uncovered. A group member who hesitates or remains silent during a group discussion may be doing so for various reasons. Silent group members could be preoccupied with their personal considerations. They may be bored and have lost track of the conversation. Perhaps the group member objects to the direction the discussion is taking and decides to be silent. If the group accepts the silence, it will not be able to consider those objections, because it has no idea what the objections are. In the opening narrative, Jim Osgood reported that when he led the jury, he was unwilling to accept silence from a group member. A question directed to the quiet member and designed to uncover the reasons for the silence would be in order:

> *Aaron, you have not said anything recently. What do you think?*

Ethical Consideration

In a support group, being forced to contribute before one is ready to do so voluntarily can be harmful to a group member. However, in a task group, the silence of a group member interferes with the goal of gathering as much information as possible before making a decision. The entire group is responsible if it chooses to accept silence: the member who begins by being silent and the others who do not question it. Members of a task group should, therefore, encourage a silent group member to contribute. Moreover, the silent individual has a responsibility to participate even without encouragement.

This question gets the attention of the silent member and lets him know that the group values his opinion. Yet it does not force an elaborate response. Nichols (1995) recommends that quiet group members be addressed without intensity, so that they will realize it is safe to speak up.

After an Irrelevant or Inaccurate Response, the Group Member Can Be Pushed for an Accurate Answer to the Question Asked.   Sometimes a group member provides an irrelevant response, whether by design or by accident. In such a case, a secondary question is needed to refocus attention on the question asked. Suppose, for example, that you have asked,

> *How can we get permission for the trip from the parent groups at each elementary school?*

and the answer you receive is

> *Well, each teacher could sign an agreement to take his or her class and indicate which day and time would be best.*

In this case, the answer does not relate to the question being asked. Assuming that you asked the question for a good reason (you wanted an answer to it), the secondary question needs to refocus attention on the original question. It is helpful, however, to acknowledge having heard the response already given. Therefore, a good follow-up might be:

> *That might work to get* teacher *agreement, but I am wondering how we can get* parent *approval.*

The first phrase acknowledges that you have heard the response given, thus discouraging the group member from continuing on the irrelevant course, just to be sure you have heard; the second phrase restates, this time with emphasis, the point of your original question.

Suppose, though, that a group member provides an answer that is relevant, but you believe is inaccurate, such as this:

> *We should just go without parent approval.*

Of course this answer might be a possible solution, but if the group believes that such behavior violates rules for the school or community, then it is necessary to challenge the apparently inaccurate answer with a secondary question, perhaps one like this:

> *Jane, I do not think that action would be legal. Do you have some information that suggests otherwise?*

Whether they are used as follow-up questions after an initial primary question or anytime in a discussion after someone in the group gives an unsatisfying response, secondary questions play an important role in advancing the communication of a group. It would be difficult to plan secondary questions ahead of time because, in each case, the appropriate question depends on accurately analyzing the reason the original response was not satisfying and then formulating a means of drawing out the kind of response that is sought.

Ethical Consideration

A group is hurt by basing a decision on information that is false. It is not hurt, however, by considering contradictory positions. In fact, considering contradictions can improve the total group product. It is important, therefore, to challenge a contribution that appears to be inaccurate.

The Responsibility for Asking Questions. If a group is engaged in a discussion led by a moderator, the moderator will have primary responsibility for asking both primary and secondary questions. In a focus group, for example, the group's facilitator will formulate a series of primary questions (typically open questions) that will function as a guide for the discussion. The facilitator is then responsible for posing secondary questions

> as needed to probe for additional information, stimulate group interaction, encourage the involvement of all group members, keep the discussion moving and on target, summarize issues covered, and help the group reach conclusions without influencing or biasing members' responses unduly. (Kreps, 1995, p. 181)

In less formal group meetings, group members share responsibility for asking questions. That makes it possible for the discussion to explore issues until group members can come to a shared understanding of the ideas they are considering.

Responses

Creating shared meaning is most possible if the contributions that group members make meet certain standards. Harnack, Fest, and Jones (1977) identified qualities of desirable contributions, which form the basis for the qualities described here. Good responses are (1) informative, (2) clear, (3) appropriate in length, (4) relevant, (5) related, and (6) open to evaluation.

Informative. A contribution should add to the resources of the group. Group members are not in a competition to fill time; they are engaged in a cooperative activity to allow them to analyze ideas, make decisions, or implement decisions. If a comment provides additional information for the group, then it truly is a contribution to the group.

However, contributors should exercise some caution about the amount of information added at any given time. Information overload can paralyze a group. It will be essential to ensure that a contribution is understood before moving on.

Clear. A group member aids others in the group by increasing the clarity of a contribution. Eisenberg (cited in Civikly, 1992) explained that clarity

> is a *relational* variable which arises through a combination of source, message and receiver factors. . . . In trying to be clear, individuals take into account the possible interpretive contexts which may be brought to bear on the message by the receiver and attempt to narrow the possible interpretations (p. 139).

Ethical Consideration

It is one thing to reduce the directness of your message in order to help another group member save face. It is quite another to be purposefully ambiguous so that group members do not understand what they are agreeing to until later. Purposefully misleading a group is unethical.

Several factors interfere with clarity, including vague wording, ambiguity, insufficient examples, and stops and starts in delivery. The same behaviors found to increase the clarity of classroom teachers can also enhance a group member's clarity: a careful explanation of the point and the contributor's goal, repetition of key points, providing time to process the information before continuing, and checking for understanding before continuing (Civikly, 1992).

Interestingly, there are cultural differences in the importance given to clarity of comments. Kim (1994) noted that in some cultures, concern for hurting another's feelings, for minimizing imposition on others, and for avoiding others' negative evaluations all can take precedence over concern for clarity. Cultures with strong group orientations, such as Asian cultures, will emphasize face-saving strategies over direct and efficient strategies. In contrast, those with an individualistic orientation, such as the general United States culture, give more emphasis to clarity. In comparing Korean, Hawaiian, and mainland United States respondents, Kim found "the most striking cross-cultural differences [to be] in the perceived importance of clarity" (p. 142). The cultural group that rated clarity of least importance was the Koreans; respondents from the mainland United States gave clarity its highest rating.

Appropriate Length.   A comment made during a group discussion should be long enough to allow the contributor to make a point clearly, but not so long as to discourage the other group members from staying involved in the discussion. In the opening narrative, Jim Osgood mentioned that jurors who wanted to communicate were able to listen better if they knew when their turn was coming. In some groups, members may stop listening when one person's contributions go on at length. Reynolds's (1984) study of the length of a typical contribution within a small group revealed how short the typical contribution is: surprisingly, less than ten seconds long. In groups that meet face-to-face, time is a limited resource. When one group member uses it, it is lost to other members.

In face-to-face groups, size affects the length of comments. Reynolds found that more long contributions occur in dyads and in groups of six than occur in groups with three, four, or five members. In large groups, however, two or more people are often making comments at the same time.

Although many people imagine that group leaders make longer contributions, actually group members who emerge as leaders of a group typically fall within the norms for brief contributions. They differ from other group members in the *frequency* of their comments—and in providing more suggestions to the group on processes the group might follow.

Technology Note: Length and Mode of Communication

Groups that communicate by E-mail do not have to worry as much about the length of members' comments. They can communicate simultaneously without interrupting the other person and at length without denying the other members the chance to create equally long messages. The medium guarantees each member equal opportunity to participate.

Ethical Consideration

Comments that are excessively long interfere with a group's ability to invite the participation of all group members. Monopolizing a group discussion does not merely annoy other group members; it also hurts the ability of the group to function as a group.

Relevant. Comments made by group members should have a connection to the subject matter the group is considering. In any discussion, there will be times when the group gets sidetracked momentarily. Those moments can even be beneficial for the group's decision-making processes if they allow members to reflect on the issue at hand at the same time that they interrupt the group's unified, intense focus on the issue. Nonetheless, because a contribution should typically add to the understanding of the subject at hand, group members who regularly interject irrelevant comments frustrate the rest of the group members.

At times, a relevant comment may get delayed while the rest of the group members follow a divergent path. The contribution should still be made, in as timely a fashion as possible. Of course, there are also times when the topic should change—when the group has completed its consideration of one issue and is ready to move on to the next. Palmer (1989) found that individuals who changed the topic were perceived to be most dominant, while those who seldom changed the topic were perceived as giving way, but also as more friendly.

Related. Even comments relevant to the topic at hand should be related to the comment or comments made earlier. Harnack, Fest, and Jones (1977) suggested using *hook-on* phrases to create the connections. Here are some examples to show how a hook-on works:

> *"I see things differently from the way Jamil does. To me . . . "*
> *"My perception is quite similar to Aya's. I think . . . "*
> *"I agree. And, in fact, I can think of a second reason we might do that."*
> *"A little while ago, we were talking about ___; I wanted to get back to that and suggest that . . . "*

Verbal strategies such as these allow others to process our ideas more easily, because the group members know whether our idea adds to the previous one or contradicts it.

In studying devices that create coherence in a conversation, Planalp, Graham, and Paulson (1987) found that even if no connecting devices have been used by a speaker, other individuals will struggle to make sense out of conversational moves. The difficulty is that if our purpose is to have others *share* our intended meaning, then we achieve that most effectively if we use hook-on devices to clarify the relationship we intended between our comment and those that preceded it.

Open to Evaluation.   If a group member suggests, either by language or vocal tone, that a contribution is not to be questioned, then the member undermines the very purpose of the group's discussion. If one group member had had all of the necessary information to make a decision and there was no question about the validity of that information, then there would really have been no need for the discussion. Therefore, when a group *does* engage in discussion, it should be assumed that a clearer, more complete, and more accurate understanding can emerge from the discussion. In the opening narrative, Jim Osgood mentioned that both on work teams and in the McVeigh jury, group members were expected to be open-minded during the discussion, and their communication was to reflect that openness. Comments during a discussion should be made in a manner that invites their exploration rather than demanding their endorsement. Here are some examples of wording that invites exploration of ideas:

> "*It* seems to me *that the problem is more serious than that*" rather than "*The problem is obviously more serious than that.*"
> "*Well*, one possibility *is that . . .*" rather than "*Well, there is only one possibility.*"
> "*We* could *get funding from an outside agency.* Would that work?" rather than "*We will get funding from an outside agency.*"

There are some situations in which we do not need to be as concerned with cutting off discussion with the wording of our contributions. For instance, in a formal group that is following parliamentary procedure, a group member might say, "*I move that we get funding from an outside agency.*" Making a motion invites exploration of an idea, because the procedural rules require time for discussion of a proposal after it has been moved and seconded. It is in groups that do not offer such a procedural protection of members' rights to disagree that we must be especially careful to express our ideas in such a way that other members feel welcomed to disagree with us.

There are likely to be some gender differences in group members' use of phrases that suggest that an idea is open to evaluation. Such phrases as "it seems to me" and "it could be that" are qualifying phrases. They have been identified more frequently in the speech of women than in the speech of men. However, they may be perceived differently when used by one sex or the other. Bradley (cited in Andrews, 1992) "found that qualifying phrases were perceived as indicators of uncertainty and nonassertiveness when used by women, but as tools of politeness and other-directness when used by men" (pp. 84–85). If such devices encourage discussion rather than stop it, then group members of both sexes need to use them.

When group members contribute with informative and clear comments, appropriate in length, relevant to the discussion at hand, related to the earlier comment, and presented in such a way that evaluation of the contribution is encouraged, then their talk assists the group's effective communication. However, effective communication also requires good listening.

Listening

The importance of listening is well documented. DeFleur, Kearney, and Plax (1993) say that "listening is a requirement for social efficacy. . . . being competent as a social person—being able to form, manage, and maintain all kinds of social relationships in a positive manner" (p. 105). Individuals in relationships with others count on the others to provide them with the feeling of being listened to, even when—or perhaps especially when—their thoughts are jumbled. A group member's listening behaviors will affect how the group responds to that member. Belcher and Johnson (1995) found that "members perceived as poor listeners appear to have been eliminated at some point during [the leadership] emergence process . . . , whereas those who were perceived as being leaders were also usually perceived as being good listeners" (p. 83). Listening is so important that even the communication skills already described in this chapter cannot be exercised effectively without good listening: a group member cannot formulate appropriate secondary questions without listening to the initial response; contributions are unlikely to be relevant and cannot be related to previous comments if the group member has not been listening. Moreover, if group members have any hope of constructing shared meaning, listening is essential. Banville (1978) supported this concept: "I as a listener to your message have an obligation to attempt, at least, to identify your reality and the affect, or feeling, that your message is intended to relate—not merely what your words mean, but what *you* mean" (p. 11).

Terrie, Helena, and Dawn have learned the importance of listening to all that is said (and left unsaid) and of asking questions in order to create shared meaning.

Technology Note: Listening at a Distance

There are added difficulties involved in listening when a group is not meeting face-to-face. Bostrom and Searle (1990) explain that in face-to-face interaction, the sense of the "social presence" of another communicator stimulates interest in interaction, increasing attention to the message of the other. When a group is communicating by technological means, the sense of social presence is diminished. That is especially true if group members do not have access to visual and aural messages simultaneously, as when they communicate in an audio conference. And when a group communicates by computer, they have neither the visual image of the people with whom they communicate nor an audible message, so it seems that there is no chance to listen. Nonetheless, the messages must be processed so that their full meaning can be "heard."

Despite its importance, listening is difficult. That is due, in part, to the complexity of the process. It involves perceiving a signal (with our ears *and* eyes), selectively attending to the signal, remembering it, and then assigning it both an initial literal meaning and, later, a deeper meaning before we can say we comprehended the message (Fitch-Hauser, 1990).

Overcoming Potential Problems.   Listening is also difficult because we fall victim to problems that interfere with good listening. We will consider six problems likely to interfere with our listening efficiency and the means of avoiding or compensating for each. Overcoming the potential problems requires us to (1) listen as the context requires, (2) avoid environmental distractions, (3) suspend a self-focus, (4) delay interpretation, (5) avoid a combative attitude, and (6) manage the information load.

Listen as the Context Requires.   In Chapter 1, we identified four different purposes of small groups: social, learning, personal growth, and task accomplishment. The purpose of the group establishes a context that will require different listening outcomes, at least at times. Members of a learning group may be listening to retain information for a long term. They need to listen for factual information and check idea relationships. A member of a support group who listens to another's stories only for the facts of the story and misses the tone of sadness in which the story was told would be failing to listen well. Listening in order to interpret information was essential to the process of critical analysis for the jury led by Jim Osgood, but such interpretation may be unwelcome among a group of friends when they seek simply to be heard. Therefore, the first step to improved listening is to identify the listening context and the requirements for group members to process the information shared within the group, and then to listen with the goal of processing information as appropriate to the group's context.

Avoid Environmental Distractions.   When the group of women you read about in the opening narrative met to reflect on their experiences during the summer, they met in a campus coffeehouse. A waitress interrupted them on two occasions. A friend of theirs interrupted them at another point. Background music and noise were present throughout their discussion. None of those factors actually interfered with their ability to accomplish the task they faced that day. However, if they had been trying to polish a presentation or to make a difficult decision, any one of the factors might have caused them difficulty.

One step to improved listening is obvious: a group should control its environment to ensure that members are comfortable and that distractions are at a minimum. That may necessitate moving to a new meeting space or simply closing a door or window. It may require control of the natural tendency of groups of people to engage in side conversations during a discussion. The jury in the McVeigh trial agreed before discussing the case to control all side conversations in order to listen closely to the juror whose turn it was to speak. When a group can meet in comfort, as free from distractions as possible, then listening can be focused on the group's discussion.

Suspend a Self-focus. If a group has any hope of constructing shared meaning, its members must focus on the messages of others and work to identify the intentions of those group members who initiate the messages. Focusing on the meaning and intentions of others leads you to listen empathically—to feel with the other member as you take the role of the other member. Yet each group member enters a meeting with other concerns in mind—an inner struggle, a recent experience, a pressing obligation. If those issues, which lead to a focus on self, cannot be put aside, then they will interfere with effective listening. If you begin to think about how you will pay your tuition bill during a group meeting, your mind is *sidetracked* away from listening to what the other members discuss. Or, you might interrupt a group member's contribution to make one of your own, which may or may not be related to the topic the group is considering. Not only will you be unlikely to empathize with the other group members, you are unlikely to hear what they say at all.

Ideally, it would be best if you could resolve other concerns before you attend a group meeting; but even then, your mind could wander as you recall your success in resolving your personal concerns. Perhaps a more practical suggestion would be to get the issue off your chest by mentioning it to the other group members during the early moments of a group meeting, when members typically take a short time to reorient themselves to the group. You will still need to monitor your own mental behavior and avoid sidetracking in order to follow the group's train of thought. When your own concerns come to mind suddenly, in the midst of another's comments, it will simply require concentration on the other's comments and a recognition that a group member who feels unlistened to will continue to seek attention and will be unavailable to listen to you.

Sometimes our desire to empathize with other group members combines with a self-focus to create another listening problem: owning, and sometimes outdoing, the other's experiences. Imagine that you are a member of a group that is trying to find a way to reduce the costs of textbooks for students at your university. As your group is trying to understand the nature of the problem, you report on a situation that occurred at the beginning of this school year, when your textbooks cost twice what you had budgeted for them. If another group member follows your comment by saying, "I know exactly what you mean. The same thing happened to me!," you may feel relief at being understood. On the other hand, you may come to wonder how the other group member could know *exactly* how you felt, since his or her circumstances would certainly have been somewhat different from your own. You are likely to become annoyed that the person has, in essence, "owned" your experience. At times, it may feel as if our comments serve only as a springboard for another group member to tell a "better" story. Comments that attempt to outdo our own are also annoying. Instead of expressing empathy (feeling *with* us), these comments feel *for* us; they replace our feelings rather than acknowledging them.

We can learn to control this problem by temporarily suspending our own agenda, deferring our contributions until other group members have been heard and understood. Furthermore, we may need to check with the first contributor about his or her feelings—and meaning—*before* moving on to another contribution. Then we have better grounds for knowing how our comments relate to those of the other group members. Finally, we may need to remind ourselves that we are separate from the other members of our group, with different experiences, ideas, and feelings. We cannot know their thoughts unless we listen to them first.

Delay Judgment.   Prejudging a contribution another makes in a discussion prevents us from listening to the actual comment. We may make a premature judgment if we believe we know the other group member very well. Married couples have the experience of finishing the sentences of their partners, all too often with a completion not at all related to what the partner had intended to say. Members of groups who get along well may also feel that they can anticipate the contributions of the other members; they may share with the married couples the negative outcomes if they fail to listen to what is actually said.

Premature judgments can also be caused by negative judgments about the group member. A team leader may feel that a new team member could not possibly have anything of value to add to a group discussion and thus not listen to the contribution. A person who decides not to listen to another person who "never has anything interesting to say" will be sure to miss the one exception that proves the rule! Murphy (1995) explains that minority members of culturally diverse groups have frequent experience with being judged prematurely. It occurs when there is a fundamental distrust of members who are different. Their contributions are judged inadequate because the member is judged inadequate—before having been attended to at all.

In both cases, listening is improved if we assure ourselves that every group member has an individual perspective and then we make a point of discovering what that perspective is. To wait to judge a comment until after a person has been heard does not deny the listener his or her own selfhood; to the contrary, it affirms the thinking, rational self of a person, one able to choose how to respond rather than reacting automatically.

Avoid a Combative Attitude.   Small groups joined to accomplish some goal are, by definition, cooperative. Nonetheless, there will be times during group interactions when differences among group members are highlighted and may appear to threaten the unity of the group. There is no danger to the group in exploring the members' differences. But if group members assume a combative stance, two dangers arise.

First, a group member may stop listening to what another is saying, either to prepare a response or to interrupt another's comments with a response. But what the first person has said, then, will have to be assumed. A group member may assume that opposition exists where concurrence actually exists. And when opposition does, in fact, exist, its nature can not be understood if it was not heard. It is important to listen to a position taken by a group member and to check on whether the meaning is understood *before* any decision is made or action is taken to dispute it.

Second, a group member who takes a combative stance may transform the intent of the message, even when listening to the message in its entirety. A reasonable difference of opinion can be assumed to be a personal attack if one group member's defensiveness colors his or her perceptions of the comment. To some extent, the classroom group experiencing conflict over handling their exam experienced this problem. Because of the group's tension, the statement "I want to take the exam independently" was transformed to mean "I do not want to take the exam with *you*," and further, "because as a person of your race, you can not be trusted to contribute effectively to an exam." That statement was never made, nor was it intended, but it was heard.

Frequently group members become defensive because they lack experience as a member of a group that argues about ideas. Yet when a group tests the ideas of its members, the group is likely to make a better decision, one that avoids creating negative by-products the group had never anticipated. Therefore, disagreement should not be feared by group members. As we increase our tolerance for disagreement within a group, we can reduce our defensive posture. It is still important, when we begin to assume intentions that suggest deep divisions within the group, to check our assumptions about another's intent with the other.

Manage Information Load.   Visualize a situation in which you are mailing a package. If you try to squeeze too much into the box, the contents will be damaged. On the other hand, if you send the package with too little in the box, the contents are still likely to be damaged as they bounce around in the box. A parallel situation occurs for a listener: with too much information to process, ideas are likely to be jumbled; with too little information to be processed, a group member's mind is likely to wander, and key elements of the actual message may be missed. Thus, both information overload and underload cause problems for listeners. Underload problems occur naturally because we can think at about twice the rate that we can speak (Barker, 1971). Overload problems are more likely if the discussion covers a topic relatively unfamiliar to the group member and if meetings continue at length with little opportunity for a break.

Although responsibility for these problems does not originate with the listener, the problems do affect listening effectiveness. Moreover, listeners can use strategies to overcome the difficulties. When too much information is coming at too fast a rate to manage, listeners should rein in the speaking group member. A question that seeks clarification can signal concern over the rate of information flow. A move to restate the key ideas can let a contributor know what the listening group member remembers and what part of the message is being processed. Together, group members can negotiate an appropriate rate for the discussion.

However, there are likely to be individual differences in the processing rates of group members. An ideal rate for many members can result in information underload for others. A group member who perceives the rate to be too slow can make use of the time by increasing the depth of information processing. Mentally repeating an idea, identifying the implications of the idea—its strengths and weaknesses—and checking for proof of the point can all make good use of the listener's time.

A Listening Strategy: Active Listening.   Many of the problems associated with poor listening can be avoided or resolved by using *active listening.* Active listening involves both a change in attitude and a change in behavior from typical listening patterns. Frequently we think of listening as passive ("I am not doing anything, just listening," or "I will just sit back and listen"). Active listening requires us, first, to acknowledge that good listening requires hard work. It requires us, second, to develop the practice of paraphrasing the ideas of our conversational partners so that they can check our understanding before we carry the conversation forward. For instance, in a discussion about the cost of college textbooks, a member of your group might make a statement like this:

> *"It seems to me that there is a big problem, because we're required to purchase too many books with prices that are sky high, and then the books are not even used in the class."*

Using active listening, you might say,

> *"So you are saying that there are really three problems: assigning too many books, assigning books that are not used, and the books' high prices, right?"*

or you might say,

> *"From the way you said that, it seems to me that you would be willing to put up with the high cost of textbooks if the books were at least used in the class. Am I right?"*

Both statements paraphrase the original comment and provide an opportunity for you to check your interpretation of the comment. After all, the two interpretations included are both possible, but they are quite different from one another. Using either paraphrase of the comment allows you to check your perception of the other group member's meaning before you proceed with the discussion. Notice, also, that the second comment refers not only to what the speaker had said, but also to how it was said. In order to effectively paraphrase what has been said, a listener needs to attend to the nonverbal behaviors of a speaker. Sometimes the meaning of a speaker is not fully clear from one or two comments, but by listening to recurring themes that may unfold throughout a discussion a group member can grasp the full meaning. In that case, the paraphrasing strategy would draw together several comments and check the perception of the unifying theme.

Ethical Consideration

Some group members may be well-practiced at behaving as if they are listening (by looking attentive, maintaining eye contact with the speaker, and nodding) without actually attending to the comments of others at all. Appearing to listen is not enough. To deserve the trust of fellow group members, we must actually attend to others' comments and work hard to listen well. Nichols (1995) argues that "Listening to others is an ethical good, part of what it means to have just and fair dealings with other people. Listening is part of our moral commitment to respecting each other" (p. 250). When distractions cause us to fail at good listening, we should admit it, so the discussant has a chance to make the point again.

Active listening is difficult in any context, but it is easier in dyadic communication than it is in a group context. It simply is not possible for every group member to paraphrase all group members' contributions. There are times, however, when the process of active listening is especially useful. When the group is about to arrive at a decision on the nature of a problem it is exploring or the solution it is recommending, then active listening can help the group to be sure its members agree. For instance, it would be important for the group in the bookstore example to know whether they want to solve three separate problems or just one problem.

Also, when a group is experiencing conflict, active listening can help the group to understand the differences they have. It can also help to dispel some tension in the group. Tracy (1984) considered the role of asking a question to clarify another's meaning. She found that "at the explicit level, a direct query is an attempt by the respondent to gain greater clarity about the speaker issue; at the implicit level, it informs the speaker that the respondent feels that what he or she said is important and worth clarifying and dwelling upon" (p. 285). Therefore, knowing that someone has listened to you and understood what you said makes it harder to be angry at that person.

Listening requires attention to the entire communicative act. Obviously, a listener attends to the verbal messages in the group. But if shared meaning is to be created, the listener must identify the intentions of the communicator, which often requires attention to nonverbal behaviors as well.

Attending to Nonverbal Messages

You are probably already aware of the communicative potential of the nonverbal code. If you have ever looked around a restaurant at a group of people eating together and played a game of deciding why they are there and what their relationship to one another is by watching them for a while, then you have used the nonverbal code. Similarly, you might consider the following actual situation to see how much you could tell about a group without hearing a word exchanged among the members:

> The group forms in a classroom when students move from their normal seats to meet in a group. Four people, one male and three females, gather in a corner of the classroom. They begin to move their chairs together. The male and the two females on either side of him scoot their chairs into a circle. The fourth member barely moves her chair. A comment is directed toward her by one of the females. She moves her chair in minimally, but sits down when the chair is—for all intents and purposes—still positioned behind the backs of the other two women. She looks down at her desk. The other group members exchange comments, occasionally looking at this one while speaking. At those times, she looks up tentatively, speaks, and then looks down again. Soon the rest of the group stops looking her way. The rest of the group is wearing shorts and T-shirts, but she is wearing long pants and a long-sleeved shirt. As she sits without involvement, her face begins to redden.

It is not difficult to conclude that one of the group members is estranged from the group. Many of the elements involved in the nonverbal code provide clues: the eye behavior of group members and the use of space, silence, and even clothing suggest that one member of the group is apart from the group rather than a part of it. By noticing that three of the members look toward the "outsider" and direct their comments toward her, you might conclude that the rest of the group is trying to draw her in; the estrangement appears to be selected by her rather than imposed on her by the group— at least initially. Yet the reddening of her face suggests that she is not happy to be on the outside; is she angry? embarrassed? While attention paid to nonverbal behaviors cannot tell us everything about what is happening in a group, the nonverbal signals can provide useful information, available quickly, to group members and observers alike.

Elements in the Nonverbal Code.   Many elements are involved in the nonverbal code. They include

- Eye behavior—Are the group members making eye contact or avoiding it? Are members staring at each other or glancing quickly away?
- Facial expression—What emotion seems to characterize individual members? Are they thoughtful? happy? surprised? Do group members seem to share the same emotional response, or are there differences within the group?
- Posture and body lean—Do group members sit or stand up straight, or are they slouched? Are they turned toward or away from others?
- Gestures—Are hand movements animated? How do they reinforce, modify, or substitute for verbal messages?
- Use of space [or proxemics]—including both territoriality [the marking of physical space as one's own] and personal space [maintaining a physical distance from others consistent with one's psychological space needs]—Have some group members occupied more space—or nicer space—than others? How close together are the group members? Does the arrangement of the room in which the group is meeting encourage or discourage communication? Does it increase or decrease the formality of the interaction?

- Clothing and artifacts [such as a briefcase or jewelry]—Are there indications of social class or occupation conveyed by these items? Do group members appear to be similar to or different from each other? Do the artifacts and clothing identify other groups that have a claim on the members' time?
- Touch—Do members hug each other? shake hands? pat each other on the back? Do they seem to be emotionally close or distant? Do they seem to respect the personal boundaries of each other?
- Use of time—Does the group begin and/or end on time? Do the members act as if time is plentiful or scarce? Do they respect the demands on other members' time?
- Paralanguage [vocal tone, pitch, rate, fluency, resonance, and volume]—Do members sound interested? angry? relaxed? Does the way a statement is made seem consistent with the content of the statement?
- The use of silence—Do members seem to be avoiding issues? Or is there comfort conveyed by their quietness?

Frequently the data sent through nonverbal channels add redundancy to the verbal message. There are desirable outcomes of such redundancy: it makes messages easier to remember and clearer. In fact, the loss of nonverbals for groups that communicate over electronic channels presents some difficulties for group members (Hollingshead, McGrath, & O'Connor, 1993).

Patterns of Meaning from Nonverbal Behaviors. Some communication researchers have studied isolated nonverbal signals to identify the messages sent by the signals. Unfortunately, the research often results in contradictory findings and findings with limited value. After all, each individual uses multiple nonverbal behaviors at once; these messages are perceived as a whole, rather than in isolation. Moreover, in small groups, each member is contributing to the pool of nonverbal data. Fortunately, it is not as important to classify the specific messages sent by each nonverbal behavior as it is to be aware of the important patterns of messages that can be conveyed nonverbally in the small group setting. Four patterns are communicated nonverbally: (1) the impressions of group members, (2) the relationships among group members, (3) the direction of the conversational flow, and (4) the attitude of group members toward the group's decisions. We will consider how each pattern is communicated and how you can make use of this information to monitor your nonverbal behaviors within a group.

Impressions of Group Members. Because "all behaviors in the social-setting are acts of communication . . . *all* become our acts of self-presentation from which others draw conclusions about us" (Raghu, 1989, pp. 101–102). You may believe that the group member who wears baggy pants, beads, and dreadlocks would be a creative but undisciplined thinker; that the group member who avoids your eye contact dislikes you; and that the group member who arrives at group meetings early and dressed in a suit regards the meeting as a serious event. Each of these judgments may be inaccurate, but each is likely, nonetheless, to affect your initial impression of your fellow group members, and, in turn, your communication with the members.

Technology Note: Forming Impressions When Nonverbals Are Reduced

Groups that communicate at a distance face some disadvantage because the nonverbal information available to members is limited. A videoconference may preserve most of the nonverbal data, but perceived distances between group members may be created by camera shot. Although much nonverbal information is missing from audioconferences, they still preserve the information conveyed by paralanguage which is absent if computers are the channel used for interaction. Nonetheless, groups not meeting face-to-face still form impressions of one another, although perhaps at a slower pace. Some verbal behaviors—such as spelling accuracy—take on added importance in impression formation for computer-mediated communication (Walther, 1993). Students in groups required to communicate by E-mail without having met face-to-face have developed negative impressions of other members from abrupt, impersonal messages, messages that go unanswered, those who SEEM TO BE YELLING, or those E-mailers who assume an unjustified level of familiarity.

Knowing that others will form their impressions of you based, in part, on your nonverbal behaviors should lead you to make choices about the messages you prefer to send. Often, we are not conscious of our own nonverbals, but some are certainly within our control. For instance, we can choose to arrive at meetings on time, to convey the impression that the meeting is important to us; smile at other group members, to appear congenial; and take with us to meetings the artifacts, such as paper and pen, that prepare us to work at a group meeting. As we attach meaning to the nonverbal behaviors of others, we should be careful to check for consistency by comparing verbal and nonverbal messages and noting consistency among nonverbal messages. We should be willing to adjust our initial impressions as new information about our group members becomes available to us.

Relationships among Group Members.   Individuals who enjoy each other's company will usually sit close to one another. The distance members place between themselves can be reduced by forward lean and eye contact or increased by averted eyes and crossed arms. Group members who feel a close relationship to one another will often mirror each other's nonverbal behaviors. Manusov (1995) found that reciprocation of nonverbal behaviors occurred with proxemics, body orientation, vocal warmth, and facial expressions. If you perceive yourself to be different from others in the group, or if you are at a point of disagreement with the others, then your distance from others is likely to increase. Even if you carefully monitor your verbal behavior, your feelings toward the other members are likely to be apparent in your nonverbal behaviors. A group member attentive to nonverbal behaviors of group members may be able to identify members who are forming new alliances within the group or those who feel distanced from the group.

Power relationships can also be observed by attention to eye behavior and territoriality. If you have ever been glared at by another person, you know that eye behavior can be used to exert control over others in a group. Thompson and Kleiner (1992) compared the behaviors of dominant individuals—relaxed, sprawled out, usually at the head of a rectangular table, using large gestures, and maintaining a lot of eye contact while speaking and less while listening—with the opposite behaviors of more submissive members. Space alone can be a factor in conveying power: group members who emerge as leaders are most likely to be sitting in "high interaction positions," where they can see and be seen by the greatest number of group members.

Not only can these relationships be observed, but they can also be managed within the small group. For instance, a group meeting around a round table is more likely to interact as equals than one that meets around a rectangular table with one member "heading" the discussion. Thompson and Kleiner (1992) noted that even people who randomly sit at the ends of a rectangular table "begin to act more forcefully than they usually do" (p. 82).

A historical example makes the point about the importance of the table's shape even more forcefully (McCroskey, Larson, & Knapp, cited in Tubbs, 1984). Peace talks that would end the Vietnam War were delayed for months as the parties to the talks disputed the shape of the table over which peace agreements could be reached. The United States and its ally, South Vietnam, wanted a rectangular table; they would take one side of the table and the other would be occupied by the parties from the north. But those parties wanted to use a square table so that the representatives of North Vietnam and those of the National Liberation Front would each have a separate side; that would give nonverbal recognition to the National Liberation Front as a legitimate party to the negotiations. A round table finally resolved the dispute, allowing parties to claim each was equal or, if they wished, to claim that no dividing lines existed to separate the two northern entities. Clearly, table shape has symbolic significance.

Seating areas can also have symbolic significance. A group that meets in someone's living room may find that whoever sits in the largest, most comfortable chair comes to be treated more as a leader than do any of the members seated next to each other on a sofa. Closeness can also affect a group's effectiveness. An office group will have increased difficulty communicating if team members are spread throughout the office, with workers who do not belong to their team mingled among them. Whatever the nature of the group, it is important to be sure that all group members can see each other.

The Direction of Conversational Flow.   Managing the flow of conversation requires the use of nonverbal behaviors to negotiate the subtle rules of turn taking. Finding an opportunity to speak and knowing when to stop speaking both require attention to nonverbal behaviors. If you wanted to speak while someone else still had the floor, you might increase your eye contact with group members, lean forward, clear your throat, open your mouth as if to speak, or gesture. Group members who are naturally quiet may still signal a desire to get involved in the discussion. Those who speak more freely need to be especially attentive to the nonverbal cues of the less-talkative group members, and then invite their contributions.

You will notice that the group wants you to end your turn if they are not looking at you (especially if they are looking at their watches instead). If you are in a group in which one member is monopolizing the discussion, then you should be sure you are sending clear nonverbal signals that discourage further comments. Nodding and maintaining eye contact may lead the speaker to continue. If the nonverbal messages are not being attended to, then a verbal message may be necessary to equalize the opportunity to speak. Most often, however, the flow of conversation can be regulated nonverbally.

Technology Note: Getting the Floor in a Teleconference

When a group is using a channel of communication other than face-to-face, many of these signals are not visible or audible to the other group members. The difficulties are exacerbated by the fact that the microphone system typically picks up only one sound at a time, sending a jumbled signal when there is competition for the microphone. Some groups have found that supplementing an audioconference with computer access allows groups members who cannot gain the floor to interject their ideas into the exchange nonetheless.

Altering the arrangement of chairs within a room can also have an impact on the conversational flow. In some rooms, the seating arrangement makes interaction easy. Such arrangements are described by environmental psychologists as "sociopetal" (Burgoon, 1996), meaning literally "seeking companionship." Arrangements that direct the focus away from others, making interaction difficult, are described as "sociofugal" or "fleeing companionship." Figure 4.2 illustrates three seating arrangements. The first, the sociopetal arrangement, directs the flow of communication to the group as a whole, making interaction easier. But suppose you belong to a community group that meets in the cafeteria of a local school. Your members might be distributed around several tables. Conversation among the members sitting at the same table is easy; but the seating directs the flow of conversation into clusters, rather than to the group as a whole. For that reason, as you can see in the second image, the seating mixes sociopetal with sociofugal forces. The third seating arrangement represents an arrangement we found in a local high-school library. There are comfortable seats for nine members of a small group, but they obviously would not make communication easy for a group meeting there. Perhaps less obviously, three or more members sitting in a row on a sofa are not able to direct their conversation toward one another with ease. To enhance the flow of communication, groups should choose to meet in rooms with sociopetal arrangements or should rearrange the room in such a manner. Of course, if a group is meeting in a large, public room, a sociopetal arrangement may invite outsiders into the group, perhaps inhibiting the work of the group.

Attitude of Group Members toward the Group's Decisions.   Even though our society permits freedom of speech and even though groups may freely engage in discussion, we should not assume that group members will always say what is on their minds. For one thing, the concerns of a single group member may get overlooked when the rest of the group enthusiastically supports a particular course of action. An excited vocal tone, increased volume, and increased physical activity may all be signs of enthusiastic support. But there will be other nonverbal behaviors important to attend to if the group is to consider the attitudes of all group members. The group member who inches a chair away from the other group members, who remains silent, or whose vocal tone and facial expression convey anger or disinterest is signaling a negative attitude toward the group. By ignoring those signals, the group prevents itself from reconsidering its direction and reaching a decision that all group members can support.

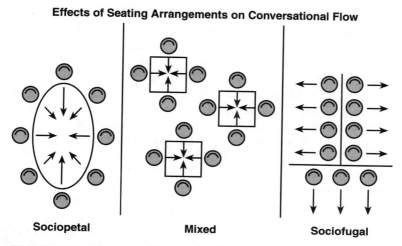

Effects of Seating Arrangements on Conversational Flow

Sociopetal   Mixed   Sociofugal

FIGURE 4.2 The seating arrangements of a room can have an impact on conversational flow.

It is important for groups to check any discrepancy between verbal and nonverbal messages. A group member may say, "I do not care" or "It does not matter to me," when in fact it matters very much. The nonverbals may convey the true message—as long as group members attend to them.

Precautions about Interpreting Nonverbal Messages. Three precautions are important to remember about the messages communicated nonverbally: the meaning of nonverbals is ambiguous; the meaning varies from culture to culture; and the message is affected by the communication channel used.

Ambiguity. First, nonverbal messages are ambiguous: their multiple potential meanings make deciphering the specific meaning difficult. A group member who frowns may be responding negatively to a comment from another group member, but might simply be concentrating on the ideas or might be experiencing stomach pains after a spicy meal. The frown need not be ignored, but its meaning needs to be ascertained. Paying attention to the context in which the communication is occurring can help us to determine the meaning of nonverbals. Comparing the nonverbal cues to the verbal message can help us narrow the possible interpretations. If you notice an excessive use of a particular behavior, that may alter your interpretation of the behavior. So the smile that you first assumed meant friendliness may, in excess, come to represent subservience. Sometimes, however, you will need to ask the group member what his or her nonverbals mean: *"Jodi, I thought I saw you frown just now. Do you have a concern about the proposal you have not mentioned yet?"*

Cultural Variations. Second, nonverbal behaviors vary from culture to culture. For instance, Thompson and Kleiner (1992) tell the story of a Chicano clerk who averted his eyes while being reprimanded by his supervisor. The white supervisor did not initially realize that the clerk's lack of eye contact was intended as a sign of respect, not of disrespect. The clerk's cultural rules were that direct eye contact is inappropriate with a superior. Some other cultures follow the same rule for eye behavior. Rules for use of space differ among cultures. In the female subculture, sitting close together is the norm more than it is for members of the male subculture. Arab students in the United States find their fellow students moving away from them; in Arab cultures, the rules for personal space require conversational positions close enough to reach into what is regarded as a more intimate distance in general United States culture. A person from Thailand would be insulted by being patted on the head or by a group member whose crossed legs resulted in the sole of the foot pointing at the Thai.

Even rules for silence differ culturally. In those cultures in which "maintaining the face" of one's partner is important, silence is a way of avoiding having to disagree and causing the partner to lose face. In other cultures, silence may be taken as a sign of agreement. In interpreting the intention behind a nonverbal message in order to assign meaning to the act, it is critical that group members consider the cultural meanings of specific behaviors, difficult though that may be. Kim (1994) notes that we may be more attuned to cultural differences in the verbal message, because pronunciation differences or grammatical difficulties faced by a member of another culture will be noticeable. When a nonnative speaker speaks fluently, we may not recognize that a difference in culture exists, and erroneously assume that the differences in the nonverbal code are due to impoliteness, unfriendliness, or ineptness of the individual.

Impact of Communication Technology.   Third, because the channel over which groups interact can alter the amount of nonverbal information transmitted, groups need to be conscious of the fit between the task they are tackling and the nature of the channel they will use for communication. Hollingshead, McGrath, and O'Connor (1993) studied two groups, one working face-to-face and the other working by computer. When the two groups switched communication channels for two weeks, those who began to use face-to-face interaction adjusted more easily. That was partly explained by the discomfort felt by the groups that were just adjusting to computer communication, but it was also explained by the fact that the addition of the nonverbal cues, which provided redundancy, eased the communication. The researchers also noted that when membership changes occurred, the groups communicating electronically faced greater difficulties (see Figure 4.3). Therefore, they cautioned that, particularly in situations in which work groups would be experiencing personnel turnover, groups communicating electronically should not be expected to perform as well as those groups meeting face-to-face. Groups needing to negotiate did not perform as well when communicating by computer. They were not less effective, however, when the task required them to generate ideas or to make decisions.

Communicating Climate

You are already familiar with the impact of a region's climate on the activities of its residents: a hot, muggy climate slows down some activities, and a frigid climate discourages

FIGURE 4.3   Groups communicating electronically face greater challenges.
Cartoon by Cor Hoekstra; reprinted with permission from The Rotarian.

other activities. Groups are also characterized by a climate, although a psychological one, not a physical one. The psychological or emotional climate of a group does have an impact on the group's activity—encouraging some behaviors and discouraging others. A comfortable group climate encourages easy communication; a chilly climate does not. Actually, the climate of each group will be unique to that group. There is no one kind of appropriate climate. A very formal group can be just as effective as a much less formal one, for instance. But it is desirable to create a group climate that allows the members to focus on the task of the group and to communicate effectively within the group. A positive communication climate is confirming, rather than disconfirming; cooperative, rather than competitive; and supportive, rather than defensive.

Confirming versus Disconfirming Communication.   Imagine a group meeting in which each time you try to make a comment someone in the group interrupts you. Finally you get a chance to say something, and no one else even seems to notice that you have spoken. Such a meeting might begin to make you feel angry, but more than that, it is likely to make you feel unvalued. When Evelyn Sieburg studied communication patterns in small groups for her doctoral dissertation (cited in Trenholm, 1991), she was able to distinguish some communication behaviors that made a group member feel more valued (or confirmed) from others that led to a person feeling less valued (or disconfirmed). You could probably predict that when other group members support our comments and agree with them, we feel confirmed. But even if others disagree with our position, we can still feel confirmed if they have at least acknowledged our comments, tried to clarify them, and/or expressed positive feelings toward us (despite our ideas). The strategies involved in active listening (checking our perceptions through paraphrasing another's contribution) and asking appropriate probing questions result in feelings of confirmation for the other person.

In contrast, disconfirming behaviors include failing to acknowledge a group member's response, interrupting the group member, and following the group member's comments with responses that are incoherent, totally irrelevant, or only partially relevant. Therefore, some of the communication behaviors described earlier in this chapter help to create a favorable climate, such as allowing another member to finish a comment rather than interrupting, making comments that are relevant to the discussion at hand, and using hook-on comments to acknowledge the relationship between a previous comment and our own. When group members feel valued by the group, they are likely to work comfortably on the task at hand. When they do not feel valued, another agenda item takes precedence over the group's task: proving that they are worthy of the group's respect. The climate of the group suffers as the focus turns toward personal issues.

Cooperative versus Competitive Communication.   By definition, a small group has a common goal that requires interdependent activity on the part of its members to be achieved. Effective groups, then, need to cooperate. But, because individual members also come to a group with individual needs, there may be times when a group member comes to feel that his or her own needs will not be met without winning a competition against the other group members. To communicate in a competitive manner, however, damages the climate of the group.

Cooperative communication is characterized by content that stresses common goals. The focus then turns toward what unifies the group rather than what divides the group. Language that reflects the common goals would also be natural. Ellis and Fisher (1994) write that changing "the language to 'we' when talking about the group" (p. 242) is a simple way to improve the communication climate.

A competitive climate exists when one group member wants to "win all the marbles" at the expense of the other group members. Taking all of the credit for the successes of the group and placing blame on other group members for any failures create the win-lose orientation that characterizes a competitive climate at the expense of cooperation. A blamed group member will begin to focus on regaining a positive image in the group. Again, the climate of the group suffers as the members' attention turns toward such personal issues.

Supportive versus Defensive Communication.   When individuals feel that they have the support of the group, they will respond in a manner that improves the climate of the group. Some of the communication behaviors recommended earlier in this chapter contribute to a feeling of support, such as expressing empathy (rather than a lack of interest). When members communicate defensively, the communication climate suffers. Such behaviors as making contributions that are open to evaluation are associated with reducing defensive behaviors.

One problem that all groups face is that members do not always perform in a manner that advances the goals of the group, whether by accident or by design. Consider the case of a string quartet rehearsing for an upcoming performance. Even if all

The members of the Kocapelli Quartet face a difficult communication task: in rehearsals, they must criticize the work of each member in order to reach high performance standards; at the same time, they must try to maintain a cohesive group. (Photo compliments of the University of Michigan School of Music.)

members of the group arrive at the rehearsal on time with their parts practiced, there may be countless areas for discussion of each individual's performance. Did the first violinist rush a particular passage? Did the cellist play two measures too loudly? Was the second violinist out of tune on one note? Did the violist use the wrong bowstroke as the piece was ending? The way the group members talk to each other about their performance can contribute to either supportiveness or defensiveness. Overall, therefore, the factor that has the greatest influence on reducing defensiveness is the nature of the feedback in the group: the way group members respond to one another's behavior within the group.

Haslett and Ogilvie (1996) write that "feedback from others enables us to understand how our behavior affects them, and allows us to modify our behavior to achieve desired goals" (p. 254). More specifically, they indicate that feedback can cue a group member that a particular behavior is not desired so that it can be corrected; can motivate members to reach a new goal; and, by providing new information and establishing new goals, can help members develop their potential.

Because feedback has the potential to be very useful to group members, it is important that it be presented in ways that improve the climate of the group. Even when the information communicated to group members is negative, the feedback should be presented in such a manner that it is confirming of the group member and avoids triggering defensive responses. Five qualities of feedback lead to a positive climate: its presence, timing, descriptiveness, appropriateness to the receiver, and link to the source of the feedback.

Technology Note: Getting the Point by Seeing Feedback

At times it may be easy to ignore feedback that is given to us by others in our group. We can imagine that other members understand and agree with us; the ambiguity of nonverbal behaviors gives us some room to reinterpret them so as to confirm our preconceptions. In the Computer Automation Team (CAT) at Houston's Texaco offices, the group's leader, Sarah Reinemeyer, discovered that using a group decision support system helped her to see the feedback more clearly. One of the capabilities of the system allows members to rank proposed projects according to their priority. Reinemeyer was surprised when she discovered the projects that team members had ranked as having low priority; some of them were the very projects she regarded as most important. She thought she had communicated their importance to the team members. Seeing the team members' rankings displayed on a computer screen first allowed her to realize that there was a communication gap and then to correct it (Hoffman, 1991).

Ethical Consideration

Ray (1993) described ways in which supportive comments actually can undermine the recipient. Offering support to a fellow group member should not be used intentionally as a means of making that group member seem weak or dependent. To do so violates the trust of the group member.

Feedback Should Be Present.   To fail to acknowledge the behavior of individuals within the group is to signal disinterest in the individuals. It is important to respond to behaviors with feedback. Both *appreciative* (positive) and *improvement* (negative) feedback are appropriate. Mesch, Farh, and Podsakoff (1994) found that groups (and the individuals within them) who receive negative feedback respond to it by setting higher goals, developing more strategies for dealing with the task, and, in turn, performing better than do groups (and members) who receive positive feedback. They caution, however, that negative feedback has also been found to lead to dissatisfaction among group members, who may even end their relationship to the group. Therefore, the feedback given should not be solely or continuously negative. The presence of appreciative feedback is also important.

Feedback Should Be Timed Appropriately.   Feedback should be presented soon after the behavior to which it is responding was performed. If a group member completes or fails to complete a task for the group, group members should not delay in acknowledging that. If a group member's communication is perceived as offensive by another member, no time should pass before that is mentioned. As time passes, one's memories of his or her own actions are altered, so that late feedback will have reduced meaning. As time passes, our concern about the negative behavior may fester, and our pleasure with a positive behavior may pass unexpressed.

Feedback Should Be Descriptive.   Rather than evaluating another's behavior, our feedback should describe the specific behaviors to which we are responding. For instance, if we tell a group member that she is irresponsible, we have evaluated her behavior, but she has no idea what the basis of our judgment is. By saying instead, "You agreed to have the paper typed for today, but you have not done that," we provide the basis for our judgment. This is an important characteristic even for positive feedback. Telling a group member that she showed a lot of responsibility without describing the behavior that led us to that judgment leaves the recipient of the feedback feeling that the compliment was hollow.

Feedback Should Be Appropriate to the Receiver.   As we give another feedback, we should be attuned to that person's capacity to process the feedback and to control the behavior to which we are responding. If comments are made to us in writing, we can refer to them again and again. Most feedback to members of a small group, however, should be presented in the face-to-face situation in which the group is meeting. The point at which information overload is reached is likely to come sooner when the comments relate to one's own behavior than when they are impersonal comments about the task. The number of points made at any one time should not exceed the group member's ability to process the feedback.

There are some behaviors over which a group member has no control. Perhaps a member of a work group has been required by the supervisor to go to a conference out of town. When the member's absence affects the progress of the work group, that should be feedback given to the supervisor. It is inappropriate criticism of a group member who was not in control of the situation.

Link Feedback to Its Source.   Ideally, feedback should be presented by the group member who originated the feedback. If you were to say, "Tim, the members of your subcommittee feel that you are not living up to your responsibilities," then Tim is likely to have two questions: (1) How do *you* feel about this issue, and (2) Why were you talking to his group members about him? He would begin to worry about those questions rather than listening to you describe the specific behaviors that led Tim's coworkers to that conclusion. If the negative perception of Tim originated with one of his group members, then it is preferable for that group member to give the information to Tim.

At times, however, a group leader may have the official responsibility for giving feedback (especially negative feedback) to group members. Whoever gives feedback should express it in such a way that he or she is taking ownership of the perceptions and the comments. Feedback that begins with an "I" is most likely to do that:

> *"Dawn, I felt upset when you said you wanted to take the exam independently. I saw that as limiting our ability to work as a group."*
> *"Candice, I was annoyed that first you said you wanted to take the exam alone, but on the day of the exam said we should take it as a group. I saw that as a change of position."*

It may seem to be a slight difference to say, "Dawn, you upset me . . . " or "Candice, you annoyed me . . . ," but the difference in impact is not slight. After all, the group members cannot dispute the fact that you were upset or annoyed; they *can* dispute their role in causing those feelings. By taking ownership for your feelings in the feedback you give, you are eliminating some grounds for disruptive conflict.

When feedback is provided well, then group members are less likely to respond to it defensively. However, it is important to remember, when receiving feedback, that others take risks by being honest about their perceptions of us. We should appreciate the risk our group members are taking by being honest. We should understand that multiple perceptions of an event are possible, so another's perception is just as valid as our own. We should not challenge the other's perception, and we need not defend our own behavior. We should, instead, look for the information that will allow us to improve our performance in the group and ask questions to clarify feedback that is not clear to us (Ray & Bronstein, 1995).

Because providing feedback appropriately is important, but very difficult for most group members, work groups may turn to an outside facilitator to handle feedback sessions. A facilitator can schedule regular feedback sessions (which the group might otherwise avoid), model appropriate behavior, and encourage others to provide feedback. The facilitator will not make judgments about the group members or contribute to the content of the feedback but will be responsible for the process. Ray and Bronstein (1995) note that once group members become used to sending and receiving feedback appropriately in scheduled meetings, they begin to respond on their own without waiting for a meeting.

Groups can improve their climate by taking time—either with a facilitator or on their own—to talk about the communication behaviors of their group as a whole. Jim Osgood, in the opening narrative, mentioned the importance of talking about the process of the jury at each break as a means of improving it. Communicating about the group's communication—called **metacommunication**—is a means of providing effective feedback to the group as a whole. If the feedback is positive, it will contribute to increased cohesiveness in the group. The same can be true even if the feedback is negative, as long as it is provided in a fashion that allows improvement in the behaviors and underscores a commitment among the members to effective communication.

Appropriate feedback reduces defensiveness in group members, creating instead a supportive climate. When a climate is supportive, cooperative, and confirming, group members will be in an environment that encourages productivity. The physical climate in which we live may be controlled by factors over which we have no control. But the psychological climate within a group is controlled by communication behaviors, and those are factors over which we can exercise total control.

Summary

Effective communication in a small group is important. When groups have homogeneous members who will reach consensus quickly on an easy, familiar task, then communication functions only as a means of combining the members' information, and the members themselves are of more importance than their communication. But when groups are heterogeneous and face a task that is difficult or unfamiliar and thus high in ambiguity, then communication is especially important as a tool to obtain clear information (Salazar, 1995).

Despite its importance, communication is not an easy task. That is true, in part, because the nature of the communication process is complex, requiring the creation of shared meaning. Within the small group, when meaning needs to be shared by three or more people, the complexity is even greater. It is no wonder that the jury led by Jim Osgood began by establishing rules for communication before they began deliberating in order to work successfully on a difficult task. Nor is it surprising that the classroom group you met at the beginning of this chapter experienced so much confusion about the meaning of taking their exam together or independently. That group overcame its difficulty when it met over the weekend after they had taken the exam. Initially, the group members had not realized the importance of expressing their concerns openly. As they learned about the importance of communication and learned strategies for communicating effectively, the group members—like the jurors—began to use the wide range of skills required in the process: asking primary and secondary questions, supplying responses, listening effectively, attending to nonverbals, and creating a comfortable group climate.

It is difficult for any group member to improve all communication behaviors simultaneously. It is possible, however, to analyze one's own behavior to identify areas needing improvement, to work on each of those skills separately, and to improve step-by-step the overall communication behavior.

QUESTIONS FOR DISCUSSION

1. Mead believed that humans communicate in a fundamentally different way than other creatures do. Do you agree?

2. Is it necessary for group members to share exact meanings, or is it possible for them to function effectively without doing so? Could it even be desirable, in some situations, for a group member to not know exactly what the others have in mind?

3. Why is it difficult for group members to give negative feedback to each other? Why is it important to learn to do so?

SUGGESTED ACTIVITIES

1. Observe a group interaction (or a photograph of one). Draw five conclusions about the group from the nonverbal behaviors evident. Explain how you came to those conclusions.

2. Form groups of three to discuss a topic you feel comfortable talking about as a group. (It can be something as simple as roommates, family, a political campaign, or a television show or movie.) Videotape a brief interaction (five minutes or so) on the topic. Watch the videotape. Write a paper in which you describe and evaluate your communication behaviors. Consider your use of primary and secondary questions, your responses, the messages you are sending with your nonverbal behaviors, and evidence of your feedback and listening behaviors.

3. Watch a televised group discussion (such as *The Capitol Gang*). In a paper, analyze the communication skills of the participants.

4. Have your instructor place you into E-mail groups with students known only to you by their E-mail addresses. Exchange ideas about some topic. Write a brief paper in which you compare the communication by E-mail with communication in a face-to-face group.

5. Develop a set of primary questions to lead a focus group discussion. The focus group could evaluate a program on your campus or in your community. For instance, you might have a group of graduating seniors meet in a focus group to talk about their major. In teams of two, lead a focus group. Write a paper in which you evaluate your performance.

SOURCES CITED

Andrews, P. H. (1992). Sex and gender differences in group communication: Impact on the facilitation process. *Small Group Research, 23*, 74–94.

Banville, T. G. (1978). *How to listen—How to be heard.* Chicago: Nelson-Hall.

Barker, L. L. (1971). *Listening behavior.* Englewood Cliffs, NJ: Prentice-Hall.

Belcher, C., & Johnson, S. D. (1995). Leadership and listening: A study of member perceptions. *Small Group Research, 26*, 77–85.

Bostrom, R. N., & Searle, D. B. (1990). Encoding, media, affect, and gender. In R. N. Bostrom (Ed.), *Listening behavior: Measurement and application* (pp. 25–41). New York: Guilford Press.

Burgoon, J. K. (1996). Spatial relationships in small groups. In R. S. Cathcart, L. A. Samovar, & L. D. Henman (Eds.), *Small group communication: Theory and practice* (7th ed., pp. 241–253). Dubuque, IA: Brown & Benchmark.

Buttny, R. (1985). Accounts as a reconstruction of an event's context. *Communication Monographs, 52*, 57–77.

Civikly, J. M. (1992). Clarity: Teachers and students making sense of interaction. *Communication Education, 41*, 138–152.

DeFleur, M. L., Kearney, P., & Plax, T. G. (1993). *Fundamentals of human communication.* Mountain View, CA: Mayfield.

Ellis, D. G., & Fisher, B. A. (1994). *Small group decision making: Communication and the group process* (4th ed.). New York: McGraw-Hill.

Fitch-Hauser, M. (1990). Making sense of data: Constructs, schemas, and concepts. In R. N. Bostrom (Ed.), *Listening behavior: Measurement and application* (pp. 76–90). New York: Guilford Press.

Harnack, R. V., Fest, T. B., & Jones, B. S. (1977). *Group discussion: Theory and technique* (2nd ed.). Englewood Cliffs, NJ: Prentice-Hall.

Harré, R. (1984). *Personal being: A theory for individual psychology.* Cambridge, MA: Harvard University Press.

Haslett, B., & Ogilvie, J. R. (1996). Feedback processes in task groups. In R. S. Cathcart, L. A. Samovar, & L. D. Henman (Eds.), *Small group communication: Theory & practice* (7th ed., pp. 254–267). Madison, WI: Brown & Benchmark.

Hoffman, D. (1991). Play it again, SAMM. *Brainstorm: The Quarterly of ITD's Group Decision and Collaboration Research, 1* (2), 15–16.

Hollingshead, A. B., McGrath, J. E., & O'Connor, K. M. (1993). Group task performance and communication technology: A longitudinal study of computer-mediated versus face-to-face work groups. *Small Group Research, 24*, 307–333.

Kim, M-S. (1994). Cross-cultural comparisons of the perceived importance of conversational constraints. *Human Communication Research, 21*, 128–151.

Kreps, G. L. (1995). Using focus group discussions to promote organizational reflexivity: Two applied communication field studies. In L. R. Frey (Ed.), *Innovations in group facilitation: Applications in natural settings* (pp. 177–199). Cresskill, NJ: Hampton Press.

Lewis, R. D. (1996). *When cultures collide: Managing successfully across cultures*. London: Nicholas Brealey.

Littlejohn, S. W. (1996). *Theories of human communication* (5th ed.). Belmont, CA: Wadsworth.

Manusov, V. (1995). Reacting to changes in nonverbal behaviors: Relational satisfaction and adaptation patterns in romantic dyads. *Human Communication Research, 21*, 456–477.

Meltzer, B. N. (1972). Mead's social psychology. In J. G. Manic & B. N. Meltzer (Eds.), *Symbolic interaction: Reader in social psychology* (2nd ed. pp. 4–22). Boston: Allyn & Bacon.

Mesch, D. J., Farh, J-L, & Podsakoff, P. M. (1994). Effects of feedback sign on group goal setting, strategies, and performance. *Group & Organization Management, 19*, 309–333.

Murphy, B. O. (1995). Promoting dialogue in culturally diverse workplace environments. In L. R. Frey (Ed.), *Innovations in group facilitation: Applications in natural settings* (pp. 77–93). Cressskill, NJ: Hampton Press.

Nichols, M. P. (1995). *The lost art of listening*. New York: Guilford.

Palmer, M. T. (1989). Controlling conversations: Turns, topics and interpersonal control. *Communication Monographs, 56*, 1–18.

Parker, G. M. (1994). *Cross-functional teams: Working with allies, enemies, and other strangers*. San Francisco: Jossey-Bass.

Planalp, S., Graham, M., & Paulson, L. (1987). Cohesive devices in conversation. *Communication Monographs, 54*, 325–343.

Raghu, S. G. (1989). Trainer needs and other factors affecting communication in training. *Small Group Behavior, 20*, 101–111.

Ray, D., & Bronstein, H. F. (1995). *Teaming up: Making the transition to a self-directed, team based organization*. New York: McGraw-Hill.

Ray, E. B. (1993). When the links become chains: Considering dysfunctions of supportive communication in the workplace. *Communication Monographs, 60*, 106–111.

Reynolds, L. T. (1993). *Interactionism: Exposition and critique* (3rd ed.). Dix Hills, NY: General Hall.

Reynolds, P. D. (1984). Leaders never quit: Talking, silence, and influence in interpersonal groups. *Small Group Behavior, 15*, 404–413.

Salazar, A. J. (1995). Understanding the synergistic effects of communication in small groups: Making the most out of group member abilities. *Small Group Research, 26*, 169–199.

Stewart, C. J., & Cash, W. B., Jr. (1997). *Interviewing: Principles and practice* (8th ed.). Madison, WI: Brown & Benchmark.

Thompson, P. A., & Kleiner, B. H. (1992, September). *The Bulletin of the Association for Business Communication*, pp. 81–83.

Tracy, K. (1984). The effect of multiple goals on conversational relevance and topic. *Communication Monographs, 51*, 274–287.

Tracy, K., & Naughton, J. (1994). The identity work of questioning in intellectual discussion. *Communication Monographs, 61*, 281–302.

Trenholm, S. (1991). *Human communication theory* (2nd ed.). Englewood Cliffs, NJ: Prentice-Hall.

Tubbs, S. L. (1984). *A systems approach to small group interaction* (3rd ed.). New York: Random House.

Walther, J. B. (1993). Impression development in computer-mediated interaction. *Western Journal of Communication, 57*, 381–398.

5 Conflict in Small Groups

CHAPTER OBJECTIVES

After reading this chapter, you should be able to

- Distinguish between affective and substantive conflict and between experienced and expressed conflict
- Explain why conflict is inevitable in groups
- Explain how uncoordinated meanings may lead to conflict in groups
- Identify the advantages and disadvantages of conflict
- Define groupthink
- Identify the symptoms and causes of groupthink and strategies for avoiding it
- Distinguish among the typical approaches for conflict management
- Identify strategies for effective conflict management
- Utilize communication strategies to manage conflict effectively

The Narratives

At the beginning of Chapter 4, you read about the (mis)communication among a group of students about an exam—a source of major conflict within their group. Here they continue their conversation, describing the role of conflict in their classroom group.

> **Candice:** *What kinds of conflict did we have? We had leadership conflict, that was one. And, second, we had . . .*
>
> **Helena:** *Personality conflict. It's not that we hated each other. We just didn't always complement each other.*
>
> **Letitia:** *The initial conflict for me came when we met at someone's house and got on the topic of houses. Then someone said that the rest of the class felt we were going to fail because of our different ethnic backgrounds. For me, that was the first conflict, internally as well as in the group. I guess I got on the defensive, feeling that if I started seeing any prejudice exhibited by anybody, that was it; I was not having it. At the same time, on the inside I was saying, "Here*

we go again." I'm always the odd one out of a group because of my race. I've been in a group where I've been the only black woman . . . or the only black, period. So I've had those conflicts before. We were aware of the potential for a problem. It was on the table.

Dawn: *But conflict had advantages for our group.*

Candice: *Absolutely. It really built cohesiveness.*

Dawn: *Resolving our conflict really set us apart. Other groups didn't do it, and we did.*

Letitia: *When we talked in class at the end about what had happened in each of our groups, I thought we were the most real and honest group there was.*

Terrie: *I remember when I was walking past one group. I wasn't eavesdropping. (The group laughs at her.) I swear I wasn't eavesdropping, but I overheard one woman say, "I'm tired of coming here—all the way here—all the time, and we never get anything accomplished when I come. We have that conflict, and what are we going to do?" I overheard that, and I thought, OK. Other groups have problems, too.*

Letitia: *When we had conflict, we'd get it out in the open. I'd start, and we'd go around in a circle. On the weekend after we had taken the exam individually, we had a meeting. We worked first and were very productive. Then, when the meeting seemed to be about over, I said, "Well, before we go, we need to talk." Then we went around the table.*

Dawn: *And then we ended it by saying something positive. We didn't just leave and say we'd all complained, and now it's over. We all did something positive.*

Helena: *We had our differences, but we didn't hate each other. We just couldn't leave mad. The day we left the classroom after the exam mad, it was just . . . evil.*

Candice: *There were other strategies we used to handle conflict. In the beginning, brainstorming was a strategy that helped us to resolve conflict about what we were doing—so we weren't just stuck on one idea.*

Dawn: *Sometimes we invited conflict. I remember when I made an outline for our presentation, I called Letitia and said, "How do you think this is going to go?" I figured she was going to tell me straight out, "It's horrible. It needs this or that." I needed honest feedback. I wanted to know what was wrong with it.*

Helena: *I think our most effective strategy was having just the right communication. If we had never talked about our conflicts, I think we probably still would have done well at the end. But we wouldn't have had the same feelings that we got. It was like a rush for me to talk about our conflict and to resolve it.*

Dr. Masayuki Nakanishi, 44, teaches communication at Tsuda College in Japan. After graduating from International Christian University in Tokyo, he did graduate work in communication studies at the University of Virginia and the University of Kansas. His doctoral dissertation concerned the relationship between group interaction patterns and group decision-making effectiveness. Here he discusses the nature of conflict in small groups in Japan and the United States.

There's a basic cultural difference between the United States and Japan when it comes to conflict. In Japan, the majority of people believe that conflict is bad and, therefore, should be avoided. In the United States, conflict is regarded as healthy—a natural consequence of communication; it's thought that by overcoming conflict, a relationship will be strengthened.

When I began my graduate work in the United States, I became worried when I first saw people arguing over an issue in a small group setting. I was surprised to see those people go out for a drink after arguing so hard! In Japan, that kind of thing wouldn't happen so easily. One difference is that most Japanese people cannot distinguish between substantive (task-related) and affective (emotion-related) conflict. So once we start arguing over an issue, we might end up name-calling and having a big argument—which is very damaging to our relationships. In the United States, you can more easily distinguish between substantive and affective conflict, so disagreements can more easily be expressed without damaging a relationship.

If we do have a disagreement with someone in Japan, we are very careful about expressing the conflict. We have to read the situation to discover how the other party will respond when we act to express conflict. Because we don't want to confront others directly, we will express conflict indirectly. One strategy we might use is silence. Silence is a final disagreement, in a sense. Japan is a high context culture (one in which the situation constrains and gives meaning to the interaction). Nonverbals will provide clues to the meaning of silence. We are pretty good at reading people's nonverbals. That's a skill one develops over the years, living in the Japanese culture. Face-saving is something we are concerned about, too. We don't want to make anybody lose face in the process of conflict management, especially when someone older or higher in status is involved. In a group discussion, if we start worrying about making somebody lose face or losing our own face, the discussion may not go anywhere from that point. We might adjourn a meeting, hoping that time will resolve the problem. We might meet later after figuring out how to deal with the conflict without making anybody lose face in the process. So we often end up using compromise as a conflict management strategy.

Another indirect strategy I might use would be to talk to somebody else first, testing the water by discovering how an independent person feels about my position. If it is OK, then I could go to the person and express conflict to him or her. Even then, I'd express my disagreement gradually, while monitoring the person's behaviors to see how much he or she can accept. For me it's very difficult to express conflict without knowing the other person and how the person would react to what I'm going to say.

However, based on my experience in the United States, I believe that conflict is good and constructive in some situations and that we should not avoid conflicts if we can solve them. Because I still tend to express conflict much more directly than average Japanese do, I might end up in a very tough situation here in Japan. Most Japanese people are not used to that kind of communication style. At Tsuda College, there are 26 faculty members in my department. The four of them who are from the United States or Britain understand me, but the rest of the department members may have difficulty understanding my style.

In Japanese organizations, a group meeting is not the place to discuss issues. Group meetings are where we make a final commitment to whatever decision has been made. In Japan, there is a process called "nemawashi," which literally means "root-binding," but is more like "doing the spadework" or "doing the preliminaries." The root of a plant is hidden and cannot be seen easily. And, as Edward Boyer explained in a 1983 Fortune International *article, a gardener who will transplant a tree binds its roots very carefully. Similarly, the nemawashi process involves painstaking behind-the-scenes efforts designed to achieve consensus. Using nemawashi, whenever you want to make a decision as a group, you first need to contact and communicate with each person who will eventually be affected by the decision, in advance of the decision, to gain approval. That way the differences of opinion will be worked out in the process of nemawashi. When nemawashi is done, everybody knows what's going to happen at the upcoming meeting. Nobody will express any disagreement there.*

The person in charge of the decision starts the nemawashi process. He or she will be called a leader; but in most Japanese small groups, the leader is more like a facilitator who has no authority in making a decision. The leader will approach each member, saying, "We are going to decide this or that. This is what we will be doing. Would you agree with it? Would you accept it?" He or she will not ask for any input. Instead, he or she will ask for approval—or beg for approval, in a sense. Usually, the proposal itself is not something that is disagreeable. It would have been carefully formulated in the first place by the leader, perhaps in consultation with some others who may or may not be group members. If, during the process of nemawashi, I heard a proposal that I had some concerns about, then I might ask for some changes. That's rather difficult because the proposal might have been made by somebody up in the hierarchy—some senior member of the group. Junior—younger—members are not supposed to contradict senior members of the group, unless they have good enough reason to do so or unless they are willing to accept the negative consequences of their actions. So it's kind of difficult to point out the flaws in the proposal. In that case, I might approach another senior member whom I trust to express my concerns about the proposal. That senior member may relay my concerns to the leader who started the nemawashi.

I've thought about whether this process encourages groupthink. We don't have the concept of groupthink in Japan. When I analyze the groups I am involved in, my conclusion is that groupthink might not be a problem as long as the nemawashi process works well. It is time-consuming, but nemawashi is an effective way of building consensus by thoroughly informing the group of what's going to happen once the decision is made. There's no strong leadership, no strong conformity pressure, and no strong group cohesiveness present in the process.

At Tsuda College, where all the students are women, I teach a seminar on intercultural communication. One of the sessions deals with cross-cultural differences in the way people approach and resolve conflict. I take examples from my experiences in the United States, of course. Most of my students believe that conflict is bad. In girlfriend-boyfriend relationships, they might experience some conflict, but they don't know how to express conflict to a partner. Whenever I tell them that it's good to express conflict and directly confront the other person about what you feel and what the problem is, they tell me that it's very difficult for them to do that. Asked why, some of my students simply said, "He's going to hate me for that." There might be a male-female difference involved in the issue. Japanese females are not supposed to be very direct and straightforward in communication, so they may have more difficulty expressing conflict. The Japanese way of expressing conflict works for Japanese people as long as they live in Japan. What I point out is that the Japanese way of dealing with conflict may not work in different cultures. That's something everybody should be concerned about.

Both of the narratives in this chapter focus on the experience of conflict in groups. Normally, conflict generates our interest. If we choose a book to read or a film to watch, we often seek one in which there is an interesting conflict. The opposing forces at work on the characters provide the basis for developments in the plot. But the conflict we appreciate when we see it at work on others is something many of us hope to avoid in our own small group activity. Such hopes can seldom be realized, however, because conflict is an inherent element in small group interactions. In other words, as long as a small group exists, conflict will be an element of the group. To understand why, you must first understand the nature of conflict and then recognize the factors that ensure its existence in small group interaction.

The Nature of Conflict

Like the opposition of forces in a novel or film, conflict within a small group is created when some factor creates opposition within the group so that a state of incompatibility exists. Conflict can exist within a group and also between groups. Boardman and Horowitz (1994) define **conflict** as *"an incompatibility of behaviors, cognitions (including goals), and/or* *affect among individuals or groups that may or may not lead to an aggressive expression of this social incompatibility"* (p. 4). Their definition acknowledges that intragroup **conflict** can be the result of real or perceived differences among members about the goals of the group or behaviors acceptable within the group. The conflict that relates to task issues is called **substantive conflict.** Factual disagreements or differences in the interpretation of the information that group members have gathered are included within the realm of substantive conflict. So also is disagreement about procedures the group should follow. But Boardman and Horowitz indicate that conflict may also be the result of emotional responses toward group members; this is called **affective conflict.** It seems reasonable that if, as Masayuki Nakanishi mentioned, individuals cannot distinguish between these two types of conflict, their difficulty in resolving the conflict increases.

The definition also makes it clear that conflict may be expressed aggressively, but need not be; in fact, it may not be expressed at all. Therefore, it is possible to distinguish between **experienced** and **expressed** conflict. All conflicts within groups are experienced, as members feel the tension with others in the group. Only some of the experienced conflicts will be expressed. O'Connor, Gruenfeld, and McGrath (1993) note that some groups have a "no-conflict" norm and may punish dissenters. In those groups, members "may experience conflict but not express it. Although the occurrence of conflict in these groups may not be obvious to an observer, it may still be present and affect group interaction" (p. 363).

The Inevitability of Conflict in Small Groups

Even when group members do not express conflict, it is bound to exist within a group because small groups make choices, small groups involve individuals, and—increasingly—small groups incorporate diverse members.

Small Groups Make Choices

The fact that small groups engage in tasks requiring the members to make choices automatically invites conflict into groups. In fact, Kirchmeyer and Cohen (1992) write that "all organizational decision making involves some form of controversy" (p. 156). To understand the reasons for this, consider that in its Latin origin, the word "decide" means "to cut off." When groups make decisions, they cut off one or more choices or paths. A sense of the trauma of dismemberment may accompany the cutting off of some options, especially when our inability to know the future leaves us uncertain about whether the choices we have rejected might have been the best options, after all. Even when we make difficult choices individually, we feel a sense of internal conflict about our decisions. When we make choices as groups, and when members' initial preferences differ, the level of conflict we feel is likely to be multiplied.

Small Groups Involve Individuals

Individual group members may come to group meetings burdened by internal conflicts. Kraus (1997) argues that we may project onto others the qualities we dislike or fear in ourselves and come to see other members of our group as individuals to avoid, compete with, or defend ourselves against. But even in groups whose members accept themselves, differences among the members can plant the seeds for conflict. Apparently we begin to experience the social nature of conflict very early in our lives; Caplan, Vespo, Pedersen, and Hay (1991) found conflict evident in the interactions of children as young as one year old. O'Connor, Gruenfeld, and McGrath (1993) catalog some of the causes for conflict between individuals in groups: "Group members get jealous or bored with one another, they feel insulted or wronged by other members, they disagree on task solutions or approaches to the problems, they discover serious differences among themselves in values and attitudes, and so on" (p. 362). It is no wonder that, when the members of the classroom group described in the narrative identified the nature of their conflict, they mentioned personality conflict as one form they experienced.

The classroom group also mentioned experiencing conflict about leadership. Because leadership is so closely connected to issues of power, and because the desire for power and inequities in power are both likely to generate conflict, leadership is frequently a source of conflict for small groups. In addition, conflict about other roles is typical during the process of group development. In a study of conflict between groups, Thalhofer (1993) suggested that intergroup conflict is heightened when groups compete to fill the same role; she added that intergroup conflict can be reduced when different groups occupy separate niches. The same principle can be applied to intragroup conflict: when members' roles are indistinct, conflict is more likely than it is when each member has a unique role to fill in the group and is recognized as important to the overall group performance.

Still, the very interdependence of group members accounts for some conflict. The need to rely on others whose acts will impact our lives creates tension, too. For instance, in studying the very interdependent small groups that are involved in NASA space missions, Stewart (1988) found that in "isolated groups there is often not enough opportunity to release tension, so it builds up" (p. 443). Because groups are composed of individuals—who may be experiencing internal conflicts, who may have disagreements with other members of their group, who face issues of leadership and role expectations, and who are interdependent with other group members—there will always be conflict within groups.

Small Groups Are Increasingly Diverse

We live in a society in which geographical distances are being overcome by travel and international communication systems. Organizations may well have within them work groups that span international boundaries. Within national boundaries, some workplaces face the issue of social distance head-on with a workforce that reflects the diversity of society. The confluence of these factors led Boardman and Horowitz (1994) to predict that "much of the conflict in the 1990s and beyond will involve cultural diversity at some level" (p. 2). Their prediction seems justified, given the observation of Kirchmeyer and Cohen (1992) that multicultural and other heterogeneous groups experience increased difficulties.

Two factors are at work to increase the experience of conflict within diverse work groups. First, differences in communication patterns, values, and attitudes are more likely between group members with different demographic characteristics. Such differences increase the chances of misunderstanding. Second, the small group is not immune to the problems between social groups in the outside environment, and those external conflicts may be reenacted within the small group (Donnellon & Kolb, 1994).

The observation of increased difficulties in heterogeneous groups did not lead Kirchmeyer and Cohen (1992) to recommend the creation of groups whose members are all similar. In fact, they complained that an effort by organizations to homogenize work groups "represents a form of conflict avoidance" (p. 155) that is undesirable. Despite the increased conflict experiences of diverse groups, diversity within small groups—when managed well—can heighten creativity and improve productivity.

The nature of small groups—as decision-making bodies composed of individuals who are increasingly diverse—ensures that conflict within small groups is unavoidable, even if it were desirable to attempt its elimination. Therefore, the remaining sections of this chapter explore a communication theory that can help to explain the experience of conflict in small groups, describe the potential advantages and disadvantages conflict may bring to a group, and identify strategies that can be utilized to manage conflict effectively while avoiding undue conformity within a group.

Coordinating the Management of Meaning or Experiencing Conflict: A Theoretical Perspective

In the 1970s, W. Barnett Pearce and Vernon E. Cronen, at the time both faculty members at the University of Massachusetts, began to develop a communication theory that they called the *coordinated management of meaning,* or CMM. The theory focuses on the problem of coordinating the rules that individuals follow to construct meaning within their systems of interaction. Pearce (1976) used an analogy to describe the difficulty of coordinating conversations:

> The coordination problems in the management of meaning are like those of five musicians suddenly thrust before an audience, who must simultaneously perform and collectively decide what numbers to play, how fast to play them, and who should play what parts. The element of surprise . . . is that people so frequently produce such good music. (p. 20)

To explain how individuals achieve coordination in communication—and the potential for efforts at coordination to fail—Pearce and Cronen and their colleagues identified the constituents of communication and the patterns that give them meaning (see, for instance, Cronen & Pearce, 1981; Cronen, Pearce & Harris, 1979; Cronen, Pearce & Snavely, 1979; Pearce, 1976; Pearce & Conklin, 1979; and Pearce & Cronen, 1980).

Constituents of Communication

Our communication occurs within the context of an **episode,** *a structured segment of life identified by answering the question, "What does the communicator think he or she* *is doing?"* For example, if you are a member of a small group engaged in interaction, you might define your episode as "having a discussion," "having a brainstorming session," or "having a fight." Group members might have different episodes in mind when they interact. If someone in a group defines the episode as deciding on a solution while others define it as having a brainstorming session, the group members will not be likely to coordinate their actions very well. If they do not recognize the problem and adjust their behaviors, then the potential for conflict is high.

Within an episode, a communicator produces one or more **speech acts,** *units of communication that an individual uses to accomplish a communicative goal.* Examples of speech acts are agreeing, disagreeing, joking, praising, criticizing, threatening, and promising. Certain speech acts are appropriate within a particular episode and inappropriate within others. For instance, "disagreeing" is an appropriate speech act in an episode of "having a discussion" or "having a fight," but not when the group is "having a brainstorming session." As Masayuki Nakanishi explained in the opening narrative, culture may affect our notions of which speech acts are appropriate within a given episode. In Japan, expressing disagreement might be an appropriate speech act within an episode of nemawashi, but not during a group meeting; in the United States, a group meeting is likely to include disagreeing. Thus, even if communicators agree on what episode they are enacting, they may have different understandings of how to construct the episode, again leaving room for conflict to develop.

Speech acts are interpreted by **constitutive rules,** *rules used to define the acts other communicators have performed.* Suppose you make a suggestion in the midst of a group discussion and someone in your group responds by saying, "Now, *that's* an idea!" You will quickly interpret that remark, perhaps deciding that the speech act is a "compliment" of your suggestion. Or, if you detect sarcasm in the other person's voice, you will decide that the remark is not a compliment, but rather is ridicule.

If no one comments on your idea, you will have to interpret the silence to determine what kind of speech act it constitutes. Does the silence constitute disagreement? disinterest? or does it mean that the others are seriously considering your ideas? When you assign meaning to a particular speech act, you have used constitutive rules.

After interpreting one speech act, we generate another in response. We use **regulative rules** *to determine what act would be an appropriate response and to create the response.* If, for instance, you have interpreted someone's comment as ridicule, you might use the regulative rule that "ridicule should be responded to with a defense." Then your rule would lead you to construct a defense of your idea, perhaps by restating it calmly and clearly and providing sound reasons for your position. Another group member less argumentative than you might follow the rule that "ridicule should be responded to with a threat," and thus indicate that an undesired outcome will occur in the future. The two of you would be following different regulative rules.

In some cases, we may feel that several different responses to an act are possible and equally legitimate. In other cases, the preceding speech act seems to call for a specific response, perhaps because we are enmeshed in a repetitive pattern such that the act of another calls forth the same response time and time again, or perhaps because our culture constrains our behavioral choices. For example, as Masayuki Nakanishi explained, in Japan a direct challenge of a superior is inappropriate, so a group member would be silent until such time as another superior could be consulted in a private conversation about the concerns.

Patterns That Assign Meanings

You may have begun to suspect that coordinating our communication can be especially difficult if other people in your group have communication rules different from your own. In fact, Pearce and Cronen (1980) have identified a range of factors that can affect our interpretation of, and response to, a speech act. They describe these factors as elements in the **hierarchy of meanings.** The factors that may have particular influence on small groups include (1) raw sensory data, (2) communicator contracts, (3) life-scripts, and (4) culture.

The sights and sounds (and other sensory stimulations) created by the speech act are described as **raw sensory data.** For instance, if you say, "I am pretty upbeat about Tom's idea," but Tom hears you say, "I am pretty upset about Tom's idea," then he is likely to respond differently than you might expect him to. As you anticipate his gratitude, but he demands your explanation or expresses his irritation, you may have difficulty coordinating your responses.

The relationships that exist between communicators are described as their **contract.** The way we create and interpret certain speech acts is affected by the nature of our relationships with our communication partners. For instance, Deutsch (1994) noted that individuals often have different rules for communicating with members of their own group from those they have for communicating with outsiders.

Within a group, members are likely to have contracts as equal team members. Some groups, however, involve contracts between superiors and their subordinates. The act of expressing criticism may be performed differently in the two cases. Or consider a church group in which one member may have a contract as the spouse of one of the group members, the neighbor of another, the child of a third, and the coworker of a fourth. In creating a joke, for instance, the member has difficulty communicating in a way that seems clear and appropriate to the spouse, parent, coworker, and neighbor all at once.

The self-views of the communicators, called the **life-script,** also affect communication. When a group member thinks, "The kind of person I am would respond to that by . . . , " the group member is relying on a life-script to identify the appropriate regulative rule. For instance, if the dominance of one member has begun to annoy a man in the group who considers himself to be shy, he might select his response after thinking, "A shy person such as I am would not speak up about that annoying behavior." If his life-script was a "take-charge kind of guy," his response would be quite different. In some cases, an individual's life-script may lead to a consistent selection of one approach to conflict and consistent rejection of other strategies. Deutsch (1994) explains that individuals with strong interpersonal needs frequently select hostile responses to others within a group and overlook more cooperative responses to conflict.

General patterns, or archetypes, developed within the communicator's culture also affect the creation and interpretation of speech acts. The use and meaning of silence in interaction certainly varies from one culture to another. Also, Wong, Tjosvold, and Lee (1992) explain that the codes of behavior within Chinese culture lead to a greater likelihood for Chinese group members to avoid conflict with strangers, to avoid face-to-face conflict in general (but especially with those of higher status), and to use compromise to shorten and diffuse conflict situations. Deutsch (1994) writes that cultures define some acts as "appropriate or inappropriate, respectful or disrespectful, friendly or hostile, praiseworthy or blameworthy" (p. 20) and that differences in the cultural or subcultural backgrounds of group members may therefore complicate the group's ability to manage conflicts successfully.

Although Pearce and Cronen (1980) did not develop the coordinated management of meaning to explain conflict specifically or to relate specifically to small group communication, it is relevant on both counts. When we acknowledge the difficulty of coordinating a conversation between two individuals, we understand that achieving coordinated interactions within a group multiplies the difficulty.

In his classes, Masayuki Nakanishi explains that rules for managing conflict vary from culture to culture. His students, Japanese women, find it difficult to express conflict openly. (Photo compliments of Tsuda College.)

Further, by understanding the explanation of communication that CMM provides, we can anticipate areas in which misunderstandings can lead to conflict:

Group members have divergent assumptions about the episode they are enacting.

Group members have different ideas about what speech acts belong within the agreed-upon episode.

Group members differ in their constitutive and their regulative rules—so that what one intended to communicate is not what another perceives has been communicated.

The differences between communicators increase because of differences in raw sensory data, contracts, life-scripts, and culture.

Furthermore, understanding the coordinated management of meaning lays the basis for some of the discussion later in this chapter: an individual may (because of life-script or culture) feel constrained to respond to each conflict in the same manner, regardless of how productive that approach is. A useful approach in studying small group conflict is to discover a range of possible responses and to develop a larger set of regulative rules that can be tapped to respond to conflict. First, however, it is important to discover the disadvantages and advantages associated with conflict in small groups.

The Outcomes of Conflict

When we consider the outcomes associated with conflict, we are likely to recognize its disadvantages first. After all, internal tension accompanies conflict; if it does not *feel* good, we reason, it must not *be* good. And, in fact, conflict can have some disastrous results.

Disadvantages of Conflict

Consider the actual case of one university department. It was a department in which power was determined by the seniority of the members. For instance, when faculty members decided who would teach what classes, the member who had worked at that university the longest got the first choice; newcomers got the leftover courses. Department members became resentful of the unequal power distribution; strong personality conflicts developed. Interpersonal relationships were typically competitive; the successes of individual faculty members were met with jealousy rather than with praise. Tension was so high that some members actually feared that physical violence might occur. Weekly faculty meetings were often not the place where issues were decided. Instead, some faculty met in small groups, behind closed doors, to develop coalitions that could determine the outcome of policy votes.

Although problems existed throughout the year, the tension ran especially high when teaching assignments were determined. The department taught most of its classes on the school's main campus, but a few upper-division classes each year had to be taught at night on an extension campus an hour away from the main campus.

Faculty members were not eager to travel to the extension campus. Nor were they eager to teach the lower-division service course the department offered that accounted for most of the sections to be taught. Therefore, when faculty chose classes, they wanted to select upper-division classes, and they wanted the main campus classes. Yet someone had to teach on the extension campus, and someone had to teach the lower-division service classes. When the department was able to hire an additional faculty member, the members agreed that the new faculty member, whoever it would be, would not have a choice about classes at all; that faculty member would be allowed to teach only lower-division classes on the main campus and would be required to teach most of the upper-division classes on the extension campus.

It may not surprise you to discover that there was fairly high turnover among the faculty of that department. Qualified faculty members able to get jobs elsewhere usually left. It also may not surprise you to discover that ultimately the department split in half in the hopes of reducing the conflict they experienced. This example illustrates clearly the disadvantages that can come from unresolved conflict within a small group.

Conflict Can Make Group Interaction Uncomfortable—and Sometimes Even Unsafe—with the Effect of Undermining Democratic Processes.

At first, individual members feel as if their views are ignored; later, the discomfort may grow so high that they choose not to communicate at all. Individuals do all that they can to reduce the amount of whole-group interaction, often resorting to secretive meetings between portions of the group. Then, the divisiveness within the group increases as a result of the coalitions. Gossip within one faction about the other factions helps drive the wedge between subgroups. Gastil (1993), in studying communication within a food co-op, identified such behaviors as a primary factor in obstructing democracy in a small group, even one committed to democratic processes.

Conflict Can Lead to Poor Solutions.

Group members make quick compromises to avoid the extended discussion they would need if they were to resolve the conflict. In the faculty group, for instance, much of their conflict could have been eliminated if they had worked out a fair means of distributing teaching opportunities and responsibilities. Their compromise solution of keeping the opportunities for themselves and sticking the newcomer with unwelcome responsibilities was not only unfair to the new faculty member, but was, potentially, a disservice to the students.

Group Members Lose a Sense of Commitment to the Group, Diminishing Cohesiveness within the Group.

Meetings in which each member becomes the target of others become easier to avoid than attend. Moreover, when the group itself is divided, members are unlikely to feel commitment to the group as a whole. The contract among group members changes and becomes strained. As cohesiveness drops, the members' motivation to be productive is difficult to generate. Also, group members are more likely to leave the group. In work groups, such departures can be costly, for the investment made in hiring and training new group members is lost as members leave the group.

High Levels of Unresolved Conflict May Cause the Group to Disband.   If there was any value in the original group, then that is lost when the group ends. The faculty group lost important ties with colleagues when the department split. And although the smaller departments experienced a honeymoon period during which they pretended that their problems had been solved, they soon returned to their earlier tensions. After all, their conflicts had not really been resolved.

Advantages of Conflict

Despite the fact that unresolved conflict can have disastrous effects on the members of small groups, conflict can also be advantageous for small groups. Both of the opening narratives stress that fact. Masayuki Nakanishi, who first marveled at the fact that members of the small groups he observed in the United States could argue hard and then socialize together, has come to appreciate the direct expression of conflict as a means of resolving problems facing a group. The classroom group acknowledged that conflict was an advantage for them and mentioned several of the advantages common to groups that are able to express and resolve conflict.

Conflict Can Build Cohesiveness within a Group.   In a group that manages conflict effectively, members discover that they can express their ideas and feelings. They feel that they have been heard and understood. Therefore, they come to trust the members of their group (Kraus, 1997). With increased trust comes increased commitment to the group and its members. The feeling can come on powerfully (the "rush" Helena described in the opening narrative) when group members realize that they have managed to overcome a barrier that might have pulled them apart.

Conflict Can Serve to Motivate Group Members.   In a group where nothing happens, we may feel little motivation to remain involved in the group's activities. In a group in which conflict is expressed openly, something is nearly always happening. Missing a meeting not only means missing some potentially dramatic action; it also means missing an opportunity to be involved in crafting a solution. When a group is attempting to resolve conflict, all members are important. Any one of them may have the answer the group is looking for.

Conflict may also provide motivation by allowing group members to recognize the importance of their task. Such was the case for a group of creative television writers working on the development of a bicultural version of *Sesame Street* for Arab and Israeli children. Meeting the day after Israeli army planes had killed more than one hundred civilians in a United Nations peacekeeping camp in Lebanon, members of the work group expressed the tension they felt. As they discussed the conflict, members were able to arrive at the conclusion that their work was especially important: it was a chance to teach respect and tolerance and the dehumanizing role of violence (Mifflin, 1996).

Conflict Can Invigorate a Group by Removing Obstacles to Effective Functioning.
Often the source of conflict within a group is something within the group's structure that inhibits effective functioning. Perhaps the group is hindered by unequal distribution of

power. Perhaps it is hindered by a norm that discourages critical evaluation of ideas. Or maybe members have become dissatisfied with the style of leadership in the group. If the group members experience conflict but fail to express it, the tension each feels continues to grow, and the problems of the group continue as well. Expressing conflict allows individuals to release their pent-up emotions; but it does more than that: it allows members to transform their group. Restructuring a group is not an easy task, but it becomes possible when members express their conflict and work to resolve it.

Conflict Can Lead to Personal Growth. Several factors contribute to achieving this advantage. When we engage in conflict expression and resolution, we learn to see things not only from our own perspective, but also from the perspective of someone who disagrees with us. Firsthand we discover that there are multiple sides to a story. We may discover that, without even knowing it, we have engaged in behaviors that are annoying or detrimental to others. Suddenly our awareness is increased. As we discover the need to change, we enlarge our behavioral flexibility (Ostmann, 1992).

Conflict Can Lead to a Better Outcome. Individuals who do not challenge the information and opinions of others in their group may make a poor decision based on misinformation. Conflict about information motivates members to gather additional data and to analyze the data they have gathered more carefully. Groups that experience conflict about proposals they are considering usually expand their search for alternatives, ultimately selecting one that avoids the concerns voiced about the earlier suggestions. In fact, the role of conflict in improving decision making has come to be widely recognized through analysis of decisions made under conditions of high conflict avoidance. A commitment to avoid conflict leads to a phenomenon known as *groupthink*.

The Groupthink Phenomenon: A Theoretical Perspective

Irving L. Janis was on the psychology faculty of Yale University, involved in the study of small group processes, when he read Arthur M. Schlesinger's 1965 memoir of the John F. Kennedy presidency, *A Thousand Days*. Janis paid particular attention to the chapter in the book that described the ill-fated Bay of Pigs invasion, an attempt to land a small group of U.S.-supported Cuban exiles on the coast of Cuba (at the Bay of Pigs) with the goal of toppling the government of Fidel Castro. Planned by the CIA before President Kennedy's election, but approved after he took office by Kennedy and his advisors, the Bay of Pigs invasion was a failure from the outset. When Janis read Schlesinger's account of the decision making leading up to the invasion effort, the account brought to mind some of Janis' own research on small group decisions flawed by the pressure to conform. He began to develop the hypothesis that some foreign policy blunders might be caused by similar group dynamics. His teenaged daughter, following her father's suggestion to study the Bay of Pigs invasion for a high school history term paper, uncovered additional evidence that confirmed her father's notion that group dynamics provided an explanation for the flawed decision.

Janis pursued his hypothesis by studying other flawed policy decisions (the invasion of North Korea, the failure to prepare for the attack at Pearl Harbor, the escalation of the Vietnam War, and, later, the Watergate cover-up) and comparing them with two policy successes (the U.S. response to the Cuban missile crisis and the development of the Marshall Plan). [Subsequently, analysis of such decisions as the one to launch the *Challenger* space shuttle in temperatures too cold for the equipment has discovered similar patterns (Moorhead, Ference, & Neck, 1991).] Janis's book, *Groupthink: Psychological Studies of Policy Decisions and Fiascoes*, (1982) develops his argument that the nature of the dynamics within the decision-making groups accounted for the successes or failures of the decisions he analyzed.

Definition of Groupthink

Janis (1982) coined the term **groupthink**

> to refer to a mode of thinking that people engage in when they are deeply involved in a cohesive in-group, when the members' strivings for unanimity override their motivation to realistically appraise alternative courses of action. . . . Groupthink refers to a deterioration of mental efficiency, reality testing, and moral judgment that results from in-group pressures. (p. 9)

In essence, then, groupthink exists when members discourage the existence of substantive conflict within the decision-making process. Although Janis developed his theory by examining public policy decisions made by the United States federal government, the phenomenon can occur in groups of all types in all places. One classroom group, for instance, enjoyed its cohesiveness so much that members decided not to challenge each other's ideas—and in some cases, not even to check each other's work. During a presentation their group made to the class, when one member usurped half the group's time and the presentation suffered as a result, the members realized the error of their ways. They defined themselves as classic victims of groupthink.

Symptoms of Groupthink

Not all poor decisions result from groupthink, as Janis (1982) acknowledged. However, flawed decisions are more likely when symptoms associated with groupthink exist. Janis identified eight such symptoms:

1. An illusion of invulnerability shared by most or all the members, which creates excessive optimism and encourages taking extreme risks
2. An unquestioned belief in the group's inherent morality, inclining the members to ignore the ethical or moral consequences of their decisions
3. Collective efforts to rationalize in order to discount warnings or other information that might lead the members to reconsider their assumptions before they recommit themselves to their past policy decisions

Ethical Consideration

A decision-making group should base its decision on the information available at the time. If you have information the group needs to make an informed decision and do not share it with the group, you have violated one of your fundamental responsibilities as a group member.

4. Stereotyped views of enemy leaders as too evil to warrant genuine attempts to negotiate, or as too weak and stupid to counter whatever risky attempts are made to defeat their purposes
5. Self-censorship of deviations from the apparent group consensus, reflecting each member's inclination to minimize to [him- or herself] the importance of his [or her] doubts and counterarguments
6. A shared illusion of unanimity concerning judgments conforming to the majority view (partly resulting from self-censorship of deviations, augmented by the false assumption that silence means consent)
7. Direct pressure on any member who expresses strong arguments against any of the group's stereotypes, illusions, or commitments, making clear that this type of dissent is contrary to what is expected of all loyal members
8. The emergence of self-appointed mind-guards—members who protect a group from adverse information that might shatter their shared complacency about the effectiveness and morality of their decisions (pp. 174–175)

Cline (1990) compared the communication behaviors of groups with and without groupthink pressures. She discovered some ways in which group members created an illusion of unanimity: verbalizing one's own agreement with oneself, interrupting in the form of a simple agreement, and asking questions that solicit statements of agreement. In contrast, groups without groupthink expressed agreement by stating the position with which they agreed and offering the reasons for their support. In those groups, which had fewer statements of agreement from the members, statements of agreement led to real, not illusory, unanimity. As a consequence of groupthink, group members are unlikely to search thoroughly for information relevant to their decisions and are more likely to process the information they do have with a selective bias that confirms their preconceptions. They are unlikely to generate a very complete list of solution options or to evaluate the risks of their proposed solution, preferring to assume that their choice will succeed. They are even willing to continue to commit themselves to decisions that have proved to be poor risks in the past (Street & Anthony, 1997). No wonder a group under the influence of groupthink frequently makes bad decisions.

Causes of Groupthink

How does groupthink develop? Janis (1982) identified three antecedent conditions. The first is *the existence of a cohesive group*, which Janis called a necessary but not sufficient condition for the creation of groupthink. In other words, groupthink does not occur in all cohesive groups, but it does not develop in groups that are not cohesive. Still, the link is somewhat surprising, because cohesive groups are typically more tolerant of conflict: group members can freely disagree and still be accepted by the rest of the group. The connection becomes clearer when you remember that cohesiveness is a multidimensional concept. Several research studies have explored the connection between groupthink and cohesiveness and have been able to pinpoint the specific dimensions of cohesiveness that are connected to groupthink. Mullen, Anthony, Salas, and Driskell (1994) found that only cohesiveness based on interpersonal attraction between group members led to groupthink; when the cohesiveness was based on members' shared commitment to the tasks of the group, groupthink was thwarted. Bernthal and Insko (1993) and Mohamed and Wiebe (1996) reported similar results: cohesiveness based on amiability, prestige, and personal attraction led to groupthink; cohesiveness stemming from competence of the members and previous effective performance led away from it.

Neck and Manz (1994) warned that self-managed teams are prime candidates for developing the groupthink phenomenon since their high interaction rates are apt to increase their cohesiveness, and their interdependence could decrease their desire for conflict. It is comforting to realize that, by itself, cohesiveness does not lead to groupthink and is unlikely to do so in a self-managed group that maintains a high commitment to doing its task well.

The second antecedent condition of groupthink is the *existence of structural faults within a group*. These faults include factors that limit the members' access to a clear picture of reality, such as restrictions on access to diverse points of view. Groups composed of homogeneous members do not have built-in diversity of opinions; normally, sorting through diverse positions will automatically force members to test each other's perceptions. If, in addition, a group is insulated from other groups, then the members' view of reality cannot be checked against the views of reliable experts external to the group. Inadequate time to make a decision also inhibits a group from exploring a diversity of ideas, whether they come from inside or outside the group (Moorhead, Ference, & Neck, 1991). Another kind of structural fault is any condition that makes individual members anxious about expressing their opinions freely. For instance, if you had no idea how your group made its decisions, or if you thought that your job depended on your agreeing with your group leader (as in the cartoon in Figure 5.1), then you would probably be anxious about expressing your opinion freely (unless it did actually agree with that of the leader). When Anderson and Balzer (1991) studied teams of residence hall staff members, they asked them to devise plans of action for solving typical residence hall problems. If the team leader began the meeting by stating his or her preferred solution, then team members rather quickly agreed to support the leader's recommendation. In contrast, teams generated more solutions—and solutions rated higher on feasibility and the likelihood of adoption—when the leader delayed stating a preferred course of action. The structural faults identified by Janis (1982) work to discourage thorough critical evaluation of information and ideas by the members of a small group.

The third antecedent condition is *a provocative situational context* within which the decision is to be made. A group that has experienced recent failures, is having excessive difficulty in making the current decision, or sees no promise of solutions

FIGURE 5.1   In some groups, the leader's behavior encourages groupthink.
Reprinted with permission of King Features Syndicate.

Ethical Consideration

As a leader, you have every right to expect your followers to commit themselves to the group. However, expecting group members to serve as a rubber stamp for your decisions and denying them the right to express disagreement is an abuse of your power.

except those that violate their ethical standards will feel inadequate to the task of making a good decision. Members of groups operating under a high level of stress are likely to feel as if they will not be able to come up with a better solution than their leader has proposed. In any of these cases, members who, under ordinary circumstances, are capable of critical evaluation will be discouraged from thinking critically by the context in which they find themselves. The way out of the situation will seem to be to support the plan of the leader and gain strength from the unity of the group.

Tests of the groupthink model suggest that cohesiveness alone does not produce groupthink. Nor is any other of the antecedent conditions by itself sufficient to produce groupthink. However, Mohamed and Wiebe (1996) argue that when either (or both) of the latter two antecedents is combined with cohesiveness, then the stage is set for groupthink to develop.

Avoiding Groupthink

Janis's (1982) analysis of the Cuban missile crisis identified some of the strategies that can be used to avoid the development of groupthink. The strategies became clear because the group involved in making decisions about the missile crisis was the same one that had approved the Bay of Pigs invasion. In the Cuban missile crisis, occurring just 18 months after the Bay of Pigs invasion, the Kennedy cabinet was faced with responding to a threat of nuclear attack created when the Soviet Union placed offensive nuclear missiles on Cuban soil. Yet in the time after the first crisis, President Kennedy had made four major procedural changes in his Cabinet's decision making that altered the dynamics of the group and enabled a successful outcome to follow the dismal failure of the invasion. First, all members of the policy-making group were expected to function as critical evaluators of all ideas, not simply as advocates of their own personal proposals. Two members were asked to be especially vigilant, serving as devil's advocates in raising challenges against even the most popular ideas.

Second, closed sessions were replaced by ones in which outside experts were invited to group meetings and their involvement was solicited. This strategy worked to reduce the insulation of the group and enhance the diversity of viewpoints available to members.

Third, independent subgroups were formed to create competing proposals. There may be times in the life of a group when subgroups are formed to speed up the work of a group. One subgroup tackles one of the full group's responsibilities while the other subgroup tackles another responsibility. In this case, however, the process of the group may actually be slowed down, because both subgroups are assigned the same task. Each formulates a proposal. When the full group meets, the two proposals compete with one another initially, so conflict of a sort is built into the subsequent group meetings.

Fourth, on occasion the group met without its leader, especially in the early stages of consideration of a proposal, so that President Kennedy would be unable to exert influence over the policy-making group. A group meeting without a leader avoids the constraints felt when the leader's preferences are made clear to group members who then try to please the leader by conforming. Together these four changes transformed the group meetings so that Kennedy and his advisors engaged in a thorough analysis of the situation and the proposed solutions.

These strategies, along with some others, can be used by other groups as well to avoid the dangers of groupthink. Janis recommended that groups take the time to suggest alternative scenarios, including a worst-case scenario, so that they identify as many risks associated with their proposals as they possibly can. They can then identify remedies for potential problems and also decide whether the proposal is worth the risks associated with it.

Janis also recommended that after coming to a preliminary decision, a group should hold a "second-chance" meeting. At this meeting, "the members are expected to express as vividly as they can all their residual doubts and to rethink the entire issue before making a definitive choice" (p. 271). The making of a decision does cause some internal mental conflict. Rather than ignoring those concerns and rushing to implement a solution it later regrets, a group that holds another meeting to share the concerns is clearer about the impact of its decisions and is able to correct its course before taking action.

Ethical Consideration

Every group has connections to its outside environment. Therefore every group should be accountable for its actions. Even if no one requires you to develop a justification of your decisions, you should still be able to do so.

In their analysis of the jury deliberations of the case against John DeLorean, Neck and Moorhead (1993) found that a methodical procedural approach was an antidote to groupthink tendencies. The case concerned whether DeLorean, with his car company in financial crisis and desperate for cash, had been entrapped by the government into drug trafficking or was responsible for his own involvement in that illegal activity. Although the jury quickly became highly cohesive, their initial position against DeLorean was altered in a process of thorough, careful analysis. Neck and Moorhead concluded that it was the use of well-defined procedures that was responsible for the group's avoidance of groupthink. In Chapter 7 of this book, a variety of decision-making formats are described. Selection of any one of them would lead a group to use a systematic process that could counter tendencies toward groupthink.

Another suggestion develops from the work of Kroon, Kreveld, and Rabbie (1992), who found that when group members were required to be accountable for their actions, they became more rigorous critical evaluators. The researchers suggested that when group members had to provide justifications of their decisions, the members no longer felt as if the group was insulated from those external to the group to whom they were accountable. Moreover, the demand of accountability reduced each member's reliance on the leader, however partial that leader was to his or her own proposals. Therefore, groups should be made accountable for their actions and required to develop clear justifications for their decisions, which can be presented to those to whom the group is accountable.

The research of Kameda and Sugimori (1993) leads to the suggestion that adoption of a non–consensus decision rule may be a sufficient strategy to avoid groupthink. At the beginning of Chapter 7, we discuss three different decision rules: consensus, majority vote, and negotiation. Kameda and Sugimori found that groups that had a

Technology Note: A Tool to Avoid Groupthink

One recommendation for thwarting groupthink is the use of computer systems as an aid to decision making. Miranda (1994) explains that "group support systems [GSS] are an advanced information technology that combine communication, computer, and decision technologies to support decision making and related group activities" (p. 106). Several factors allow groups using GSS to avoid the tendency toward groupthink. Because ideas are communicated over a computer, the communication is more anonymous. Members communicate with greater security and less fear of censure. Several group members can communicate simultaneously without cutting each other off; as the freedom to communicate is increased, so is the generation of alternative solutions. The nature of cohesiveness within the group is affected because the decision technologies focus a group's efforts on the task, not on socio-emotional factors. Therefore, the causes of cohesiveness that give rise to groupthink are diminished, and those that protect against groupthink are enhanced. In short, group support systems might be considered as a means of attacking the fundamental cause of groupthink: the pressure to conform. As Miranda writes, "conformity in itself is not harmful. However, when it subdues the meaningful discussion of issues and opinions directly related to the task at hand, conformity can produce disastrous results" (p. 107).

consensus decision rule imposed on them were more prone toward groupthink than those that decided by voting. Their research focused, in particular, on the decision to continue an unproductive approach arrived at in an earlier decision. In those cases, groups following a majority vote rule were more apt to heed the minority voices when problems with the initial decision became apparent than were those groups that had followed a consensus rule.

You may have noticed that the strategies for avoiding groupthink are ones that introduce substantive conflict into the group. The conflict may come from a group member assigned to challenge all ideas, from an outsider who introduces a new perception, from the interaction of two subgroups each committed to a different proposal, or from the acknowledgment of concerns individuals have but might otherwise have kept silent about. Therefore, the lesson from groupthink is that decisions are likely to be better when substantive conflict is welcomed into group meetings. In such a way, the advantages of conflict can be realized. However, it is still necessary to consider strategies that will allow groups to avoid the dangers that may develop if conflict gets out of hand.

Management of Conflict

You have probably noticed that groups differ in the way they handle conflict. For instance, your own family may handle conflict quite differently from the way other families do. And within a group, you may respond differently than others in the group do. Obviously, there is more than one way to manage conflict.

Five Approaches to Conflict Management

Deutsch (1994) identified five different approaches to conflict management that we can distinguish by their relative emphasis on satisfying our own needs versus satisfying the needs of our conflict partner. The approaches are competition, accommodation, avoidance, compromise, and collaboration.

Competition.   This approach places the emphasis on satisfying our own needs at the expense of other group members' needs. It is described as a win-lose approach, because when we resolve a conflict through competition, we win and our partners lose.

Accommodation.   The approach most directly opposite competition is *accommodation*, which emphasizes satisfying our partner's needs at the expense of our own needs. A group member who resolves conflict by accommodating gives in to the demands of another member, perhaps in the interest of bringing the conflict to a quick end. However, because the group member's own needs are not resolved, the approach is described as a lose-win approach.

Avoidance.   In this approach, the needs of neither party are emphasized. Individuals who feel a high level of discomfort with conflict are likely to use avoidance strategies if they do not use accommodation. By ignoring the conflict issue, the group may be able to temporarily move on to other concerns. The danger, however, is that the seed of the conflict will grow, and what might have been resolved quickly and easily if dealt with immediately will be more difficult to resolve subsequently. Therefore, avoidance is considered a lose-lose approach.

Compromise. This approach balances the needs of both sides to a conflict but does not satisfy the needs of either party completely. When groups resolve their conflict through a compromise, they typically begin the conflict management process with two different proposals. They end up with a proposal that includes some elements of each of the initial proposals. Each party gives in to some degree, so the approach might be described as a "win-a-little–lose-a-little" approach for each party.

Collaboration. This approach places a high regard on the needs of all parties. Groups that use collaborative approaches to manage conflict identify the needs of each party to the conflict, generate solutions with the potential to meet the needs, and select a solution with which all parties are satisfied. The process, therefore, is quite different from the process used in compromising. Collaboration is a win-win approach, but it requires time and skill to accomplish. Therefore, other approaches may be preferred by some groups in some circumstances or for some issues.

Conflict management approaches that are cooperative, such as collaboration and compromise, are more likely to encourage constructive conflict; they are referred to as **integrative** strategies because they *integrate the needs of all parties in the solution.* Conflict management approaches that are competitive are referred to as **distributive strategies** since they *distribute the winnings to one party or another;* they are more likely to encourage destructive conflict. In addition to selecting integrative approaches, there are some specific strategies that can be used to create the conditions for constructive conflict. It is possible that you have a preferred mode of managing conflict, regardless of the nature of the conflict. It might be useful, however, to consider enlarging your repertoire of regulative rules so that you can select from the wider range of conflict management strategies the one best suited to establishing the conditions for constructive conflict.

Creating the Conditions for Constructive Conflict

Constructive conflict involves disagreements about information a group has gathered or about the group's goals and the methods to be used to achieve them. Engaging in constructive conflict requires mutual respect. It involves the exploration of alternatives and the exchange of arguments (claims, reasoning, evidence) to try to clarify ideas. In contrast, **destructive conflict** obscures ideas because individuals distort their perceptions by relying on stereotypes and searching for scapegoats. It involves a hostile climate of mutual disrespect as each member seeks the advantage over others through the use of revenge, trickery, and threats (Rosen, 1989).

There are some situations in which a group or its members are more likely to resort to an expression of conflict that is destructive: (1) if a group member feels

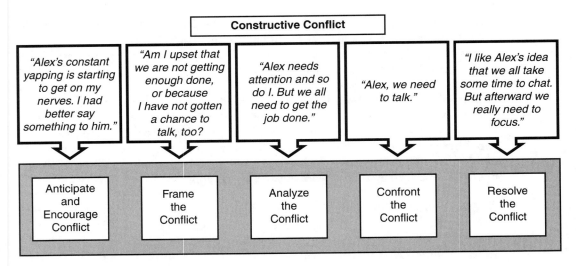

FIGURE 5.2   Five steps are useful in creating the conditions for constructive conflict.

ignored by, or alienated from, the rest of the group and believes there is no other way to be heard by the group or have an impact on it; (2) if the issue the group is facing involves the power, status, or identity of members, so that individuals feel threatened; (3) if the conflict has grown and taken on a life of its own; and (4) if the group members lack the skills necessary to engage in constructive conflict expression. By creating the conditions for constructive conflict, even these situations can be transformed. Five steps are useful in such a process: (1) anticipating and encouraging the expression of conflict; (2) framing the conflict; (3) analyzing the conflict; (4) confronting the conflict, and (5) resolving the conflict. These steps are visualized in Figure 5.2 and are then described more fully.

Anticipate and Encourage the Expression of Conflict.   If we fear conflict within a group, then its appearance is likely to make us defensive. Defensive behaviors can turn a benign disagreement into a malignant conflagration. Recognizing that conflict is inherent in small groups should lead us to anticipate its appearance.

Understanding that conflict can benefit the group should lead us to welcome its expression and to respond to it with an attitude of open inquiry. Differences between group members can then be addressed as they first emerge. The conflict is less likely to expand beyond the specific, limited cause of concern; the limited conflict can be addressed rather easily if dealt with immediately.

Frame the Conflict.   When we experience conflict, we may first recognize only a sense of discomfort that accompanies the incompatibility involved in conflict. It may take us a while to pinpoint what exactly is at issue for us. When we are able to put that into words, we have *framed* the conflict. However, there are multiple ways of framing any dispute. For instance, Drake and Donohue (1996) illustrate the concept of framing with excerpts from divorce-dispute mediations during which a wife might initiate a complaint about the amount of child support she was promised (a factual issue) and then transform the complaint to one about the dominance her husband had during the marriage (a relational issue). It is also possible for one spouse to see the issue as factual and the other to perceive it as relational, particularly if their life scripts are quite different from one another. Drake and Donohue report that if individuals in conflict have divergent frames, their conflict is likely to escalate in severity and expand in length. Groups in conflict have the same experiences as divorcing couples: without careful attention to framing the conflict, coordinating the frames, and restricting the conflict to the issue that has been framed, the conflict is harder to resolve constructively.

In contrast, "frame convergence is associated with disputants' ability to reach substantive agreements in their conflict" (Drake & Donohue, 1996, p. 309). Although Drake and Donohue recommend the use of mediators to keep talk within the limits of the established frames, group members may be able to play the same role of keeping the talk between disputing members within the frame they have agreed upon. But even the initial step of determining how the issues are to be framed is a step toward constructive conflict management.

Analyze the Conflict. Because conflict, by definition, involves some level of incompatibility, it is possible that group members who experience conflict have divergent needs at issue. Even more likely, the parties to the conflict develop distinct positions that are incompatible. Imagine the situation that might have confronted the faculty members described earlier in this chapter as they determined who would teach what classes in their department. One member might have a need to be intellectually challenged by his job, while another member might have a need for her colleagues to respect her as an equal member of the faculty. Those distinct needs are not necessarily divergent. However, when the faculty member in need of intellectual challenge takes the position that he must teach a specific upper-division course (in order to be challenged) and his colleague takes the position that she must have the opportunity to teach the same course (in order to be treated as an equal), then their positions are incompatible.

In the process of analyzing a conflict, group members identify the needs involved and distinguish them from the positions members have taken. By focusing on the needs involved as distinct from positions, group members free themselves to consider a wider range of alternatives as solutions. For instance, the faculty member desiring an intellectual challenge could be encouraged to initiate a research project or to mentor younger faculty; the faculty member desiring equal treatment might be happy teaching the lower-division service course, as long as it was her choice to do so. In the process of conflict analysis, members may also discover that there is as much to unite them as there is to divide them. As Deutsch (1994) noted, "most conflicts are mixed-motive conflicts in which the parties involved in the conflict have both competitive and cooperative interests" (p. 13). Identifying the interests that group members share is an important outcome of the analysis stage.

To be effective, conflict analysis requires competent communication. Fisher (1994) writes that "conflict analysis requires clear and honest communication in which parties remain sensitive to common errors in perception and cognition and develop

Ethical Consideration

If you have a hidden agenda—individual goals unrelated to the group's goal—and you fail to share those during the process of conflict analysis, you automatically impede the group's ability to resolve its conflict.

---

empathic understanding of each other" (p. 52). By communicating openly, group members are likely to discover some instances of uncoordinated meaning at the base of their conflict. Differences in episode definition, speech act selection, and in constitutive or regulative rules, caused by differences in life-scripts, in understanding of the contract of the group members, and in their culture lead to conflicts that can only be overcome once their fundamental cause has been identified. Moreover, using the communication skills described in Chapter 4, including providing confirming feedback and employing active listening, can help a group member feel listened to and understood. Then he or she is more willing to engage in constructive conflict management.

Confront the Conflict.   Once a conflict has been analyzed, it should be confronted. Several factors important to the success of this process are identified by Fisher (1994). Group members should meet face-to-face, as equals. It is important, therefore, for the group to be sensitive to their meeting environment to ensure that nonverbal messages do not imply inequality of members. They should follow norms of mutual respect and be committed to resolving their conflict. The goal should be to maximize the gains of all parties while resolving their mutual problem. Rather than trying to follow a predetermined agenda, a group engaged in conflict confrontation should work through the issues as they arise, maintaining flexibility in their approach.

In some situations, confronting the conflict is a long and difficult process. That is especially true if the conflict focuses on power or identity issues. Donnellon and Kolb (1994) write about the difficulties involved in resolving disputes that are, at their base, diversity issues. They acknowledge that groups often prefer to attribute diversity-based disputes to individual differences because, in doing so, they avoid threatening the social order. But it may be that alterations in the social order are the only tool capable of chiseling away at the dynamics of the dispute. They add,

> Because issues of social diversity are central to identity and rights, the exploration of such conflicts is likely to be emotional for all parties concerned. It takes longer to process such conflict thoroughly, assuming that it can be brought to some mutually satisfactory closure. It also requires considerable expertise to handle emotional issues. (pp. 147–148)

Group members confronting any conflict, but especially ones involving these sensitive issues, should utilize a full range of effective communication skills. Deutsch (1994) identified skills important to the conflict management process, many of which are of particular importance during the confrontation stage. *Using "I messages"* rather

Technology Note: A Time to Avoid Technology

When a group has to complete a task in the face of conflict, use of technological tools may be helpful since they allow interaction to take place while the interpersonal relationships are given the distance to cool off. However, when a group is trying to resolve conflict by confronting it, meeting face-to-face is important. In fact, Lipnack and Stamps (1997) mention that the absence of face-to-face communication hinders the ability of virtual teams to resolve conflict. This is one situation in which having the fullest access to both verbal and nonverbal communication—as only face-to-face communication allows—is desirable.

---

than "you messages" ("I feel as if I am not an equal member of this group," not "You treat me as if you are superior to me") encourages an individual to express personal feelings instead of making charges against another group member. After all, we can only be certain about our own feelings. If we try to explain to our opponents what they are feeling, we risk enlarging the dispute.

Perspective taking allows a group member to examine the issue through the eyes of another group member. After one group member has used "I messages," then it is possible for others to begin to discover that person's life-script and to understand that individual's perspective. With that in mind, we can more effectively imagine the rules that member is using to define and produce speech acts. We can also see what needs the other might have in the conflict, which we might not have recognized earlier.

Focusing on common ground rather than on individual interests directs attention toward mutual goals and encourages collaborative efforts, not divisive ones. Even if a group is not able to overcome all of its divisive concerns quickly, it is able to function if there is motivation to reach a shared goal. *Controlling expressions of anger* allows the group to consider the issues rationally rather than becoming embroiled in emotions. *Checking for feedback* from other group members allows individuals to discover the development of misperceptions and misunderstandings. Feedback provides clues to the lack of coordination in the meanings of members, which then allows for renegotiation of meaning. If groups have members who lack effective communication skills, they may need the services of a facilitator who can model appropriate behaviors, train members in such skills, and enforce the use of these behaviors.

Engaging in **metacommunication**, *communication about the communication processes of the group*, is also a desirable strategy. Suppose that feedback has revealed that group members have divergent understandings of the communication episode they are enacting. One member thought the group was arriving at a final decision, and the others thought they were brainstorming; one member believed that criticism was appropriate at the meeting, whereas others expected only support to be communicated. While communicating about those differences is a prerequisite to negotiating coordinated meanings, the communicators may also, in the process, become more conscious of their own behaviors and the manner in which they can contribute to the conflict. Knowing that others have observed us and will continue to do so encourages us to monitor ourselves more carefully. Moreover, knowing that how the group functions is important to other members increases pride in group membership, which helps to cool off the disagreements.

Resolve the Conflict.   In the final stage of the conflict resolution process, members select the mechanisms that best meet the needs of all parties and that transform the relationships of group members. As members make suggestions, the proposals should be treated as hypotheses. Hypotheses are meant to be tested, not accepted without question. Proposals should also be treated as group property, so that if a change is made in a proposal, it is clearly not an attack on the individual who initially proposed the idea. Throughout this process, the group should make clear its procedures and make sure the procedures are fair.

If the climate of the group becomes hostile, then more specific rules may need to be instituted. These might involve allowing each member a chance to present a position free from interruption, followed by questions of clarification from any member before the next member is allowed to speak. Restricting individuals' communication opportunities is normally not desirable, but if the freedom to speak is so abused by some that it is denied to others, then some restrictions need to be employed.

If a dispute involves interpersonal issues rather than task issues, then the group needs to follow the strategies of providing specific descriptive feedback to allow a member to understand what is bothering the rest of the group. Moreover, in the phrasing and timing of the feedback, all members must be sensitive to the needs of the group members being addressed. It is not just in the Japanese culture that people hate to lose face. Destroying the image of a group member in front of others does not improve the working relationships of the group.

Although some groups may have the norm of resolving conflict competitively, they should realize that competitive conflict management strategies decrease the group morale, disrupt work relationships, and increase the danger of the group's destruction (Wong, Tjosvold, & Lee, 1992). When groups use competitive styles, communication is strategic; after all, exaggerating one's position is advantageous, and disclosures of information may be exploited. Groups that use collaborative, cooperative styles of conflict management realize that misrepresenting their position does them a disservice; it is open communication that is valued in collaboration (Rubin, 1994). If group members are not willing to communicate openly, it

Ethical Consideration

If you are concerned about an issue within your group, then you should certainly express your concern. That is your responsibility as a member of the group. At the same time, prohibiting others from responding to your concerns or expressing their own violates their right to free speech and denies the group members the opportunity to hear all ideas.

may be necessary to make use of an outside facilitator. As Rubin explains, "it is precisely the disruptive effect of introducing a third party that often helps get disputants unstuck . . . [and] makes it possible for disputants to make concessions with reduced risk of losing face" (p. 41).

When these strategies are used within groups, they will counter the conditions that might encourage use of destructive conflict approaches. Group members are all given an opportunity to speak and will be considered as equals within the group. There is no need for an aggressive response just to gain attention. Nor should group members develop the feeling of being misunderstood. The use of active listening allows members to hear that they have been heard and heard accurately. In fact, Kirchmeyer and Cohen (1992) found that Asian ethnic minorities, who might normally avoid conflict, increased their contributions within groups that used constructive conflict management techniques. In the process, they increased their commitment to the group and its decisions. By dealing with issues as they emerge, rather than avoiding them, the size of conflicts can be kept manageable. Practicing good communication behaviors helps to develop the skill to manage conflict effectively. If additional help is needed, then the group can enlist the assistance of a facilitator.

Summary

Many of us initially fear the eruption of conflict in groups to which we belong. We may think it best not to rock the boat, even if we disagree with decisions our group is making. Unfortunately, such an attitude creates bigger problems for a group than does the experience of conflict. Conflict is an unavoidable experience for group members. It occurs because groups make decisions, are composed of individuals, and are increasingly diverse. It also occurs because the members of groups misunderstand the speech acts others create and have difficulty coordinating their interactions. Cultural differences certainly have an impact on the existence of conflict and on the manner in which it is expressed and resolved.

Uncontrolled, conflict can create dangers. Resolved, it leads to better decisions and improved relationships within groups. Although agreeing with others to avoid tension within a group may be tempting, the dangers of groupthink are clear. Therefore, it is to the group's advantage to learn how to manage conflict effectively.

The classroom group you met in the opening narrative ended its intensive three-week class by presenting an excellent training session on managing diversity within groups. Their presentation was creative, informative, and professional. They earned the respect of their classmates for the high quality of their product, but also for the skill they evidenced in dealing with conflict. They did not ignore it. They talked about it directly and openly. Their trust in each other grew from the process. They learned to invite disagreements to their meetings, for in that way, their performance could improve. They learned from experience how valuable a tool conflict can be when it allows a group to test its ideas and to grow as a team.

QUESTIONS FOR DISCUSSION

1. Discuss the university department described in the section on disadvantages of conflict as it relates to CMM. Imagine yourself as a faculty member new to that department. How would your expectations of the contract between faculty members coordinate with the others' expectations of contract? How would your expectations for a faculty meeting episode coordinate with the others' expectations for that episode?

2. To the extent that conflict comes from uncoordinated meanings, it seems to be unavoidable. To what extent can such conflicts be avoided?

3. We have suggested that unrestrained conflict is damaging to groups, but so also is avoiding conflict. Is finding the perfect balance of conflict a matter of avoiding extremes in the degree of conflict? Does it relate instead to welcoming certain types of conflict and avoiding others?

4. Masayuki Nakanishi said that the Japanese approach to conflict does not lead to groupthink. Develop an argument that either supports or challenges his statement.

5. Is the danger greater from uncontrolled conflict or from groupthink?

6. Why is it that when we are engaged in conflict it is so easy to shift the frame of the original conflict?

SUGGESTED ACTIVITIES

1. Analyze the conflict and conflict management strategies used in the movie *Twelve Angry Men*. What kinds of conflict were evident? What advantages and disadvantages did the conflict have for the jurors? What recommendations would you have made to the jurors about managing the conflict more effectively? (You could also analyze the role of conflict in the Guarneri Quartet, as revealed in the movie *High Fidelity*.)

2. In your journal, describe your own individual attitude toward conflict. Explain how that has affected your group's conflict management strategies and/or your attitude toward the way your group deals with conflict. If you are experiencing conflict but not expressing it, discuss the way you will try to express the conflict in an effective way. After you try to implement your suggestions, describe how successful your efforts were. If conflict has been expressed but has been damaging the group, develop a plan for improving the conflict management strategies; implement the plan, and evaluate it.

3. In your journal, describe a recent decision you were a party to and discuss whether you felt the pressures associated with groupthink. If so, explain how you might have altered the group dynamics to resist those pressures.

SOURCES CITED

Anderson, L. E., & Balzer, W. K. (1991). The effects of timing of leaders' opinions on problem-solving groups: A field experiment. *Group & Organization Studies, 16*, 86–101.

Bernthal, P. R., & Insko, C. A. (1993). Cohesiveness without groupthink: The interactive effects of social and task cohesion. *Group & Organization Management, 18*, 66–87.

Boardman, S. K., & Horowitz, S. V. (1994). Constructive conflict management and social problems: An introduction. *Journal of Social Issues, 50*, 1–12.

Caplan, M., Vespo, J., Pedersen, J., & Hay, D. F. (1991). Conflict and its resolution in small groups of one- and two-year-olds. *Child Development, 62*, 1513–1524.

Cline, R. J. W. (1990). Detecting groupthink: Methods for observing the illusion of unanimity. *Communication Quarterly, 38*, 112–126.

Cronen, V. E., & Pearce, W. B. (1981). Logical force in interpersonal communication: A new concept of the "necessity" in social behavior. *Communication, 6*, 5–67.

Cronen, V. E., Pearce, W. B., & Harris, L. M. (1979). The logic of the coordinated management of meaning: A rules-based approach to the first course in interpersonal communication. *Communication Education, 28*, 22–36.

Cronen, V. E., Pearce, W. B., & Snavely, L. M. (1979). A theory of rule-structure and types of episodes in a study of perceived enmeshment in undesired repetitive patterns (URPs). In D. Nimmo (Ed.), *Communication Yearbook 3* (pp. 225–240). New Brunswick, NJ: Transaction Books.

Deutsch, M. (1994). Constructive conflict resolution: Principles, training, and research. *Journal of Social Issues, 50*, 13–32.

Donnellon, A., & Kolb, D. M. (1994). Constructive for whom? The fate of diversity disputes in organizations. *Journal of Social Issues, 50*, 139–155.

Drake, L. E., & Donohue, W. A. (1996). Communicative framing theory in conflict resolution. *Communication Research, 23*, 297–322.

Fisher, R. J. (1994). Generic principles for resolving intergroup conflict. *Journal of Social Issues, 50*, 47–66.

Gastil, J. (1993). Identifying obstacles to small group democracy. *Small Group Research, 24*, 5–27.

Janis, I. L. (1982). *Groupthink: Psychological studies of policy decisions and fiascoes.* Boston: Houghton Mifflin.

Kameda, T., & Sugimori, S. (1993). Psychological entrapment in group decision making: An assigned decision rule and a groupthink phenomenon. *Journal of Personality and Social Psychology, 65*, 282–292.

Kirchmeyer, C., & Cohen, A. (1992). Multicultural groups: Their performance and reactions with constructive conflict. *Group & Organization Management, 17*, 153–170.

Kraus, G. (1997). The psychodynamics of constructive aggression in small groups. *Small Group Research, 28*, 122–145.

Kroon, M. B. R., Kreveld, D., & Rabbie, J. M. (1992). Group versus individual decision making: Effects of accountability and gender on groupthink. *Small Group Research, 23*, 427–458.

Lipnack, J., & Stamps, J. (1997). *Virtual teams: Reaching across space, time, and organizations with technology.* New York: Wiley.

Mifflin, L. (1996, June 30). Muppet diplomacy: Israelis, Palestinians work to create a bicultural "Sesame Street." *Detroit Free Press*, pp. 1J, 4J.

Miranda, S. M. (1994). Avoidance of groupthink: Meeting management using group support systems. *Small Group Research, 25*, 105–136.

Mohamed, A. A., & Wiebe, F. A. (1996). Toward a process theory of groupthink. *Small Group Research, 27*, 416–430.

Moorhead, G., Ference, R., & Neck, C. P. (1991). Group decision fiascoes continue: Space shuttle *Challenger* and a revised groupthink framework. *Human Relations, 44*, 539–550.

Mullen, B., Anthony, T., Salas, E., & Driskell, J. E. (1994). Group cohesiveness and quality of decision making: An integration of tests of the groupthink hypothesis. *Small Group Research, 25*, 180–204.

Neck, C. P., & Manz, C. C. (1994). From groupthink to teamthink: Toward the creation of constructive thought patterns in self-managing work teams. *Human Relations, 47*, 929–950.

Neck, C. P., & Moorhead, G. (1993). Jury deliberations in the trial of *U.S.* v. *John DeLorean*: A case analysis of groupthink avoidance and an enhanced framework. *Human Relations, 45*, pp. 1077–1091.

O'Connor, K. M., Gruenfeld, D. H., & McGrath, J. E. (1993). The experience and effects of conflict in continuing work groups. *Small Group Research, 24*, 362–382.

Ostmann, A. (1992). On the relationship between formal conflict structure and the social field. *Small Group Research, 23*, 26–48.

Pearce, W. B. (1976). The coordinated management of meaning: A rules-based theory of interpersonal communication. In G. R. Miller (Ed.), *Explorations in interpersonal communication.* Beverly Hills, CA: Sage.

Pearce, W. B., & Conklin, F. (1979). A model of hierarchical meanings in coherent conversation and a study of "indirect responses." *Communication Monographs, 46,* 75–87.

Pearce, W. B., & Cronen, V. E. (1980). *Communication, action, and meaning: The creation of social realities.* New York: Praeger.

Rosen, N. (1989). *Teamwork and the bottom line: Groups make a difference.* Hillsdale, NJ: Erlbaum.

Rubin, J. Z. (1994). Models of conflict management. *Journal of Social Issues, 50,* 33–45.

Stewart, R. A., Jr. (1988). Habitability and behavioral issues of space flight. *Small Group Behavior, 19,* 434–451.

Street, M. D., & Anthony, W. P. (1997). A conceptual framework establishing the relationship between groupthink and escalating commitment behavior. *Small Group Research, 28,* 267–293.

Thalhofer, N. N. (1993). Intergroup differentiation and reduction of intergroup conflict. *Small Group Research, 24,* 28–43.

Wong, C. L., Tjosvold, D., & Lee, F. (1992). Managing conflict in a diverse work force: A Chinese perspective in North America. *Small Group Research, 23,* 302–321.

6 The Problem-Solving Process

CHAPTER OBJECTIVES

After reading this chapter, you should be able to

- List the steps in the reflective-thinking process and the tasks accomplished in each step of the process
- Describe recent research findings on the problem-solving process
- Frame a problem-solving question
- Determine how to gather information about a problem
- Discuss the importance of sharing information
- Apply the tests of information
- Describe how to reason from information to an analysis of a problem
- Describe the rules for brainstorming
- Describe the process of developing and applying criteria to evaluate solutions
- Develop and apply criteria to evaluate possible solutions
- Develop an agenda for a problem-solving discussion

The Narratives

Thea Gast, 65, is a resident of Arcata, California, where she moved in 1961 when her husband started the oceanography program at Humboldt State University. Thea is active in a variety of community groups, ranging from her church fellowship to the League of Women Voters. In 1982, she was elected to the city council and served two four-year terms, including two years as mayor. Here she describes a problem faced by one of the groups of which she is a member.

An activity I'm especially proud of is my involvement with a Sister City project between Arcata and Camoapa, Nicaragua. The cities of Arcata and Camoapa adopted each other as sister cities in May of 1986; as mayor, I signed the official resolution. At the end of 1987, we had our first exchange. Somebody donated an old school bus that the community filled full of medical and school supplies, materials for remodeling the health clinic, and other things. Several people went with the bus to Camoapa, and others flew. After the bus arrived, the group used the materials to help in remodeling and cleaning up the health clinic. I decided that, to make this really official, the mayor needed to go. So I flew there on that first group trip. Later trips focused on various projects. Groups of doctors and dentists went to do medical work. One group built an addition to the health clinic. Another worked on a latrine project. We also paid some volunteers to stay in Camoapa for several months each to teach English as a second language.

However, as we approached our tenth anniversary in 1996, the participation in the project had slacked off. About six of us were really actively involved, and we were getting burned out. We knew it was a valuable project and did not want to see it die. But we could not continue to spend as much time on it as we had in the past. We had a problem we needed to solve: how to reactivate a group of people that would be involved in the Sister City project.

We realized that there was a problem because even when we contacted people to come to our monthly meetings, using our calling list, they would not show up at the meetings. Earlier, anywhere from a dozen to twenty people had gone to meetings, but now only six of us were there. Also, our annual fund-raiser, the I Street Block Party, had made most of the money for the Sister City project. But we began having fewer volunteers, making it more and more difficult to put on that event. So we were not getting the funds we needed. We needed to get more people involved so that we could get the funds needed to continue our relationship with Camoapa.

At our January meeting in 1996, we decided to look at the positives first. We listed all of our accomplishments. Then we said, "What are our main problems?" What we came up with was that we had a waning leadership. We just did not have enough people involved. So we began talking about what we could do about it. We decided we needed to ask for help to revitalize the project and give it a new direction. We planned to address this issue at our February meeting.

For that meeting we decided to invite people who had been involved in the past—past members or participants in groups that had gone to Nicaragua, people who were interested or had in some way participated. At the February meeting we would brainstorm solutions.

In February, about the same number of people showed up, even though we had tried to get more to come. However, a couple of older members had come. One person who had been involved at the beginning and had not been coming for years was there; he was committed to keeping the project alive, although he was not able to become part of the leadership himself. At least he was there to try to help figure out what to do. Another person there was Julie Fulkerson, who had been on the council with me, was mayor, and currently was on the Board of Supervisors. She was known for her problem-solving ability, so I made sure that we met when she could come.

In our brainstorming, we talked about what we could do. We had generated some ideas during our January meeting, so we began by listing those. Then we wrote other ideas down on the chalkboard as we got them. We talked about cooperating with other organizations, like the Rotary Club. We discussed targeting certain people to get them involved. Then Julie asked, "Do you have money?" We said we did. And she said, "Why don't you hire somebody who would help with this?" When that idea was mentioned, it felt like a big relief to all of us. We knew a lot of work was needed to keep this program going, and the few of us that were there did not really have time to do those things—approach the media, whatever it was—necessary to keep this going.

When we heard Julie's idea, we thought it was a great idea. We agreed to it, but not without some discussion. One of my concerns was just how this could be done. How do you really get an organization going by hiring somebody to do something? I've felt that our group lacked structure and that was something that needed to change. So the rest of the meeting we talked about how we were going to do it. We suggested names of people that we knew to contact about getting *us a proposal. We talked about what someone we would hire would do—approaching other clubs and schools, putting out publicity, perhaps organizing a new project to stimulate interest.*

Ultimately we hired someone who had been to Camoapa more than once and knew all about the Sister City project. We felt very comfortable with her taking the project on. We agreed to work with her in getting started, trying to stimulate more activity and getting more people involved. She worked last summer and fall, organizing slide shows that were presented to various community organizations.

A lot has happened since then. We have built an association with another organization, called El Porvenir, which works in Nicaragua, mainly with water and wastewater projects. About six people from here went to Camoapa with them in January during the break at Humboldt State University. Most of them were students. When they returned, they became active in the Sister City project and organized a student group at Humboldt State University. The Planned Parenthood organization here adopted the clinic in Camoapa as their sister clinic. The Rotary Club agreed to fund a project. With the new people involved in the organization, I think that we will be talking more about the structure of the group and how we want that to change.

During our brainstorming meeting in 1996, someone mentioned that one solution to our problem would be to give up the Sister City project. But we did not want to do that because things in Nicaragua have gotten worse instead of better over the years. They can use as much help as we can give. But we are not only helping; we get a lot from them too. When you learn a different way of living—a new culture—it is very broadening to one's own sense of the world.

Raymond Kennelly, 36, was hired in 1995 as Director of Admissions at Xavier University, a Jesuit institution in Cincinnati, Ohio. Here he describes the problem-solving efforts made as Xavier worked to increase its student enrollment.

Up until 1969, Xavier University was all male and almost strictly a commuter school. In our fairly recent history, quite a transformation has occurred. The Xavier of today is a fundamentally different place from the Xavier of 30 years ago. We are now coeducational and more of a residential campus for our undergraduate population. When our current president arrived here in 1993, he set out what he referred to as "Xavier 2000," a plan for the university from that point until the year 2000. A big portion of the plan related to enrollment. In 1993, the school had about 2700 full-time undergraduates. But the president said that, with the classroom capacity we had, we should be at about 3200 full-time undergraduates by the year 2000. The entire campus community has collaborated in efforts to meet the goal set by the president. The part of his vision related to enrollment was turned over to the enrollment services area, which includes the admissions office.

It was apparent that we could not really increase our recruiting within the Cincinnati market. We were already recruiting a very large number of students from within a 30-mile radius of the campus. Relying on local commuters to increase our enrollment was not realistic. So we knew that we had to go outside of our region and become more national.

Whenever visitors come to campus, we ask them to fill out an evaluation. From the evaluations we were receiving, it became apparent that, although our campus was nice, it certainly was not as welcoming as it could be. Busy, active streets dissected campus. To increase the attractiveness of the campus and add to its residential nature, those streets were closed, then torn up and replaced with red brick walkways. Trees, benches, fountains, and new entrance gates were put in. The physical transformation was incredible. But the impact on the visitors has been just as incredible. Now visitors come away with a much stronger sense of place.

I came to Xavier when these plans were in their early implementation stages. After I got here, I was part of a decision to shift our athletic conference. The athletic director wanted the reaction of our office to the impact on enrollment that would come if we changed from the Midwest Collegiate

Conference to the Atlantic Ten. We supported the change for a number of reasons. In our efforts to grow enrollments, we were looking heavily to the east, to places like Philadelphia, Pittsburgh, the D.C. area, and Boston. We felt there was a great potential for recruiting for Xavier in those areas that was not being realized. We knew that from looking at the number of high-school graduates and the general willingness of students in those areas to travel beyond their borders for college. They were cities with fairly high Catholic populations. That ia a big draw for Xavier—the large number of Catholic high schools in those areas. Other Jesuit universities are located in those areas, so people are more familiar with a Jesuit education. Some other schools in Ohio were having success at attracting students from the east, including Wittenberg, where I had spent seven years prior to coming here. From that experience, I felt Xavier certainly could be effective, too.

Being in the Atlantic Ten offered us some exposure that we knew would only help us. We knew that if Xavier was out playing basketball games in the east, it would only enhance anything else that we might be doing out there. Besides, the conference itself has a higher profile and greater TV exposure. When you go into new markets, from an admissions point of view, name recognition will make or break you. If students do not recognize the name of your school—if it is not even remotely familiar to them—the reality is that it is not likely that they are going to consider you. We knew that when the basketball team started playing out there on a fairly regular basis and in televised games, the name recognition would help us. Not that people would come here because we have a good basketball team, but when they got something in the mail from Xavier, at least they would say, "Oh, yeah, I have heard of that school." And that increases the likelihood that they will open and read what you send them. That could translate into enrollments.

I think it was a fairly creative idea. USA Today did a story on us because they had not encountered any other campus that incorporated a conference-affiliation shift as part of a strategic plan. It was actually a stated part of a plan to enhance the university.

In the fall of 1995, we had 701 new students, below the goal of 750. In the fall of 1996, we had 787 freshmen—the largest freshman class in Xavier's history. We barely had space for all of them. We converted study rooms and computer lounges into bedrooms. We had to be creative, because it was beyond our expectations. I got a lot of congratulations. It was a huge increase from one year to the next. The interesting thing is that as classes have grown, they have been academically stronger as well, so it is not as if we are filling up the spaces just to fill them up.

This has been a four-year process so far, and it is still ongoing. I think the key is that we are all incredibly excited at the results we are achieving. It is working in ways that people could not have envisioned when the plans were initially put in place. My assessment as a more recent entry to the process is that this is working because of broad-based collaboration. Everybody at Xavier has to play a part in this. This is not the president alone or the board of trustees implementing this . It is not just the basketball team going out and winning some games. There is a sense here that all the oars are pulling together. And that takes time. It has taken three, four years of ongoing meetings, deliberations, and communications to gain the support of an entire community. I think this would have failed miserably if it had just been a presidential mandate. Without the support of everybody else, it just would not have worked.

The Importance of Problem Solving to Small Groups

Small groups regularly face situations in which they need to solve problems. Sometimes the problems are internal to the group and relate to its own future. For instance, you have just read Thea Gast's description of the problem the Sister City Committee faced when, after ten years, energy had drained from the committee. Committed to continuing the Sister City project, the committee itself represented a problem in need of solution. Groups that struggle to become productive, as well as those that have passed beyond the stage of productivity into issues of quality and fairness, discover—upon self-reflection—that the group itself has internal problems in need of solution.

Still other groups are formed with the charge of solving a problem external to the group. The campus groups Ray Kennelly described at Xavier University have worked on the general problem of increasing student enrollment and on the many specific issues related to that broad task. Work groups frequently form to tackle a problem, such as increasing efficiency, broadening a market, or developing a new product. Similarly, community groups often form because there is a problem affecting the lives of the citizens. Groups that hope to reroute traffic to increase pedestrian safety or to find ways to attract physicians to an area that can then have adequate health care are examples of groups that charge themselves with solving a problem.

If you are a member of a group in a small group communication class, you are undoubtedly asked to solve problems on multiple occasions. Some may be problems that can be resolved within a brief period of time (if you are given all of the information necessary and do not need to implement the solution). Some problems, if they relate to long-term projects you must complete, require several meetings and a good deal of persistence to resolve. Yet even classroom groups can be successful in remedying problems. For instance, student groups from classes such as yours have succeeded in getting a traffic light installed at a dangerous intersection, getting the cooperation of the university library staff to extend study hours during exam time or to monitor noise levels in the library, and increasing communication within their university by organizing and hosting an informal forum with their university president. Other groups have developed successful training sessions for their classmates on subjects ranging from managing diversity in small groups to adapting small group communication skills to the therapeutic group setting.

In short, whether a group is a classroom group or a community group, a short-term or a long-term group, it is probably faced with the task of solving a problem, one either internal or external to the group. This chapter considers the process involved when small groups solve problems. The material in this chapter is also relevant to the task facing some groups who must make a decision on an issue (which applicant to hire, which equipment to purchase, which students to admit). As you will discover in reading this chapter, the latter stages in the problem-solving process involve making a decision about which solution to implement. For groups faced with the task of making a decision, Chapter 7 is also useful, because it will consider a variety of formats that groups can employ to assist them in making their decisions. In this chapter, however, we first consider a process described nearly a century ago and then focus on the skills group members must utilize to solve problems effectively.

The Reflective Thinking Process and Beyond:
A Theoretical Perspective

John Dewey's Reflective Thinking Process

Early in the twentieth century, in 1910, an educational and political philosopher by the name of John Dewey published a book entitled *How We Think;* decades later, Frey (1996) wrote that "the impact of Dewey's ideas on group communication and decision-making research . . . cannot be underestimated" (p. 21). Dewey argued that educational systems needed to direct attention to teaching students to think critically, not just to memorize facts. Dewey described the kind of mental activity he was encouraging as **reflective thought,** which he defined as *active, persistent, and careful consideration of any belief or supposed form of knowledge in the light of the grounds that support it, and the further conclusions to which it tends* (Dewey, 1910, p. 6). Dewey explained that such thinking was initiated when some difficulty arose that inspired individuals to think their way out of it. In the process of thinking reflectively, the individuals would "maintain the state of doubt and . . . carry on systematic and protracted inquiry" (p. 13) in order to test inferences and select among alternatives.

Dewey (1910) outlined "five logically distinct steps" (p. 72) central to the reflective-thinking process: (1) a felt difficulty arises; (2) it is located and defined; (3) possible solutions are suggested; (4) the implications of the suggested solutions are reasoned; and (5) after further observation and experimentation, a solution is accepted or rejected. With the development of courses in small group discussion in the early twentieth century, Dewey's reflective-thinking process was adopted as a process that groups ought to follow in solving problems. Consider, for instance, how the five steps relate to the process Thea Gast described when the Sister City committee attempted to solve its problem.

As committee members realized that there were too few of them and that each of them felt overcommitted, they were experiencing "a felt difficulty." By asking themselves how they could reenergize the Sister City committee, they were locating and defining the problem. Dewey explained that

> the first and second steps frequently fuse into one. The difficulty may be felt with sufficient definiteness as to set the mind at once speculating upon its probable solution, or an undefined uneasiness and shock may come first, leading only later to [a] definite attempt to find out what is the matter. (p. 72)

In this particular instance, the felt difficulty was perceived with enough specificity that its definition was closely linked to its perception. However, if the group members had defined the difficulty differently—perhaps by asking themselves how they could reduce their own stresses—they might have had a very different sense of what problem they were trying to solve.

After deciding what their problem was, the committee members held a special meeting to discuss possible solutions. Dewey argued that "the essence of critical thinking is suspended judgment" (p. 74). Judgment can be suspended, first, by delaying attempts at solution until the nature of the problem has been determined and, second,

After traveling to Camoapa, Nicaragua, and meeting with its residents, including this hatmaker, Thea Gast (right) felt committed to retaining the Sister City Program. The problem, however, was finding a way to reenergize the Sister City Committee. (Photo compliments of Thea Gast.)

by exploring a variety of alternative solutions. In the case of the Sister City committee, the group understood its problem prior to considering solutions. In the meeting at which they considered solutions, multiple solutions to the group's problem were proposed, but the group quickly recognized the appeal of hiring someone to help the group. Still, they did not rush to implement it. Instead, they talked at length about the implications of that option. Only after considerable deliberation did the group proceed to implement its solution, and even now they continue to appraise its impact. The processes of the group followed those advocated by John Dewey quite closely.

In recent years, as U.S. educators have explored the need to improve students' critical thinking skills, they have returned to the philosophy of John Dewey. In the field of small group communication, Dewey's prescriptions for reflective thinking have been tested by researchers who have tried to determine whether problem-solving groups typically follow the five steps of the reflective-thinking process and whether there is a difference in the quality of solutions devised by groups that do follow the reflective-thinking process and those that are less systematic or that follow a different system.

Contemporary Research on Problem Solving

One scholar who has devoted research and theory development to the study of decision processes is Marshall Scott Poole. Poole (1983) has argued that rather than following the systematic, step-by-step process envisioned by Dewey (1910), decision-making groups follow three distinct tracks at once—a relational track, a topic track, and the task-process track. He wrote that "when the development of the tracks converges in a coherent pattern, phases similar to those in classic research may be found. However, at other points there may be no relationship among the tracks and therefore no recognizable phases" (p. 326). Even within a given track, there will be break points created by delays in group members' comprehension of issues, by the incubation period preceding highly creative or difficult work in the group, and/or by disruptions caused by conflict or failure within the group. However, Poole recognized that accomplishing the decision task required a number of steps, including those identified by Dewey: recognizing the need for a decision, defining and diagnosing the problem, searching for and generating solutions, adapting the solution to the group's needs, reaching consensus on criteria to be used in evaluating the solution, selecting the solution, and then planning its implementation.

Another scholar whose research agenda has been closely tied to studies of group problem-solving processes is Randy Y. Hirokawa. Among the studies Hirokawa has done are several in which he recorded the interactions of groups of students who were asked to solve a problem he gave them. Experts then evaluated the quality of the groups' solutions on grounds such as the workability of the solutions, their financial feasibility, and their political potential. Next, Hirokawa compared the interactions of the most effective groups (those judged as having the best solutions) with those of the least effective groups (those judged as having the poorest solutions) to discover how their processes differed.

In one study, for which group members were asked to rank the usefulness of a series of items for travel on the moon, Hirokawa (1980) found that effective groups interacted on procedural issues more than ineffective groups did. However, in a later study, when students were asked to solve a problem related to the highway system in an urban area, Hirokawa (1983b) found that it was the ineffective groups that spent greater time on procedural issues. In this case, with a more complex problem—and constrained by a time limit—effective groups devoted a greater portion of their time to analyzing the problem and the potential effectiveness of their solution than they did to discussing the procedure to follow in making a decision. Although the studies did find somewhat contradictory results, they are consistent in discovering that groups must have a clear idea of what they are up against before they consider possible solutions. That finding was confirmed in another study in which Hirokawa (1983a) discovered that ineffective groups began their deliberations by evaluating possible solutions. Their more effective counterparts began, instead, by analyzing the problem. Only after they had a good sense of the difficulty they faced did effective groups begin to consider specific solutions.

In yet another study, Hirokawa and Pace (1983) found that effective and ineffective groups shared some communication behaviors: members of both types of groups participated relatively equally, tried to identify relevant facts and information, generated several alternative solutions, and used criteria to evaluate solutions. What distinguished the effective from the ineffective groups in that case was the thoroughness of the effective groups' evaluations of possible solutions in contrast with the quick, superficial evaluations made by ineffective groups.

Hirokawa did not find that successful groups all operate in the same manner, nor that they follow the reflective-thinking process systematically. In fact, in one study, when groups were trained to use the reflective-thinking process or other systems of problem solving, the format used did not explain the effectiveness of the groups (Hirokawa, 1985). Instead, it was the completion of specific requirements—or functions (specifically, a thorough understanding of the problem, identification of possible realistic solutions, and discovery of the positive and negative outcomes that might come from an alternative)— that distinguished effective from ineffective groups. Such findings led Hirokawa and his research colleagues to articulate and test a **functional perspective,** *a set of theoretical assumptions that identify the role of communication in small groups as a tool that can lead groups toward effective decision choices and away from poor ones by ensuring that important functions in the decision-making and problem-solving processes are completed* (Gouran, Hirokawa, Julian, & Leatham, 1991).

Together, the findings of Hirokawa's research support the idea that thorough ("vigilant") critical thinking is related to effective problem solving, that effective groups engage in problem analysis prior to considering potential solutions, and that the kinds of thought Dewey had identified are involved in the critical evaluation processes that effective groups use (see also Hirokawa, 1987, 1988, 1990). Therefore, the remainder of this chapter focuses on the basic steps involved in the effective problem-solving process and the skills involved in thinking critically about a problem and its solution.

The Essential Stages of Effective Problem Solving

By definition, all problem solving entails, first, a consideration of the existence, nature, scope, and consequences of what is initially perceived to be a problem and, second, the devising, evaluation, implementation, and (if necessary) subsequent revision of the solution to that problem. This is not to say, however, that all problem-solving discussions end with a solution. Indeed, it is possible that the perception that a problem exists is changed as a result of a group's analysis of the problem.

The essentials of the problem-solving process include three distinct stages: (1) the framing of the problem-solving question, (2) analysis of the perceived problem, and (3) consideration of possible solutions to the problem. So that you can understand both the importance of each stage and how each is enacted, each of these stages is examined in further detail.

Stage One: Framing the Problem-Solving Question

Individuals and groups may begin to use a problem-solving process or format overtly when they perceive that a problem exists—that is, when they develop that sense of a problem that Dewey (1910) called the "felt difficulty." It is the purpose of the framing stage for a group to articulate these perceptions of the problem so that the process may continue productively. Otherwise the group members may take stabs at actions that they hope might solve their problems, but waste their efforts with stabs in the dark. You can understand how that might happen if you consider times when you start to feel a little out of sorts. If you select a standard response (perhaps you treat yourself to an ice cream cone or you go for a jog), you may get lucky, and your problem may evaporate. But if the cause of your undefined but unpleasant feeling is that you have not prepared for an upcoming exam, these diversional tactics could add to your "felt difficulty" rather than diminish it. Until you can articulate your difficulty, you cannot realistically and productively consider how to solve the problem.

You might frame a very general question such as, "What, if anything, should I do to put my feelings on course?" Such a question does not provide much direction for your efforts at remedying the felt difficulty, however. After a bit of introspection you would probably be able to identify the nature of your problem more specifically and formulate a more specific problem-solving question such as, "How can I increase my mastery of the exam material?" The more specific question could then lead you into the next stages of the problem-solving process in a more direct and specific way. It is also possible that upon reflection, you discover that your feeling out of sorts was a simply a passing mood and no further action to resolve a problem needs to be taken.

Comparison with Framing a Conflict.   Framing a problem-solving question bears some resemblance to framing a conflict, as discussed in Chapter 5. Both framing processes are attempts to put a finger on the problem at hand, to identify what is amiss and in need of resolution. In both cases, the framing process draws boundaries around the issues to be considered, narrowing and structuring the range of the subsequent discussion. There are differences between the two processes, however. In the case of a conflict between group members, framing the conflict identifies the nature of the issue on which the parties disagree (perhaps a relationship issue; perhaps a factual issue). In contrast, framing the problem-solving question identifies both an area of agreement (that there is a problem) and the area of uncertainty (as to how it should be resolved) that the group members will need to resolve through discussion. It may be that members of the group will initially disagree on the answer to the question, and it may even be that the group will never reach consensus on a solution. By framing the problem-solving question, however, the group at least has a focus for its subsequent discussion.

Wording a Question.   Your group will have framed a problem effectively when you have formulated a question that acknowledges the existence of a problem (such as a lack of mastery of the exam material) and asks—in an open-ended manner—how the problem might be solved ("How can I increase my mastery . . . "). To further understand the nature of a good problem-solving question, contrast the following pairs of questions:

How can we reactivate the Sister City committee?	*Should we cease the Sister City program?*
How can we increase applications to Xavier University?	*Should we change basketball leagues?*

Both of the questions on the left effectively frame the problems faced by a group you read about in the narratives. The first one identifies the problem as a lack of energy and asks how to alter the situation. The second one identifies the problem as too few applications and asks how to increase them. In contrast, each of the questions on the right identifies a specific course of action and, with a closed question, asks whether the group should support or reject that alternative. Although each question on the right was ultimately considered by the problem-solving groups, neither question framed the problem for the groups. In fact, a group that begins its deliberations by focusing on a single possible solution before it has analyzed the problem is engaging in one of the behaviors which Hirokawa's (1983a) research found to be characteristic of ineffective groups rather than effective ones.

As terms are used in the problem-solving question, they should be defined so that the participants can develop a common vocabulary to describe their understanding of what it is they expect to accomplish. Language unfamiliar to some members of a group naturally needs to be defined so that each member of the group understands what issue they are considering. Sometimes, even familiar language requires definition for the group to have a shared understanding of the question. For example, in the fall of 1997, the city council in Mt. Pleasant, Michigan, met to consider this problem-solving question, "How can we ensure that off-campus housing for university students does not lead to the deterioration of family neighborhoods?" An important step in their problem-solving process was developing a definition of "family" that all members of the council could understand and agree to as an acceptable distinction between neighborhoods for families and neighborhoods for nonfamilies.

Adjusting the Question. Often, as the problem-solving process continues, the members of the group return to the question's wording and revise it to reflect understandings and opinions that emerge from the later stages of the process. For instance, when the new president of Xavier University established a goal of increasing the student body so as to make better use of the campus facilities, the group charged with meeting his goals was trying to answer this question: "How can we increase the student body by 500 students?" As the group discovered that there was not a problem with retaining students once they were admitted to the university, the question could be narrowed to ask, "How can we attract 750 first-year students?" When further analysis revealed that the local market of students had already been tapped to its fullest potential, the question was reframed once again: "How can we increase our attractiveness to high-school graduates from other areas?" Finally, when the group discovered that the eastern region was an untapped source of potential students, the question became "How can we increase our attractiveness to high school graduates from the East?" In this example, the question became narrower with each step, but other changes are certainly possible. A student group that initially believes that they want to increase parking spaces on their campus might discover that the real problem is that current parking regulations are not enforced. They will need to reframe their problem-solving question to focus the group's attention on the new understanding of the difficulty.

Stage Two: Analysis of the Perceived Problem

In the second stage of the problem-solving process, group members try to determine whether a problem actually exists, i.e., whether the perception of a problem is confirmed upon analysis of the relevant facts. If a problem does, in fact, exist, the members also seek to determine its nature, scope, and effects and its cause or causes. In essence, the group answers such questions as, "What happened that led us to consider this to be a problem?," "Who has been affected by this problem?," "How have they been affected?," "How serious are the impacts?," "Why did this problem develop?," and "How did the problem develop?" The process of analysis begins with the data related to these questions that group members have gathered from research and leads to judgments about the data that have been gathered—or answers to these questions. The essential processes involved in a group's analysis of the problem include gathering, testing, and sharing information, and reasoning from the information. Each of these steps in the analysis process is considered.

Gathering Information.   Group members cannot make sound judgments about the nature and causes of a problem—or, for that matter, about later stages of analysis—unless they have sound information to serve as the basis for those judgments. They should not assume, however, that the process of information gathering is entirely external to themselves.

Assessing Member Information.   In fact, the starting place in the information-gathering process should be careful reflection by each group member about his or her own experiences and understandings relevant to the topic at hand. Most likely, a wealth of information already exists within the group.

The narratives at the beginning of this chapter provide adequate illustration of the tremendous resources groups have at hand prior to engaging in systematic data collection efforts. No amount of library research could have given Thea Gast more information on the value of the exchange program with Camoapa than the information she had gained from being there herself. The Sister City committee members already knew, also, the limits of their own busy schedules and the amount of money they had in their treasury. Ray Kennelly did not have to begin a study of the potential for an Ohio university to attract students from the East Coast; his own experience in admissions at another college in the state had given him that information. The staff at Xavier University also already knew how successful they had been at recruiting students from the Cincinnati region, the importance of name recognition in recruiting potential students, and the amount of television exposure available to basketball teams in the Atlantic Ten. In your own case, when you are involved in a problem-solving process, you should begin to gather data by stopping to think about what you already know that is relevant to the topic. And, because well-constructed groups include members with diverse backgrounds and information resources, a second step should be to reflect on the information other group members are likely to know that is relevant to the topic that you can draw out from them with effective questions.

Acquiring Additional Resources.   It is possible that the group has within its membership all of the information necessary. It is more likely that some added information will need to be gathered to fill in holes in the database the group needs for making well-informed decisions. Among the resources that can be used at this point are libraries, electronic sources, organizations with an interest in the subject, and surveys. Books, magazines, journals, newspapers, and government documents are among the resources available in libraries. Relevant sources can be identified in most college libraries through the use of electronic databases. Electronic databases are regularly updated, which is both an advantage and, potentially, a disadvantage to you. The advantage is obvious: up-to-date information is continually added. But as new information is added to some databases, less-recent information will be deleted, even if it is information that might still be relevant to the search you are conducting. To have access to that material, you may need to search through indexes in print form. For instance such volumes as the *New York Times Index*, the *Education Index*, or the *Humanities Index* could lead you to some older but still valuable information. Even if you are trying to solve a local problem, it is quite possible that there is published information about a similar problem in other places that will be helpful to you. For instance, a group concerned with an issue of free speech on its own campus is likely to find information about other campuses with similar problems in news magazines and in the weekly newspaper, *The Chronicle of Higher Education*, which covers subjects relevant to colleges and universities.

Information is available on the Internet that could be useful to you, too. You need to be certain, however, that you keep a record of both the information itself and its source. The fact that something appears on the Internet does not stand as proof of its validity. As is the case with all information you might gather, you need to evaluate it carefully yourself and encourage the group to evaluate it in the process of discussion, using the standards discussed later in this chapter.

Organizations may be valuable resources to use as you gather information. For instance, a group that is trying to reduce the dangers of secondhand smoke in your community would find useful information in publications of the American Lung Association and the American Cancer Society. A group addressing a problem of date rape on your campus might find relevant information available at a rape-crisis center, women's shelter, police department, or campus counseling office.

There are times when surveys of others outside your group can be used to generate valuable information for your group. At Xavier University, surveys of prospective students who had come to campus for a visit provided useful information about

Ethical Consideration

The purpose of research is to enable the group to arrive at the best possible analysis of the subject. To that end, group members should be open to all relevant information, even if it does not lend support to their own positions, and should use only information that passes the "Tests of Information."

visitors' perceptions of the campus. Similarly, a committee working on improving child-care options within a community might interview a cross section of individuals to gauge the nature and extent of the problem for the respondents. Carefully worded questions are important if useful information is to be generated by the survey. The suggestions given in Chapter 4 on asking good questions can serve as a useful checklist in evaluating your survey. In administering the survey, avoid simply asking a few people you know (whose positions you already know) to confirm your preconceptions. You might test your sample survey on those people so that you can detect problems with the survey before using it with a broader group of respondents, but then seek reactions to the survey from respondents who best represent the group impacted by the issue you are considering.

After you have added the information from libraries, electronic sources, organizations, and survey results to your own store of information, you are prepared to tap another resource: the expertise of others whom you can interview. Although some experts are willing to give you a lot of generally available background information, others will be annoyed if you use them just as a shortcut. Moreover, your time is not likely to be used well if you have not developed a solid grasp of the issues through background research before the interview occurs. When using an interview as the source of information, you may find these recommendations helpful:

1. Identify who the best source(s) of the information you need will be.

2. Arrange for an interview ahead of time that is convenient for everyone involved. Your group may want more than one member to attend the interview. Be careful, however, of having a larger group present than you need to accomplish the task.

3. Develop a set of questions you want to ask. You might even share these with the person you have arranged to interview so that he or she has a chance to think about them ahead of time.

4. If having the exact wording of the answers is important to you, seek permission to tape record the interview. If exact wording is not important, or if permission is not granted, you should still be prepared to take notes so that you do not rely only on your memory to recall the points made during the interview. If several members of the group are present, their shared recall may be sufficient to ensure an accurate representation of the responses.

5. Listen carefully to the answers you are given and adapt your planned questions to the answers you have received. If there is more than one group member present, you will need to have developed a strategy for handling the interview that is comfortable for your group members and your respondent. When an answer is given, if it is not clear to you, ask for clarification rather than pretending to understand.

6. Follow the guidelines for good questions and follow-up questions described in Chapter 4 of this text.

Student groups have access to experts in a variety of academic areas on their campus. Any community contains residents who have developed expertise in a wide range of areas. Using their knowledge can add to the resources of a group.

It is important to consider the wide range of resources available to a group and attempt to gain access to the information. Even a group with members skilled in the use of appropriate analytical methods is constrained in its problem solving if it is unable to access all the relevant data. The resultant incomplete or inaccurate analysis of the problem may lead to an ineffective solution. In fact, Hirokawa and Keyton (1995) found that members of work teams reported inadequate information as one of the most important factors inhibiting their success—second only to inadequate time to meet as teams.

Dividing the Information-Gathering Efforts among the Group.   Groups have an advantage over individuals in the data-gathering process because they can distribute the responsibilities for discovering information among the members. It is useful, first, to distribute the responsibility for generating a list of resources to be examined and, second, to distribute the responsibility for examining those resources. Suppose that a four-member group has decided to address a problem on their campus of intolerance for diversity. They might first decide on these responsibilities:

Abbas: Check to see whether the Minority Student Advisor and the Office for International Education have information. Check copies of the campus newspaper for stories about relevant incidents on campus.

Beth: Check to see what information is indexed in the library's electronic databases.

Cameron: Check the *New York Times Index* and the Internet.

Darcy: Develop a rough draft of a questionnaire to use in surveying students. Check the index of *The Chronicle of Higher Education.*

Together: Generate a list of individuals with information on the topic who might be interviewed.

After the group members have generated the list of sources available, then they can again divide their responsibilities for gathering and processing the actual information, perhaps in this way:

Abbas: Read the booklets gathered from the offices visited. Interview the leader of the Arabic student group about the harassment members received recently. Survey 15 students. Compile a list of relevant incidents from the campus paper.

Beth: Read the government hearings on hate-crime statistics and hate-crime sentencing. Survey 15 students. Interview member of the Gay and Lesbian Coalition about the harassment members received recently.

Cameron: Skim through the two books Beth discovered in the library. Read the Winter 1996 issue of *Diogenes*, which is devoted to the topic of intolerance. Survey 15 students.

Darcy: Read a series of articles in the *New York Times* on hate crimes on campuses and an article in the *Journal of Interpersonal Violence.* Interview sociology faculty member who teaches a course on resolving cultural conflicts. Survey 15 students.

By distributing (and sometimes redistributing) information-gathering responsibilities among the group members, a wealth of data can be gathered in much less time than any one group member alone would need to process that amount of material. This information, in addition to that already known by the members, can then be shared during a group discussion.

Sharing Information.   At any point in the analysis of a problem, it is seldom the case that any one group member has all of the information needed to make an informed decision. If a team—in which the members have divergent backgrounds, skills, and responsibilities—is engaged in problem solving, it is likely that each member comes to the meeting with different knowledge in store. Frequently, individuals are appointed as members of a group created to solve a problem precisely because each individual has a distinct interest and perspective on the problem not shared by other members, but valuable to the group as a whole. In any group, it is likely that the members have divided the responsibility for gathering information. There may be overlap in the information some members have; but if the whole group is to develop a shared sense of what the problem is, then group members must share their information.

You can avoid a trap into which many groups fall if you are aware of—and work to overcome—the fact that typical groups do not tap the full range of information available to them. For instance, Dennis (1996) studied information exchange in experimental groups he established. The groups were composed of six members, each of whom was given an information sheet containing data relevant to the task assigned to the group (selecting one of three student applicants for admission to the university). Some of the data were given to all group members and thus constituted "common information." Other pieces of information were "unique," that is, given to only one group member. Groups interacted to come to a decision as to which applicant should be admitted to the university. A lot of the available information was overlooked entirely. But in addition, rather than focusing on exchanging data not held by all group members, the groups emphasized common information in their discussions. Dennis found that, on the average, 64% of the common information was discussed within the groups, but only 35% of the unique information was discussed. The groups' decision making suffered as a result of the poor information exchange. Group members also restricted the information they shared to information that supported their individual decision preference, a practice which works to limit a group's opportunity to make a decision based on the fullest amount of information. A problem with the groups Dennis observed, as with others like them, was that they did not use communication within the group to its full potential, because good group discussion has the potential to allow "group members to distribute and pool informational resources needed for effective decision making and problem solving, . . . to identify and remedy errors in individual judgment, . . . [and] provide an opportunity for intragroup persuasion" (Gouran, Hirokawa, Julian, & Leatham, 1991, p. 581).

Even when a group member does speak up to integrate unique information, there is a danger that other members may not process it fully. Dennis (1996) observed that groups had particular difficulty integrating the unique information

Ethical Consideration

Members of groups should challenge themselves to discover (to the best of their abilities) the truth about the situation they are considering. Concealing information in order to protect their personal interests or the interests of a subgroup they represent deprives the group of information necessary to make freely a fully informed decision.

into their decision making. In other words, it was common for each member to make an individual decision based on the information received prior to the discussion. During the discussion in which unique information (or at least some of it) was exchanged, the new information was typically overlooked and members stuck with their early impressions. This observation led Dennis to recommend that decision-making sessions should not be held right on the heels of information-exchange sessions, but time should be provided to allow groups to integrate the new information into their thinking.

When individuals fail to share the information they have with other group members involved in a problem-solving or decision-making process, the results can be disastrous. Hirokawa, Gouran, and Martz (1988) describe the failure to communicate relevant information as one of the factors that led to the disastrous launch of the *Challenger* space shuttle in 1986. Another problem they identified was that available information was not heeded when it conflicted with the prior beliefs of group members. Obviously, sharing all of the information every group member has about a topic is difficult. But certainly, it is important for group members to share *relevant* information, particularly information that is unique to them. A standard test you can use to decide what is relevant is to ask this question: Does knowing this information make me *less* inclined to make the decision I had planned to make? If the answer is yes, then the information is relevant and should be shared. Groups then need to give attention to all shared information, especially information that challenges their initial assumptions. Only in that way does the group develop an accurate sense of the situation they confront.

Testing Information.   Before a group uses information gathered in research and shared within the discussion as a basis for a decision, the group members should take a preliminary step: to assess the source of the information and the information itself. Problem solvers need information that accurately describes and/or interprets the subject under investigation. Conclusions based upon inaccurate information can lead to inferior decisions about the existence, nature, causes, and extent of a problem and about ways and means of attempting to deal with it. For example, the 1990 census in the United States has been criticized because it may have underrepresented persons living in urban areas. Since decisions about the distribution of federal appropriations is based upon census data, such an undercount would seriously harm states with large urban populations.

Tests of Source.   Information always has at least one source—the person who has generated or gathered the raw data. Sometimes another person is responsible for interpreting the data and a third person for reporting these conclusions. At times, a single individual performs all three functions; at other times, the functions may be distributed among several people and only an organization is identifiable as the source. It is important that the problem solvers be aware of the real possibility that information may be unreliable either because the source lacked competence in gathering, interpreting, or reporting the information or because the source had a reason for misrepresenting or "slanting" the facts. The chain of information needs to be examined as closely as possible to exclude unreliable information from the decision-making process.

Two questions that group members should ask about sources are these:

1. Is the source of the information competent to gather, interpret, and report the information?
2. Is the source willing to gather, interpret, and report the information fairly?

If the source of the information fails either of these tests, the information is likely to be unreliable. When the Sister City committee in Arcata met to select someone to manage the group's activities, if one member of the group had had a relative applying for the position, that committee member might still have been competent to interpret the data about the qualifications of all applicants. However, due to the personal connections, he or she would have been suspect in the willingness to interpret and report the information fairly.

Of course, no source of information is likely to be ideal. Even competent persons can make mistakes, and no person is totally free from bias. In this sense, no information can be viewed as totally reliable. Passing the tests of source does, however, create a presumption that the information is probably reliable and able to be used by a group or individual. For example, suppose that a student has plans to eat dinner with his parents after classes one evening. If his mother informs him in the afternoon that his father will be home an hour late because he has to stop to get the car's oil changed, then the student might reasonably plan to study at the library for an hour after classes. He is relying on the information from his mother because she probably spoke with her husband and has no particular reason to mislead her son. But what if the father's plans have changed or if he can leave work early? Then the information provided by the mother may no longer be accurate. Thus, after testing the source(s) of information, it is also necessary to assess the information itself to determine its degree of accuracy.

Tests of the Information Itself.   In the example just given, the mother is relaying information based on a conversation she had with her husband before he left for work. Although the student received the information in the middle of the afternoon, his mother had received it in the morning. In the hours between, circumstances may have changed. Similarly, information appearing in a book published in 2000 may have been drawn from a study done in 1998 based upon data collected in 1996. The accurate date for the information is 1996, not the publication dates 1998 or 2000. These examples illustrate the **test of recency:** *Is the information sufficiently recent?*

There are some situations in which older information can be valuable to a group, but if the circumstances reported have changed since the observations were made, the information will fail the test of recency and ought to be discounted.

In addition to the test of recency, there are other tests for evaluating information that should be used. A second test, the **test for external consistency,** is related to an old saying that 50 million Frenchmen cannot be wrong. It is likely that when most sources of information agree and supply consistent information (as would be the case if 50 million Frenchmen shared one opinion) then the information itself is probably accurate. Thus, a test for external consistency can be applied to any given piece of information. The test asks this question: *Is the information consistent with information from different sources?* However, problem solvers need to be careful here. They should be careful not to assume that simply because some information is frequently repeated, it is accurate. Arkes (1993) called that faulty assumption the "validity effect." After reporting the results of studies in which frequently reported bits of inaccurate information were perceived as valid simply because of their frequent repetition, Arkes concluded, "I find this result to be quite troubling. . . . Note that no attempt has been made to persuade. No supporting arguments are offered. Mere repetition seems to increase rated validity" (pp. 13–14). Furthermore, it may be that the one piece of information that is inconsistent with the other information is the only accurate information available. Think of the many who thought the sun revolved around the earth until Copernicus proved otherwise. Or the several sources in agreement may actually be deriving their information from a single common source, so that there really are only two pieces of information inconsistent with one another. Despite these very real possibilities, it is usually prudent to question the accuracy of information that is inconsistent with most others' information.

A third test to apply in evaluating data is a **test of context.** When gathering information, a person doing research usually selects the information that is most likely to be useful in the problem-solving process. This act of selection needs to be measured against the test of context by asking the question: *Is the selected information consistent with the context in which it was found?* If, for example, you are working in a group on the problem of increased tuition costs for students at your college, you might have interviewed a representative of the budget office. She might tell you that three factors have contributed to a recent increase of tuition at your school: first, increased utility and maintenance expenses associated with a new building on campus; second, technological costs for updating computer services for the administration and students; and third, minimal costs involved in meeting the salary increases for faculty. If you selectively omit the first two causes and report to your group that faculty salary increases have caused student tuition hikes, then your information fails the test of context, for what you reported would not be consistent with the context in which it was presented. Student group members may not recognize the problem, but your underpaid instructors certainly would! More seriously, any solutions your group would recommend or attempt to implement could fail to address the most significant causes of the rising tuition.

It is important for individuals and the group as a whole to evaluate the information members have gathered. One of the factors Hirokawa (1987) identified as distinguishing between effective and ineffective groups was that effective groups engaged in

second-guessing—*the process of questioning information introduced by other members* (as well as questioning earlier decisions made by the group).

Reasoning from the Information.   Information alone often does not provide sufficient grounds for making a judgment. It is necessary at times to draw inferences from the information to arrive at conclusions. Three specific types of inferences, or forms of reasoning, are especially useful in coming to conclusions when a group is in the process of analyzing the problem: reasoning by sign and reasoning by example to identify the nature and extent of the problem, and causal reasoning to determine the cause of the problem.

Sign Reasoning.   In a court of law, a person can be convicted of a crime even if there is no eyewitness testimony or if the accused does not confess. Such convictions are based on circumstantial evidence or what is called **sign reasoning.** Signs (or circumstances) are indicators that something exists or something has happened. Thus, if you see the U.S. flag flying at half-mast, you are likely to conclude that someone important has died. The lowered flag is usually a sign of mourning. Rarely are signs certain however; a single sign by itself seldom indicates that something necessarily exists or has happened. For example, the flag might be flying low because a rope got caught as the flag was being raised. It is important then to have a sufficient number of signs all pointing to the same conclusion and to be able to account for inconsistent signs. Thus, in the case of a crime, you can convict someone of murder on circumstantial evidence, but that evidence must be substantial (that is, there must be many signs), before the sign inference is considered reasonable.

In problem solving, sign reasoning is especially useful when direct evidence of a problem is lacking. We can establish that a problem exists from its signs. For instance, what conclusion might you infer from the following bits of information (signs): the average number of people being fed daily at the community soup kitchen has increased from 60 to 80; more downtown business owners are complaining to the police about people sleeping overnight in their doorways; and the two local thrift shops report a sharp increase in customers? Sign reasoning would help you to determine that poverty has increased in the community, just as sign reasoning helps doctors diagnose illness (because the symptoms they notice are signs of the ailment), teachers to detect child abuse, and lovers to suspect infidelity.

Reasoning from Example.   In determining the extent of a problem, a variety of information is likely to be useful, including informed opinions, statistics, and examples. Examples can be especially useful when combined with inference. It is often neither possible nor practical to acquire all the information that might be available about a particular problem. For example, the Bureau of Labor Statistics reports monthly the number of unemployed workers, but this statistic is based upon a survey of sample households, not of all the households in the United States. In determining the extent of the 1996–1997 famine in North Korea, the U.S. government and international aid agencies had to rely on anecdotal reports from the few visitors permitted to enter some regions of the country. In these two illustrations, the data (examples) combined with inference to arrive at conclusions that go beyond the data.

Ethical Consideration

Selecting language to report the data gathered that distorts the data is a subtle means of depriving a group of the opportunity to base a decision on accurate information.

Reasoning from example begins with examples in a particular, definable class (unemployed workers, death from famine). If the examples typify the class and are sufficient in number, it is reasonable to infer that what is true about them is true about the class as a whole.

Generalizing based on specific instances should take into account negative instances. Thus, if one discovers a number of students in a fraternity who are known for their rowdy behavior at rush parties but others who are not, it is important to use language that properly reflects the database. A conclusion that "many" members of Zeta Zeta Zeta are rowdy at rush parties might be a reasonable inference, whereas concluding that "most" or "all" members are rowdy would not be reasonable.

Causal Reasoning. Information can be used to establish a strong and consistent correlation between two events. Reasoning connects them causally. If you see a child eat too much cake and ice cream at a birthday party and then complain of a stomachache, it is easy to connect the overeating with the discomfort. To do that is to make a causal inference. It might seem at first that no inference is involved, because it seems so obvious that the two things are causally related. But the information only proves that a correlation exists between the two. It is your mind that reasons that, in light of the correlation, the overeating probably caused the stomachache.

Causal inference is often used to determine *why* a problem exists. Since solving problems often requires eliminating causes or devising ways of preventing causes from producing their effects, it is important to be careful in making causal inferences. A causal inference is reasonable if the cause occurs prior to the effect, if the cause is sufficient to produce the effects, and if no other cause could account for the effects. The use of all three tests of causal inference can avoid what is known as the **post hoc fallacy.** The name comes from the Latin phrase, *post hoc ergo propter hoc,* which literally means *after this therefore because of this.* The fallacy identifies the flaw in reasoning that exists when a person assumes that an act that occurs subsequent to another is a consequence of the first act. Certainly the group charged with increasing Xavier University's admissions would have needed to be careful about assuming that changing a basketball league would *cause* an increase in applications. An increase in applications following basketball games in the East could be merely coincidental. However, discovering that playing basketball in the East provided name recognition that was sufficient to increase applications (and without which applications do not increase) allowed a reasonable causal inference to be drawn.

A group that has gathered, shared, and tested information and then reasoned from the information can identify the existence, nature, and extent of a problem. The cause of the problem can also be identified. These skills are useful in later stages of problem solving or decision making, but they are also critical in the problem-analysis process.

Outcome of the Problem-Analysis Process.   Often, upon a thorough investigation and analysis of the relevant facts, a sense of the problem is revealed to be accurate. At that point, the problem not only has been identified, but is also understood. As a result, group members are in a good position to begin consideration of the solution to the problem, for two reasons. First, they *have a sense of what needs to be changed in order to resolve the problem.* For instance, the admissions staff at Xavier University realized that the university needed name recognition beyond its immediate region in order to attract additional numbers of prospective students and also that the university needed to change its commuter campus image in order to make a positive impression on visiting prospective students. Careful analysis of the problem allowed them to consider creative ideas relevant to the specific nature of the problem they confronted. Other problem-solving groups are able to determine whether the problem they face warrants a local solution or a national one. Having identified the causes of the problem they face, they know precisely what needs to be changed to resolve the problem and are ready to consider how the changes should be made.

Second, when the group has completed its analysis of the problem, it is usually *motivated to resolve the problem,* if there is a problem. For instance, a campus group might discover that it is not just an occasional student who worries about safety when walking back to the dorm from the library in the dark, but that it is a serious concern for many students. A community group might discover that in addition to the few homeless individuals they have seen and worried about, there are additional people who have found hidden housing in decaying, condemned buildings and need help. Such discoveries should provide added motivation for the groups as they try to identify solutions to the problems they have identified.

There are times, however, when analysis reveals that a problem does not, in fact, exist or that it lacks sufficient significance to seek solutions and the group need not pursue the matter further. But this discovery is, in itself, significant because the members have, by using appropriate methods of analysis, resolved their *sense* of a problem. One classroom group, for instance, began their problem-solving efforts with the belief that the staff of their university's library failed to help students having trouble with computer searches. To gain a clearer sense of the scope of the problem, members pretended to be helpless at computers on different floors of the library and at different times of the day. To their surprise, each "helpless" student gained quick assistance from a staff member. The group's sense of the problem was resolved by their efforts to gather information about it.

Stage Three: Consideration of Possible Solutions

Once a group has determined that a problem of sufficient significance exists, the members proceed to the third stage of the problem-solving process: the search for and selection of an appropriate solution. This stage requires, first, the identification of alternative courses of action and, second, the evaluation of these alternatives to determine which would be most likely to be the optimum solution available.

Identifying Alternatives. Groups may begin to identify alternatives by considering solutions that others have used when faced by similar situations. Ray Kennelley, for instance, realized that other schools had encountered increased applicants when the schools' athletic programs gained national recognition, so he knew the effects such a solution might generate for Xavier. Additional research might uncover proposals from experts that have yet to be tried but that appear to be promising. Using the skills of searching for information described earlier in this chapter helps groups locate alternatives that others have devised.

It may be necessary, however, for group members to resolve the unique problems they encounter by devising alternatives unique to them. In devising solutions, groups may find **brainstorming** a helpful tool. Brainstorming, a device for generating ideas, is associated with Alex Osborn, who was head of a large advertising firm and the author of *Applied Imagination* (1957). Osborn shared with John Dewey (1910) a conviction that individuals should be taught to think; like Dewey, he associated the process he described with the principle of suspended judgment. However, whereas Dewey described a thought process leading to reasoned judgments, Osborn described a process of creative thinking.

Rules for Brainstorming. Osborn (1957) believed that groups could generate more ideas than individuals operating in isolation, as long as rules for brainstorming were followed that freed the imaginations of group members and that reduced their fear of social judgment while they generated ideas. Therefore, he recommended that brainstorming be done in informal sessions. He established five rules to encourage group creativity:

1. *All ideas should be recorded.* If we do not have a record of an idea, it is easily forgotten and is unavailable for later analysis.
2. *Criticism of ideas is ruled out during the brainstorming session.* If someone criticizes our creative ideas, it takes us a long time to venture forth with another idea. Besides, it interrupts the flow of creative juices.
3. *"'Free-wheeling' is welcomed. The wilder the idea, the better"* (p. 84). An idea that at first seems ridiculous may, after refinement, be quite reasonable, not to mention highly effective.
4. *"Combination and improvement are sought"* (p. 84). Contributed ideas become the property of the group to alter. One member's contribution also functions to stimulate brain activity in another group member.
5. *Quantity, not quality, is the initial goal.* If we think that we can contribute only ideas of high quality, we will engage in self-censorship and hinder our productivity. As Osborn said, when more ideas have been generated, the chances of having a winning idea increase.

Osborn (1957) did not say that groups should never be interested in the quality of their ideas or that brainstormed ideas should never be criticized. He simply recognized that when we sit in judgment of our own or others' ideas, then the flow of ideas is hindered. Nor did Osborn dismiss the value of analysis. In fact, he mentioned that analysis can spur the imagination by identifying exactly what needs to be resolved. Also, Osborn did not recommend that all creative thinking should be done in groups. In fact, he recommended that to "insure maximum creativity in teamwork, each collaborator should take time out for solitary meditation" (p. 75). Individual thinking should precede a group brainstorming session, and it can be used in small doses as breaks in the group sessions. The sessions themselves are envisioned as relaxed, enjoyable, free-wheeling events in which members contribute at a quick pace with the ideas of one member sparking creativity in the other members' minds. In *Applied Imagination*, Osborn provided a number of additional suggestions for maximizing creative productivity. They include

- Providing in advance a short memo for participants to spur independent thought prior to the session.

- Using a leader to guide the session. The leader can suggest the kinds of thinking the group might be doing, without acting as a proponent of his or her own suggestions. The leader can also set goals ("Let's reach 100 ideas"; "Let's not stop until we get l0 more ideas") to motivate the group.

- Inviting outsiders to the brainstorming session to increase heterogeneity of ideas.

- Keeping each session focused on a single goal rather than trying to generate solutions to multiple problems at once.

- Supplying each participant with a notepad so that ideas can be remembered if they are generated in the midst of another participant's contributions.

- Limiting each member to one idea at a time so that all members can stay involved.

- Holding a subsequent meeting or making subsequent contact with participants to record all of the creative ideas that came as afterthoughts of the brainstorming session.

Although brainstorming has become widely used by groups of all kinds, some research has raised questions about the value of group brainstorming. A body of research has compared the number of ideas produced by brainstorming groups with the number of ideas produced by *nominal groups*. A **nominal group** is *a collection of individuals who are a group in name only*. When groups use the **nominal group technique**, *the individuals work independently, and then their individual products are summed* to represent the total product of the nominal group. The most common result of the research has been that the nominal groups have produced more ideas than have brainstorming groups.

One explanation for the limits on the success of brainstorming groups lies with qualities of individual members. For instance, Comadena (1984) found that group members high in communication apprehension made few contributions in brainstorming groups. Brown and Paulus (1996) have developed a model of the group-brainstorming

Technology Note: Computer-Assisted Brainstorming

When groups use computers in their brainstorming activity, proper use of the channel can enhance the productivity of the group, as Roy, Gauvin, and Limayem (1996) discovered. Because members working at individual terminals are able to contribute ideas simultaneously without interrupting each other, there is no blocking effect.

The presence of a "public" computer screen on which group members can view the full list of brainstormed ideas has a positive motivating effect on the group. When members know that they will see the screen, but it will not be shown until the end of the session, then social loafing is less likely to affect the group members. The effort to match the productivity of others takes the positive form of social facilitation.

---

process that integrates some additional factors that influence the productivity of brainstorming groups. Their model assumes that any individual eventually runs out of ideas ("output decay"); that would hold true for members of nominal groups as much as for members of brainstorming groups. But other factors can alter the number of ideas contributed by an individual. When one member attempts to mention an idea in a brainstorming session, another contributor taking a speaking turn may (inadvertently) interfere with that attempt ("blocking"). As group size increases, blocking leads to a greater loss of productivity for the group members. A sense of social pressure leads one member to adjust his or her rate of idea generation to the rate of the typical group member ("matching"). If the typical rate is lower than the individual's rate, the individual will produce fewer ideas ("social loafing"). If the typical rate is higher than the individual's rate, the individual soon increases idea production ("social facilitation").

Additionally, the use of trained facilitators and brief pauses inserted in the brainstorming session—allowing for periods of individual reflection—were found by Offner, Kramer, and Winter (1996) to raise the productivity of brainstorming groups to the level of nominal groups. When Kramer, Kuo, and Dailey (1997) studied brainstorming groups, they found some parallels between the positive outcomes achieved by groups trained in brainstorming and those using nominal-group techniques. In both types of groups, individuals reported feeling that they had communicated effectively, used an effective process, and were satisfied with their results. The researchers concluded that because the rules of brainstorming (like those of the nominal-group technique) stress equal and free participation, group members trained in these behaviors accept them as normative; use of the process then carries over to create a positive climate that can aid the group in its further efforts at problem solving. But the key element is that the brainstorming groups must be following the rules of brainstorming. Holding a session intended to generate ideas but failing to follow the rules that enhance creativity leads to a brain drizzle, not a brainstorm.

Evaluating Possible Solutions. Once alternative solutions have been identified and generated, the group needs to begin the process of evaluating the various options. In evaluating possible solutions, groups must derive relevant criteria and apply them to the alternatives, ultimately selecting the alternative that best satisfies the criteria.

The Nature of Criteria.   **A criterion** is *a standard that provides a measurement tool for use in evaluating alternatives.* In the opening narrative, Ray Kennelly mentioned a couple of standards that college students typically use in selecting colleges: the school should be one they have heard of, and it should have an attractive campus. Of course this is an incomplete list of the criteria most students consider when making a choice about colleges. You probably used additional criteria, such as how affordable the school would be, whether it had a good academic reputation, whether its size was appropriate for you, and whether it had a major in your area of interest. It is useful for groups to word criteria as questions that, when answered yes, indicate that the alternative meets the criteria.

Sources of Criteria.   Since the first step in evaluating alternatives is to derive relevant criteria, it is important to consider the sources of criteria. A group can begin to derive criteria from four sources: the nature of the decision question, the group's analysis of the subject, the group members' preferences, and the constraints on the evaluators (Greg & Renz, 1993). The **nature of the decision question**—or the kind of decision a group is making—is the first source of criteria. Compare, for instance, these lists of qualities Arcata, California, might have used in selecting a sister city and those Xavier University might hypothetically use in selecting a prospective student:

Does the Prospective City Have	*Does the Prospective Student Have*
A need for financial assistance?	The ability to afford tuition at a private university?
A culture quite different from our own?	A background consistent with a Catholic institution?
Leaders who would welcome our involvement?	Leadership experience?
A population that could benefit from increased academic resources?	Demonstrated academic excellence?

Although we do not know what criteria are actually used by the Xavier admissions staff (and so our list of questions is hypothetical), the contrast between the two lists is enough to illustrate that the kind of decision question a group is asking itself will be the source of some criteria. In some cases, before a group is able to identify what criteria are relevant for selecting among alternatives, it may need to do some research. For instance, most college students know more about what is important in selecting a good college than they do about what is important in selecting a good investment account. Before you could consider possible investment choices, therefore, you might need to do some preliminary research to discover how such options are typically evaluated.

Because implementing most decisions involves creating some kind of change, a standard criterion generated at this stage might be "Does the solution involve risks that are acceptable?" or "Are the outcomes of the solution ones we are willing to accept?" Later analysis of the alternatives against this standard requires group members to identify the possible negative outcomes of each alternative and determine whether the group is willing to live with those potential outcomes.

Changing basketball leagues may seem to be an unusual approach to increasing college admissions, but at Xavier University it met the creiterion of increasing name recognition outside of the Cincinnati metropolitan area.
(Photo by Greg Rust, Xavier University).

A second source of criteria is **the group's analysis of the problem.** The primary reason that it is important to analyze a problem prior to focusing on its solution is that without understanding the nature of the problem, it is impossible to establish all of the criteria to be used in evaluating solutions. After deciding that the nature of the "admissions problem" at Xavier was not local, the admissions office knew it needed an approach that met the criterion of generating name recognition outside of the region. Determining the cause of the problem is an equally important source of criteria. For instance, the Sister City committee had identified waning leadership as the cause of its problems. Therefore, a solution to their problem of reactivating the committee had to meet the criterion of providing a consistent source of the leadership needed to make contact with other organizations and individuals. If, instead, they had defined the cause of their problem as the inability of the project to generate sufficient community interest, then the solution would have needed to meet the criterion of increasing project interest throughout the community. When a group uses its analysis of the problem as the source of criteria, then it increases its chance of making appropriate decisions and of selecting alternatives able to overcome the specific problems the group faces.

The preferences of group members are a third source of criteria. All of us are familiar with some decisions made by groups in which individual or group preferences have come into play: some workplaces celebrate employee birthdays in an official way, while others prefer to leave birthday recognitions up to individual coworkers; some classroom groups prefer to meet only in their classroom, while others decide to meet in more relaxed, social settings; some families prefer to celebrate holidays by visiting other people and places, while others value more intimate celebrations in more familiar surroundings. Groups of all types should let the preferences of individual members and of the group as a whole generate some criteria to use when choosing among alternatives. In deciding which trees to plant on the newly closed area of Xavier University, it is likely that personal preferences affected the decision. The music director of the National Symphony Orchestra, Leonard Slatkin (1997), has indicated that when making decisions about orchestra members, preferences on factors such as the amount of movement a performer makes while playing may be used to decide between highly qualified orchestral applicants. It may seem to you that such preferences are not always "rational" and should not be considered in the decision-making process. However, if preferences are ignored, group members are likely to feel less committed to the decisions they make, reducing the ultimate effectiveness of the choice over time. Moreover, individual preferences are likely to affect the preferred choices of individual group members. When the group as a whole discusses the individual members' preferences, the group can understand the perspective of each member and can identify common preferences that should influence the group's decision. Without such a discussion, group members are likely to have separate sets of criteria or a set that each member uses differently. In such a case, a group is likely to find itself unable to agree on a decision and unable to understand what is keeping the members apart.

A final source of criteria is **the limitations on the group.** When people join together voluntarily or by assignment to solve problems, they are not necessarily fully free to decide on the theoretically best solution. Groups are not sovereign; they are constrained in a variety of ways that limit their freedom. These limits should lead the group to generate some criteria that solutions must meet in order to be selected, ultimately, by the group. Four limitations are especially important: (1) limitations on the group's authority, (2) limitations of resources, (3) limitations from the values of the larger system, and (4) limitations of prior decisions.

Limitations on the authority of the group exist because no group is ultimately self-creating; each is the product of the authority of an individual or other group. Thus, for example, the Congress of the United States of America exercises its legislative power by authority of the federal Constitution. Should the Congress exceed that power as it legislates to solve a problem, the Supreme Court of the United States would declare such a solution to be unconstitutional and therefore invalid. Similar limitations are faced by smaller groups. A community group that is given the responsibility for planning the design of a neighborhood park has to choose solutions that fall within their powers; if their power does not extend to determining the location of the park, then their design must fit within the space they have been allocated. If a classroom group is required by the instructor to implement a solution to a campus or community problem before the end of the term, then its solution must meet the criterion of being able to be implemented in a short time regardless of how much time the members are willing to spend on the task.

Limitations of resources available to the group may also constrain the group. Solutions to problems need to be doable—otherwise the problem remains unsolved. In evaluating alternatives, a group needs to recognize constraints—whether in personnel or budget—that may make an "ideal" solution impractical. These constraints should be reflected in the criteria that the problem solvers employ. For instance, one factor that allowed the Sister City committee to solve its problem by hiring an individual was the fact that it had financial resources to do so. A group might decide that its solution must cost less than $10,000 or less than $10, depending on the resources it has available. Time is a resource the group may have in limited quantity, leading it to become the basis of another criterion. The Xavier 2000 plan committed the admissions office at the university to increasing admissions quickly, so solutions that could create change in a short time became preferable to longer-term options.

The **values of the larger system** can also be a source of criteria that put limits on the group's freedom of choice. A single work group located within an organization cannot act free from the value structure of the larger organization. For instance, the committee working to increase student enrollment at Xavier University might have done that by lowering admissions standards. The committee's immediate goal (increased student body) could have been met, but only at the expense of violating broader university goals about the kind of student body desired and the kind of education to be offered at Xavier.

Prior decisions by the same group frequently restrict future choices. Unless a group is truly ad hoc, it—or the authority that convened it—has a history. That history includes prior decisions made by the group or the convening authority. A group is usually bound—to some degree—by these prior decisions, if only for reasons of continuity and stability. Thus, the Supreme Court of the United States usually gives precedence to its own prior rulings in deciding new cases by following the principle of *stare decisis* ("let the decision stand"). Similarly, formal groups often maintain minutes that are consulted prior to a group's decision to be certain that consistency is maintained in the group's approach to problems. For instance, when the Interpersonal and Public Communication faculty at Central Michigan University met to consider a timetable for implementing its process of assessing learning outcomes of their students, they were limited by their previous decisions about what elements were to be included in the process. Those decisions were reported in the group's minutes. Previous actions, then, along with restrictions imposed by external authorities, by external group values, and by the group's resources provide limits that are reflected in the criteria of the group. These limitations, along with the nature of the decision question, the group's analysis of the problem, and the preferences of group members, constitute the sources of criteria for a group.

Agreement on Criteria by Group Members.   A group that is preparing to evaluate alternatives needs to reach agreement on the criteria to be used in the evaluation process. Not only does the group need to agree on which standards it will be using, but it also needs to agree on the meaning of each standard. Consider, for example, an advertising group deciding on an advertising jingle. It may agree that the jingle should be memorable. Committee members need to be in agreement about what *memorable* means. Is it acceptable if consumers remember it as obnoxious? (The group may decide that is fine, if it has evidence that consumers' product recall is more important than the particular product image in explaining purchase patterns.) A group deciding on a line of company cars may decide that good gas mileage is important, but, having reached that agreement, they are still miles apart if some members of the group believe that anything over 20 mpg is "good gas mileage" and others believe that only if the car reaches 35 mpg does it get good mileage.

A group also needs to agree on the relative importance of the criteria on their list. Some groups may distinguish between *essential* and *preferred* criteria. Others may decide to weight the most important criteria more heavily than those of moderate and least importance.

Groups that find it impossible to reach consensus on preferred alternatives frequently discover that their discussion about criteria has been inadequate. Consensus is impossible because each group member is looking for something different in a solution. Working out the relevant criteria, along with the meaning and importance of each criterion, goes a long way to helping the group agree on a solution to the problem they are hoping to solve.

Applying Criteria.   The actual evaluation of solutions occurs when group members apply each criterion to each alternative to ascertain whether the alternative passes the test posed by the criterion. It is necessary for a group to gather some data about the likely effects of their proposal. That is difficult, because the proposal has yet to be implemented. However, a group can make use of data on the projected effects of such an action and on the actual effects of similar proposals instituted elsewhere. By comparing these effects, the group is using **reasoning by analogy.**

For the inference reached through reasoning by analogy to be reasonable, it is necessary that the proposed solution and an already implemented plan of action be similar in their essential features. Thus, for example, a student currently living in a dorm on campus may decide to move into off-campus housing. When her parents question whether she can afford to do this, her answer is that a classmate who moved last semester has experienced no financial difficulties. However, her classmate's experience may or may not accurately predict her own future experience. If her classmate can cook but she cannot, or if her classmate is splitting the rent with three others and she would split rent with only one, her expenses may be considerably higher. Significant differences between the instances would lead to a rejection of the analogy. When Ray Kennelly reasoned that Xavier University could have similar success recruiting students from the East Coast to that of another private college in Ohio at which he had worked, he was reasoning by analogy. The essential similarity of the two admission offices' efforts allowed him to make a warranted prediction about the success of the proposed effort at Xavier.

As a group evaluates its options for solving a problem, it needs to be thorough in its analysis of the extent to which each option meets the relevant criteria. In a study of the interaction-based explanations for faulty decisions in groups, Hirokawa (1987) found that low-quality decisions were made by groups that were careless and superficial in analyzing their choices. His study required several groups of three students from an outdoor survival course to determine which of several items they should salvage from a hypothetical winter plane crash in a remote area of Canada in order to survive (without leaving the area of the crash) for five days until help arrived. One group made the poor decision to salvage a compass, which would be unnecessary for the group since the instructions clearly indicated that the group was to remain at the crash site and that rescuers knew where they were. An excerpt of the group's interaction revealed that the member who first suggested the compass gave no reason for its selection. A second member concurred with the selection, adding the false, but unquestioned, explanation that the compass would have value to the group in getting its "bearings and stuff" (p. 13). The third member announced that selection of the compass was a group decision and then moved the group forward to another item. The group was quickly able to make a decision, but it was a poor decision they made.

In contrast, the high-quality decisions in Hirokawa's study (1987) were made by groups that were "careful, thoughtful, and systematic" (p. 10) in their analysis of options. An excerpt of one group's analysis of the value of plastic trash bags revealed that the member who first suggested the bags was questioned about their value. After responding that the bags could protect the group from the elements, the member was challenged again to establish that trash bags would meet that criterion more effectively than the blankets and lighter (for a fire) they had already selected. A lengthy explanation of the reasons for the trash bags' superiority (in keeping out water and air) followed and led the challenging group member to acknowledge the wisdom of the choice. These examples should clarify the point that it is not enough simply to use the criteria of the group as a quick checklist to confirm a group's early solution preference. The criteria should serve as the starting point in a discussion that is thorough in its analysis of the degree to which a solution avoids negative outcomes (fails to meet the criteria) and promises positive outcomes (meets the criteria).

Some groups move systematically through this analysis process, examining each solution in turn. It is more common, according to Hirokawa (1988), for groups to eliminate the solutions that fail to meet important criteria first and then to compare the positive features of the remaining solutions. But all groups that made effective decisions were able to provide a clear rationale for their choices.

In fact, analyzing the degree to which proposed solutions meet essential criteria is important because it provides groups with a rationale for their decisions. Such an outcome may be of critical importance to a group. Suppose, for instance, that contributors to the Sister City project challenged the group about a supposed "misuse of funds" in hiring an individual to work on the project. The committee could defend its choice by referring to the way in which the criteria were met or not met by the options considered. Suppose that a candidate for a job sues a hiring committee for not getting the job. The committee can defend its decision in court by identifying the criteria it used in its decision and revealing the degree to which candidates met the criteria. And remember that when Ray Kennelly (whom you met in the opening narratives) was hired, he was in a position to implement decisions made prior to his tenure at Xavier University. His commitment to the task could be increased by his discovery of the manner in which the plans met the goals (or criteria) of the administration. In short, a systematic decision-making process that applies the criteria to proposed solutions allows a group to develop a clear and consistent rationale for its decisions. The rationale may be important in generating support from others, in reminding the decision makers of their reasons for the decision, and perhaps even in supporting the group against legal challenges.

Avoiding Errors of Judgment.   Even when a group has applied the criteria carefully and gathered sound data about the impact of a proposed solution, the members may create problems for themselves if they are careless in reasoning from the data. In their analysis of the flawed decision to launch the *Challenger*, Hirokawa, Gouran, and Martz (1988) concluded that "the problem was not so much that they ignored information, but rather that they drew the wrong conclusions from it" (p. 419). Two typical judgment errors found frequently in reasoning about economic matters, but relevant to reasoning about other issues as well, have been identified by Arkes (1993). The first is a *"windfall-spending" error*, the perception that unexpected "earnings" are more expendable; thus, risks of loss are more likely to be taken with "found money." If Arcata's Sister City committee had obtained its money from an unexpected donation, rather than from the hard work of the block party, this judgment error could have increased their willingness to use the money, even without careful discussion of the way in which their investment could solve the problem.

The second judgment error is the *sunk-cost effect*, the notion that prior investments, even if they have proven faulty, justify continued investment. Analysis of the decision to launch the *Challenger* revealed that error in operation. Given the fact that the *Challenger* program had required tremendous investments, it seemed reasonable to continue the program. The judgment error was compounded by the facts that there had been a promise that increased flights would reduce the cost per flight and that some recent flights had been canceled; thus, the risk of certain economic losses was perceived by some at the time to outweigh the risk of uncertain danger from the launch (Renz & Greg, 1988).

Technology Note: Selecting Solutions on the Computer

There are software programs available that can assist a group as it moves through the process of selecting a solution by applying relevant criteria to the possible solutions. By the early 1990s, a research group at the University of Minnesota had developed a program (mentioned in Chapter 2) called Software Aided Meeting Management (SAMM) and was studying its effectiveness. The SAMM program included "multicriteria decision analysis" for comparing solution alternatives to multiple criteria (along with options to use in formulating the problem and brainstorming for solutions). The researchers found that well-functioning groups that were introduced to the decision aids as the group was learning how to function together and that received help from a facilitator began to use the programs often and effectively, often inventing uses of the tools not originally anticipated by their developers (Poole, DeSanctis, Kirsch, & Jackson, 1994). In the face of more recent funding limits for project development, the research team has ceased its work on SAMM. However, other similar systems are now available commercially.

Selecting and Implementing the Solution. The process of analyzing the manner in which the possible solutions meet the criteria established by the group leads group members to select their preferred solution. Under ideal conditions, the group is able to select an ideal solution. Frequently, however, a group must select a less-than-optimum solution. That is, there may be no solution that meets all criteria the group has established. Limited resources of the group may lead the members to select a less-than-ideal solution that they have the potential to implement with available resources. The more ideal but resource-extravagant solution is one the group simply cannot afford to select. However, if a group has been careful in its analysis of the problem and possible solutions, then the solution it selects should be the best possible solution in terms of the criteria established by the group and in face of the limitations imposed upon the group. The selection process may be simple if the group has been thorough in its analysis of proposed solutions. It is quite possible, however, that a time of group debate will be required before a choice can be made by the group members. The debate will be productive if it is focused on a consideration of the way in which contending proposals meet or fail to meet the criteria devised by the group.

Under some conditions, a group—if it has the authority—implements the solution agreed to. This chapter does not consider the process involved in implementation efforts. What is important to note at this point, however, is that the analysis process is not complete even once the solution has been implemented. An effective group later returns to its decision, reevaluating the solution while it is in place. Previously, the group had to make guesses about the way the solution would operate. Now, however, the group has details at hand about the actual operation of the solution. It is able to confirm the wisdom of its choice or make adjustments in the solution so that it works more effectively. If the enacted solution has met only a portion of the group's goals, then additional proposals may need to be considered. For instance, in the opening narrative, Thea Gast mentioned that the hiring of a coordinator by the Sister City committee had succeeded in reactivating the

Ethical Consideration

A group engaged in problem solving should allow its members the opportunity to reject the decision the group is about to make. Even if, ultimately, the group agrees on the original suggestion, the process of critical examination of the proposal is an essential prerequisite to a freely made informed decision.

committee; she suspected, though, that changes in the structure of the committee itself might still be necessary and could be considered as time went on. The implementation of a solution to one problem by any group does not mean that the case is closed on that solution, nor that the group will face no other problems in need of solution.

An Agenda to Move through the Problem-Solving Process

As a member of a classroom group, you may be called upon to demonstrate your understanding of the problem-solving process by engaging in an analysis of a significant issue in order to identify reasonable solutions to the problem. As a citizen, you may participate in meetings designed to select a solution that can be implemented to resolve a problem. In either case, it should be helpful to you to realize that the stages in the problem-solving process can be the foundation for a set of questions that form an agenda for your group's deliberations. The following generic questions illustrate the nature of such an agenda for discussing problem X:

To Frame the Problem-Solving Question
What factors have led us to be concerned about X?

Why have we been asked to meet to consider X?

How can we word our problem-solving question to acknowledge our concerns and to indicate our willingness to explore a variety of answers?

To Analyze the Problem
What examples do we have that X is a problem?

How widespread does X seem to be?

What signs are there that X is a problem?

What is the significance of X as a problem?

What factors have caused X?

Do the data we have gathered satisfy the tests of source and substance?

Are we convinced that X is a concern worthy of our further attention?

To Identify Possible Solutions

What solutions to X have others recommended?

What solutions to X have been tried in the past?

What creative solutions can we devise to X through the process of brainstorming?

To Analyze Solutions

Besides considering whether the outcomes of the solution are acceptable to us, what criteria should we consider when we select a solution to X?

What does our analysis of the problem indicate our solution must do?

What personal preferences do we have for criteria?

What limitations does our group have that should be reflected in our criteria?

Do we agree on the meaning of each criterion we have listed?

Which of these criteria are essential and which are preferred?

What are the likely positive and negative outcomes of each solution?

What have been the outcomes of similar solutions in other, similar cases?

How well does each of our suggested solutions satisfy each criterion?

To Select a Solution

Which solution best meets the criteria we have identified?

Are we willing to accept the outcomes of the solution we have selected?

Summary

Small groups of all types are faced with the need to solve problems. The effectiveness of groups in such situations depends on what the members bring with them to the group and on the process used within the group. When John Dewey (1910) described the thought process involved in making decisions, he probably did not anticipate that writers on small group communication would prescribe reflective thinking as an approach for groups to use in problem solving.

The reflective-thinking process has been criticized by more recent scholars who have discovered that groups seldom are so systematic in their approach and that groups that follow a different set of steps can be successful in making high-quality decisions. At the same time, however, researchers have found that successful groups follow several steps: they understand the nature of the problem confronting them before they consider which solutions to endorse; they identify the standards (or criteria) by which they will evaluate proposed solutions; and they are vigilant analysts of the outcomes of the proposed solutions.

In addition, groups—and individuals—are often best able to resolve their problems if they generate a wide variety of creative solutions. Although meeting in a group for a brainstorming session does not guarantee the generation of a variety of creative solutions, following the rules for brainstorming allows such a session to be successful.

Effective groups are able to perform a series of behaviors in order to solve the problems they face. They frame a problem-solving question that captures the essence of the problem they face and directs the group's attention to an open-minded analysis of the problem and possible solutions. They analyze the nature, extent, and causes of the problem by gathering, sharing, and testing information, and then reasoning from the data to arrive at sound conclusions. They consider possible solutions by, first, identifying and generating possible solutions; second, identifying relevant criteria; and, third, applying the criteria, or measuring the possible solutions against the criteria so that the solution that best meets the criteria can be selected. Even when groups attempt to select an ideal solution to the problem they are addressing, they are limited in their attempts by several factors, including inadequate information and resources, constraints in their power, and the limitations their previous decisions have imposed on them. When the best possible solution has been selected, its implementation should not end the process of analysis within the group; group members should continue to analyze the solution as it operates so that modifications can be made.

Sometimes effective solutions can be arrived at in one sitting—as long as the group has been handed a description of the problem and all necessary information. Frequently, the process involves multiple meetings with time for gathering information and individual reflection between sessions. The Sister City committee took three months from the time they decided to address their problem until they arrived at an agreement on a solution. A major change has increased the effectiveness of the committee, but there is still more to be done. The Xavier 2000 project has involved constant work over four years, and, while many goals have been met, the process is continuing in full force. Successful groups are willing to devote time and effort to the process because the payoff is rewarding.

The problem-solving process described in this chapter is closely related to the process recommended for effective management of conflict and for avoidance of groupthink. Also, the final stage of the process is central to the task of decision making, because once a group has in place possible solutions and the standards by which to judge them, then they are able to make a decision on whatever issue they face. The next chapter extends the discussion of decision making by considering some issues related to decision rules and some special formats groups may select, depending on the specific decision issue they are considering.

QUESTIONS FOR DISCUSSION

1. Given the fact that group members typically have some information already gathered before any systematic research effort begins, how will the group members know when they have enough information so that more research is not necessary?

2. Evidence suggests that group members tend to exchange information common to the group members rather than exchanging information unique to a member. Why do you think this happens?

3. When one group believes that a problem exists, it is likely that others share that perception. In cases when a group's analysis of the problem leads them to realize that there is actually no problem of concern to them, what responsibility (if any) do they have to those others who, like them, may have thought a problem existed?

4. Given the fact that most groups require months or years to solve the problems they are concerned with, how can a classroom group work to solve a problem within the time frame the class meets?

5. How can groups balance the need to be vigilant decision makers against the practical demands of making an expedient decision?

SUGGESTED ACTIVITIES

1. Use a recent newspaper to identify problem areas in your community or campus. Frame questions that could focus a problem-solving discussion about three of the problems.

2. Use a book designed to help consumers select a product to buy (perhaps a car or a major appliance). Discuss the criteria used to rate products. Then select something you will evaluate and develop and apply the criteria relevant to its evaluation.

3. Interview an individual at your place of work or your school who has responsibility for hiring decisions. (An Affirmative Action officer would be a good choice.) Find out how criteria are used in making hiring decisions.

4. Attend a meeting of a community group that is engaged in a problem-solving discussion. (A city council, school board, or parent-teacher organization are possibilities.) Decide whether the discussion incorporates all of the essential steps in the problem-solving process. Evaluate the quality of the process and the solutions selected by the group.

5. In your project groups, identify a "felt difficulty" and use the steps of the problem-solving process to determine whether there is a problem and, if so, what solutions to recommend. In your journal, describe and evaluate the process you use.

SOURCES CITED

Arkes, H. R. (1993). Some practical judgment and decision-making research. In N. J. Castellan, Jr. (Ed.), *Individual and group decision making: Current issues* (pp. 3–18). Hillsdale, NJ: Erlbaum.

Brown, V., & Paulus, P. B. (1996). A simple dynamic model of social factors in group brainstorming. *Small Group Research, 27,* 91-114.

Comadena, M. E. (1984). Brainstorming groups: Ambiguity tolerance, communication apprehension, task attraction, and individual productivity. *Small Group Behavior, 15,* 251–264.

Dennis, A. R. (1996). Information exchange and use in small group decision making. *Small Group Research, 27,* 532–550.

Dewey, J. (1910). *How we think.* Boston: D. C. Heath & Co.

Frey, L. R. (1996). Remembering and "re-membering": A history of theory and research on communication and group decision making. In R. Y. Hirokawa & M. S. Poole (Eds.), *Communication and group decision making,* (2nd ed., pp. 19–51). Thousand Oaks, CA: Sage.

Gouran, D. S., Hirokawa, R. Y., Julian, K. M., & Leatham, G. B. (1991). The evolution and current status of the functional perspective on communication in decision-making and problem-solving groups. In S. A. Deetz (Ed.), *Communication Yearbook 16* (pp. 573–600). Newbury, CA: Sage.

Greg, J. B., & Renz, M. A. (1993). Critical thinking. In L. W. Huggenberg, P. L. Gray, & D. M. Trank (Eds.), *Teaching and directing the basic communications course,* (pp. 9–22). Dubuque, IA: Kendall/Hunt.

Hirokawa, R. Y. (1980). A comparative analysis of communication patterns within effective and ineffective decision-making groups. *Communication Monographs, 47,* 312–321.

Hirokawa, R. Y. (1983a). Group communication and problem-solving effectiveness: An investigation of group phases. *Human Communication Research, 9,* 291–305.

Hirokawa, R. Y. (1983b). Group communication and problem-solving effectiveness II: An exploratory investigation of procedural functions. *Western Journal of Speech Communication, 47,* 59–74.

Hirokawa, R. Y. (1985). Discussion procedures and decision-making performance: A test of a functional perspective. *Human Communication Research, 12,* 203–224.

Hirokawa, R. Y. (1987). Why informed groups make faulty decisions: An investigation of possible interaction-based explanations. *Small Group Behavior, 18,* 3–29.

Hirokawa, R. Y. (1988). Group communication and decision-making performance: A continued test of the functional perspective. *Human Communication Research, 14,* 487–515.

Hirokawa, R. Y. (1990). The role of communication in group decision-making efficacy: A task-contingency perspective. *Small Group Research, 21,* 190–204.

Hirokawa, R. Y., Gouran, D. S., & Martz, A. E. (1988). Understanding the sources of faulty group decision making: A lesson from the *Challenger* disaster. *Small Group Behavior, 19,* 411–433.

Hirokawa, R. Y., & Keyton, J. (1995). Perceived facilitators and inhibitors of effectiveness in organizational work teams. *Management Communication Quarterly, 8,* 424–446.

Hirokawa, R. Y., & Pace, R. (1983). A descriptive investigation of the possible communication-based reasons for effective and ineffective group decision making. *Communication Monographs, 50,* 363–379.

Kramer, M. W., Kuo, C. L., & Dailey, J. C. (1997). The impact of brainstorming techniques on subsequent group processes: Beyond generating ideas. *Small Group Research, 28,* 218–242.

Offner, A. K., Kramer, T. J., & Winter, J. P. (1996). The effects of facilitation, recording, and pauses on group brainstorming. *Small Group Research, 27,* 283–298.

Osborn, A. F. (1957). *Applied imagination: Principles and procedures of creative problem solving.* (Rev. ed). New York: Charles Scribner's Sons.

Poole, M. S. (1983). Decision development in small groups III: A multiple sequence model of group decision development. *Communication Monographs, 50,* 321–341.

Poole, M. S., DeSanctis, G., Kirsch, L., & Jackson, M. (1994). Group decision support systems as facilitators of quality team efforts. In L. R. Frey (Ed.), *Innovations in group facilitation: Applications in natural settings* (pp. 299–322). Creskill, NJ: Hampton Press.

Renz, M. A., & Greg, J. B. (1988). Flaws in the decision-making process: Assessment and acceptance of risk in the decision to launch Flight 51–L. *Central States Speech Journal, 39,* 67–75.

Roy, M. C., Gauvin, S., & Limayem, M. (1996). Electronic group brainstorming: The role of feedback on productivity. *Small Group Research, 27,* 215–247.

Slatkin, L. (1997, July 24). Interview. *Performance today.* National Public Radio.

7 Decision-Making Rules and Formats

CHAPTER OBJECTIVES

After reading this chapter, you should be able to

- Define each of three decision rules: decision by consensus, by majority vote, and by negotiation
- Describe the conditions under which each of the decision rules would be appropriate
- Describe the nature of communication most useful for each of the decision-rule conditions
- Select a decision-making format appropriate to the functions to be served
- Follow the steps for using a selected format
- Advise a group in the selection of a decision-making format

The Narratives

N. Edd Miller is now retired in Reno, Nevada, after a career in academic administration. When he served as president of the University of Nevada–Reno, he served on an accrediting agency for the first time. Accrediting agencies evaluate colleges, universities, and other, more specialized, educational programs. He continues to serve as a member of accreditation teams, whose decision-making procedures he explains here:

> *The whole accrediting process is voluntary, but government legislation affecting higher education nearly always reserves funding support for accredited institutions, so it is easy to see why institutions voluntarily seek accreditation.*
> *The process begins when a set of standards has been developed by the accrediting group. Institutions then do a self-study using these standards to organize their report. The reports reflect the viewpoints of several groups on a campus, including the faculty, students, and administration. Self-studies tend not to be self-praise, but an honest look at the way things are.*
> *Once the self-study is completed, a team of visitors makes about a three-day site visit. Prior to the visit, a team has had the self-study for about a month; during the visit, they check*

the accuracy of the self-study, with each person given a different assignment. If I'm assigned to look at faculty, then I will have interviews with faculty, discover what kind of faculty senate there is, how much influence it has, whether it's listened to by the administration, and what salaries the faculty get. We don't engage in dialogue or argument with the people we interview. We simply ask for additional information.

For several hours each day, we meet to hear reports about what has been observed. It's particularly important to hear about a finding that was not covered in the self-study or that seems inconsistent with the study. These are reported to the whole team because the consensus of the team is ultimately what is expected. As we hear the first two days of reports, the chair of the team may ask that a particular issue be looked at more carefully, or in a certain way, or that someone else join in the search for truth. Throughout this process, all of us listen to the reports and participate. The people looking at student services, for example, may have some insights about faculty that would not show up just from talking with faculty.

On the final day, the team gathers for a discussion to generate recommendations and commendations reported to the college and a recommendation to the accrediting commission, to be made in writing. Team members write their sections of the report, but always as representatives of the team. They're forbidden to use the words I or me. Instead they write about what the team *or* we *recommend; it is very clear that the report is a team report.*

Having a team make its decision by consensus is advantageous. Members who have been looking at isolated segments of the institution can view those elements in a larger context. The consensus is usually arrived at because of the openness of the discussion. In only a couple of instances have I seen real differences within the team. Then the chair of the team would make it clear to the commission that there were differences of opinion as to whether faculty salaries are high enough or whatever. I think making a decision by consensus about educational institutions is more satisfactory than it would be to have an up or down vote be the accepted norm. Even though I may not agree with every particular thing, I end up agreeing with the final decision.

Any decision maker should be a careful and evaluative listener. For this particular kind of decision making, it's important to try to see where the part that you became an expert on fits into the whole. People confronted with the necessity of making decisions are people who—I hope—get themselves involved in the process and, therefore, learn something about the areas in which they're making decisions. I believe that accreditation improves the quality of what happens in an institution. And I'm delighted to have some little part in that.

In Chapter 4, you met **Jim Osgood,** who served as foreman of the jury for the McVeigh trial. Jim has been involved in decision making, both in developing new products for Teledyne Water Pik (where he works) and during the trial. Here he talks about decision-making processes in both of those circumstances.

In any decision-making situation, it's important to understand the goals that the team is working toward. In project development, a number of criteria are established up front—the metrics or measuring sticks against which the outcome of the project will be evaluated. It's important to understand how one metric is prioritized versus another. At Teledyne Water Pik, I led a project team working toward developing a sonic technology toothbrush or plaque removal instrument. We had a project budget, a product cost goal, performance criteria for the product, and a schedule. At the onset, we clearly understood the importance of time: this was to be a preemptive introduction versus the competition. So schedule was the number one priority. If we could accelerate the project by investing more dollars in material development, that would be a good tradeoff, because we could better meet our schedule requirement. Also, we were willing to pay a premium for the resulting cost of the product if we could launch it with certainty by the targeted date. That was risk management.

Risk is very difficult to quantify because you're judging what may or may not happen as a result of any given decision. There may be very obvious, quantifiable results if you decide not to do something. But in a business environment, you're always dealing with a very dynamic situation. Decisions must be made without having all the facts. Rarely can you wait to have 100% of the information you need to make a fully informed decision. You may need to make it with 80% of the facts, 50% of the facts, or what have you. Engineers, including those I worked with on project development, are traditionally risk-averse people who would prefer to have all of the information in order to make the decision. But perhaps a less-than-perfect decision in a timely fashion is better than a fully informed decision that's made too late to be implemented.

I've often been responsible for decisions at work, but until the McVeigh trial, I'd never been on a jury . Before deliberations began, the twelve jurors and six alternates had spent six and a half weeks together. We were not allowed to talk about the case. When you can't talk about the one thing you have in common, the case, you talk about everything you don't have in common. It made for very interesting conversations. We came to understand what each of us stood for and got a good sense of our personalities, our sense of leadership, our sense of character.

When the case was handed to us for the first verdict, after all the closing arguments had ended, we were instructed that our first order of business was to select a jury foreman. The six alternate jurors had been temporarily excused when we retreated to the jury room. For a few moments, when it became apparent to us who the twelve deliberating jurors would be, we all had some overwhelming feelings . . . a kind of shock. After that settled, one of the other jurors said, "I don't know how you all feel, but I don't have any desire to be the foreman, and I'd like Jim to be the foreman." I thanked the woman and indicated what an honor and privilege that would be, but suggested that we go around the table and all twelve of us take an opportunity to express our interest in being the foreperson, and share for a few moments how each saw the position being handled and what values we believed we would contribute as foreperson. I was last to speak. I said that I had mixed feelings because, on the one hand, I would be honored to serve in that function and apply my team and project management background. On the other hand, inherent to being foreperson of such a big trial, the responsibility would be pretty overwhelming. But in the end, after we took a blind vote, I was elected foreman.

After I was elected foreperson, I started gathering my thoughts as to how I envisioned handling the job. The most important goal I had was to make sure that we all start at the same page and stay on the same page through the whole course of deliberations. That was the only way I saw us being successful in the deliberations. The testimony was so riveting and so touching that you couldn't help but be moved by the impact that this event had on the lives of the victims' families, the families and friends of the surrounding area of Oklahoma City, and the nation in general. How could we focus on facts and testimony if we were preoccupied with the emotion of the case and distracted by its gravity? We had to force ourselves to be objective by divorcing ourselves from the emotion of the case. It was our duty and oath as jurors. I thought the only way to ensure our objectivity was to employ a methodical and pragmatic process that could be used as a focal point for each step. I thought by doing that, we could be more focused and more objective. It was a way to make sure that we considered the mountain of information; yet left no stone unturned. This process enabled us to review the facts and testimony in such a way that everybody could appreciate each element of the case. Then, by the time the votes were cast, we could have exhaustively considered all of the details and be ready to take a well-informed vote. After all, we began with a presumption of innocence and had to determine beyond a reasonable doubt that the defendant was guilty of the charge presented in this case. It was a huge responsibility, far greater than any I've ever had.

We began our deliberations by studying the judge's instructions and identifying a number of issues that we had to consider carefully. From the instructions we created an agenda. We reviewed and prioritized the items on the agenda and allocated time for each discussion. This helped ensure that our following deliberations would be logical, efficient, and appropriate. That agenda became our charter for managing our deliberations. We kept it on an easel, visible throughout our deliberations.

When it came to capturing the essence of our deliberations, I used a technique called mind-mapping, which is a simple and efficient way of gathering a lot of detail in a visual format, which allowed me to illustrate the relationship of one fact to another. Doing so helped us all understand the relative importance of one thing to another. With mind-mapping, you start with one central idea. This central idea is broken down into subconcepts and connected together with lines like spokes on a wheel or a spider's web. From those subconcepts, we added additional subtopics, relevant facts, issues, testimony, and exhibit numbers. So we would start with a general issue and dissect it into four or five subissues, and then detail the relevant evidence, testimony, facts, et cetera, so that there was a visual record of how we summarized that particular facet of the case. We had dozens of these diagrams lining the walls of the jury room. These diagrams were the essence of our deliberation. It was a visual map of our discussions, with the correlation of facts and testimony intertwined that ultimately supported or diluted certain aspects of the prosecution's case. There was a lot of interconnection from one mind-map to another, layering corroborating evidence but also highlighting gaps or conflicting information. That interconnection is really what gelled the relationship and the chronology of the facts and issues of the case.

We had to go through an overwhelming number of pieces of evidence and testimony without the benefit of taking notes during the trial. The judge ordered us to pay close attention and prohibited us from taking notes. I believe he wanted to eliminate any possible distractions and force us to pay very close attention and retain as much as we could. We had to rely on our collective memory and hope that at least one of us was going to remember a particular detail or aspect of the case. And we did.

The mind-mapping technique is one I have used for both work and personal decision making. It helps put facts and issues down on paper so they can be visualized and objectively reviewed more effectively. By dumping your thoughts on to paper, you no longer rely on your mind to keep track of a lot of details. You can inspect them in a more logical format and then make a more informed, less emotional decision. For me, the most paralyzing part of decision making is thinking, "I've got so much to consider here. How do I get through it all?" The emotion of a decision tends to adversely impact your ability to make a good decision.

Having 12 people on a jury seasons out any singularly skewed opinion. There are checks and balances in the collective opinion of 12 individuals. Twelve people summoned to duty are just average citizens, most of whom (I suspect) have never served on a jury before. It's a huge responsibility. There is no training or crash course on "How to be a Juror" or "Deliberation 101." You just have to rely on each other to find a way to arrive at a decision that's the right decision. And that is the essence of collective reasoning. One person cannot possibly derive a decision that represents the "collective conscience of the community."

I believe that consensus— a unanimous decision—is entirely possible if a jury is committed to a process that keeps them focused on contemplating the facts and testimony presented in the trial. By using a process, you maintain a discipline in the deliberations and can minimize tangent discussion and the influence of irrelevant observations. I would like to think that anyone who is selected to serve as a juror would take that responsibility very seriously. The responsibility begins with presuming the defendant's innocence. The responsibility ends when you have objectively rendered—by whatever process or means—a verdict based solely on fact and testimony.

The Importance of Decision Making to Small Groups

A central feature of small group activity is the making of decisions. Even a social group, which does not have task accomplishment as a primary focus, commonly undertakes some activities and needs to decide what to do (go bowling? have a party? just talk?) and how, when, and where to accomplish it. For problem-solving groups, decision making is part and parcel of the problem-solving process described in Chapter 6. Other groups are formed to make a decision among alternatives without going through the full problem-solving process; such groups might decide how to allocate a state's money earned from a lottery, whom to hire for a new position, which product to recommend as a good choice for consumers—or (as the narratives suggest) which products to develop, which schools to accredit, and whether a person charged with a crime is guilty. In each case, the information on establishing and applying criteria (described in Chapter 6) is relevant to the task the group faces in making a decision, as is the material on information gathering and testing. For instance, when Edd Miller describes (in his narrative) the process of campus interviews to test the data in self-studies, he makes clear how important gathering and testing information is to a decision-making group. This chapter extends the information on decision making considered earlier by first discussing the choice a group makes about decision rules and, second, by identifying special formats groups might use to enable the form of their decision-making process to follow its function.

Selection of Decision Rules

Groups differ in the rules they follow about how decisions are made. In the accrediting agencies Edd Miller described and the jury Jim Osgood led, decisions were made by consensus, with the groups following the rule that unless all members of the group supported the decision, the group had not reached a decision. In some groups, however, decisions are made by majority vote; and in others, decisions are negotiated. In yet other cases, such as some project groups Jim Osgood has led, a group offers its advice, after which a unilateral decision is made by a single member of the group (or by an outsider of the group). If an individual makes an independent decision for a group, then the group itself is not engaged in decision making; if the group advises, then it may arrive at its recommendation by one of the three other means—by consensus, voting, or negotiating. While there may be other decision rules in force within a particular group, the most typical approaches are these three. Each of the three types of rules varies in its impact on the group and differs in its appropriateness for a particular situation, so much so that Gerald Phillips and Julia Wood, in their jointly edited 1984 book on *Emergent Issues in Human Decision Making*, argued that different conditions should lead to different decision rules. The differences are described carefully by Wood in her lead essay in that book.

Decision by Consensus

Wood (1984) defined a **consensus decision** as "*one that all members have a part in shaping and that all find at least minimally acceptable as a means of accomplishing some mutual goal*" (p. 4). In his history of the concept of consensus, Rawlins (1984) noted that decision by consensus is based on the assumptions that reaching agreement among the members of a group is desirable and that opposition to a position taken by other group members should not be the basis for exclusion from the group. Rather, group members talk through their disagreements to achieve a mutually agreed upon decision. Wood added that consensus also assumes that agreements among reasonable persons are possible and that group members have a true commitment to the goals of the group.

Some group members assume that their groups have reached consensus when, in fact, they have not. If a group leader pressures the group to approve a position, if a group member assumes that all members agree without soliciting opinions from the group, or if a group concurs on a decision without discussing or analyzing it, then the group has converged on a decision but has not actually reached consensus. In the accrediting agencies that Edd Miller mentioned in the opening narrative, consensus came from the openness of the discussion among group members. Similarly, Jim Osgood said that the jury he led adopted a process of open, thorough discussion that allowed true consensus to be reached within the group. The jury did not simply converge on a position; it shaped its decision as a group and thus decided by consensus.

The nature of the decision rule affects the nature of communication within a group. In groups deciding by consensus, communication that reviews points made by others, clarifies ideas, coordinates points made by various group members, and offers support for others' ideas is useful in forging agreement among group members. Communication that expresses negativism toward the ideas of others, seeks to separate group members, or serves to advocate one's individual position at the expense of others' positions is destructive of the process.

When groups are able to achieve consensus, there are advantages to the group. Members whose positions have been taken into account in the crafting of the decision are more likely to feel committed to implementing the decision and, in turn, more committed to the group. There may also be an improvement in the quality of the decision if it is reached by consensus. Thompson, Mannix, and Bazerman (1988) found in their research on decision rules that the subjects arrived at better decisions when they had reached decisions by consensus than when they had used a majority vote as the deciding factor. Hirokawa (1984) did not support the claim that consensus decisions were inherently superior, but he did argue that decision quality improved when groups reached consensus through the use of "a 'vigilant' decision-making strategy (that is, one characterized by careful reasoning and analysis, intensive exploration of alternatives, and systematic examination of evidence)" (p. 41).

Given the advantages of decision by consensus, you may prefer to adopt consensus as the decision rule for groups you join. That may work for you, if the following conditions that Wood (1984) identified describe your group: (a) it is composed of members who are equals and who openly express their opinions about and interests in the group decision; (b) the members have a strong commitment to reaching agreement as a group; (c) they approach the decision-making process with open minds about the solution, rather than being committed ahead of time to a particular position; (d) they are focused on the group's goals, not on their independent, individual goals; and (e) there is time available for extended discussion. If those are not the conditions that exist within your group, then another decision rule may be more appropriate for your group. Or, it may be that over time your group may improve its ability to operate by consensus. When Hall and Williams (1966) compared the performances of established groups with those of ad hoc groups, they found that established groups were better able than ad hoc ones to integrate members' opposing views in their final solutions and to achieve consensual agreements. The members' history together had developed a body of operating procedures that made it easier for them to acknowledge opposing viewpoints and respond to them.

Decision by Majority Vote

Decisions by **majority vote** are *ones in which more than half of the members support a decision.* (For decisions that require a broader range of support, it is common to require a larger proportion of votes in support of a proposal.) Making decisions on the basis of a vote is common in our society. Voting is a more efficient means of reaching a decision than is consensus decision making. Moreover, it may prevent an impasse within a group. Jim Osgood alluded to that fact when he hesitated about endorsing consensus for all jury trials; if a single juror refused to base a decision on facts and reasoning in the case, he said, a miscarriage of justice could occur when the jury reached an impasse in its deliberations. The importance of voting as an option in a democratic society was stressed by Phillips (1984) when he said, "politically speaking, a society cannot stand if it depends on reasonable discussion achieving unanimity. There must be a fail-safe built into the system, a way of getting a decision made when no agreement appears possible" (p. 113).

In some cases, however, decisions by majority vote may undermine democracy in a group. That is the case when groups vote as a means of bypassing discussion of an issue about which there is some disagreement. Nemiroff and King (1975) reported that groups uninstructed in the strategies for reaching consensus often reached quick decisions by voting. The difficulty for such groups is that minority positions may be overlooked, even in cases when the minority position is valid or when the majority has weak support of one position that the minority strongly (and legitimately) opposes. Groups that follow a voting rule in making decisions, therefore, are best served if they encourage expression of minority positions. The advantages are to allow modification of proposals in response to minority concerns. Nemeth and Kwan (1987) found that when group members had access to minority views, the minority did not need to win to have an influence on the group; access to the minority view led the group to "use more strategies in solving a problem and, in the process, come to detect more correct solutions" (p. 797).

Making decisions by voting assumes that there will be winners and losers as an outcome of a decision. Therefore, a group member's communication during the decision-making process is designed to increase the chance that he or she ends up a winner. Communication involves advocacy of a single position, efforts to solicit allies or to form a broader coalition (perhaps through making promises in exchange for

Technology Note: Voting by Computer

The danger of group members altering their positions to coincide with the majority position is lessened when members cast their votes by computer. Each member votes independently, and the totals can be concealed until after all votes have been cast.

support or by calling in past favors), and drawing lines between group members whose positions vary.

In contrast to decision making by consensus, voting leaves a group with less commitment to the decision it has made and, thus, to the group itself. Nonetheless, there are conditions under which voting is an appropriate approach. Your group might choose to decide by voting in cases in which (a) closure on an issue is more important than harmony within the group, (b) time is of the essence, (c) members enter the decision-making process already having a high commitment to a particular position, (d) the goals of group members are inconsistent and incompatible, and (e) long-term support of a full group is not needed for implementation of the decision. The conditions that make voting appropriate contrast directly with those in which decision by consensus is appropriate. If conditions lie somewhere between the two, then the third approach, decision by negotiation, is appropriate.

Decision by Negotiation

Groups that decide by **negotiation** reach agreements that are *compromises of the positions members had at the beginning of the decision-making process.* Like groups that decide by consensus, negotiating groups recognize the interdependence of group members. Like groups which decide by voting, negotiating groups recognize that their members have competing goals. The decisions that result recognize the interests of individual members, but in a more piecemeal manner than does a decision that results from consensus. For example, if an accrediting group made decisions by negotiating with the faculty and the administration rather than (as they actually do) by consensus within the accrediting group, it might support the faculty request on teaching load in exchange for accepting the administration position on teacher salaries. Thus, members are likely to disagree with certain aspects of a decision, but "find enough of value in that decision to support it" (Wood, 1984, p. 6). Support for the decision is moderate and lasts only as long as the group members continue to perceive themselves as interdependent.

As is the case in each of the other approaches, decision by negotiation influences the communication of group members. An effective communicator within a group using a negotiating decision rule is one who can persuasively present his or her own position, clarify the priority of members' goals, identify the minimal expectations of each group member, compare alternatives and project their consequences, and help members revise their positions.

Your group might want to adopt the decision rule to negotiate if the following conditions are present: (1) members are committed to divergent positions when the process begins, (2) they are moderately committed to the group itself, (3) there is a moderate amount of time available for decision making, (4) different members of the group have different amounts of power, and (5) the group's interdependence is sufficient to allow support for the implementation of the group's decision. These conditions form the midpoint between the conditions in which the other two approaches are preferable.

As Wood (1984) summarized the point,

> each of these three methods—quite distinct in assumptions and implications—is a legitimate mode of making decisions in groups. They proceed in different ways and produce distinct outcomes, yet judgments of worth must be contingent upon a variety of issues extrinsic to the methods themselves. (pp. 17–18)

Choosing the decision rule appropriate for your group should take into account the conditions in your group at the time a decision is to be made and the outcomes associated with each decision rule. Those factors in relation to each of the decision rules are summarized in the chart in Figure 7.1. In addition to choosing an appropriate decision rule, your group should select the format most suitable for the decision it is making. Understanding how that decision should be made requires, first, that you understand the principle of form following function.

FIGURE 7.1 Factors Associated with Each of Three Decision Rules

	Consensus	**Majority**	**Negotiation**
Prior Commitment to a Position	No	Yes	Yes
Goals of Most Importance	Group	Individual	Subgroup
Primary Focus	Maintaining Process	Reaching Closure	Balancing Power
Type of Communication Most Valuable	Open, Clarifying, Coordinating	Coalition-Building, Advocating, Distinguishing	Revising; Perhaps Exaggerating; Clarifying and Advocating
Time Available	Yes	No	Moderate
Intragroup Relationships	Harmonious	May Be Difficult	Factions, but Interdependent
Difficulties with Approach	Time-Consuming	Lose Full Support	Fragile Agreement

Form Follows Function:
A Theoretical Perspective

In other chapters, the theoretical perspective comes from communication theory. In this chapter, however, a principle from architecture forms the theoretical foundation. Louis Henry Sullivan was an architect who was born in Boston in 1856 and worked in Chicago until his death in 1924. He worked at a time when new developments, such as the invention of the elevator, made it possible to alter the design of buildings. Yet most architects continued to design buildings in the same pattern as before; so an office building might have an elevator, but it still looked like a Greek temple. In contrast, Sullivan designed skyscrapers, office buildings that not only made use of the new developments, but that were also efficient areas intended to allow for efficient work. In his designs, Sullivan attempted to realize this principle: *form follows function*. This principle, at its simplest, means that the form (design, shape, arrangement, organization, or format) should derive from and be appropriate to its function (its intended use or purpose).

You can see the application of the principle that form follows function in your everyday activities. The shapes (forms) of a football and a basketball differ from one another. The oval shape of the football is well-suited to its purpose—to be thrown accurately at long distances (function). Its shape would be ill-suited to swishing through a basketball net. Toothbrushes have been designed with a bent head (form) to help you reach behind your teeth when brushing (function). A wide array of tools, like scissors, have been redesigned in form so that a left-handed person can use them more effectively and comfortably. The principle of form following function should also be applied to your choice of decision-making formats. To optimize the decision-making process, your group should select an appropriate format, one designed to suit the purpose your group has in that particular decision-making situation.

Decision-Making Formats

A variety of formats useful in decision making exists. New formats are generated fairly regularly by individuals and groups seeking a new way to make a decision. Some gain momentary popularity, and then their use may fizzle out. If a new format is likely to be effective, it requires the form, or design, necessary to achieve its function. For instance, if your purpose is to generate a long list of possibilities for fund-raising events for your student organization, you might select the brainstorming format. It is designed to help generate ideas. If your purpose is to ascertain whether a recent troubling incident of assault on campus indicates a safety problem, reflective thinking might be the appropriate format because it is designed to help a group decide whether a real problem exists and, if so, how it might be solved. Both of these formats should be familiar to you from their descriptions in Chapter 6. But what format should you use if you are deciding about an issue of high risk, such as the development of a new product (as described in the opening narrative of Jim Osgood)? What if you are trying to narrow the number of options quickly? or test the soundness of your thinking?

Other formats are devised to serve those specific functions. Although all formats may share the steps of analyzing data and evaluating alternatives, they differ in the manner in which those steps are performed so that the form can best follow its specific function. Understanding this principle allows a group to evaluate new formats as they arise, modify old formats to suit new purposes, or select from the formats described in this text the ones best suited to the needs of the group.

The formats described here are not exhaustive. They do represent some of the key approaches developed over a period of years. As you read about each format, you will learn about its background, the situations in which it should be most useful, and the steps used for that particular format. Even the most widely known formats have been modified to meet the particular needs of a group engaged in decision making, so you should feel free to adapt the format to the needs of your group, too. At the end of this chapter there is a chart that summarizes the functions, form, and outcomes of each format.

Satisficing, Elimination by Aspects, and Paired Alternatives: Formats Designed to Narrow Solution Options

In Chapter 6, the general process of decision making was described: all possible solutions are evaluated, using the set of criteria the group has devised as standards in the evaluation. Under ideal circumstances (when the group has unlimited time), that is exactly what the group will do. Each alternative is thoroughly considered against a full set of criteria. However, Payne, Bettman, and Johnson (1993) note that decision makers frequently cannot afford such thoroughness, particularly when a large number of alternatives exists for their evaluation. Suppose, for instance, that you have decided to buy a book as a gift for a friend. Your local bookstore has thousands of books, each of which is a possible alternative. Rather than examining each alternative in turn, you need a strategy that reduces the time involved in evaluating solutions. Such a strategy is **satisficing,** *a strategy that selects the first choice that suffices in meeting the group's most essential needs* (Payne et al., 1993).

Situations in Which Satisficing Is Used. When the only way a group has the opportunity to make a sound decision among alternatives is to quickly reduce the number of alternatives available, then satisficing can be used.

Steps in the Format. A group determines which of its criteria are essential criteria—and may decide that there is a single criterion that is essential. For instance, a group selecting a book as a gift might decide that the book should be written well, priced economically, and on a topic of interest to the recipient. Perhaps the group, if composed of financially strapped college students, decides that being economically priced is the only important criterion the book need meet. The group decides how it will know when each criterion is met. For instance, if being "well written" is an important standard, the group might decide that a book meets that standard only if critics have reviewed its style favorably.

Once the essential criteria have been identified, the group begins to compare the first alternative to the essential criteria. If the alternative does not meet the essential criterion or criteria, then it is eliminated from further consideration. The first alternative that does meet the criteria is selected by the group as being satisfactory enough to suffice. If no alternatives meet the essential criteria (so that all have been eliminated), then the group lowers its expectations and begins to examine the alternatives again.

Related Strategies.   A time-saving strategy closely related to satisficing is called **elimination by aspects** by Payne, Bettman, and Johnson (1993). In this case, the group identifies its first criterion (or the first aspect). The alternatives are examined in relation to that criterion alone. Any solution that does not meet the first aspect is eliminated. When the examination is complete, the option that is the "winner" in the evaluation is chosen. If there is a tie, then the group measures the tied alternatives against the second criterion.

A third strategy for limiting the number of options may not save time as much as it saves the group's sanity. Sometimes groups begin to feel frustrated when some options seem very closely related. The strategy of **paired alternatives** *forces the group to choose between the most closely related options.* When a decision has been made between one pair of alternatives, the group moves on to another pair. The "winners" selected from the first two pairings can compete against one another, much as the winners of semifinals compete against each other as finalists in later rounds of competition. When some alternatives share several of the same attributes, enough so that it seems they are nearly duplicates, the group benefits from pairing the alternatives. Otherwise, the group may dismiss one of the pair without examining it thoroughly.

Advantages and Limits of the Methods.   Reducing the amount of time involved in decision making is the primary reason for using the satisficing and elimination by aspects approaches. If there are clear differences in the importance of some criteria in relation to others, then the techniques can speed up the decision process without endangering its quality. If the criteria are more equally weighted, then these approaches risk a group's eliminating a solution that would be, overall, the most satisfying solution before the group has had the chance to realize that. This is particularly true when satisficing ends with a group selecting the first solution that it finds to meet the criteria reasonably well. On the other hand, that technique is helpful if any number of solutions could reasonably be chosen and serve the group satisfactorily. (The gift buyer in the bookstore, then, might do a careful analysis of the stock and find 50 books that would reasonably meet the needs for the occasion. Unless the recipient and the occasion are especially significant, the first of those books found might be a perfectly acceptable purchase.)

In the case of paired alternatives, the group forces itself to look at closely related options. In the process, it may clarify its own criteria. (The pairs are similar in many aspects, but differ in a few. The differences may allow the group to identify some additional criteria of importance to the group.) Ultimately, a number of options are eliminated. However, the speed at which this is accomplished may not be as fast as it is with satisficing and elimination by aspects.

Two Formats Designed to Increase Independent Work by Group Members

Nominal Group Technique (NGT). After observing the difficulties that citizen involvement groups experienced in decision making, Andre Debecq and Andrew Van de Ven developed an approach to decision making that they called the *nominal group technique.* Developed in 1968 and tested the following year on groups concerned with community action, health care, and student affairs, the approach takes its name from the fact that for a good portion of time, the groups using the technique are groups in name only (only nominally groups). That is, the group members operate independently much of the time and actually interact for only brief periods.

Situations in Which NGT Is Useful. Several conditions might motivate the use of the nominal group technique. If a group (1) is experiencing conflict to such an extent that members cannot talk openly about their ideas, (2) has conformity pressures high enough to discourage members from expressing unique ideas in the course of a discussion, (3) includes one or more members who dominate discussions so that a quieter member has difficulty getting involved, or (4) needs closure on an issue, but not necessarily a high level of individual commitment from each member, then NGT is useful. For instance, Hickson, Worrall, Yiu, and Barnett (1996) used NGT to pool ideas from elderly individuals and professionals who work with them about the content to include in a course designed to improve communication behaviors of the elderly. In another case, NGT was used at Appalachian State University, when the campus counseling center was in the midst of changing its procedures, to try to identify the needs the center ought to strive to address (Skibbe, 1986).

Steps in the Format. The technique begins when a group needs to develop ideas and has time available to meet. Estimates range from 45 to 90 minutes to complete the process. It begins with the group leader placing the issue needing resolution before the members and directing them to write down their ideas silently for a specified period of time (perhaps 10 minutes). Group members can be given slips of paper or notecards for this process and record only one idea on a each slip or card; members can also record all ideas on a single sheet of paper.

Once the time allotted for silent writing (sometimes called "brainwriting" as opposed to "brainstorming") is up, the group is led through a round-robin process of assembling a group list from the individuals' items. In other words, each group member has a turn in which to contribute one idea. As each idea is contributed, the leader lists it for all to see. When each member has contributed one idea, then a second round of contributions is solicited, and then a third, and a fourth, and so on until no further ideas remain. Any group member may pass at any time but should be asked for further ideas on subsequent rounds, since further ideas may be stimulated from hearing those mentioned by other members.

Up until this point, there has been no discussion of ideas by the group. In the next stage, the group may ask questions about any idea (one at a time) for the sake of clarification, and explanations should be given. Therefore, even though there is some interaction within the group at this point, the discussion is quite structured.

Once ideas have been clarified, group members vote with a secret ballot for the preferred ideas. Groups may limit the number of ideas members may vote for to their favorite three to five ideas. The leader then tabulates the results and announces the winning ideas. It is possible to complete the process at this point, but it is also possible to continue it by allowing members to discuss the factors that led some to their votes. By providing their reasons for voting one idea high and another low, individuals provide their fellow group members with an increased understanding of their perceptions of the ideas. A final vote can follow this step and complete the procedure.

Advantages of the Format.   Nominal group technique encourages group members to stay focused on the task at hand. Task focus may be difficult to maintain when individuals are in conflict or when they are getting along very well, because in either case, the group diverts its attention to relationship issues. When relationship issues are getting in the way of a group's focus on the task, NGT can redirect the focus to the task. It also prepares the individuals for divergent points of view, because it creates an expectation for more than one idea to be placed on the list. And, in those situations in which conflict levels in the group are such that the group could not achieve consensus, the use of a voting decision rule allows the group to reach closure despite the conflict.

In tests comparing NGT to brainstorming, NGT usually outperforms brainstorming in the quantity of ideas and the uniqueness of ideas. Its advantages come from the fact that individuals develop ideas prior to communicating them, so ideas are generated without interruption and without being censored by the individual or by others. (Of course, leaders of groups using NGT need to recognize the possibility that a member will not divulge an idea during the round-robin step of the process if the atmosphere is unwelcoming of unique ideas.)

Typically, NGT is useful in groups of heterogeneous members. In an introduction to a book on NGT (Delbecq, Van de Ven, & Gustafson, 1986), Dr. Alberta Parker of the School of Public Health at the University of California–Berkeley described her experience using NGT in Guam with individuals from very diverse cultural backgrounds. Some were English-speaking urban dwellers who were active in civic affairs. Others were residents of small villages who had limited skill in English. Even these latter individuals, who would have had difficulty participating in a fully interactive group, became comfortable contributing items from their lists and clarifying the items. The satisfying outcome is possible both because NGT equalizes participation among all members and because it allows ideas to be clarified (and misunderstandings to be erased) before any other reaction to the ideas occurs.

Limitations of NGT.   Nominal group technique does require group members to meet for a segment of time. If the block of time is unavailable or members cannot meet, its usefulness is limited (as is the case for most approaches to decision making). Although members who have never used the procedure may find its first use quite satisfying, it becomes less satisfying subsequently (Hornsby, Smith, & Gupta, 1994). Even initial uses of the process may not be satisfying to those who seek increased interaction within a group (Toseland, Rivas, & Chapman, 1984). Although group members can avoid conflict by clarifying misperceptions, they do not have the opportunity to work out real differences of opinion. Therefore, the decisions may represent a false consensus (Gargan & Brown, 1993). They are acceptable if the point is simply to pool ideas—such as suggestions about what subjects can be included in a program being planned. They present problems if they are perceived to represent a single point of agreement for a group whose individual members are not committed to the decision.

The Delphi Method.

Development of the Delphi method is attributed to Norman Dalkey and his colleagues at the RAND corporation in the early 1950s (Dalkey, Rourke, Lewis, & Snyder, 1972). It was developed as a means of involving varied perspectives on issues while avoiding the errors in group judgment that can occur when individuals alter their opinions to conform to the positions expressed by other vocal members. Because it has been used with attempts to forecast developments, the approach takes its name from the mythic oracle at Delphi. In many ways, it parallels the nominal group technique; but unlike NGT, the individuals using the Delphi method need never be present in the same room and may never even realize that they are in a group together.

Situations in Which the Delphi Method Is Used. In situations in which opinions of a variety of experts are sought, the Delphi method is useful. There are two key conditions: (1) the decision to be made is not able to be determined by undisputed facts, so decision makers need to rely on opinions in coming to a decision; and (2) a variety of opinions might legitimately be held by those with some expertise on the issue. The Delphi method has been used recently to generate ideas about the role to be played by the community Hebrew school of Minneapolis (Passig, 1997), the use of reflecting teams during family therapy (Jenkins, 1996), and the appropriate content of social science courses (Martolla, 1991) and social work field experiences (Raskin, 1994). The Delphi method is also used when groups must make decisions but have little if any opportunity to meet as a group.

Steps in the Format. Use of the Delphi method typically begins by identifying individuals with expertise in a particular area and asking them to serve as members of a Delphi group. Experts might be recommended by others working in the field or might be identified by their publications on a given topic. In some cases, membership in an existing group qualifies an individual as an expert. For instance, in Passig's study (1997), students at the Hebrew school in Minneapolis were viewed as experts about the role the school played in their lives as Jews.

Once the initial group has been identified, the group is asked to respond, in writing, to the decision question to be resolved. For instance, individuals active in coaching competitive intercollegiate speech teams might be asked to identify ways in which the activity could attract more minority students. Group members send their responses to the individual who has formed the group, either electronically or by regular mail. The members themselves often remain anonymous to one another; even if their names are revealed, they do not meet in person as members of the Delphi group.

The responses from the initial group of experts are then compiled. The responses can be transformed into a series of statements that form the basis of a questionnaire to be sent to a broader group of respondents. In the example, respondents might be asked whether they agree or disagree with statements such as these:

- Scholarships should be designated for minority students who participate on a speech team.
- Workshops on competitive speech events should be given in urban high schools.
- A mentoring relationship should be established between current participants and new recruits.

Not only would respondents indicate their degree of support for each strategy in some numerical form, but they would also be encouraged to add comments about the way such strategies would work. Although typically the respondents at this stage are a different (and larger) group than the experts polled in the first stage, the Delphi method sometimes uses the same group throughout.

The next step involves resubmitting the questionnaire to the group just polled, but with some additional information provided. Respondents are told the average of the members' responses to the first version of the survey (frequently by way of a mean score, along with standard deviations) and get a chance to see the comments contributed in the previous step. With that information in mind, group members are given one more opportunity to respond to the survey. The summarized results from this round are generally taken as the conclusions of the group.

When a Delphi group is formed to generate a list of issues to be considered, the method may be completed through the process just described. However, a modification of the Delphi method could be used by a group that usually meets face-to-face and expects to identify a single solution to which the group agrees. In this modification, after it has completed the written activity, the group meets so it can thrash its ideas out. The modified Delphi method can be a time-saver for the group, because the face-to-face meeting can skip over areas on which members have already agreed in writing and focus attention on those areas where written comments indicate disagreements among the group members.

Advantages of the Delphi Method.   Groups using the Delphi method can generate ideas without needing to meet in person, which saves both time and money. It may be the only practical way for geographically distributed members to interact. The independent work involved in the process leads to many of the same advantages that NGT has for its users: more equal distribution of participation and the generation of more ideas and more unique ideas than interacting groups might devise. The anonymity of members allows them to be free from the pressure of dominant members. The statistical reporting of results allows each individual's position to be reflected in the final judgment.

Limitations of the Delphi Method.   If groups need to make a decision quickly, the Delphi method is not a good choice. Although the time each member devotes to completing a decision by the Delphi method is usually shorter than the time an interacting group would require of its members, the overall time that elapses before a group finishes the

Delphi process may be months—as members lose surveys on their desks, forget to respond, or make other activities priorities. Electronic communication in groups that habitually use such tools can speed up the time involved, but there is still a loss of time involved in the compilation of responses after each round. Another significant limitation exists for groups that hope to develop some cohesiveness: use of the Delphi method diminishes the chances for cohesiveness as it eliminates face-to-face interaction.

Two Formats Designed to Visualize the Decision Process

Mind-Mapping. In his opening narrative, Jim Osgood described a process called mind-mapping, which he used to structure the decision process of the jury he led. As Wycoff (1991) explains in her book on the process, Mindmapping is a registered trademark belonging to Tony Buzan, formerly the editor of a journal for Mensa, an organization whose members have exceptionally high IQs. Buzan became interested in whether there were strategies individuals could use to enhance their intelligence. He was aware of research on the brain that had discovered that particular activities are centered in particular areas of the brain. Centered in the left hemisphere of the brain are those activities we might normally link to decision making, such as language, logic, and judgments. Such brain activity seems to proceed in a linear manner. The right hemisphere is the center for images, emotions, rhythms, and creative activity. Finding a means of integrating the activity of both hemispheres seemed to Buzan to be a way of enhancing creative decision making. That was the primary goal of mind-mapping.

Situations in Which Mind-Mapping Is Used. Mind-mapping can be used by individuals or groups who seek creative ideas and want to find a way of capturing them on paper. Because the process allows individuals to see relationships among the ideas that have been generated, it is also a technique that can be used to organize decision-making efforts, particularly ones that require the group to organize a wealth of data and consider a variety of decision issues, as was the case for the jury considering whether Timothy McVeigh was guilty of bombing the Federal Building in Oklahoma City.

Steps in the Format. If mind-mapping is used to capture creative efforts, it begins when the group places the topic on which ideas are to be generated in the center of a piece of paper. Anderson (1993) explained how a team using mind-mapping to develop an advertising campaign for an eye shadow product might placed the words "The lady has eyes" in the center of the paper. The next step is to generate ideas as a brainstorming group would do, but to record them on the paper in relation to the central term. Each of those terms then becomes the stimulus for additional brainstorming, and the ideas generated are visually depicted as stemming from the earlier idea. When the central idea has generated a variety of connected ideas and they, in turn, have generated other ideas, then the mind-map visually depicts several ideas in a rather systematic way. For an advertising team, the interconnections among these ideas can be useful; the ideas they have generated can be transformed into advertisements that use slogans and images to suggest similar connections to viewers. The mind-map in this case is used to enhance the creativity of decisions.

The process of mind-mapping used by the McVeigh jury was somewhat different, because the jury was more interested in a systematic process than a creative one. In that case, each of the central issues in the case became the concept in the center of one piece of paper. Stemming out from the center issue was each subissue, just as a spider's legs come out of the central body of the spider. And from each leg, additional lines were drawn for the evidence relevant to that point. The visual image allowed the jury to see more clearly how each piece of evidence was related to each point in the lawyers' case and how each point was ultimately connected to the major issues in the case. In this manner, the mind-maps helped structure the decision process for the group by visually "taming" the complexity of the case.

To see how the process might work in other situations, imagine yourself as a member of a group planning to rehabilitate an old building in your city. The number of issues you need to decide might be depicted in the mind-map (that is admittedly incomplete) shown in Figure 7.2.

Advantages of Mind-Mapping. As a tool for increasing creativity, mind-mapping is much like brainstorming, except that it encourages a somewhat more systematic recording of ideas than brainstorming does. By putting down thoughts in a visually organized way, a mind-mapper is encouraged to think of related thoughts more easily than would be the case for a brainstorming group that creates a more randomly organized list. When ideas are flowing too quickly to discover the "logical" placement of the idea as it is being recorded, mind-mapping encourages rapid recording to be followed by an organizing process of visually grouping ideas (drawing a circle around related ideas or color-coding ideas to reveal relationships among them).

Using mind-mapping to structure a decision-making session allows group members to see the key issues throughout the discussion and to keep in mind the way in which indi-

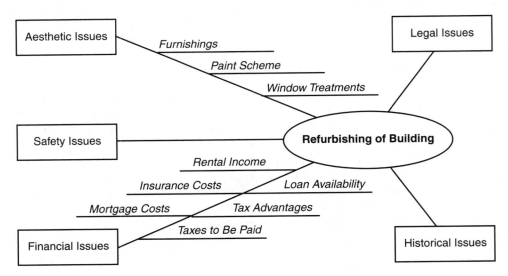

FIGURE 7.2 Mind-mapping can be a useful tool for recording ideas.

vidual pieces of information relate to the whole picture. It provides a content focus for the group. Because the map allows group members to see each issue as a separate issue, it becomes easier for individual group members with greater expertise on a given issue to lead the discussion of that issue and then yield to another group member on another issue.

Limitations of Mind-Mapping. Even individuals who use mind-mapping regularly mention that not everyone is comfortable with a technique that is so visual ("Mind mapping," 1992). Because mind-mapping is often done by individuals, creating a group map may be somewhat difficult when a number of members have their own preferred method of creating a map.

Decision Trees.

The decision tree is a technique used to visualize alternative courses of action and their consequences. It has been used in businesses in which the risks of various alternatives need to be considered, especially in devising sales and marketing approaches or making decisions about product development (Mittra, 1986). Health-care–related agencies use decision trees when considering treatment options, drug safety, and insurance coverage for various treatments (Keeler, 1996). Decision trees would be useful to city councils trying to select among various options for highways in and around town. A committee of military personnel would find the format useful in evaluating the risks of possible responses to an international crisis. A classroom group trying to decide between two different solutions to a campus problem could use a decision tree to help visualize and assess the outcomes of each format.

Situations in Which Decision Trees Are Useful. Whenever your group is considering mutually exclusive alternatives that have multiple consequences, decision trees can be used to visually lay out the options and the consequences of each option. Particularly when a series of decisions needs to be made, decision trees help groups visualize the sequence of decisions and the outcomes of each.

Steps in the Decision-Tree Process. Creating a decision tree requires that you first identify your possible choices. For example, if you are on a committee that is selecting performers to appear in a concert series, the choices might be narrowed, for the sake of this example, to two performers, a well-known performer who demands a high fee and a less known performer whose fees are lower. The committee wants to decide whether to risk the higher-priced performer. A decision tree created to visualize the team's decision would first identify the two choices, as illustrated in Figure 7.3.

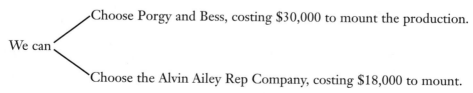

FIGURE 7.3 A Decision Tree begins by identifying options.

In the second step, you identify the possible outcomes of each choice. Your committee would be concerned with how its choice affects ticket sales. When these outcomes are added to the decision tree to describe the initial outcomes, the tree could appear as shown in Figure 7.4. The tree at this point should meet two criteria (Jones, 1995): (a) each of the outcomes should be mutually exclusive; and (b) together, the outcomes should be collectively exhaustive.

With some knowledge of attendance at concerts, your committee could progress to step three in the design of a decision tree: adding calculations for the probability of each specific outcome occurring. Mittra (1986) explained that the infrequent nature of many decisions makes it difficult to calculate probability figures in a truly objective and rigorous fashion. Using previous experience and generally accepted patterns, you can subjectively calculate the probability of a specific action's being taken. In this case, the better-known performer is more likely to lead to a sellout crowd, which would be reflected in the figures. Probabilities are usually represented as a decimal, so a one-in-two chance, or 50% probability, would be written as ".5"; at any decision point, the sum of probabilities for the possible options would total 1.0. In our example, previous experience could lead you to assign a .5 probability to Porgy and Bess selling at least 1200 seats and a .5 probability to its selling at least 1000 seats; the probabilities for the Rep company filling the seats might be lower. Because initial decisions lead to other subsequent decisions, it is possible to continue laying out subsequent outcomes and their probabilities. In our case, however, we consider only the primary outcome: the income to be generated by the performance in comparison with the financial risk involved in hiring the performers.

Finally, the value of each option can be entered into the decision tree. For our example, calculating the total value attached to each option requires two steps. This process is purely mathematical; first, you calculate the total possible value for each outcome. In this example, you would multiply the total number of purchasers possible by the amount each would pay for the ticket. For the sake of simplicity, we will assume that all tickets for the Porgy and Bess performance would sell for $35; for

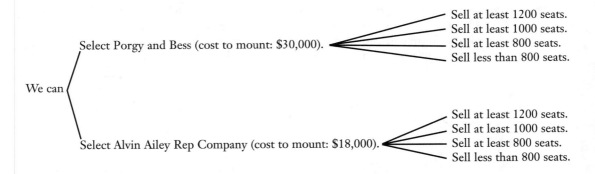

FIGURE 7.4 The second step in using a decision tree is to identify possible outcomes.

the performance by the Alvin Ailey Rep Company, all tickets would sell for $15. The next step is to multiply the total possible value by the probability of each option. By summing the possible outcomes for each option separately and then comparing the options, we could discover whether we could afford the risk of contracting with the higher priced performance. In this case, the completed decision tree would appear as shown in Figure 7.5. These calculations indicate that the greater risk is not in contracting with a higher-priced group able to fill the auditorium, but with a group less able to fill the seats. Of course, the probability projections in our example are purely hypothetical; actually, Alvin Ailey dancers would also be likely to generate a lot of ticket sales. Nonetheless, use of a decision tree can reveal some information about risky decisions that might not be obvious without the use of the format.

Advantages of Using Decision Trees. When a decision is accompanied by a number of "what ifs," some more likely than others, a group may need some way of visualizing the various possible choices and likely outcomes. By laying out the options in a systematic way, a group can consider the complicated issues systematically. As is the case with mind-maps, the visual elements of the decision-tree process tend to allow a group to maintain its focus more easily. The format is useful because it allows groups to go beyond the members' initial, off-the-top-of-their-heads judgments; they may discover that what first seemed to be too risky is, in the long run, the least risky response of all.

Limitations of Decision Trees. Obviously, the mathematics of using a complete decision tree can become complicated, and the process may be more involved than many groups may be interested in. Notice also that the decision tree does not make the decision for you. A decision tree is useful only if the decision maker has generated all reasonable alternatives, discovered all the possible consequences, and analyzed and evaluated them properly.

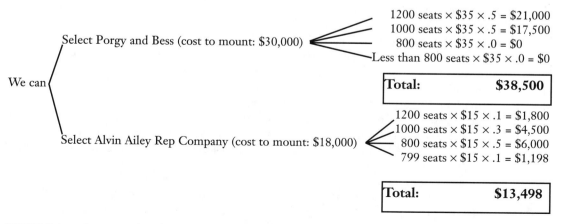

FIGURE 7.5 In a completed decision tree, the outcomes of each option can be compared.

The decision tree provides a format into which information can be organized and visually presented; it does not generate the information any more than it makes the decision itself.

The example we have given here identifies all outcomes in terms of income produced by ticket sales. Not all outcomes are parallel in nature; some may be difficult to compare. For example, a decision tree could be used in health care to assess the risk of surgical versus nonsurgical treatments of angina. The probability of mortality for each option would need to be calculated. But mortality is not the only possible outcome of angina treatment. A patient might actually prefer the greater risk of mortality in surgery if nonsurgical treatment would lead to a life of considerably reduced activity. The form of the decision tree, visually representing all consequences as the same size and shape on a page, might distort the group's perception of all outcomes as being equal in impact. This limitation might be dealt with by altering the size or shape of outcomes as they are listed on a page, thus reflecting their probability of occurring and their divergent value for the group.

Formats Designed to Enhance Critical Thinking: Devil's Advocacy and Dialectical Inquiry

Chapter 5 of this text stressed the importance of building conflict into the deliberation process in order to avoid reaching a decision prematurely, before the group has had a chance to thoroughly consider its decisions. Two related formats, *devil's advocacy* and *dialectical inquiry*, utilize methods that are traditionally associated with debate as a decision-making format, methods that include evaluation of premises, evidence, and reasoning as arguments are weighed during the deliberative process. Both extend Janis's (1982) recommendation of using competing subgroups as a tool for avoiding groupthink; in extending the recommendation, the formats suggest specific steps that competing subgroups can use to structure their activities.

Situations in Which Devil's Advocacy and Dialectical Inquiry Are Useful.   If the decision to be made deals with a matter on which equally reasonable alternatives may be presented and defended, dialectical inquiry and/or devil's advocacy would be appropriate. It is especially useful when the decision is of sufficient import that the group needs to make every effort to foresee potentially dire consequences.

Steps in the Format.   For both approaches, the first step involves dividing the full group into two subgroups, both of which discuss the issue. The second step in both cases requires one subgroup to develop its position in writing, making clear both its recommended decision and its bases for the decision (specifying assumptions, evidence, and reasoning from the evidence). In the third step, the proposal is presented to the second subgroup, which, meeting independently, criticizes the proposal.

At this point, devil's advocacy and dialectical inquiry diverge. In the case of devil's advocacy, the second subgroup critiques the assumptions, evidence, reasoning, and recommendation of the first subgroup. It presents the critique in writing as well as orally to the first subgroup, then leaves the first group alone to revise its recommendation in response to the criticisms. The procedure is repeated until the two subgroups have reached agreement (Priem & Price, 1991).

In the case of dialectical inquiry, the second subgroup goes one step further to introduce conflicting ideas: it develops an alternate position supported with its own set of premises, evidence, and reasoning. The subgroup does this even if the members would have initially agreed with the first subgroup's position. The second subgroup presents its position to the first subgroup, and both subgroups join together to debate their positions. Priem and Price (1991) indicate that the purpose of this debate is to "arrive at a final list of assumptions that is acceptable to both subgroups" (p. 221). Based on the common, and now tested, assumptions, the full group develops a recommendation that represents the decision of the whole group.

Advantages of the Formats. Both devil's advocacy and dialectical inquiry have the advantage of using debate as a decision-making format. Debate involves systematic inquiry into a position and the grounds that have led to the development of that position. The clash inherent in debate is designed to result in the selection of a position for which the premises, evidence, and reasoning have been fully tested and have survived that testing. The resultant decision is one that can be relied upon as both reasonable and defensible.

Limitations of the Formats. When college students engage in academic debate, an independent third party (the judge) assesses the relative merits of the two positions being debated. However, when debate is used in decision-making groups, the advocates are also the decision makers. Thus, devil's advocacy and dialectical inquiry have limited effectiveness if the advocates are unwilling to reach agreement between themselves and insist on supporting their individual positions without attending to the reasonableness of the position or adapting to the criticism of the opposing subgroup. Conversely, the approaches also have limited effectiveness if the subgroups are so intent on reaching a decision that they prematurely select an alternative that further analysis would find to be an inferior alternative. Obviously, when quick action is necessary, these approaches would not have adequate time to function properly.

Use of devil's advocacy and dialectical inquiry techniques may also affect the social relationships within groups. Priem and Price (1991) found, when testing the use of these two techniques against a standard consensus approach, that group members anticipated more social conflict with the use of these two specialized formats. If the anticipated conflict becomes a self-fulfilling prophecy, then group members' commitment to the group may be negatively affected. This negative outcome can be minimized if groups providing critical feedback do so in ways likely to limit the defensiveness of the first subgroup and if those receiving the feedback are taught to value conflicting perceptions of the issue as a means of strengthening the group's final product.

Format Designed to Plan Solution Implementation: Performance Evaluation and Review Technique (PERT)

In the late 1950s, the U.S. Navy was attempting to develop the Polaris missile system, a weapon system for use on a nuclear-powered submarine. The project was a complex one, in part because those in charge had to deal with hundreds of contractors and thousands of subcontractors (Levin & Kirkpatrick, 1966). How long would it take each to develop the part it was expected to produce? How did the responsibility of each relate to the responsibilities of others? These uncertainties posed difficulties for the development of the project, but they were directly addressed by the 1958 development of the PERT model in a joint project with Lockheed Aircraft and the Chicago consulting firm of Booz-Allen & Hamilton (Evarts, 1964). The success of PERT in leading to the timely completion of the Polaris system has led to its implementation in other governmental agencies and private businesses. Small classroom groups have found it to be useful as well in getting their members on track to complete a task within the allotted time.

Situations in Which PERT Is Useful.   If a group has not yet decided on its solution to a problem, then PERT is not useful. Only after a group has decided on its solution is the use of PERT possible. Nonetheless, it can still be considered a decision-making format, because it is used when the group is making decisions about implementing the agreed-upon solution. It focuses the group's attention on considering what steps and what sequence of steps are involved in implementing the decision, allotting the appropriate time for each step, and assigning group members to complete the tasks. PERT is unnecessary in situations that the group faces regularly. For example, a publishing group that puts out a daily newspaper can follow its routine procedure each day without using PERT. But if the group has to publish a special edition that makes its routine procedures useless, then special attention to the details of organizing its activities may lead the group to use PERT.

Steps in the Format.   PERT begins with looking to the future and identifying the *end point*, or "final event," of the task it is facing. For instance, a group planning a fundraising event for the local animal shelter might identify as its final event "the money has been given to the director of the animal shelter." A group hosting a party might have as its final event "cleanup after the party is completed." A group hoping to extend hours in a library could identify as its final event "the library has longer hours." In each example, the final event is the signal that the task of the group has been completed. You might also notice that in each case, at a particular moment in time, a group could recognize that the event had (or had not) occurred, but the event itself does not involve elapsed time. The time involved in reaching the final event is taken up in activities, which are processes that do involve time (Levin & Kirkpatrick, 1966). Thus, cleaning up after a party is an activity and involves elapsed time; "the cleanup is completed" is an event that can be recognized at one moment in time but does not involve, itself, elapsed time.

The second step in the PERT process requires the group to identify the predecessor events necessary if the final event is to be reached, usually through brainstorming.

For example, a group putting on a training program in a classroom might identify the following events:

Final Event:
The training program is completed.

Predecessor Events:
Group members gather research.
Available resources on the topic are identified.
The goal of the training is identified.
Activities to include in the training are selected.
Activities are rehearsed.
Means of evaluating the effectiveness of the training are identified.
The effectiveness of the training is evaluated.
Information to include in the training program is organized.
Visual aids to reinforce key concepts are completed.
Packets for class members are prepared.
Contents of the packets are selected.
The training program is rehearsed and timed.
Alterations in the program are made to polish the program.

You have probably noticed that there is not a logical order for the events in this list, because brainstorming does not usually proceed in an entirely logical order. Putting the events in a logical order is the next step of the process. The steps can be numbered to reflect their relationship to one another. Here you can see the way one group might number the previous steps:

3. Group members gather research.
2. Available resources on the topic are identified.
1. The goal of the training is identified.
6. Activities to include in the training are selected.
10. Activities are rehearsed.
13. Means of evaluating effectiveness of the training are identified.
14. The effectiveness of the training is evaluated.
5. Information to include in the training program is organized.
8. Visual aids to reinforce key concepts are completed.
9. Packets for class members are prepared.
7. Contents of the packets are selected.
11. The training program is rehearsed and timed.
12. Alterations in the program are made to polish the program.
4. **Information to include in the training is selected.**

Notice that in the process of numbering the events, an additional one—item 4—has been identified. To accomplish that event, it might be necessary for a group to have an additional meeting. Having numbered the events, a diagram can be drawn (Figure 7.6)

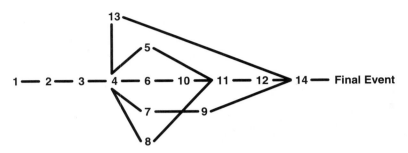

FIGURE 7.6 Diagramming the predecessor events leading up to a
final event helps to illustrate the relationships between the events.

that shows the relationships between the events. The lines from one event to another
represent the activity involved in accomplishing each event.

Groups should next estimate the time required to complete each activity. PERT
handbooks make varied recommendations as to how to do each estimate. If a given
activity has been done with some regularity before, then the group can use a single time
estimate—the time it regularly uses to complete that task. If the task is unfamiliar, then
the group might estimate time in this more complex fashion: figure the time the task
will take if everything goes as quickly as it could (optimistic time); add to that the time
the task will take if barriers occur that might interfere with efficiency (pessimistic time);
then add a weighted estimate for the most realistic amount of time needed (the realistic time is weighted by multiplying it by 4); then divide the sum by 6 (since it represents six total times: 1 optimistic time + 1 pessimistic time + 4 realistic times). The time
estimates for all of the activities are added and then compared to the actual time the
group has available to it. Typically, the group will need to make adjustments at that
point. The group might make an adjustment by altering its final event (instead of having the library hours extended as the final event, the group will settle for having made
its proposal to the library board). It might adjust by eliminating one of the predecessor
events. For instance, in the example, if preparation of packets left the group with inadequate time to complete the task, the group might decide to omit the packets. The
group might adjust by reorganizing the distribution of effort, either by allocating more
members of the group to accomplish one task more quickly or by dividing up resources
to accomplish more tasks at once. Once the adjustment has been completed, group
members can be assigned to specific activities identified in the diagram.

Advantages of PERT.   PERT focuses the group's attention on the steps involved in
implementing a decision, the time involved in the task, and the distribution of human
resources to accomplish the tasks. By focusing on both long-term and short-term goals (in
the form of the final event and the predecessor events), the format assists with time management. By focusing on the time available, the format should reduce the tendency a
group may have to procrastinate. Comparing available time to estimated time may force
groups to become realistic about what they can actually accomplish in their allotted time.
Individual members of the group also discover how their parts in the task relate to the tasks
of others. They see, with the diagram, who is counting on them to complete a particular

Technology Note: Decision Support Systems

Most of the formats described in this chapter, along with the strategies used in problem solving, can be used by groups communicating by means of computers, because a variety of computer programs are available that provide the necessary tools.

Brainstorming groups can contribute ideas that are then displayed on a common, large screen. Many decision-support systems have a tool that allows a group to chart the ways possible solutions meet the group's criteria. Groups can use computers when they employ either the nominal group technique or the Delphi technique. There are also tools that allow groups (or individuals) to create decision trees and PERT diagrams on computer. The market is developing quickly and changing constantly, but there are many decision-support systems available for use. Groups will not find in the tools a panacea for problems in the group. In fact, groups experiencing difficulties of any kind are likely to use the decision-support system as a scapegoat for their problems. Analysis of groups that have made use of the systems indicates that groups adapt the tools for their own uses and make better use of them if the tools are introduced early in the life of the group (Poole, DeSanctis, Kirsch, & Jackson, 1995).

task and why it must be done by a particular time if the whole job is to be completed on time. A sense of responsibility should emerge; if it does not, then at least the group can pinpoint the cause of delays with greater ease and adjust again to the new situation.

Limitations of PERT. This decision-making format does not help a group arrive at a solution to a problem. It can only be used once that decision has been made by a group. If a group is not careful in identifying all predecessor events or in making reasonable time estimates, group members may think they are well prepared to implement their decision when they are not. Using the process effectively requires that time be devoted to completing each step carefully.

Summary

Whatever their type, small groups regularly engage in decision making. They may be formed precisely to make decisions (such as what copy machine to purchase for the office or which candidate to hire for a job), or they may need to make decisions in the final stage of a problem-solving process. Even social groups may need to decide where to meet or eat or what to do for fun.

The nature of decision making is heavily influenced by two factors: the decision rules of the group and the format used in the decision-making process. Typically a group selects its decision rules from three options: decisions by consensus, decision by majority vote, and decision by negotiation. None of the decision rules is appropriate in all situations. The conditions within the group and the goals of the group should be considered before determining how to decide. Once that decision is made, it has an impact on the kinds of communication that are valued within the group.

The format followed also influences the group's decision making. A number of formats have been devised already, and more will be created each year. You might even devise a format yourself. Each of the formats described here—satisficing, elimination by aspects, paired alternatives, nominal group technique, the Delphi method, mind-mapping, decision trees, devil's advocacy, dialectical inquiry, and performance evaluation and review technique—has been designed to accomplish a specific function: from limiting the number of solution options to increasing the diversity of proposals, from visualizing the decision process to planning the solution's implementation. You should become familiar with the variety of formats available and the functions that each serves best or least. The formats are summarized in the chart in Figure 7.7. You may be able to use many of the formats when you communicate by means of computers, since programs are available that allow you to do so, as long as you develop facility with their use. Above all, you should be aware of the importance of having the form of the tool well matched to the function of the group at the point of making its decision. Armed with the understanding that *form follows function*, you should be able to devise, evaluate, modify, and select the format most appropriate for the needs of your group.

QUESTIONS FOR DISCUSSION

1. How might the decision rules of a group influence the likelihood that groupthink will occur?

2. How can a group effectively determine whether the form of a decision-making format fits its functions?

3. Consider the following situations and, for each, answer these two questions: (a) *What decision rule should the group adopt?* (b) *What decision-making format seems best suited to the group's needs?*
    a. A Senate committee is meeting to consider the future of the office of Independent Counsel. The committee will decide whether to eliminate or maintain the position.
    b. A college has decided that all incoming freshmen will be required to read the same book (either fiction or nonfiction). The book will be used as a stimulus for discussion in orientation sessions before school begins. You are advising the committee that will select the book.
    c. A city commission is deciding between two candidates for Director of Parks and Recreation. The commission, which has experienced a lot of conflict in recent years, is now strongly split in their support for the two candidates.
    d. Your family is selecting the destination for a two-week summer vacation.
    e. A company wants to develop a new product, but to beat the competition will require a sizable increase in investment.
        (1) They are trying to decide whether it is worthwhile to commit the necessary resources.
        (2) The decision was made to increase investment and proceed with development. Now the development plans need to be decided upon.
        (3) Development is nearing completion. Now an advertising campaign must be designed. A new committee must decide on the design.

FIGURE 7.7 A chart summarizing the decision-making formats described in this chapter.

Function	Format Name	Form	Advantages/Disadvantages
To narrow choices among possible solutions	Satisficing	1. Identify essential criteria. 2. Select standard(s) for deciding whether each criterion is met. 3. Evaluate alternatives against criteria. 4. Select first option to meet criteria.	+ Saves time in decision making when several choices could be satisfactory. − May overlook the best options.
	Elimination by Aspects	1. Identify the most important criterion. 2. Measure alternatives against that criterion. 3. Select alternative that best meets criterion. 4. In case of a tie, compare alternatives against second most important criterion.	+ Saves time in decision making. − Can shortchange decision process. − If multiple criteria are important, may exclude solutions with the best chance of meeting more than one criterion.
	Paired Alternatives	1. Group alternatives in pairs that are most alike. 2. Choose the best of each pair. 3. Compare remaining options.	+ Group is forced to recognize differences between quite similar options. + May clarify criteria. − Does not save time.
To increase independent work by group members ■ Avoiding pressures of conformity ■ Allowing work despite high conflict ■ Equalizing group power	Nominal Group Technique (NGT)	1. Announce topic to group. 2. Members work alone generating ideas silently. 3. Assemble ideas through round-robin listing. 4. Group communicates to clarify ideas. 5. Group votes on ideas. [Process may end here, or may go on to . . .] 6. Explain votes. 7. Take a final vote.	+ Maintains task focus rather than relationship diversion. + Allows group to reach closure. + Allows divergent members to interact effectively. − Time-consuming. − Lack of interaction may decrease satisfaction and ability to work out real differences.

continued

FIGURE 7.7 Continued

Function	Format Name	Form	Advantages/Disadvantages
To increase independent work by group members (continued) ■ When the opportunity to work together is limited	Delphi Method	1. Invite individuals with expertise on topic to form a group. 2. Group responds in writing to the decision question. 3. Compile answers from members. 4. Send compiled answers to members. 5. Members respond to indicate support for items. 6. Summed reactions are distributed to members who respond once again. 7. Final responses are compiled as the group decision. 8. Group may meet face-to-face to work out areas of disagreement.	+ Allows decision-making process to occur even when face-to-face meetings are not possible. + Equalizes opportunity for influence among group members. + Increases idea generation. − Elapsed time from start to finish is high. − Hinders development of cohesiveness.
To visualize the decision process ■ Capturing creative ideas on paper organizing a wealth of data around decision issues	Mind-mapping	1. Place key topic in center of paper. 2. Place related ideas around the key topic, as spokes of a wheel. 3. Place related ideas or data as stems off these legs.	+ Stimulates added creativity and/or systematic handling of ideas. + Allows group to see idea relationships more clearly. − Less comfortable for nonvisual thinkers.
■ Laying out options, the sequence of decisions, and the outcomes of each	Decision trees	1. Identify possible choices. 2. Identify mutually exclusive and collectively exhaustive potential outcomes of choices. 3. Calculate probability of each outcome. 4. Enter the value of each outcome. 5. Compare likely outcomes of options to determine whether risks are warranted.	+ Encourages systematic evaluation of choices. + Evaluates risk more carefully. − Process is too complicated for simple decisions. − Difficult if outcomes are not easily compared.

Purpose	Technique	Procedure	Evaluation
To enhance critical thinking about decisions between two reasonable courses of action	Devil's Advocacy	1. Divide group into subgroups. 2. One group develops a position in writing. 3. Second group critiques that position and its assumptions, evidence, and reasoning. 4. After reading critique, first group revises recommendation. 5. Repeat procedure until agreement is reached	+ Enhances systematic inquiry through use of debate. + Increases confidence in the defensibility of final choice. – Limited effectiveness if group becomes caught in roles as opposing subgroups. – Limited effectiveness if group shortchanges the process to avoid disagreement.
	Dialectical Inquiry	1. Divide into subgroups. 2. Each group develops its position in writing. 3. Subgroups join together in a debate. 4. Full group reconvenes to create joint recommendations.	– May reduce cohesiveness in group.

To plan solution implementation	Performance Evaluation and Review Technique (PERT)	1. Identify the final event.
		2. Brainstorm for predecessor events.
		3. Order the events chronologically.
		4. Diagram events to reveal sequential relationships.
		5. Estimate the time required to complete activities between events.
		6. Compare required time with available time.
		7. Make adjustments.
		  ■ Reassigning personnel
		  ■ Altering final event
		  ■ Omitting unnecessary predecessor evemts
			+ Assists with time management.
			+ Forces realistic and specific consideration of commitments.
			+ Increases sense of responsibility to task.
			– Only useful when solution has been selected.
			– Requires time if it is to be done well.

SUGGESTED ACTIVITIES

1. Interview individuals involved in a college-wide or program accreditation effort. Discover how the campus group makes decisions about what to include in its self-study.

2. Watch the movie *Twelve Angry Men*. Consider whether a decision rule other than consensus would have been desirable for the jury to use in making its decision.

3. Identify the decision-making formats most suitable for your project groups to use in making decisions it is facing. Employ those formats. Analyze their effectiveness. Are there ways in which your group could adapt the formats to improve their utility?

4. Analyze an important decision that you personally have made or that has been made by others. Describe the process that was used in making the decision. Evaluate the quality of the decision. Identify the factors responsible for the decision's quality.

SOURCES CITED

Anderson, J. V. (1993, January). Mind mapping: A tool for creative thinking. *Business Horizons, 36*, 41–46.

Dalkey, N. C., Rourke, D. L., Lewis, R., & Snyder, D. (1972). *Studies in the quality of life: Delphi and decision making.* Lexington, MA: Lexington Books.

Delbecq, A. L., Van de Ven, A. H., & Gustafson, D. H. (1986). *Group techniques for program planning: A guide to nominal group and delphi processes.* Middleton, WI: Green Briar Press.

Evarts, H. F. (1964). *Introduction to PERT.* Boston: Allyn & Bacon.

Gargan, J. J., & Brown, S. R. (1993). "What is to be done?" Anticipating the future and mobilizing prudence. *Policy Sciences, 26*, 347–359.

Hall, J., & Williams, M. S. (1966). A comparison of decision-making performances in established and ad hoc groups. *Journal of Personality and Social Psychology, 3*, 214–222.

Hetzel, R. W. (1992). Solving complex problems requires good people, good processes. *NASSP Bulletin, 76* (540), 49–55.

Hickson, L., Worrall, L., Yiu, E., & Barnett, H. (1996). Planning a communication education program for older people. *Educational Gerontology, 22*, 257–269.

Hirokawa, R. Y. (1984). Does consensus really result in higher quality group decisions? In G. M. Phillips & J. T. Wood (Eds.), *Emergent issues in human decision making* (pp. 40–60). Carbondale: Southern Illinois University Press.

Hornsby, J. S., Smith, B. N., & Gupta, J. N. D. (1994). The impact of decision-making methodology on job evaluation outcomes: A look at three consensus approaches. *Group & Organization Management, 19*, 112–128.

Janis, I. L. (1982). *Groupthink: Psychological studies of policy decisions and fiascoes.* Boston: Houghton-Mifflin.

Jenkins, D. (1996). A reflecting team approach to family therapy: A Delphi study. *Journal of Marital and Family Therapy, 22*, 219–238.

Jones, M. D. (1995). *The thinker's toolkit: Fourteen skills for making smarter decisions in business and in life.* New York: Random House.

Keeler, E. (1996). Decision trees and Markov models in cost-effectiveness research. In F. A. Sloan (Ed.), *Valuing health care: Costs, benefits, and effectiveness of pharmaceuticals and other medical technologies.* New York: Cambridge University Press.

Levin, R. I., & Kirkpatrick, C. A. (1966). *Planning and control with PERT/CPM.* New York: McGraw-Hill.

Martolla, P. H. (1991). Consensus building among social educators: A Delphi study. *Theory and Research in Social Education, 19*, 83–94.

Mind mapping: A new way to think on paper. (1992, November 16). *Fortune, 126,* 12.

Mittra, S. S. (1986). *Decision support systems: Tools and techniques.* New York: Wiley.

Nemeth, C. J., & Kwan, J. L. (1987). Minority influence, divergent thinking, and detection of correct solutions. *Journal of Applied Social Psychology, 17,* 788–799.

Nemiroff, P. M., & King, D. C. (1975). Group decision-making performance as influenced by consensus and self-orientation. *Human Relations, 28,* 1–21.

Passig, D. (1997). Imen-Delphi: A Delphi variant procedure for emergence. *Human Organization, 56,* 53–62.

Payne, J. W., Bettman, J. R., & Johnson, E. J. (1993). The use of multiple strategies in judgment and choice. In N. J. Castellan, Jr. (Ed.), *Individual and group decision making: Current issues* (pp. 19–29). Hillsdale, NJ: Erlbaum.

Phillips, G. M. (1984). Consensus as cultural tradition: A study of agreements between marital partners. In G. M. Phillips & J. T. Wood (Eds.), *Emergent issues in human decision making* (pp. 97–119). Carbondale: Southern Illinois University Press.

Poole, M. S., DeSanctis, G., Kirsch, L., & Jackson, M. (1995). Group decision support systems as facilitators of quality team efforts. In L. R. Frey (Ed.), *Innovations in group facilitation: Applications in natural settings* (pp. 299–321). Cresskill, NJ: Hampton Press.

Priem, R. L., & Price, K. H. (1991). Process and outcome expectations for the dialectical inquiry, devil's advocacy, and consensus techniques of strategic decision making. *Group & Organization Studies, 16,* 206–225.

Raskin, M. S. (1994). The Delphi study in field instruction revisited: Expert consensus on issues and research priorities. *Journal of Social Work Education, 30,* 75–89.

Rawlins, W. K. (1984). Consensus in decision-making groups: A conceptual history. In G. M. Phillips & J. T. Wood (Eds.), *Emergent issues in human decision making* (pp. 19–39). Carbondale: Southern Illinois University Press.

Skibbe, A. (1986). Assessing campus needs with nominal groups. *Journal of Counseling and Development, 64,* 532–533.

Thompson, L. L., Mannix, E. A., & Bazerman, M. H. (1988). Group negotiation: Effects of decision rule, agenda, and aspiration. *Journal of Personality and Social Psychology, 54,* 86–95.

Toseland, R. W., Rivas, R. F., & Chapman, D. (1984). An evaluation of decision-making methods in task groups. *Social Work, 29,* 339–345.

Wood, J. T. (1984). Alternative methods of group decision making: A comparative examination of consensus, negotiation, and voting. In G. M. Phillips & J. T. Wood (Eds.), *Emergent issues in human decision making* (pp. 3–18). Carbondale: Southern Illinois University Press.

Wycoff, J. (1991). Mindmapping: Your personal guide to exploring creativity and problem solving. New York: Berkley Books.

CHAPTER

8 Managing Effective Meetings

CHAPTER OBJECTIVES:

After reading this chapter, you should be able to

- Determine whether conditions warrant holding a meeting
- Find a meeting time for groups whose members have conflicting personal schedules
- Identify the characteristics of an effective agenda
- Create an effective agenda
- Describe the communication behaviors most important to leading a meeting
- Describe the standard rules for conducting business in a meeting
- Discuss the additional responsibilities associated with holding an electronic meeting
- Identify the responsibilities groups have after a meeting is over

The Narrative

Al Lewis, 59, began to lead meetings in high school when he was class and student body president. In college, he gained formal training in leading meetings from classes in small group communication and parliamentary procedure. He is involved in voluntary organizations such as Habitat for Humanity and church groups. He has served as president of faculty unions and had a decade of academic administrative positions, especially at Central Michigan University where he currently teaches. All of these experiences have added to his understanding of the skills involved in managing effective meetings, the subject he discusses here:

> *Any organization—other than a dictatorship—conducts its business through the use of meetings. When I was a department chair, I had at least a meeting a day, perhaps even as many as 30 meetings in a month with 20 work days.*
>
> *The bad meetings are the easiest to remember. I remember one meeting I was at that had 50 items on the agenda. The scheduled two-hour meeting took four and a half hours. That was*

a very bad meeting because we made very bad decisions. We were rushing through the decisions, especially at the end. There was no need for 50 items to be on the agenda. And the time schedule was violated; there was no integrity to it.

I attended another meeting that was bad because it lacked focus. It was a meeting at which there were representatives from about seven different churches that were interested in Habitat for Humanity. I had thought the purpose was to help those people who had never been involved with Habitat for Humanity learn how they could get a group started in their churches. But there was no agenda. The person conducting the meeting merely said, "What do you have to share?" People ended up sharing some of their experiences, and there's some usefulness to that. But there was no "here's how you go about it" information for people to take away with them. As a result, I think five of the seven went away not knowing how to start a group or where resources were, even though there are plenty of resources available. Subsequently—and consequently—none of them did start a program.

In contrast with those two meetings, meetings that are skillfully managed have a clear focus. There's an agenda that everyone can look at. Everyone understands the procedure, which is clearly spelled out. People have done their homework before they get there. Things get done.

An agenda is a sort of hidden element, because it is developed before the meeting starts. The leader sets the agenda and should structure it so that there is plenty of time to consider the contentious and important issues, with time still left for other elements. How it all gets put together is extremely important—probably equally important to what is actually done in the meeting. The bell-shaped agenda described by Tropman (1980) is the best tool that I've run across now in 40 years of leading organizations. I think most of his rules are very, very practical, and I've used them now for at least 10 years, maybe 15. I remember the first time I put an agenda together where the easy items were first and the important ones were in the middle. It worked. I don't think anybody else noticed the specific changes, but they felt good because things really got done. They commented on the effectiveness of the meeting and how good they felt about how it was done. I've taught this principle to leaders of committees at my church, and several have told me afterward what a difference it's made in their meetings. Of course, no leader is always correct when predicting which issues will be contentious. That's why in the last third of the agenda, you build in the flexibility to expand or contract the discussion, depending upon what's happened before.

At the end of an agenda, I add "for the good of the order," which I got from Robert's Rules of Order. *It allows for the personal to be brought in, for compliments to be given, and things to be shared. It is what it says: it's for the good maintaining of the order of the group. It's a nice way to end a meeting.*

An occasional writer will recommend that meetings should limit their agenda to one item, but I think most organizations have to do more than a single item for most of their meetings. The length of a meeting should be limited, probably to an hour and a half to two hours. After two hours, if you don't have a significant break, you're asking for the quality of decision making to do down.

In addition to setting up a good agenda, having an understanding of the rules of order is important. I follow Robert's Rules of Order, *but I don't try to make it obvious. They are a set of rules to help the opinions of the minority be protected and help them to surface while allowing the majority still to make decisions. That's a good premise to follow. So having some sense of the rules of order is important. It's also important to have a good sense of timing as you listen to a debate so that you sense when the discussion is starting to become repetitive and to step in, start to summarize, and ask them if they're ready to vote on the issue. Some skills take some time to acquire and begin to feel comfortable with, such as having the ability to control those who want to dominate the proceedings or the conversation and having the ability to draw out people who, pushed out by the dominators, may be silent but have some contributions.*

It's also important to have the ability, as the leader, to stay out of the discussion even if you think the discussion is important, because you're supposed to be the impartial chair. There are ways that you can provide information and raise questions that will lead the organization to look at things you think are important without your becoming an advocate. But there may be times—if you know the most and feel the strongest about an issue—when you should step down and not run the meeting, but become an advocate, and turn the leadership position over to someone else for that period of time.

After an especially contentious meeting, when even informality at the meeting's end isn't enough to get people's feelings out of their systems, then you talk with people afterward. You soothe feelings. You do things that maintain groupness. That's important because in the heat of debate people may have said things that they really didn't mean. The other thing I do, within an hour or so after a meeting, is to make a list of what has to be done for the next meeting. What needs to be pulled through and dealt with at the next meeting? I forget if I don't make a note. I also double check to see what has to be sent forward if action has been taken on it. Usually you're going to be meeting within a larger system, so there are certain things you have to carry forward. I check to be sure all of those things are at least listed so I know what I have to do to see that the actions of the meeting are carried out. I might delegate some activity to others, so I might remind them of their obligations as we're leaving or call them the next day.

My experience is that two out of every three meetings probably are inefficient. I left the chair's position because the constant inefficient meetings drove me wild. I started thinking of all the things I could be doing, including teaching more classes. Leaders can improve the rate of effective meetings by forethought—creating a good agenda, calling people before the meeting starts, that sort of thing. To the extent that they do, then they are doing something that is of tremendous usefulness for any organization.

Groups of all types have formal group meetings. Unfortunately, the meetings are often less productive than they might be. Even the meetings of informal groups suffer from inefficiency. Because we attend so many meetings and so many of them are less than satisfactory, it should not be surprising to discover that someone like Al Lewis would go so far as to leave academic administration in order to reduce the time spent in inefficient meetings. And yet, there is enough potential value from meetings that groups keep on scheduling them. They are, as Al Lewis said, the means for groups and organizations to accomplish their business.

In some groups, the responsibility for leading the meeting is shared, either within meetings or by rotating the responsibility from one meeting to the next. Other groups give the duty to a single appointed leader. Whatever arrangement is made by the groups to which you belong, if you know how to lead and participate in group meetings, you can help to improve their effectiveness. The goal of this chapter is to provide you with strategies designed to help in that effort. We will consider (1) deciding whether to have a meeting, (2) preparing for a meeting, (3) handling the actual meeting, and (4) following up after a meeting.

Deciding Whether to Have a Meeting

One of the reasons meetings may seem to waste time is that some are held unnecessarily. Before a meeting is scheduled, there should be a conscious decision as to whether one is actually needed. Several questions can be asked to determine whether a meeting should be scheduled (Dewey & Creth, 1993):

1. Is there a clear goal that could be achieved with a meeting?
   - Is there a need for discussion by the group members?
   - Is there a need for a decision from the group?
   - Does the group need an opportunity to ask questions about a decision made for them and/or to hear that decision announced in person?
   - Is it necessary to gain commitment from the group for a project?
   - Does the group need some time to be together for reasons of cohesiveness or morale building?
   - Can the goal be achieved more effectively by meeting than by telephone calls, electronic mail, or memoranda?
2. Will the key people (those most essential to the decision and/or most affected by it) be able to attend the meeting?
3. Can those attending the meeting be prepared for it?

If each of the primary questions can be answered with a "yes," then there is only one more step to take before scheduling a meeting: weighing the costs of the meeting against its benefits. A face-to-face meeting may be particularly expensive for groups whose members are physically dispersed. But even those groups that do not need to consider transportation costs still lose the productivity of members who are taken away from their primary jobs during the time of a meeting.

To suggest that a decision to meet should not be entered into lightly is not to imply that meetings are unnecessary or disadvantageous. In reality, meetings do serve

Technology Note: A Meeting, but Not Face-to-Face

If some group interaction is necessary, but meeting face-to-face would be hard to justify, then a conference call, a videoconference, or several E-mail interactions might be a better choice. Such an approach could save time and money, be easier to arrange, and result in less stress or fatigue, as well as less loss of productivity, than would occur from a face-to-face gathering (Seekings, 1992).

Non–face-to-face meetings can have additional advantages of allowing interaction between people who would otherwise not be able to interact easily, if at all. Dewey and Creth (1993) reported on the use of E-mail to create what might be called virtual meetings for library staffs. They included the comments of a librarian at Cornell University's Medical Library who described the advantage their staff gained from coordinating involvement of evening and weekend staff with the weekly daytime staff; messages left in others' electronic mailboxes overcame the boundaries of time. Others reported overcoming geographic boundaries for librarians in different campuses for a university system or for those working in remote areas who could not easily have reached a common meeting place. Even status distinctions were overcome: workers too low in status to be eligible for funding to travel to meetings were able to make electronic contact with professionals at other institutions.

some important purposes. Developments that will affect members can be described to them in a uniform time, place, and manner. Concerns that surface can be responded to immediately. In addition, a meeting is a forum for decision making in which each group member can hear and be heard by others; others can respond to each person's concerns immediately. The opportunities for mutual influence, airing of disagreements, and debate are essential in making sound decisions. Then, once a decision has been made, a meeting can be used to help develop commitment to the decision. When there is conflict affecting a group, a meeting can allow the group to resolve it; it is especially important that those meetings be face-to-face. Meeting face-to-face allows feelings of group members to be read more accurately and misinterpretations to be immediately clarified rather than lingering until further contact. Even in those cases when a meeting could be replaced by memos and E-mail messages, the choice to meet together in one place at one time can be wise, for it develops a sense of "groupness" important to the cohesiveness of the group. In fact, early in the life of a team that typically meets by electronic means, face-to-face meetings are important to cement the feelings of being connected.

However, having too many meetings in which the members feel as if nothing in particular is being accomplished dulls their interest in attending any meetings, even those that may be essential. Therefore, if you cannot identify a specific purpose for having a meeting, do not have one. If there is good reason to meet, know what it is and be able to express it clearly.

Preparing for a Meeting

Once the decision to meet has been made, preparations for the meeting must begin. Planning for a meeting is of such importance that when Clawson, Bostrom, and Anson (1993) asked experienced facilitators what role behaviors were most critical to effective facilitation, the most frequently mentioned were planning and designing meetings. These tasks are just as important to a group meeting without the assistance of a facilitator. Meeting preparations include four important steps: scheduling a meeting time, securing a place for the meeting, setting an agenda for the meeting, and preparing to contribute to the meeting. The checklist in Figure 8.1 is a reminder of these important steps.

Scheduling a Meeting Time

The first decision to be made is to determine the time for the meeting. Having a standard time for a group meeting eliminates the need to decide on a time again and again. For example, the Interpersonal and Public Communication faculty at Central Michigan University have a set meeting time of Thursdays from 3:30–5:00 p.m. No classes are scheduled to be taught by full-time faculty during that time. Group members know not to schedule other appointments during that time. They do not meet every week, but the time is available whenever a meeting is needed. Classroom groups can also benefit from a set meeting time. College students often work in jobs that have variable hours for employers who schedule work hours around class obligations. If a

Premeeting Checklist

C H E C K L I S T

- Decide that a meeting is needed.
- Set meeting time so key members can attend.
- Reserve a room that
    - *Is comfortable*
    - *Is accessible*
    - *Is equipped with the necessary materials*
    - *Contains the proper seating*
- Agenda is prepared
    - *All items are included.*
    - *Arranged in a bell shape.*
    - *Worded as decision issues.*
    - *Supplemental information is attached.*
- Agenda is distributed.

FIGURE 8.1 A premeeting checklist aids in organization.

classroom group establishes a standard meeting time, students who make group membership a priority can and will include the meeting time in their class obligations.

If there is no regular meeting time, then the time chosen for a specific meeting should be one at which all members can be present, along with any resource people the group may want at the meeting. For instance, if you were in a group that was trying to improve the choice of concerts on a college campus, you might want to meet with a representative of the office that currently schedules concerts. That person's schedule would be as important as the schedule of any member of your group.

If it is not possible to find a meeting time that all members find agreeable, then you can follow the advice given by David Hon in his 1980 book, *Meetings That Matter: A Self-Teaching Guide.* Hon suggested weighting the anticipated importance of each member to the decisions to be made at the meeting, and then setting a meeting time at which the members with the greatest combined influence can be present. Consider a hypothetical community group meeting about a recreation center the city is developing. Ideally, attendance at the meeting might include 10 individuals: the project architect, the 2 primary contributors of funds to the project, the coach of the local ice hockey team, the coach of the traveling basketball team, the high-school physical education teacher, the city mayor, a community activist, and 2 teenagers appointed to the committee. But suppose that there are time conflicts that prevent all of them from meeting at once. If the meeting is called to consider a problem in the design of the ice rink, requiring additional funding for the project, then the essential members would probably include the project architect, at least one of the primary contributors, and the ice hockey coach. The time that would allow those members to attend would make the best choice. If the dynamics of the group are such that the mayor (or any one of the other members) has significant influence on any decision the group makes, then that person's schedule should also be considered in setting the meeting time.

Suppose, instead, that the problem the group faces relates to the rules for using the basketball court. Then the meeting planner might weight members' influence on the decision in this way:

> Architect: 5%
> Contributor one: 10%
> Contributor two: 10%
> Ice hockey coach: 5%
> **Basketball coach: 20%**
> **P.E. teacher: 15%**
> Mayor: 5%
> Activist: 10%
> **Teen member one: 15%**
> Teen member two: 5%

In this case, 3 of the 10 individuals would be predicted to share half of the influence over the decision, so the schedules of those 3 should be given first priority in scheduling the meeting time. Hon explained that once a time is set that works for the members whose influence on the decision will be greatest, the other members who initially thought they might not be able to make the meeting may well find a way to be there after all.

Setting the meeting time should include estimating the duration of the meeting. The length of the meeting should be appropriate for the tasks the group needs to accomplish as well as the energy level the group members can maintain over time. The number of items on the agenda should be realistic. In the opening narrative, Al Lewis recalled the failure of a meeting he had attended that had 50 items on the agenda and that exceeded his recommended hour-and-a-half to two-hour meeting length. An agenda with too many items will make the group feel rushed. If the agenda is completed, decisions are likely to be poor; if the group cannot complete the agenda, it is likely to

Technology Note: Arranging the Electronic Meeting

Finding a time to meet for a group located in the same business or college may be difficult, but arranging a meeting time for team members located in different cities or countries can be even more difficult. A team member rising early in New York City would find a fellow team member relaxing after dinner in Tokyo. But a third member of the team residing in California might object to a teleconference at 3 a.m. It becomes especially important in the case of virtual teams to determine which members are important to any given meeting so that only those with expertise and a stake in the decision need to be contacted.

feel unproductive. On the other hand, an agenda that sets out too little business will cause members to feel that they have gathered for little reason. If only an item or two needs discussion and the discussion on each would be quick, waiting for a later meeting would be a reasonable course of action. Another possibility would be to use the additional meeting time to address some less immediate issues: engage in self-reflection, take stock of where the group is, and begin to consider some long-term goals.

All in all, it may be wise to have several brief meetings at which members work efficiently than to have a single, long meeting near the end of which members are barely coherent. In fact, Gastil (1993) studied meetings of a food co-op that extended for two hours and sometimes beyond. His interviews with staff members led to his conclusion that overly long meetings are an obstacle to democracy within a small group. The length of the meetings encouraged unequal participation levels and led to a lack of involvement in the group. Nonetheless, if it is especially difficult to gather all members together for a meeting, the only way to accomplish business as a group may be to have fewer meetings at which the group works longer to complete its tasks. It is hard to imagine, however, that any group could have success in the conditions Al Lewis described, where the meeting extended beyond four hours, without breaks!

Securing a Meeting Place

When the time for the meeting has been determined, then a place for it can be arranged as well. Groups that have a regular meeting time are likely also to have a regular meeting place, scheduled for their use at each meeting. On occasion, group members may want to change the meeting place so they can interact in different ways than are typical. For instance, if a group that regularly meets to take care of its day-to-day business needs to begin some long-range planning, the members may find that being in a less formal, more relaxing setting will free their minds to think creatively.

Whatever the location for the meeting, it should be comfortable, accessible to all attending, and free from distractions. There should be enough space for everyone in the group to be seated comfortably with a place for taking notes. On the other hand, there should not be so much space that the group feels overwhelmed by its setting. The meeting place should have available the equipment and space the group needs to complete its task. If the purpose of the meeting is to do brainstorming, for instance, there should be something (a chalkboard, flip chart, or visualizer) on which ideas can be recorded. Sometimes, an on-site location might be chosen as the best way of providing the group with the information it needs. In the case of the hypothetical group meeting to resolve ice rink design problems, meeting at the recreation center location might best allow the group to understand the nature of the problem it is facing and then complete its task of making a decision to solve the problem.

Any group that is going to have a discussion should pay attention to elements in the setting such as the shape of the table and the positioning and size of the chairs. An arrangement that encourages a free flow of discussion is important. If the purpose of the meeting is to rehearse a presentation, then the space should be the same as (or very similar to) the space in which the presentation will be done. If members of the group need computer assistance or to be connected to others at a distant site, then a specially designed or equipped meeting room is necessary.

Of course, when special equipment such as that necessary for a videoconference is needed, then there may be less choice about where to hold a meeting. Still, it is necessary to confirm the availability of the space at the designated time before the planning of the meeting can proceed.

Preparing the Agenda

When the preliminary decisions about time and place for the meeting have been made and confirmed, then the group leader creates an agenda for the meeting. An agenda is important, because it gives members an idea of what they will be expected to discuss, report on, or decide about. Only when they know those things can they prepare for the meeting. The leader should talk to group members prior to creating the agenda in order to discover what is on their minds. Then the agenda for the meeting reflects

Technology Note: Teleconference Facilities

Seekings (1992) described the use of teleconferences by the British Civil Service. In 1987, when that agency first began to use teleconferences, they rented facilities. By 1992, they had built nine teleconferencing studios at a cost of approximately 80,000 pounds per studio. The studios receive heavy usage; each month there are about 140 meetings averaging 90 minutes each. From the start, staff were eager to meet in teleconferences, and most continue to like the experience. After one use, 67% of the people involved say they want to use the method again; after two uses, the number has grown to 80%.

Special facilities for electronic meetings have been built in this country as well. By September 1991, Texaco had begun using a specially designed Decision Room in Houston, Texas, which was connected by telephone and computer hookups to eight sites across the country. The features of the decision room included video screens, monitors, and cameras; computer network links; and built-in audio- and videoconference equipment. As designed, the room had space for up to 10 group members to meet at a table, with a personal computer available for each member. During brainstorming sessions, for instance, group members at all sites could generate ideas at their own personal workstations, then type them to be displayed on the large screen. All those in the room could see the screen directly, but it could be transmitted to the members meeting at different sites as well. Computer records and videotaping provided a record of the meeting to which all members, not just a recording secretary, contributed (Jackson, 1991; New Texaco decision room, 1991). In more recent years, reorganization of some departments and movement out of that facility have led Texaco to abandon its decision room.

Groups that continue to use specially designed rooms also must maintain some high-maintenance equipment. Therefore, if a videoconference is planned, it is important to make sure that there is an individual available who can provide technical assistance (should it be necessary) during the time the meeting is scheduled (Dewey & Creth, 1993).

the actual concerns of the group. In fact, each group member should take the responsibility to contact the agenda planner with items of concern. But it may still be necessary for the planner to check with members, especially those who have been chairing a subcommittee that might have a report to make, to see whether there are any items to include on the agenda. Three points about agendas are important to consider: the timing of their distribution, their structuring, and their wording.

Timing Agenda Distribution.   In the opening narrative, Al Lewis praised the suggestions he found in a book first published in 1980: *Effective Meetings: Improving Group Decision-Making*, by John E. Tropman. Tropman identified three mathematical-sounding rules related to agendas: the rule of halves, the rule of three-quarters, and the rule of thirds. The **rule of halves** states that *halfway between the last meeting and the coming meeting, members should send agenda items to the agenda planner.* If a group meets every other week, then one week after each meeting (which is also one week before the next meeting), items for the coming agenda should be in the hands of the planner. The planner then has time to gather any materials that members ought to read and consider before the meeting and then send those out with the agenda. The **rule of three-quarters** states that *three-quarters of the way between meetings, the agenda should be distributed to the members of the group.*

If group members are not given an agenda, by whatever means, long enough before the meeting to prepare for the meeting, then the meeting can be expected to fail.

Structuring the Agenda.   Unlike the first two rules, which have to do with timing of agenda preparation and distribution, the third rule has to do with placement of

Ethical Consideration

What is on the agenda is considered by the group; what is not on the agenda is unlikely to be the subject of group discussion and decision making. What ethical obligations does an agenda planner, then, have in preparing the agenda? What ethical obligations do other group members have to contribute to the agenda-planning process?

Technology Note: Aid in Distribution of Materials

Even when face-to-face meetings are to be held, the value of technological links between members should not be overlooked. E-mail, fax, and voice mail can be used to send agenda items to the planner and a completed agenda to each member and to forward relevant documents that need to be examined prior to a meeting. For example, voice mail messages can remind members to submit agenda items and can reinforce the time of a special meeting.

items on the agenda. Tropman (1980) realized that it is not uncommon in meetings for some members to arrive late and for some members to depart early. Moreover, even members who arrive on time may take a while to get fully involved in the business of the group; then, after working on business for a while, their attention begins to wander as they anticipate the meeting's end. With these factors in mind, Tropman proposed the **rule of thirds,** which states that *the most important business should be considered during the middle third of a meeting.*

Tropman (1980) elaborated on this recommendation to suggest that an agenda be thought of as a bell-shaped structure (see Figure 8.2). On the left side of the curve, in the first third of the meeting, the agenda should include the approval of the minutes from the previous meeting, informative announcements, and uncontroversial issues. This eases the group into its business and allows members to quickly accomplish some tasks. At the center of the bell-shaped curve, in the middle third, is placed the most significant business of the meeting. All members should have arrived by the time it is considered; none is likely to have left or tired of the meeting yet. As Al Lewis mentioned, it is the responsibility of the agenda planner to determine which issues belong in this middle third by predicting which are likely to be most controversial. The predictions may not be 100% accurate. Occasionally, what was thought likely to be a difficult decision for a group is made quickly; perhaps more frequently, an issue predicted to be easy (and so placed in the first third of the agenda) engages a group in controversy.

Tropman (1980) suggested that each difficult issue be given no more than 30 to 40 minutes of attention. If at the end of that time the group cannot come to an agreement, then the issue needs to be given further attention in a different forum. Perhaps it is simply tabled until a later meeting (by which time the group members

Al Lewis checks his E-mail to see whether a group member has suggested a new agenda item. (Photo by Emily Renz).

have gathered more information, clarified their perceptions, or worked out their differences); perhaps it is assigned to a subcommittee that invests time in debate and discussion before developing a recommendation to present to the whole group.

Included in the agenda for the final third of the meeting are items for discussion only, with no decision expected. In this way, members are allowed to ventilate their feelings, perhaps even the feelings generated from working toward the earlier decisions on the difficult issues. If earlier issues took more time than was anticipated, the discussion can be abbreviated in this section. If the group has been especially efficient in its decisions, the discussion can be more thorough. The interactions during this final third can allow the agenda planner to anticipate the level of controversy associated with any of the issues for discussion should they become issues on which action will need to be taken at a later meeting.

To see how the bell-shaped agenda works for a meeting, consider an athletic booster group that has called a meeting to deal with several issues. Chief among them is the issue of inappropriate parent and fan behavior at athletic events. Especially if some of the offending individuals are among those at the booster meeting, that issue will be a difficult issue to handle, so it will go in the middle third of the agenda. In Figure 8.2, notice that the items in the first third of the agenda would all go quickly. The plans for next year's fund-raiser could take a lot of time, but there is little pressure to take immediate action. By placing that item in the final third of the agenda, the group gives itself the flexibility to handle as much work on that issue as it can. Of course, as the time for the fund-raiser draws nearer, that item would move to the middle of the agenda.

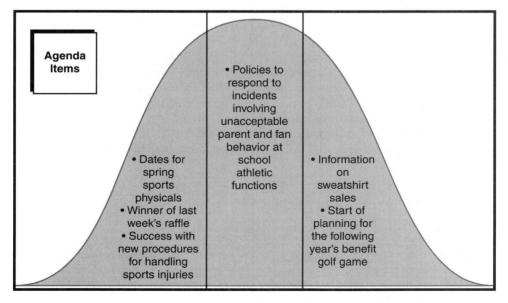

FIGURE 8.2 A bell-shaped agenda places the most important business during the middle third of the meeting.

In the opening narrative, Al Lewis mentions a final item on each of the agendas he prepares, simply called "For the Good of the Order." That item creates a time when individual members can mention events in their personal or private lives they would like to share with the group: success with a project, the upcoming graduation of a family member, a recital to which group members are invited. When an editor at Allyn and Bacon first expressed interest in publishing this book, that event was announced "for the good of the order" at a faculty meeting by one of the authors. Not all announcements that are for the good of the order need to be celebratory; personal concerns can be mentioned as well. Ending a business meeting in this way helps to cement the group as humans who not only work together, but who also care about one another.

Wording the Agenda.   The most common agendas include simply a list of items to be discussed. A leader can improve the efficiency of the meeting by wording the items on the agenda to reflect decision-issues. Consider this excerpt from a committee report that was part of an agenda for a university faculty meeting:

1. We need to decide the order we will follow in evaluating how well our major is meeting our goals and objectives We've been told that our evaluations don't need to include all of the goals and objectives each year. The committee felt that it would be wise to group goals and objectives into clusters and evaluate one or two clusters each year.
   - Do you like the idea of clusters?
   - Have we identified reasonable clusters?
   - Are the proper goals/objectives within each of the clusters?
   - How many goals/objectives should be evaluated each year?
   - In what order should they be evaluated?

This decision-issue agenda identifies the action the group has to take ("We need to decide . . . "); it provides the committee's recommendation ("it would be wise to group . . . and evaluate one or two clusters"); and it establishes specific questions that can guide the group in reaching its final decision. In many groups, a free-flowing discussion moves from one point to another and back again without ever explicitly identifying the relevant issues or making a decision about any of the specifics. To avoid those problems, a decision-issue agenda reminds the group that the meeting should

Ethical Consideration

By identifying for the group the subissues to be decided upon on the way to the overall decision, the person who is the agenda planner can wield considerable influence over the nature of the discussion and, thus, the final decision. How can that person insure that this influence is exerted in the most ethical manner?

not involve aimless talking; its approach should keep the group members more task oriented and more focused than they might otherwise be.

Sometimes, it is helpful to add to the agenda an estimate of the time each item is expected to take so that group members have added incentive to move through the business of the meeting. Time estimates should be made by the agenda planner (perhaps in consultation with the person submitting an agenda item) after determining how much controversy is likely on a particular item. The time limits should be regarded as flexible, however, so that they are never used to cut off important discussion on an item before the discussion is complete.

Completed agendas (which include the time and place for the meeting, all agenda items well ordered, and any attachments that provide members with essential information about the agenda items) should be distributed in advance of the meeting. Because even group members who have prepared well before the meeting sometimes forget to bring an agenda with them, a few extra copies brought to the meeting can be helpful.

Preparing to Contribute to the Meeting

The work of a carefully prepared agenda is wasted if group members do not then use the agenda and its attached materials to prepare for the meeting. A group member needs to invest time to read the materials before the meeting begins. If that time is not taken until the items are under discussion during the meeting, then valuable time of all group members is wasted while one member prepares. Preparation involves more than simply reading the materials. It is also necessary to think about the issues involved, to consult with others if more information is needed, and to clarify one's own position on issues before the meeting occurs.

In some groups, it is common for members to meet in informal subgroups to discuss issues prior to an upcoming meeting. That can be a helpful way to clarify the issues involved. It can be dangerous, however, if this informal process—from which some group members have been excluded—is then used to develop coalitions that quickly push through decisions to benefit special interests and to stifle full-group discussion.

Technology Note: Using Technology to Design Meetings

Clawson, Bostrom, and Anson (1993) report that recent research on group support systems (GSS) has found that one major advantage is that they do not leave meeting planning to chance. Instead, the technological tools force a group (and a facilitator, if one is present) to plan an agenda. Some groups use the agenda tool in a support system to end one meeting by planning the next meeting's agenda. Many groups also use a group display screen for the agenda during a meeting. The common visual focus seems to help keep the group work focused.

Ethical Considerations

If informal discussion among group members can be beneficial to the group as a whole but can also undermine the interests of some group members, how can members draw the line between those informal discussions that are helpful and those that are harmful?

Handling the Meeting

Chapter 4 in this text describes the communication behaviors used by skillful members during any group interaction: asking questions, providing responses, listening, and creating a comfortable climate. These behaviors are appropriate in group meetings of all kinds, no matter how formal. If every group member uses these behaviors to communicate effectively, then the group is likely to have shared leadership. However, even in groups that have shared leadership, a formal meeting is a time when a single individual is likely to take charge in order to move the group through its agenda. Therefore, the suggestions for handling the meeting focus primarily on the tasks to be undertaken by the person chairing the meeting. That person has the responsibility for setting the stage for the meeting, communicating effectively during the meeting, and guiding the group through its decisions. Effective handling of a meeting may also include adjusting to the demands of a video- or teleconference.

Setting the Stage for the Meeting

If you are going to lead a meeting, it is a good idea to arrive early. You want to be sure that the room is in order for the meeting. If it is common practice at your meetings to serve refreshments, they can be prepared before the meeting begins. Arriving early also allows you to show that the meeting is important to you and allows you to greet members as they arrive and to begin on time. Because you will have gone to some trouble to set and communicate the times for the meeting to the members, you should adhere to both the beginning and ending times you have established. That means you should begin on time even if not all members are present at the scheduled starting time. By waiting until late members arrive, you redefine them as members who arrived on time for the meeting, and lateness becomes the norm. You may need to consider, however, that there may be culturally divergent ideas about the value of beginning a meeting punctually. Lewis (1996) notes that meetings in some cultures begin briskly; in others, they begin with chatty conversations; in still other cultures, meetings "have difficulty getting going at all" (p. 115).

Before beginning a meeting, a secretary should be appointed to keep the minutes of the meeting. In some instances, the person who chairs the meeting also is expected to keep the record of the meeting. However, both chairing and recording a meeting take considerable concentration, and accomplishing one of the tasks well is likely to interfere with accomplishing the other well; therefore, it is generally better to divide those tasks between two individuals.

Communicating Effectively during a Meeting

Even when there is a single leader for a meeting, it is seldom the case that one person will be the only one moving the group through its agenda at a meeting. Typically, one person brings up an idea, another elaborates on it, and a third evaluates the idea. Each of these behaviors is involved in leadership of the group. Therefore, you should not assume that if you are leading a meeting you should be doing all of the talking—or even most of it. In fact, as Al Lewis mentioned in the opening narrative, if the usual group leader wants to speak as an advocate for a particular position, it would be appropriate for that person to step down from chairing the meeting during the discussion of that issue. The leader of the meeting should be an impartial guide. Even within these limits, the leader should communicate effectively during a meeting. Several specific communication behaviors are especially important to a leader.

Leaders should demonstrate good listening skills. They should listen actively and engage in restatement of the point of the other participants if there is some question as to what was said or meant. Leaders should not listen or respond defensively, because they should not discourage open communication within the group.

Leaders should encourage participation and direct the focus of comments by asking questions of the group. They should use orienting behaviors to encourage the group to stick to its agenda. Tropman (1980) argued that a meeting should follow the **rule of agenda integrity:** to be sure that *"all items on the agenda are discussed in the meeting for which they are scheduled and that no items* not *on the agenda are discussed"* (p. 25). Others might feel that if relevant issues are raised that were not on the original agenda, the group leader could be flexible and adapt, as long as the meeting is not prolonged excessively. The difficulties with that approach are twofold: members will then be deciding on issues for which they have not prepared; and some members who have had to be absent might have changed their other commitments in order to be present at a meeting with this added item on the agenda. Obviously, a decision to consider items not on the agenda should not be made lightly.

A good leader enforces the group's norms for interaction, such as ensuring that members can speak without interruption and that ideas are understood before they are evaluated. Leaders often engage in summarizing behavior, especially to review any decisions the group has made. They are also likely to test for consensus, as Al Lewis mentioned in the opening narrative. If other group members seem to specialize in one or another of these behaviors, that does not undermine the authority of the meeting chair; the group leader needs to fill in wherever needed, performing the behaviors the group needs performed in order to make progress.

Nelson and Economy (1995) suggest that one point about which a leader must communicate especially clearly is the nature of his or her leadership style. If the leader plans to function democratically, group members should know that their participation is welcomed. If the leader plans to make decisions autocratically, then the group members should not be led to believe that they will have influence on the decision making.

During a meeting, all members of the group may need to be willing to adapt to different styles of interaction stemming from cultural influences on the members. If it seems to you that meetings in every culture are likely to be the same, you might want to consider some of the perceptions of a British author (Lewis, 1996) about Americans in meetings:

> At meetings, Americans show the following tendencies:
>
> - They are individualistic; they like to go it alone without checking with head office. . . .
> - They introduce informality immediately: take their jacket off, use first names, discuss personal details, e.g., family.
> - They give the impression of being naive by not speaking anything but English and by showing immediate trust through ultra-friendliness.
> - They use humor whenever they can, even though their partner fails to understand it or regards it as out of place. . . .
> - They want 'yes' in principle and will work out details later. But they can be very tough in the details and check on everything in spite of apparent trust. Germans, French and others prefer to settle details first.
> - They don't like lulls or silence during negotiations. . . .
> - They are opportunistic—quick to take chances. . . .
> - They often lack patience, and will say irritating or provoking things . . . to get things moving. . . .
> - They put everything in words. But when they use words like "fair," "democratic," "honest," "good deal," "value," "assume," they feel the other party understands the same as they do. . . .
> - They are blunt; they will disagree and say so. This causes embarrassment to Japanese, Arabs, Italians and other Latins. (pp. 167–168)

These statements may seem to you to be unfair generalizations. Or they may seem to accurately describe your preferences at meetings. Either way, they point to the potential for misunderstandings if group members from one culture meet with others whose cultural background is different and do not adapt to their differences during the meeting.

At times problem situations other than cultural misunderstandings occur at a meeting—situations that a good leader can remedy. Chang and Kehoe (1993) identified four such problems: side conversations, quiet members, overly talkative members, and antagonistic members. In all cases, the leader should try to discover the group members' legitimate concerns that have influenced their involvement. For instance, someone engaged in a side conversation may have a concern that is relevant to the issue under consideration but is not exactly on the agenda. Both a quiet member and an antagonistic member may feel as if their positions have been ignored by the rest of the group. By addressing a question to the member, the leader may allow the individual to express the unheard position and return to normative behavior within the group. In some cases, these behaviors reveal the group member's boredom, stemming from slow movement through the agenda. An effective leader might determine whether the group is, in fact, able to move on and assist the group in doing so. If the group is not ready to move on, then the leader might want to explain why involvement of all group members is still necessary at that point. By remaining committed to the involvement of the group and willing to listen to the concerns of each group member, the leader can defuse the tensions that arise in the meeting.

Managing Time during the Meeting

Throughout a meeting, the leader should keep an eye on the clock to make sure that the group is making progress as anticipated and to be sure to end the meeting on time. If the business of the group is completed before the designated time for adjournment, there is no need to fritter away time until the moment of dismissal. The group can celebrate its unexpected early departure. If the work is not complete at the set ending time, the group should generally end the meeting anyway. The meeting should be extended only if all group members agree that they would prefer to stay rather than delay completion of the task. Effective progress through a meeting is more likely if procedural rules are familiar to group members.

Adapting Parliamentary Procedure to the Small Group Meeting

In the opening narrative, Al Lewis mentioned that a college course in parliamentary procedure was one tool that prepared him to lead meetings and that he continues to use, though usually not formally. In fact, formal parliamentary procedure is generally neither used nor recommended in the meetings of small groups, unless the members are taking very formal action. It might be used by a small group when the level of conflict between group members is so high that an emphasis on procedural rules is necessary to ensure the rights of all group members to be heard in a discussion. As Al mentioned in the beginning of this chapter, parliamentary procedure is intended to allow the majority to rule at the same time that it protects the rights of the minority to speak in an effort to influence the majority.

Several good manuals of parliamentary procedure exist. If you are likely to lead meetings of larger organizations, then we recommend that you familiarize yourself with one or more of these manuals so that you feel comfortable in meetings that operate according to parliamentary procedure and so that you better understand how such rules help organizations determine the procedures to follow that haven't been specified in their constitution or bylaws. We do not, however, attempt to convey these rules here. Instead, we describe some fundamental principles, based on parliamentary procedure, that groups can use even in an informal way as they move through their business at a meeting.

Initiating a Discussion of Business.
A group moves toward a decision when a member first recommends that the group make a specific decision. The recommendation is made formally through a **motion**, which is *a statement proposing an action to the group*. For instance, a member of a school board might make a motion such as this, "I move that we hire an additional teacher at the middle school." A motion is intended to focus discussion and debate within the group. If a school board were to consider the motion just mentioned, then its discussion should focus on the need for an additional teacher at that time at the middle-school level. Even if the meeting also has on its agenda curriculum development or the suspension of students from school, those items would be out of order once the motion has been made.

A group could waste time if it discussed at length every single idea that any eccentric person might have, so minimal support for a motion in the form of a *second* is required before a motion can be considered. A group member who supports the proposal made in a motion simply says, "I second that motion," or even "Second," to show that support. With a motion made and seconded, the chair of the meeting opens a discussion of the motion. Discussion both in support of and opposing the motion is allowed. It is ended when a vote on the motion is taken.

Altering a Proposal.   In the course of discussion, some members of the group may realize that they support the general position taken in the motion, but that a modification of the position would allow them to fully support the proposal. For instance, school board members might want to alter the motion mentioned earlier by suggesting that the teacher be a part-time teacher, or a temporary teacher, or an English teacher; or they may even feel that there is a need for two teachers. To alter the wording of an original proposal is to *amend* it. If an amendment has been suggested (and seconded), the group must discuss and then decide (by voting) whether it accepts the amendment before it decides whether it accepts the motion. The school board, then, might reject the proposal that the motion be amended to specify that the teacher be a part-time teacher and then support the motion that the teacher be hired. Just as possible would be support for the amendment that the teacher be a temporary teacher, followed by a rejection of the original motion. In that case, the action of the group could be interpreted to mean that if a teacher was to be hired, the group would want to do so only on a temporary basis, but that they really do not want a teacher to be hired at this point. It is possible to amend a motion in such a way that a vote on the amendment does not need to be taken. If an amendment is consistent with the intention of the motion, and in fact helps to clarify the meaning of the motion in a way that satisfies the person who proposed the original motion, then it is called a *friendly amendment* and can be accepted by the original proposer if there are no objections from the rest of the group.

Controlling Debate.   To serve their purpose of allowing the minority to be heard and the majority to act, procedural rules may control debate in three specific ways. First, each person is allowed to speak on a motion being considered. The person chairing the meeting is an exception; that role requires overseeing the debate without entering into it. Even when a person is alone in opposing the action the group is considering, he or she still has a right to express opposition. That is the way in which the voice of the minority is heard and allowed to influence the majority.

Second, an individual's right to speak may be limited in length and frequency. Usually, a small group allows discussion of an issue to continue as long as is necessary for members to feel comfortable before making a decision. However, there may be situations in which more formal procedural rules are imposed to move the group toward a decision. If the issue is extremely contentious, but action needs to be taken nonetheless, the length and frequency of comments can be limited by prior agreement of the group. The specific limits should be based upon the overall time available for discussion of that issue and the number of members in the group. It would also be possible to allow any one group member to wait until others have spoken once before taking a second turn. As a result of such limits, the group could move through the discussion to vote on a decision without any member holding the group hostage by continued harangues.

Third, the group may establish a rule that speakers representing opposing positions should alternate their speaking order. Such a procedure increases the chance of group members examining one issue at a time from the perspectives of both (or all) sides in the debate; ultimately, that allows the group to make its decision more carefully.

Debate is also controlled by the rule that comments during discussion of a motion are to relate to that motion and not to other actions already taken or to the personality of group members. Thus, even when disagreements about an issue at hand are strong, the procedural rules attempt to limit acrimonious, irrelevant, and unproductive comments.

Ending Debate.

When a group reaches the point that individuals are simply repeating themselves or each other, then the opportunity for each member and each position to be heard has been provided and the need to move the group forward takes precedence. Debate can be ended informally by the leader of the meeting saying something like, "We seem to be repeating ourselves. Are you ready to vote on this?" More formally, a procedural motion is made to end debate or to move forward to vote on the motion. Simply calling out, "Question," does not end the debate; a motion to call the question is necessary. Such a motion is not open to debate, but it does require a second from another member. Moreover, for the motion to pass, it must have more support than a simple majority of those present. In order to protect the principle of free and unlimited debate on an issue, two-thirds of the group present must support the cessation of debate.

Debate on an issue can also end short of a vote on it. If the discussion makes it clear that the group is not ready to make a decision on a particular issue—perhaps because not all relevant information is yet available—then the group could *table* the motion or, in other words, lay it aside until a later time when it will again be considered. Or, a motion can be referred to a committee, which can investigate the matter at length without taking the time of the entire group. Using formal procedural rules, both of these actions—a motion to table or a motion to refer to committee—require a second, are not debatable, and require a majority vote to pass.

Means of Voting.

In many small group meetings, decisions are reached by consensus, so voting is unnecessary. In some cases, however, voting is necessary, either because consensus is not possible to reach or because a record of the specific decision made must be reported to others. In those cases, the group should consider which means of voting is preferable. Typically, votes are taken by a show of hands, an approach that allows the group to determine both the amount of support for a particular action and the location of support. All group members know how each member voted. However, there are two situations in which it is better not to make that information available. First, some group members may feel social pressure to vote with the majority or with particular other members of a group. That pressure could make it less likely that a show-of-hands vote would reflect their true position on an issue. Second, in some cases, the role of a vote is to get the general sense of the group without distinguishing supporters from opponents. For example, if a group is voting on whether to support a member's request for promotion, it would benefit the group in the long run to know only the amount of support for the request and not to identify those who have not supported it. In these cases, the group should choose to vote by secret ballot.

The rules for parliamentary procedure are far more extensive than the brief explanation we have included here. We have limited our discussion because most small group meetings do not rely on complicated rules of parliamentary procedure that might govern the meetings of a larger group. The rules described here should be sufficient to help move most small groups through the discussion of their tasks at a meeting. Occasionally, a group member skilled in parliamentary procedure attempts to manipulate a meeting through use of special procedural rules. Such behavior interferes with the purpose of the rules, for at base they are intended to allow all members to contribute to a discussion and have the right to influence the decision while at the same time allowing business to be accomplished by the majority. Therefore, an appropriate use of procedural rules in a small group is judicious; it allows the group to guide itself through consideration of the business at hand.

Technology Note: Managing Business Electronically

When groups meet by means of electronic connections, there are some unique concerns for the leader of the meeting. When we attend meetings in the same room, we look around us to see who is there, recognize familiar faces, and cast surreptitious glances at newcomers. Electronic meetings limit the information available about those in attendance. We may not even know who is present for the meeting. Therefore, an early obligation of the leader is to orient the members to each other. If the individuals being connected have no prior relationships, then it is important for them to be introduced. Prior to a meeting, biographies of each person can be distributed; at the beginning of a meeting, brief introductions can be made. In the case of an audio conference, each member should speak briefly so that others get a chance to connect the sound of the voice with the name of the person. In the case of a videoconference, the location of the members should be indicated as they are introduced.

Teleconferences, whether audio or video, may connect individuals all in separate locations but are just as likely to connect groups of people gathered at two or more sites. The chances are good that the people gathered at one site will feel more similar to each other than to their colleagues gathered at a different site. In some cases, participants at one site may even go "off air" to caucus among themselves (Johansen, Vallee, & Spangler, 1979). The leader of an electronic meeting, therefore, needs to be sure to encourage communication among all of the members present, not just between sites.

When communicating in non–face-to-face meetings, the chairperson's role as gatekeeper of the meeting is likely to increase in importance and in difficulty. For instance, some videoconference technologies use voice-activated microphones that allow the person speaking to continue to be heard. When someone else interrupts, the microphone captures that person's voice only if the first speaker paused momentarily when the interruption began. If two people begin to speak simultaneously, the system jumbles the messages. With videoconferences, there are at least visual signals of an individual's desire to enter the conversation. With audio conferences, in which a similar microphone system can lock out voices if participants at one end rattle papers (Jackson, 1991), there are just as many problems and fewer aids to be used in predicting the flow of conversation. Therefore, finding a way into it is even harder. A leader sensitive to these difficulties can direct comments to specific members to manage the flow of interaction. In addition to having help in gatekeeping from a leader, the presence of a computer system on which group members can write to one another can give participants a voice in the proceedings, even if they are shut out from communicating by audio means.

Either the chairperson or the equipment engineer present at the meeting may also be responsible for determining who is seen on camera in the case of a videoconference. To the extent that not being seen makes one less present, those decisions can have a significant impact on the outcome of the meeting. The outcome of the entire meeting is at risk if technological difficulties are experienced during a meeting. The meeting is vulnerable to a loss of the technology on which it is dependent. Planning a backup system is important in preparing for a meeting; activating its use quickly may be necessary during a meeting.

All members of a group should be aware of the potential for the medium to carry a message that might influence the outcome of the meeting. If individuals at one site are shown in luxurious surroundings to those at another site in a modest room, or if the signals vary in their quality from one direction to the other, then differences in status are being suggested by the medium. Our self-consciousness about being on camera may influence our behavior at a videoconference. The unidimensionality of image over a telephone may affect our ability to have an influence on others during an audioconference. Even the difficulty involved in holding a telephone receiver during a long meeting may affect members' ability to concentrate (and should mandate the use of speaker phones during an audioconference of any length). The need to involve all senses, even those not utilized by a particular medium, makes attending to messages at an electronic meeting hard work. It is no wonder that Jackson (1991) recommended that electronic meetings be carefully planned, both in terms of preparing an agenda and in terms of selecting the appropriate support system tools to use during the meeting.

Following Up after a Meeting

When any meeting—whether face-to-face or electronic—is over, tasks associated with the meeting still remain to be completed. Five distinct responsibilities remain to be completed by the group leader, the secretary, and/or the membership in general: (1) assessing the accomplishments of the meeting; (2) repairing the bridges between group members, (3) representing the group to others, (4) preparing the minutes of the meeting, and (5) completing the tasks assigned during the meeting.

Assessing the Accomplishments

Once the meeting has ended, the group leader should compare the results of the meeting with the expectations for it. If decision-issues still remain, those need to be addressed at a future meeting. If the group made a decision, but perhaps too quickly, the group leader may want to encourage the group to revisit its decision at a later meeting. Spending a few minutes reflecting on the progress achieved during the meeting while the memory of the meeting is still fresh helps set the agenda for coming meetings.

Repairing the Bridges between Members

The dynamics between group members should also be evaluated once the meeting has ended. Even in groups that operate effectively, a meeting typically represents a point of division between members. Heated discussions may have taken place; a vote may have left some members feeling that they "lost." Social or emotional factors operating within the group now can interfere later with the effectiveness of the group in accomplishing its task and can diminish members' satisfaction with the process. Addressing those issues could be important to the overall success of the group.

If there is lingering disagreement over a decision or frustration within the group, it is important to continue to talk about the issues informally to let other members know that their ideas were heard and understood and to separate the disagreement on issues from the interpersonal relationships among the group members. It is even possible that by talking with each other informally, group members can come to an agreement on issues about which they disagreed during the formal meeting.

Representing the Group to Others

Especially for groups that exist within organizations, decisions made by the group have an impact on other bodies in the organization. Often the person who chaired the meeting is responsible for representing the decisions of the group to others in the broader system. Sometimes that job is required of another member who has been selected by the group to serve as a liaison with another group. For instance, after the meeting of a church budget committee, there may be decisions that affect the education programs of the church. A member of the budget committee would be expected to report the decision to the education committee.

This task seems rather straightforward: the decision of the group should be communicated clearly to those outside the group whom it affects. The task becomes more difficult if the position of the individual making the report differs from the decision made by the group. Nonetheless, the task after the meeting is to represent the group, not oneself. Therefore, regardless of what a member's personal position is, the report to outsiders should represent the group accurately.

Preparing the Minutes of the Meeting

Despite the fact that few people actively seek the task of preparing minutes for a meeting, the job is an important one. The minutes serve as the memory of a group about a meeting. It is not uncommon for a group to consult minutes of a previous meeting to recall what decisions were made at some time in the past. Therefore, the group needs to have confidence that the written memory of the meeting is accurate. To assist in creating such confidence, minutes should be prepared very soon after the meeting and should be reviewed carefully by group members to verify their accuracy. Approval of the minutes should not simply be pro forma; consistency of action by the group and progress for the group depend on accurate minutes. The agenda for a meeting can be a guide in the preparation of minutes, with each agenda item necessitating a report of its disposition.

Some groups prefer that minutes record only the actions taken by the group; however, in many cases, it is helpful to have a record that captures the flavor of the discussion as well. Jessup (1994) suggests that the minutes "document attendance, decisions made (whether by vote or by consensus), actions assigned, significant points of dissent, or unresolved issues, and summaries of important data presented" (p. 81), and that all of that be done concisely so that the minutes will actually be read by the group. As you can probably imagine, good minutes can increase the value of a meeting, and poor minutes can ensure the failure of a meeting after the fact. If the group has no record of what it decided or why, then at some time in the future the business of the meeting will probably need to be accomplished once again, this time accompanied by the feeling that the group seldom accomplishes anything. If there is no record of who was assigned to (or who agreed to) accomplish which task, then the tasks are unlikely to be completed.

Completing the Assigned Tasks

Merely remembering what tasks a person has to accomplish after a meeting is not sufficient. Action must also be taken. It is not fair to complain that meetings do not accomplish anything if group members do not act on the decisions made at a meeting. If members have been appointed to a subcommittee, then the subcommittee needs to meet and prepare its report for the group as a whole. If a member agrees to gather some information to assist the group in making an important decision, then that research needs to be done.

It is true that action will not be taken if the (ir)responsible party does not remember what was agreed to. Prompt distribution of the minutes after the meeting (with assigned tasks highlighted within them), a reminder by the person who chaired the meeting, and a final reminder of the expected presentation of results or reports in the agenda for the coming meeting should jog the memory and the conscience of even the most forgetful group member.

Summary

The frequency with which groups meet suggests that meetings play an important role in the life of a group. In fact, meetings can serve to accomplish the business of the group, develop commitment to the group and its decisions, and resolve conflict between group members. However, meetings have acquired a negative reputation because too often they are held without a clear goal or with a goal that could be accomplished without meeting. Moreover, if a meeting is to be effective, it should be prepared for, managed effectively, and followed up appropriately.

Preparation for a meeting requires that it be scheduled at a time when those with most impact on a decision can attend. The length of the meeting should also be considered; if it lasts too long, the quality of decision making by the group is threatened. A place for the meeting should be secured that is accessible to all who will attend and that allows participants the space and facilities to do well and comfortably what needs to be done at the meeting. The creation and distribution of an agenda is a critical tool for an effective meeting. Items should be accumulated and placed on an agenda, which is distributed to members in time to allow preparation before the meeting. Meetings run well if the items are placed on a bell-shaped agenda. The first third of the agenda includes routine and easily resolved issues; the middle third covers the most difficult and significant items; the final third includes discussion items that can be handled with flexibility, depending on what happens earlier in the meeting. Although the leader has most of the responsibility for preparing for a meeting, every member is responsible for knowing what is on the agenda and preparing to contribute to the discussion and decision making of the group.

Handling a meeting effectively requires that the stage be set for the meeting by an early arrival and arrangement of the space as needed before the meeting begins. A meeting should begin and end as scheduled. Time during the meeting should be managed by the leader, who acts as an impartial guide—listening to others, restating their points, encouraging participation of all members, focusing attention on the agenda, adapting to cultural differences among participants, and handling problem situations. Progress on the tasks of the meeting may be assisted by following procedural rules based on parliamentary procedure. Such rules allow the group to decide on action when a motion is made, seconded, discussed, and then voted upon by the group. Rules allow for the motion to be altered, debate to be controlled and eventually ended, and a vote to be taken by show of hands or secret ballot.

Technological advances affect the meetings of today. We may not hold a meeting if messages can be faxed or E-mailed to group members. Even when we do hold a meeting, an agenda and attached documents can be sent to members electronically. Teleconferences allow meetings of group members at sites some distance from each other. Attention to the special demands of an electronic meeting can allow such meetings to be effective.

When any meeting is over, the post-meeting demands include assessing the meeting's accomplishments in relation to its goals, repairing member relationships, representing the group to others, creating a written memory of the meeting in the form of minutes, and completing the tasks assigned during the meeting. Meeting these demands after a needed, well-prepared, and well-managed meeting help improve the success of a meeting. Upon reflection, it seems likely that individuals do not really object to meeting with others; they simply want to be sure that meetings that interrupt their work are, themselves, productive.

QUESTIONS FOR DISCUSSION

1. In which of the following situations would a meeting be called for:

   a. One business is merging with another. Does the administrative staff need to have a meeting?

   b. The president of a fraternity has family problems and will be leaving school for the rest of this academic year. The fraternity members need to hold another election. If there is to be a meeting, will the president's circumstances be discussed or should only the election be considered?

   c. Financial problems in the local school district will result in the lay-off of some teachers. Should the teachers meet? Should there be an open meeting for the citizens?

   d. Several workers were out of town on vacation when the announcement was made that a new security system needs to be installed in one area of the company. This is their first day back from vacation. Should they meet about the security system today if there is time in their schedule?

2. What factors should be considered in determining whether to meet face-to-face, have an audioconference or videoconference, or conduct business by computer?

3. How comfortable are you with arranging a meeting at which some members of a group cannot be present? To what lengths should a group go to find a mutually satisfactory meeting time?

SUGGESTED ACTIVITIES

1. Attend a meeting on your campus or in your community. Ask to see an agenda for the meeting. Evaluate the effectiveness of the meeting. What suggestions could you give to the group to improve the quality of the meeting?

2. Create an agenda for an upcoming meeting of your project group. Conduct your meeting following the agenda. In your journal, discuss the impact of the agenda on the quality of the meeting.

SOURCES CITED

Chang, R. Y., & Kehoe, K. R. (1993). *Meetings that work: A practical guide to shorter and more productive meetings.* Irvine, CA: Richard Chang Associates Publications Division.

Clawson, V. K., Bostrom, R. P., & Anson, R. (1993). The role of the facilitator in computer-supported meetings. *Small Group Research, 24,* 547–565.

Dewey, B. I., & Creth, S. D. (1993). *Team power: Making library meetings work.* Chicago: American Library Association.

Gastil, J. (1993). Identifying obstacles to small group democracy. *Small Group Research, 24,* 5–27.

Hon, D. (1980). *Meetings that matter: A self-teaching guide.* New York: Wiley.

Jackson, B. M. (1991). Computer support for a multi-site meeting. *Brainstorm: The Quarterly of ITD's Group Decision and Collaboration Research, 1* (2), 10–13.

Jessup, H. (1994). A quantum formula for improving meetings. *Journal for Quality and Participation,* 80–82.

Johansen, R., Vallee, J., & Spangler, K. (1979). *Electronic meetings: Technical alternatives and social choices.* Reading, MA: Addison-Wesley.

Lewis, R. D. (1996). *When cultures collide: Managing successfully across cultures.* London: Nicholas Brealey Publishing.

Nelson, R. B., & Economy, P. (1995). *Better business meetings.* Burr Ridge, IL: Irwin Professional Publishing.

New Texaco decision room. (1991). *Brainstorm: The Quarterly of ITD's Group Decision & Collaboration Research, I* (1), 5.

Seekings, D. (1992). *How to organize effective conferences and meetings* (5th ed.). London: Kogan Page Limited.

Tropman, J. E. (1980). *Effective meetings: Improving group decision-making.* Beverly Hills, CA: Sage.

9   Group Presentations

CHAPTER OBJECTIVES

After reading this chapter, you should be able to

- Identify the ways in which the presence of an audience does (and should) alter the interaction of a group
- Identify the delivery characteristics important in making group presentations
- Distinguish among a panel discussion, symposium, forum, and training workshop
- Determine the conditions under which each format is the appropriate choice for a group presentation
- Describe the steps involved in preparing and presenting for each of the formats
- Prepare and present an effective panel discussion, symposium, forum, and/or training workshop

The Narrative

Alicia Ferris is a student majoring in Communication Disorders at Central Michigan University. She took a small group communication class as an elective. Her course requirements included making three group presentations. Here she describes the experience of her group with the presentations:

> *For our first presentation, we analyzed the group dynamics in the movie* The Sandlot. *We knew that the movie seemed to be a basic kid's movie. We wanted the class to understand that there were some complex communication aspects involved. We used a symposium format, which was a good choice for our group because a lot of our members are ramblers. With a symposium, everyone had equal time for comments.*
>
> *We had a number of questions we were expected to deal with, and we just divided up the questions evenly. Each member prepared answers to the questions. At our next meeting, we read our answers to each other. We asked, "How can we make this better?" Everyone was willing to help out and make suggestions for additions and deletions. At our next meeting, everyone was*

prepared with the revised answers and we rehearsed the presentation. As we listened to ourselves, we found some places where there was overlap. We talked about it, saying, "Well this seems to apply more to this person than to another." I don't think anyone's feelings were hurt. As a group, we didn't really care who said what. We just wanted all the questions to be answered thoroughly and the whole presentation to go well.

Each group was expected to use at least one brief segment from the movie to illustrate what we were saying. I remember one group that relied on the VCR timer without realizing that every timer is different, a problem our group had anticipated. When I watched them trying to find their spot, at first I felt sorry for them, because I knew that could have been us. But as an audience member, I also began to feel frustrated just sitting there waiting for them to get their stuff together. It helps to be organized.

We realized that the class might have trouble following our discussion because of all of the characters in the movie. So one of our group members, Nicole, made a set of posters to help the audience. Each one looked like a baseball playing card for one of the characters. Then we added some sound effects. We had so much fun that it kept snowballing and getting bigger and bigger. There were some things that got to be too time-consuming—and even expensive. I thought we should all contribute to the cost of the posters, but Nicole said, "No, that's okay." Still, I felt bad about that.

I think the visual aids helped our group. In other group presentations that lacked visual aids, it was more difficult to stay in tune with the speakers if you were just listening to them, especially if they weren't the best speakers. The visual aids helped the audience remember. For our group, if there was a key concept, we wrote it down. It's all about repetition. The more times you hear and see something, the easier it is to remember, so you'll walk away remembering something. If all you're doing is staring at the speakers' faces and they say something you've heard only for the first time, it's hard to remember it.

But I'll tell you: one of the things that surprised me about other groups was how relaxed they were. They just got up there and talked. They didn't read their speeches. They looked totally relaxed. When our group got up there, I thought we looked nervous. My hands were even shaking. Maybe, though, we didn't look as nervous to others as we felt.

Our group felt that a lot of the success of our first presentation was due to all of the creative elements it had. So that's something we wanted to incorporate in our second presentation—a training workshop. At an early meeting, we brainstormed for ideas about content. We also made a decision to divide our responsibilities. The two most creative members of our group were going to be out of town for the weekend when we needed to get started on the work, and we also knew how much time was required to do the creative elements. So we decided that it would be an even division of responsibilities to have three members who were researchers and two who were the creative minds. In retrospect, I think it was a bad decision to divide it up that way. Until the researchers were done, the creative people couldn't do anything. That might not have been a problem if all the research had been done by the time the weekend was over, but that didn't happen. And when one of the researchers was asked by one of the creative members "What can I do with your part? How can I help you with it?," he said, "I thought that was your area." He didn't feel that he wanted to help her. When we put a label on people, others felt less willing to help each other out.

Also, preparing for the workshop presented problems because we had so many decisions to make. We had to decide what our goal was, what to teach, how we were going to teach it, what materials we needed, and how to get the class involved. There were too many choices, and when you add the time constraints . . . we just did not make some of those choices. We got some material together and somehow did a workshop. But I think our lack of unity about where we wanted to end up caused problems for us. Some people began coming to meetings unprepared. But how could they be prepared when we didn't know what was needed? I know I was worried about the big picture. I didn't know how my part would fit into the whole. I wasn't sure how we'd fit things together and how I'd tie my part to what came before it and what came afterward. I think it is really important when you're preparing something like a workshop that involves so many decisions to get started right away. And you have to be prepared for conflict and know how you're going to resolve it. You may think you'll be able to operate without it, but there will *be conflict.*

Our final assigned presentation was an analysis of our group throughout the class. We met beforehand to discuss what we wanted to talk about. We knew that we'd had a big high after our first presentation, and then, while preparing for the workshop, we'd crashed and had to build up to a high again. So we decided we wanted to talk about the conflict our group had experienced. We didn't want the presentation to be as formal as the earlier ones had been, so we didn't discuss who was going to talk for how long about what. We expected that each of us would take an equal amount of time to make an equal number of comments. We were just going to go down the row and have each person talk. Beforehand, we'd said, "Let's not go in there and drop any bombs." But then that's what happened. One member talked nonstop, and the rest of us couldn't get a word in edgewise. That was not a good day. We had a lot of surprises sprung on us. We found out that there was more conflict than we'd thought. I think it made the rest of us look foolish. So finally, I had to say something. What we'd expected would be an informal symposium evolved into more of a panel discussion. I didn't feel too comfortable with that format. You don't know what each person is going to say, and it seems a little less organized to me. But if there was someone guiding the discussion with a series of questions and monitoring the discussion so that everyone would get an equal opportunity to speak, then that would have made a big difference.

We did have some questions after our presentations, so we had limited experience with the forum format. Usually, though, one member of our group responded to all of the questions, and so the rest of us sat back and listened to her responses. I didn't have a problem with that, because she and I were usually on the same wavelength. I was satisfied with her answers.

With our presentations, I discovered how important it was to rehearse. When you rehearse, you find out whether there's overlap and whether you fit into your time frame. Just speaking your part before your group members is good practice. What you'd planned to say might make good sense in your head, but when you actually say it aloud in front of others, it might be a different story. I think it's also important when preparing for a group presentation to keep an open mind. Ask questions. Challenge each other. Be creative. Have a clear goal about what your group wants to accomplish. If everyone in your group shares that goal, then you can work hard to achieve successful presentations.

Small groups usually meet without an audience. Members interact among themselves to achieve the group's goal, whether that is to socialize or to plan improvements at work. Sometimes groups invite nonmembers to a meeting to serve as resources for the group. A lawyer could be invited to a meeting to advise the city council on the legal ramifications of a decision about to be made; a police officer could attend a neighborhood watch meeting to make suggestions about safety. In the case of a public hearing, a number of people are invited to testify before a group (usually one with legislative powers); the group, in this case, listens to the comments of the public and questions individuals to clarify their comments. On some occasions, however, groups are asked to make a presentation before a group of observers. The conditions for group interaction change dramatically in such circumstances, thus warranting our attention to the demands of a group presentation. This chapter first considers the impact of an audience on the interaction of groups and then considers the preparation and presentation of four distinct types of group presentations.

Changes Created by the Presence of an Audience

In typical small group meetings, discussion occurs in fits and starts. Periods of silence are followed by bursts of talking. Topics may shift frequently; someone may tell a personal story in between comments that are task related. Also, an individual's contributions usually vary from meeting to meeting. At one meeting, someone talks extensively who barely spoke during the previous meeting. Even in formal meetings, members are likely to make informal comments, perhaps sharing an inside joke with the group. Someone might whisper a comment to a neighbor, and another could mumble while thinking aloud.

The presence of an audience automatically transforms some of these behaviors. Just as activity changes when a camera appears to record it, interaction changes when an audience is present to observe it. Easy interaction may give way to self-conscious stiffness, and individuals who have become comfortable talking freely to members of their group may freeze with the discomfort of speaking to others. Others, eager for an audience, may warm up under the public eye. The presence of the audience creates an awareness of the audience in the minds of the group members; they realize that they need to direct some attention to the group. While some changes occur naturally (and not necessarily to the profit of the group members), other changes need to be made purposefully to create a successful presentation.

Group presentations need planning that goes beyond preparing an agenda for a meeting. A plan for interaction, like an agenda, helps to make effective use of time. Alicia mentioned the importance of careful planning for the presentations her group had to make to a small group communication classroom. In addition to creating an initial plan, if the group presentation is to create a positive impression, the group needs to organize its thoughts, prepare statements for presentation, and (in many cases) even rehearse the presentation.

In the case of a presentation, all group members need to be (nearly) equal participants. If you are present in a group, the audience expects you to participate. If the group is a classroom group making a presentation as a graded assignment, then someone who is not an equal participant has less to show to the instructor. But even in nonclassroom group presentations, if you are a member of the group making the presentation, but are uninvolved or only minimally involved, then the audience's expectations of you are unsatisfied. Therefore, each group member should be prepared to contribute. At the same time, all members should be attentive to others' needs for involvement. A public discussion should not abandon its cooperative character and suddenly become a competition for the attention of observers. Alicia mentioned the difficulty her group encountered when one member began to talk nonstop without allowing other group members the opportunity to contribute or to share their perspectives on the situation. It made her feel as if the rest of the group looked like fools.

In essence, an effective group presentation should possess both the characteristics of good contributions (as described in Chapter 4) and many features of a public speech. To help you more fully with making the transition from communicating in a small group to making a public presentation, we recommend that you consult one of the many public-speaking textbooks available. Here, we identify some of the most basic factors that are relevant to presentational speaking.

When an audience is present, delivery of the message increases in importance. A public speaker has available four different approaches to delivery, only some of which are appropriate in a group presentation setting. **Impromptu speaking,** *off-the-cuff speaking in which a speaker pulls together ideas while speaking,* is unlikely to have value in a group presentation context because participants should—at the very least—have thought through ideas and organized evidence to support claims *prior* to the presentation.

In their first group presentation, the members of Alicia's group knew that they could not count on impromptu speaking. In fact, they had prepared enough material that they worried about taking more than their allotted time for their presentation. To avoid the problem, several members wrote out timed segments of their presentation and then used a second approach to delivery: **reading from manuscript.** As a result of relying on the manuscript, they lost their ability to make contact with and adapt to their audience. Both manuscript delivery and the third delivery approach, **speaking from memory,** would be appropriate only when the language of a speech is as important as, or more important than, the ideas. Seldom does a group presentation warrant such careful and precise attention to language. Moreover, the involvement of a group presents so many chances for unexpected events to occur that delivery from memory, which severely restricts a speaker's ability to adapt to the unexpected, is especially inappropriate in a group presentation setting.

Nearly always, therefore, group members should rely on the extemporaneous mode of delivery. **Extemporaneous delivery** requires collecting ideas through research and/or introspection, organizing ideas, practicing by talking through the ideas, and creating speech notes to reinforce the speaker's memory. It is true that speaking extemporaneously involves enough flexibility to make a rigid time limit difficult to meet. However, with practice, group members gain a sense of the time they are using in the presentation. Moreover, another group member can monitor the time and move the group forward when necessary.

Group members should view their public presentations as *enlarged conversations.* If you have had some training in public speaking, you are probably already familiar with the notion that your public speaking should possess a conversational quality. If you have had no speech training and are anxious about having to make a group presentation, then this idea should help to alleviate your anxiety: those in your audience are fellow conversationalists, and you should make contact with them, one at a time. You can also take comfort from the fact that your audience seldom knows how worried you are. Certainly they are more interested in the content of your discussion than in the rate of your pulse. Alicia mentioned that other groups seemed so much more comfortable than she felt during a presentation; if those other group members had been asked, they probably would have said that Alicia looked much more comfortable than they felt.

A few changes in your delivery are necessary when you give a public group presentation. You, of course, need to modify the volume of your voice to be louder than it would be if you were speaking just to your other group members, all sitting close at hand. Your voice needs to reach beyond the rest of your group and be audible to the audience as well. Eye contact, a quality present in good conversations, should also be present in a group presentation. If the format of your presentation involves interaction among the group members, then you should make eye contact with other group members, just as you would in a less formal discussion. If the presentation format involves group members interacting with the audience, then your eye contact should be with members of the audience. You should remember that unlike your voice, which reaches all audience members at the same time, your eye contact is made with one audience member at a time. (Actually, it is possible for you to shift eye contact among several audience members at one time, giving each a feeling of being included in eye contact without being stared at; then a different section of the audience can become the focus of the eye contact.) Gestures, which most group members use naturally during private discussion, are still appropriate during a public discussion and should be visible to the audience.

If the format for the presentation involves distinct segments, each presented by a different group member, then the member speaking may choose to use a lectern, if one is available. A lectern is useful as a place to rest the speaker's notes; it is not intended as a repository for the speaker's body! The physical arrangement of the room can assist in making the group presentation effective. For instance, if the audience is large, then having the presenters elevated on a small stage can increase their visibility. However, it is worth remembering that group members who are not speaking at a particular point are still in view of the audience (even if they are not on a stage). If they look uninterested in the presentations being made by fellow group members, the message sent to the audience is not positive.

In addition to altering delivery so that it is appropriate to the group presentation context, some changes may be necessary in the content of the group's discussion. For instance, inside jokes either need to be explained or omitted so that the observing audience is not confused. Whereas an informal group meeting can tolerate frequent shifts in topic, in a presentation before the public, the relevance of contributions increases in importance. It therefore becomes increasingly important for group members to follow the plan they have created for the presentation and to explicitly link their contributions to those of other participants. The presence of an audience, therefore, creates some expectations for all group presentations, regardless of their specific type.

Group Presentation Formats

Although all group presentations are affected by the presence of an audience, they are not uniform in style or preparation. Variations in preparation and presentation result from differences in format. We consider four formats: panel discussion, symposium, forum, and training workshop. Although presentations often blend these formats, describing them in their "pure" form should help you identify the nature of each and the steps in the preparation and presentation process appropriate for each.

Panel Discussion

If you follow the news and enjoy watching televised analyses of the weekly news, you are probably already familiar with one format for a group presentation. After all, at the end of each week, representatives of several media outlets gather to review the week's news events before a television camera. The media representatives are a panel of experts; the camera is a substitute for a live audience. The discussion that is broadcast is a **panel discussion.** In a panel discussion, *a moderator leads the discussion by asking questions that one or more members of the panel can answer. Discussion flows from member to member with the moderator keeping all panelists involved and on track.* Thus, a panel discussion is quite similar to a normal group interaction, except that it adheres more closely to the agenda, involves participants more equally, may be more directed by a single person, and is likely to be more polished. If the group's topic can best be handled by interaction among the group members, then the panel discussion format is selected for a group presentation.

To prepare an effective panel discussion requires, first, preparation of participants so that each has gathered relevant information. For a class presentation, for instance, panelists might agree to read widely on the topic, though not necessarily all from the same sources. In that way, the discussion allows them to share information gathered independently.

Second, an agenda for the discussion should be developed. The agenda can consist of a series of questions that will elicit comments from the panelists. A moderator can have full responsibility for developing the agenda, or that can be a joint task shared by the group as a whole. But once the agenda has been developed, it is advisable to share it with the panelists. In that way, each panelist can organize his or her thoughts and information so that contributions can be made smoothly.

Because a panel discussion involves spontaneous interaction within the group, rehearsal is ill-advised. If a prerehearsed discussion were to be presented to an audience, group members would likely feel awkward repeating comments they made earlier (in rehearsal); but the audience would not be able to follow the idea development unless those comments were made. So, after development of the agenda, all that remains to be done before the presentation is to check with panelists to confirm that there is someone in the group who can speak about each issue and that every person can speak about some issue. During a panel discussion, participants typically are seated in chairs arranged in a semicircle. They are thus positioned so that they can interact freely with one another at the same time that they open the group to the audience, inviting the audience to listen in. Panelists should use good listening skills and ask and answer questions using sound small group communication skills. If one individual serves as a moderator, he or she can make sure that all participants have their say and that no one monopolizes the discussion.

You can see examples of panel discussions by watching the Public Broadcasting System's *Washington Week in Review*, *The Capitol Gang*, or other such programs. But to further illustrate the process, consider how a school district might develop a panel discussion to share concerns about school violence with the community and, then, how a classroom group might use a panel discussion to share a self-evaluation.

After acts of violence are reported in schools throughout the nation, each school district is likely to be motivated to explore whether its schools are prepared to avoid such dangers and to either reassure the community or ask for its assistance. A panel discussion might be presented to the community. Panelists could include teachers, administrators, and counselors, along with some community members who work in key positions with the young. Each panelist could be asked to prepare for the discussion by reading about the cases of violence that have occurred in other districts, recalling situations of actual or potential violence they have encountered, and reading for suggestions that could be implemented in their district. Then, an agenda for the discussion could be developed. In this case, an agenda that parallels the one at the end of Chapter 6 would be useful for structuring the discussion.

During the discussion, a moderator begins the presentation by introducing the issue to the audience and mentioning its importance and relevance to those present for the discussion. For example, at the 1997 International Viola Conference held in Austin, Texas, a two-part presentation was made by a group of viola scholars and performers. A symposium took place first, followed by a panel discussion. This is the way the chair of the program, Donald Maurice (1998) of New Zealand, began the first of the two sessions:

> It gives me great pleasure to welcome you to this session, the first session of two, devoted to Béla Bartôk's Viola Concerto. We are very fortunate to have a distinguished international panel of guests, each of whom has had a significant involvement with this work, either as a performer, a reviser, a musicologist, or in some cases, as all three. In today's session, guests will introduce different aspects of the history and will also include the current status of the Bartôk Viola Concerto.
>
> None of you need to be told this work has been one of the most problematic in the viola repertoire since its appearance over 50 years ago. However, the precise reasons behind this ongoing controversy may not be so well known. After hearing the speakers today you will be more aware of the reasons behind the controversy and will be all the more curious to hear the views of the panel members in the second session tomorrow. In the second session we will be discussing specific aspects of structure, note correction, orchestration, tempi, bowing, and articulation.
>
> It is now my pleasure to introduce to you the members of the panel in the order they will speak today.
>
> First, may I welcome Elliott Antokoletz, who is a professor here at the University of Texas, an internationally recognized Bartôk scholar and author . . . (p. 15)

The introduction is a good model for a moderator to follow because it connected the topic to the audience, establishing the topic's importance to the audience. It also supplied some background information on the panelists, incorporating references to the credentials of each, which added to the audience's perception of the panelists as credible. Moreover, it identified the pattern the presentations would follow so the audience had a roadmap of what would be covered in the two presentations.

As the second session began, Maurice (1998) provided another introduction, this time to highlight the nature of the panel discussion format:

> Today, rather than each of us taking turns at talking, we are going to open up some topics for debate and just have an open panel discussion. I invite members of the panel to jump in where they want to, politely of course. I will be the referee, deciding when it's time to move on to another topic, but I think once the topic has been introduced, we will let it run a little and see how it goes. (p. 32)

This description of the moderator's role as a referee is apt, for the job description involves keeping the discussion moving, on track, and fair. To begin a panel discussion, the moderator can ask an opening question designed to generate discussion. Later, he or she can ask probing questions when necessary, summarize the answers from the panelists before moving on to the next question, and monitor the time.

Howard and Barton (1992) described a panel discussion in which one of them had participated that went awry when the moderator attempted to exert too much control over the unfolding discussion. A panel had been composed of a philosopher, an astronomer, a physicist, a composer, and a graphic artist; they were brought together to discuss the relationship between art and science. A spirited exchange began when the panelists were asked about the criteria to be used in evaluating rightness and wrongness. What happened next is described by the authors:

> At about this point, the moderator interrupted what looked to become an amusing free-for-all (members of the audience were already thrusting their hands in the air) to announce that a lot of questions remained and the next one was . . . We on the panel all looked at each other in dismay while the audience squirmed in discomfort.
>
> Obviously, the moderator tried to control too closely where he should have guided. . . . he preemptively changed the subject just as it was getting interesting. (p. 50)

Exciting discussions may seem at times to lack focus. The trick, then, is to ask a question that focuses the discussion, rather than to cut off discussion by switching the topic entirely. If a good job has been done of gathering good panelists and if each of them is prepared for the discussion, the moderator will only need to provide gentle nudges to keep the discussion moving in an interesting and organized way.

As an additional example of the use of a panel discussion, suppose that a classroom group that has worked together during a course in small group communication is presenting an analysis of itself to the rest of the class. If the group chooses to make that presentation in a panel discussion format, its preparation might begin by having the group do a thorough self-evaluation. Even though it is important to retain spontaneity in a panel discussion, it is also important for a group to share and process members' feelings privately before communicating them publicly to the class as a whole. Preparation for the actual presentation could then proceed by first deciding which of the issues they have discussed should be included in the presentation. That discussion might end up with the following agenda:

1. How well did our choice of project for the term reflect each member's interests?

2. What process did we use to distribute tasks to the group members?

3. Were we effective in evaluating the information and ideas we gathered? What accounted for our level of effectiveness?

4. How was leadership handled in our group?

5. How could we have improved our leadership?

6. What norms did we have that made our group unique?

7. What do you think accounted for the level of cohesiveness in our group?

8. What stage in the group formation process presented the greatest difficulty for our group?

9. If you wanted to tell other groups how to avoid the problems we had, what suggestions would you give to them?

10. If you wanted to tell other groups how to achieve the successes we did, what suggestions would you give to them?

Another group using a panel discussion for the same purpose might end up with quite a different agenda, but whatever agenda is developed should be shared with all group members so that they can organize their thoughts before the panel discussion occurs. With an agenda developed, it is easier to ensure that every group member has something to contribute during the discussion and that someone can contribute to a discussion of each point. A moderator can keep the group organized and the discussion moving forward. With good preparation and effective participation, the interaction in a panel discussion can maintain the interest of the audience well.

Alicia's classroom group ended up making its final group presentation—one intended to be a group self-analysis—in a modified panel discussion format. The presentation was the least successful of the three her group made. A primary reason they had problems was that they had not taken enough time to discuss privately what had happened in their group during the course of their class. They knew ahead of time that they would talk about the conflicts in their group and that everyone had something to say about the topic. If they had talked about the conflict among themselves more carefully, they would have discovered how different their perceptions of the group were and that there was still some unresolved conflict in the group. The resulting problem was not that the class discovered that there had been some conflict in that group; it was, rather, that the group discovered what the conflict was at the same time that the class did. That was embarrassing for both the group and the audience.

Other problems came from the fact that the group had not developed a series of questions to organize their discussion. All of the members had agreed to focus on the

Ethical Consideration

In any group presentation, there may be information one member presents that relates to the comments of another group member, perhaps challenging the ideas of the other member or that person's behavior or character. In the case of a public presentation, does the "attacking" group member have an ethical responsibility to forewarn the other of the impending comments? to moderate the tone of the comments? to avoid making the comments?

---

topic of "conflict in our group," but a more specific agenda for the presentation had not been devised. Nor had other members developed prepared remarks; when one member began to speak at length, she did not have cause to feel that she was interfering with others' opportunity to present their prepared remarks. No moderator had been selected to keep the group on track or to move the group forward. Ultimately, the group managed to share perceptions of what had happened in their group, but much less effectively than they would have had they prepared appropriately for their discussion.

Symposium

As is the case for a panel discussion, the participants in a symposium are selected because they are knowledgeable about the topic under discussion and can present a diversity of opinions and information on the topic to be discussed. Unlike a panelist, a symposium participant is not expected to make contributions throughout the entire presentation. A **symposium** *divides the general topic into subtopics and the available time by the number of participants, so each participant is responsible for presenting one segment of the whole presentation.* If a discussion of school violence was presented as a symposium rather than as a panel discussion, the presentation might be divided into segments such as these: (1) the problems of violence at the elementary age, presented by an elementary teacher; (2) the problems of violence among adolescents, by a middle-school or high-school teacher; (3) spotting the troubled child, by a psychologist; (4) improving the police-school connection, by a police officer; and (5) new initiatives of the school district to cope with violence, by the school superintendent. A classroom group's self-evaluation could also be presented in a symposium format. In that case, separate group members would tackle separate topics. In adapting the agenda proposed earlier to the symposium format, perhaps one group member would consider the task behaviors of the group, another the group norms, another leadership, and another conflict. If the group as a whole then interacted on suggestions to future groups, the format would be a blend of panel discussion and symposium. The first presentation Alicia's group made was a symposium on the group dynamics in the movie *The Sandlot*, a movie about a group of boys who played summer baseball together in the neighborhood sandlot. Each member of the group took responsibility for describing a different dimension of the subject.

Because the symposium format involves no interaction among the participants, the role of the moderator is different than it is for a panel discussion. Prior to the presentation, either the moderator or the group as a whole makes the decisions about how to divide the topic into segments and how to order the segments. During the presentation, the moderator is still expected to begin with an introduction of the topic and of the participants. After each person is done speaking, the moderator introduces the next speaker and provides a transition between segments. The moderator also makes sure that the participants adhere to time limits, signaling a speaker whose time is running out. At the end of the symposium, the moderator can be expected to provide a summary.

Individual participants in a symposium are responsible for preparing their own segments of the presentation. Each segment is, in essence, a public speech. Therefore, each should include substantive information, be well organized, maintain the interest of the audience, be delivered effectively, and fit within the time limits allotted to it. One participant can undermine the effectiveness of the others by usurping time intended for later speakers or by covering the information assigned to another participant.

In some cases, it is possible for a group to rehearse a symposium presentation. Alicia's group found that, in doing so, they were able to identify and remedy potential problems, especially by omitting overlapping material in the presentations of some members and reducing the length of their presentations. Moreover, by getting feedback from other members of the group, each person felt more confident about the quality of the individual segments and of the presentation as a whole before a larger audience.

In a symposium format, each speaker has the floor for an extended time. Whether that speaker chooses to stand while speaking or to sit, the others in the group typically sit and listen during the times they are not active in the presentation. The participants in the symposium could be seated behind one long table (or row of chairs) or divided between two tables (or rows), one on either side of a podium, slightly angled toward each other. If you are responsible for the physical arrangement of a symposium, you might want to provide water and glasses for each participant. Also, a cloth covering the top of the table and reaching to the floor increases the comfort of the speakers who sit behind the table, especially anyone wearing a short skirt or electing to have bare feet for a few moments!

In the course of the presentations, group members may wish to use audio or visual aids to reinforce or clarify points they are making. Alicia's group noticed in rehearsal that the number of characters included in the movie they were analyzing might make it difficult for a listening audience unfamiliar with the film to keep the characters straight. They solved that problem by creating posterboard-sized "baseball cards," one for each of the players on the sandlot team. The colorful posters added both clarity and creativity to the presentation. You might use posters, overhead transparencies, or—if you have access to computer technology—computerized visuals to enhance your presentations. If you plan to use visual aids, be sure that they are visible to the audience. Letters that are too small to be read easily and colors that are not bold frustrate audience members rather than help them. Consider using multiple visual aids to allow each one to be simple, rather than crowding too much information on a single aid. Check for accuracy of spelling, because an error on display during a presentation does not help build your credibility as a presenter.

If you plan to use posters during a presentation, arrange to have a place to display them. Position yourself so that you do not block the audience's view of the poster. No matter how attractive the poster may be, continue to talk to the audience, not to the poster. The audience will also attend to your speech better if a poster is not displayed except when it is being used in the presentation. If you plan to use transparencies or a visualizer, check to be sure that both a screen and projector are available and in working order. When using either of those tools, a blank piece of paper can cover the information that is not yet being referred to to help direct the viewers' attention to the material relevant at a particular time.

Sometimes it is useful to show a videotaped excerpt during a group presentation to illustrate an idea. In that case, a VCR and large-screen television should be available, and the tape should be cued to the spot to be shown. If multiple segments are to be used, it might be worthwhile to create a tape containing only the excerpts to be shown, and in the order they will be used. As Alicia mentioned in the opening narrative, a presentation can be ruined by a group that assumes that all VCR counters are identical and ends up having the audience wait, watching the fastforwarding and rewinding of a videotape during a presentation. The promise that "we are almost there" begins to sound empty after a while.

Classroom groups are well-advised to rehearse a symposium prior to the presentation to make sure audio and visual aids are working properly and to check for overlapping, repetitious content and time violations. Groups without an opportunity to rehearse as a group can protect against these problems by (1) making sure that each person has rehearsed independently, preferably with at least one other group member present; (2) sharing outlines of each individual segment with each other, or with the moderator who can compare them, in advance of the presentation; (3) setting time limits for each segment just under the actual time available; and (4) having a signaling system to notify each speaker as the available time is about to be up. Groups that have not followed any of these suggestions regret their unquestioning faith in the group members as one member discovers there is nothing left to say that has not already been said or as group members develop the anxiety that comes from realizing that no time is left to complete the planned presentation after one of the group members took the time of three. In contrast, if the symposium was carefully organized from the start, if each member has prepared carefully, and if the group has prepared well, then the presentation is likely to be a source of interest and information for the audience.

Forum

Neither a panel discussion nor a symposium involves direct participation from the audience, unless it is linked to a **forum,** *a question-and-answer session between the group* *and the audience.* Although occasionally a forum can occur by itself, far more frequently a forum follows either a panel discussion or a symposium. You can probably imagine that in the example given earlier of a group presentation on violence in the schools, the opportunity for the audience to ask questions is an essential step if the presentation is to meet its goal of responding to community concerns.

A moderator may take charge of the question-and-answer session. That task involves recognizing those who want to ask questions and ensuring that no one monopolizes the session. By stating that it is time to give others a chance to ask a question and then averting eye contact from the frequent questioner to others in the audience, the moderator can encourage involvement from a wider number of audience members. Repeating a question that an audience member has asked may be necessary for two reasons: first, so that all can hear it and, second, to verify that it was correctly understood. A moderator may find it appropriate to direct the questions to the group member most qualified to answer the question, or the moderator can ask the audience members to do that. In some cases, a moderator may need to sift through questions, filtering out those that are actually personal attacks on a group member or a position statement of the audience member. The moderator can direct attention back to the substance of the presentation by making a comment such as, "Clearly, you have a difference of opinion with the speakers today. Perhaps we can give the panelists a chance to clarify their points of view by asking questions about the substance of their presentations."

To prepare for a forum, anticipate audience concerns and know more about the topic than was presented in the earlier discussion. Good answers to questions often link the answer back to information presented earlier, add information, and include a concise summary of the answer. If you are asked a question to which you do not know the answer, it is fine to ask others—in the group or in the audience—for their opinions. You could also give the audience your best guess on an answer, prefacing the answer with a statement like this, "I do not have a precise answer to that question, but from what I have read, I think it would be safe to assume that . . . " Group members who feel anxious about communicating in a forum should try to develop a positive attitude. After all, a forum is an opportunity to clarify earlier statements and adapt to the concerns of the audience; without the forum, the group could not achieve the goals of its presentation.

Ethical Consideration

When a group is making a public presentation about a current issue of relevance to the audience, then the group invites the audience to become a party to the decision-making process. The same ethical responsibility of providing accurate information without distortion holds for the group in relation to the audience as holds for the individual member in relation to the rest of the group.

Training Workshop

A fourth type of presentation that groups may be asked to make is a **training workshop.** In this case, *the group has information that is useful to the audience members and presents it to the audience in a manner that increases the audience's understanding and skill.*

Because a training workshop is expected to be a learning experience for the audience, preparation begins with an assessment of the audience's current level of understanding and skills and their future needs. Not until the group discovers what the target audience already knows and what it needs to know can it identify appropriate goals for further learning. For example, if you were required to present a workshop to a small group communication class, you could easily identify a number of topics that group members need to know more about that you have already gathered some background on during the course of your study of small group communication. Broome and Fulbright (1995) asked human resource workers who were experienced in working in groups about the problems they frequently encountered in groups. These problems, any one of which could be the basis for a training program, included issues with cultural diversity, lack of focus for the group and its meetings, problems with listening, lack of cohesiveness, lack of supportive communication or of participation, and behaviors linked to groupthink. Because those are common problems in groups, it is likely that even groups meeting in a small group communication class would find that further training in those areas could improve group performance. Rather than assuming that the group you will be training has one of these "generic needs," asking the potential trainees about their needs allows you to take the first step toward a successful training program (Klopp & Roth, 1997). Once assessment is complete, the group can formulate precise objectives for the training program. The objectives are vital in preparing the training workshop. If material does not link to the central objectives, it should not be included in the workshop.

Of course, the group must also know enough about the topic to be a competent source of additional knowledge. Research efforts may be necessary to reach the desired level of competence. Gathering additional information, beyond that provided in this book, could provide the necessary expertise for the group members. During the research process, group members should also identify materials useful in teaching both concepts and skills. Information that does not capture the audience's interest will not be absorbed. Examples, ideas for role plays, and film excerpts relevant to the concepts and skills can all be uncovered while researching.

With materials in hand, a group can devise a training workshop that balances substance with creative delivery. Hall and Nania (1997) noted that a training program effective at altering the systems in which audience members communicate has a cognitive component, a behavioral component, and an attitudinal component. After the workshop is complete, the audience members will understand new principles, be able to apply them, and want to do so. Absence of any one of these components means that the training has failed. It is not able to be adapted to the needs of the group if the cognitive component is absent, not able to be performed effectively if the behavioral component is absent, or will be gladly abandoned if the attitudinal component is absent.

Success of the group presentation is enhanced if the group follows these central principles:

1. Link the concepts and skills to be taught to the needs of the audience members. If they understand the relevance of the material to themselves, audience members are willing listeners.

2. Clarify the general principles involved so that the audience will understand not just what to do, but also why it should be done. In that way, the audience can go beyond the specifics taught in the workshop lesson and make sound decisions about similar situations they encounter in the future.

3. Because not everyone learns in the same way, integrate activities that involve multiple senses into the workshop. Learners should be active participants, not just passive listeners. After using an activity, a group member should lead the audience in a discussion of the activity to discover what they experienced and identify key concepts evident in the activity.

4. Provide multiple applications of the general principles. Audience members get greater practice with the concepts and skills in that way; they also can envision additional applications on their own (Hollingshead, 1998).

5. Vary the pace of the presentation to maintain the interest of the audience. This can be accomplished by having variety in the length of the segments in the workshop and variety in the type of segment. A series of 5 minilectures, each 10 minutes long, is less likely to maintain the interest of an audience than 3 minilectures interspersed with a role-play activity to test skill development and a discussion to consider applications of the skills. If interest is not captured and maintained, then the substance of the workshop misses its mark.

6. Reinforce the skills and concepts. A handout to take home can help remind an audience member of the ideas long after the workshop is over. An activity to practice the skills can also serve as reinforcement. Cooley (1994) suggests that a multistage process is useful if group members are to learn the new skills in which they are being trained: "conceptual presentation, modeling, observational training using examples from their own videotaped meetings, written practice and role playing" (p. 14)

7. Test understanding of the concepts; test skill ability. Either incorporated in the workshop or administered afterward, such a test provides feedback to the group that is important in adapting the workshop materials to future audiences or adapting additional materials to this audience.

Workshop agendas developed by two different classroom groups on the same topic can help you see how a workshop might be designed by a group. The agendas, found in Figure 9.1 and Figure 9.2, follow the audience assessments and goals for both groups.

Workshop A: Diversity in Small Groups

Audience Assessment.   The audience is a small group communication class evenly divided between males and females. They are all presently working in small groups in the classroom. In the future they will work in both classroom and work groups. They attend classes on a campus that is working to increase diversity but currently has few minority students. Few of the students in class are minority students. Although they have read about the influence of cultural differences on group members, many of the students do not have experiences working with individuals from different cultures; some students across the campus have expressed negative feelings toward the university's efforts at diversity.

Goals
- The audience members will realize that we are an increasingly diverse society and that they will need to be able to work with others from other cultures or subcultures.
- The audience members will understand the value that diversity can bring to a small group.
- The audience members will be able to identify behaviors in a work group that may differ depending on the cultural background of the group member.
- The audience members will be able to use three strategies for checking to see whether perceptions of an issue vary according to the cultural background of the group member.

Workshop B: Diversity in Small Groups

Audience Assessment.   The audience is composed of residents of the university dorms. They attend classes on a campus that is working to increase diversity but currently has few minority students. Students are aware of recent events in the dorms that have been hurtful to minority students. Several residents have told their Resident Assistants that they feel uncomfortable talking about racial differences; minority residents report feeling ostracized.

Goals
- The audience members will realize that we are an increasingly diverse society and that they will need to be able to live and work with others from other cultures or subcultures.
- The audience members will realize how uncomfortable it feels to be ostracized.
- The audience members will begin to feel comfortable talking about cultural differences.

On the next two pages, workshop plans for both groups have been included so that you can see that even if two workshops cover the same topic, they will include different components if the goals for the workshops differ. And the goals of two workshops will differ if the needs of the two audiences differ. Notice as you compare the sample workshops that both include all group members. Both workshops utilize varied teaching/learning strategies, all related to the overall goals of the workshop. And each includes some means of testing the achievement of the goals—in the first case, through the skill practice session; in the second, through the open discussion.

FIGURE 9.1 Workshop A plan was developed by the first classroom group.

Time	Description	Who
Setup: 3 minutes	Opening Activity: Each audience member will be given one piece of information on a color-coded card. Divide audience into five groups, according to the color of the cards. They complete a diversity quiz within five minutes. For four of the groups, the cards have information related to one cultural group. The cards for the fifth group have one piece of information from each of the cultural groups.	One member per group
Quiz: 5 minutes	The diversity quiz has questions from each cultural group.	
Processing: 5 minutes	Processing of the activity will help audience to see that the group that came together with knowledge of different cultures was more successful on this task.	Trina
7 minutes	Minilecture: 1. The workforce is increasingly diverse. 2. Diversity can be advantageous to organizations facing a variety of tasks.	John
8 minutes	Video: Three segments showing behaviors of workers consistent with their Asian, Hispanic, or Native American values.	Autumn
3 minutes	Questions/interaction about the video	Autumn
6 minutes	Minilecture: Describe each of three strategies to be used in checking for influence of culture on perceptions.	Jeff
8 minutes	Skill Practice Session: Audience volunteers will be placed in groups to role-play situations involving cultural differences. After the first role play, we try to discover what the volunteer observed, wondered about, and felt. Then we use the three strategies just described. In the other scenes, we will expect the volunteers to use the strategies, but we provide feedback afterward.	Crystal in charge; whole group is involved.
5 minutes	Interact with audience to summarize and reinforce the points of the workshop.	Trina

FIGURE 9.2   Workshop B plan was developed by the second classroom group.

Time	Description	Who
3 minutes	Welcome; Introduction of the group members	Nate
5 minutes	Opening Activity: Scavenger hunt; talk to others to find answers to questions.	Jennifer
5 minutes	Processing/Points to be Made: The more varied the people you contacted, the more answers you found; you may have stereotyped people in seeking answers from each one; some differences are cultural, but others are individual.	Jennifer
5 minutes	Minilecture: 1. Progress toward diversity on campus 2. Advantages of learning to live with diversity	Denae
5 minutes	Activity: Four audience members asked to leave room; there they are told that when they return they will stand in the center of the group and do whatever they can to get involved in the conversation. The rest of the audience members will be asked to form a large circle and begin talking to one another about an amusement park in the region, but they should *not* look at or talk to the returning individuals in the center of the circle.	Christopher Nate
3 minutes	Processing Activity: How did it feel to be ostracized?	Christopher
4 minutes	Full group discussion of the ways cultures affect us. During the discussion, all the participants with blue eyes will be ignored after they comment. All of the others will be told how great their comments are.	Denae leads; all others help.
3 minutes	Processing of the Activity: Subtle and not-so-subtle reactions involving prejudice can hurt everyone.	Jennifer
15 minutes	Open Forum: After one member describes her own stereotypes of whites, based on her limited observations of her sister's boyfriend, the audience will be asked to talk about their own experiences with prejudice, racism, sexism, etc. Open atmosphere will invite questions.	Brandi; then all others are involved.
5 minutes	Summary and sources of additional information.	All Members

Discussion.   In the course of a workshop, the way space is arranged in the room varies according to the needs at the time. When audience participation is desired, there should not be physical barriers between the audience and the group members in charge of the workshop. Flexible seating that allows the group to move from whole group discussion to small group activities and back again is important to achieving the goals of the workshop.

In the opening narrative, Alicia mentioned that developing a training workshop was a difficult task for her group. It is no wonder that a group of students would find it difficult to identify training needs for the target audience, develop the expertise necessary to be qualified to train others, organize a workshop so that it has the potential to enhance skill development and conceptual understanding while maintaining the interest of an audience, and then actually present the workshop. Even groups of professionals employed as trainers know the challenges involved in preparing and presenting such a program. However, a group that has learned to work together can benefit from embracing the challenge of all group presentation formats, including a training workshop.

Summary

When a group makes a public presentation, communication behaviors common to the normal, private interactions of the group change. By recognizing the public nature of the communication context, planning carefully for the presentation, and using good public speaking skills, group members can create a successful presentation, whatever the format used.

Four formats are particularly useful in small group presentations. A panel discussion involves interaction among individuals with expertise on the topic being discussed. A symposium involves separate presentations made by each expert. A forum invites questions from the audience to the group, usually following either a panel discussion or a symposium. A training workshop involves interaction between the group and the audience as the group attempts to increase the learning of the audience. All four formats require careful preparation by all members working together. That is followed by an execution of the plan, again involving each member of the group. Completing the challenges involved in preparing and presenting material in any one of these formats will prove rewarding for any group; being a party to a successful group presentation will prove rewarding for the audience.

QUESTIONS FOR DISCUSSION

1. Some televised panel discussions seem to violate the rules for communicating to achieve a positive climate in a group. How do the behaviors of the panelists affect your interest in the resulting discussion? How do they affect the quality of the interchange? How are they likely to affect the satisfaction of the panelists with the process?

2. Just as a meeting can make use of communication technology to bring together group members in different places, group presentations can use technology to make a presentation before an audience meeting in another place or to allow panelists in different locations to participate together in a group presentation. How would the use of technology affect the ease and quality of group presentations?

3. Student groups may face a difficult task if the training needs of a group are different from the expertise of the group members. How can a student group required to present a training workshop respond to that difficulty?

SUGGESTED ACTIVITIES

1. Join the audience for a group presentation, either one presented on television or one presented live in your community. Afterward, evaluate the presentation, paying particular attention to the factors that contributed to its success and those that hindered its success.

2. Interview an individual who has been a participant in a formal group presentation. (For instance, talk to a faculty member who has been on a panel at a convention program.) Try to discover the process that was used in deciding which format to follow, the method of preparation used, and the problems that occurred in preparing for and presenting the discussion.

3. With your project group, prepare and present a panel discussion or a symposium on a current issue of significance to your audience.

4. With your project group, prepare and present a training program for the rest of your class.

5. With your project group, prepare and present an analysis of your group throughout the time you have been working together.

6. As your group begins preparation for a group presentation, use the PERT format to identify and organize the steps required in the presentation. In your journal, evaluate your group's efforts in completing the group presentation.

SOURCES CITED

Broome, B. J., & Fulbright, L. (1995). A multistage influence model of barriers to group problem solving: A participant-generated agenda for small group research. *Small Group Research, 26,* 25–55.

Cooley, E. (1994). Training an interdisciplinary team in communication and decision-making skills. *Small Group Research, 25,* 5–25.

Hall, M. L., & Nania, S. (1997). Training design and evaluation: An example from a satellite based distance learning program. *Public Administration Quarterly, 21,* 370–385.

Hollingshead, A. B. (1998). Group and individual training: The impact of practice on performance. *Small Group Research, 29,* 254–280.

Howard, V. A., & Barton, J. H. (1992). *Thinking together: Making meetings work.* New York: William Morrow and Company.

Klopp, S., & Roth, W. (1997, June). In the new world traditional training hurts the bottom line. *Journal for Quality and Participation, 20,* 6–10.

Maurice, D. (Transcript Preparer). (1998). Panel discussion: The Bartôk viola concerto: From the 1997 International Viola Congress in Austin, Texas. *Journal of the American Viola Society, 14 (1),* 15–49.

10 Facilitating Small Groups

CHAPTER OBJECTIVES

After reading this chapter, you should be able to

- Define small group facilitation
- Distinguish among the types of facilitators
- Describe the components of preparing to facilitate a group
- Prepare to lead a focus group
- Identify the skills needed while facilitating a group
- Lead a focus group
- Present appropriate recommendations to a group you have observed
- Discuss the factors that affect a group's willingness and ability to change in line with a facilitator's recommendations
- Describe the process by which an individual can become prepared to be a small group facilitator

The Narrative

Ruth Hunt, 41, has worked in the field of consulting for 14 years. From her office in Minneapolis, Minnesota, she works as a principal and National Communication Practice Leader for PricewaterhouseCoopers, L.L.P., a global professional services consulting firm. The firm, the world's largest professional services firm, provides services in several areas, from the Global Human Resource Solutions group (of which Ruth is a part) to various types of financial advisory and business strategy services. Here, she describes her role as a group facilitator:

> *Clients contact our firm because of the combination of talent that we can bring to their needs for creative problem solving. In my line of the business, Global Human Resource Solutions, we specialize in helping employers with their people-related issues—their organizational issues.*

Because we can partner with our experts in areas such as corporate finance and strategy, we're able to provide a broad range of consultative support.

At present, facilitating groups is a major part of my work. Some of that relates to internal work groups. As the National Practice Leader for Organizational Communications, I often conduct meetings for the people who report to me as part of planning processes or as part of implementing strategies that we are undertaking to further the business. I also facilitate client project or task teams, where we're working on a problem-solving activity for a client. I typically facilitate two types of groups for clients. The first involves facilitating communication strategic planning sessions. We're increasingly doing work with companies involved with mergers and acquisitions. The announcement of a merger creates uncertainty that can translate into lost productivity at the very time that the organizations are trying to capitalize on the synergies of the merger, so that they fully realize its value. I facilitate the development of a communication strategy to support the integration of the organizations. We hope that eventually the client will become self-sufficient in executing and adapting the plan. The other type of facilitation for client groups is conducting focus groups to collect data. I enjoy the opportunity that presents to take the pulse of employees in a wide range of organizations.

To illustrate how I work, I'll describe a merger between two organizations. Two businesses were going to combine, and the representatives from the corporate communications functions on both sides were brought to the table to figure out how to work together to develop the strategic communication plan. What was interesting about the process was that they needed to get acquainted with one another in what could be perceived as a bit of an adversarial environment, knowing that the companies were going to be merged and there would be overlapping functions. They certainly did not know at the time they got together whether they all would still have jobs. Who would be the survivors if it seemed that there was overlap? And to complicate it, the stronger, more experienced and broad-based communication team worked in the company being acquired, not the acquirer. Yet they had less power than the company doing the acquiring. So that was a difficult situation. There was truly both a task and a relationship set of issues. We needed to come up with an effective communication strategy and to determine the relationship between these people and how they could work together most effectively. Added to the dynamic was the fact that they needed our expertise to support them, since they had not ever experienced a merger before.

In the first full-day working session, we began with introductions—who's who? What's their background? What are they bringing to the table? We confirmed our objectives, both for the immediate task of planning the communication process and the larger objectives of ensuring the success of the merger. Then we worked on the typical elements of a communication plan: understanding the audiences and the various subgroups within them, both internal and external to the organization, and determining our objectives in communication with each of them, what messages were needed, and what media would be available on both sides. We developed some new ideas they hadn't considered before that could be successful. We determined who was going to be responsible and what our ongoing process would be as events occurred. We had to work very efficiently under tight time constraints in order to achieve our objectives proactively and make the announcement when the deal was closed, which was literally a few days away. It was a highly charged environment—very short-fused. I needed to help facilitate consensus in the development of the strategy and to apply my knowledge and experience with mergers and acquisitions, giving them advice that could be applied to the unique attributes of their situation.

In consulting, you roll with the punches. Things don't always happen quite the way you might plan. The next day, the CEO decided that he needed to put everything else aside to prepare his remarks for a meeting with key members of the organization being acquired, since there was concern that some of the best people in that organization would be fearful of their future and leave the company. So we dropped everything else, and I facilitated a management team meeting in which the CEO and his top reports worked through their key messages so as to give some reassurance that a very thoughtful process was under way to address employee concerns. Over the next several weeks, we met periodically to evaluate the success of the communication efforts, modify the plan, and conduct focus groups with a cross section of the employees in a number of different locations. We might be there for two to three days and then come back in another week, and then maybe come back again a couple of weeks later.

We frequently lead focus groups in the case of a merger and to get employee feedback about other issues as well. Focus group facilitation follows a sort of formula. Typically, I am a third party, there to facilitate the process without a management representative present. As we kick off the focus group, we typically introduce ourselves, describe our backgrounds, our role and objectives for that meeting, and provide reassurances regarding the confidentiality of all comments. Then we explain the process we are going to follow. Next, we might go around the room and have the participants introduce themselves, maybe telling their role within the organization and perhaps the number of years they've been with the organization. That helps us get a sense of their perspective. Then I begin with a pretty highly structured set of questions, followed by a more free-flowing set of probing questions on particular items.

Typically members of the group will respond pretty freely if we've been successful at the outset in reassuring them that we are an impartial third party and that their remarks are confidential. From time to time, we may be involved in a situation where there is a credibility gap, perhaps with management. In those cases, we might have to probe more deeply to try to get them to open up and feel comfortable enough to share their real opinions.

In trying to summarize responses, we might verbally summarize by saying, "So, I'm hearing you say that most of you feel you do not have a good understanding of the reasons for the merger. Is that correct?" We might ask for a show of hands so that rather than relying on the people who have been more outspoken, we can assess the strength of various positions.

In some groups, we might use exercises to support the process. We could use a case study or pair up individuals on tasks and then bring the group back together again. We could use brainstorming to get the group to explore various possibilities before narrowing them down. We'll also use flip charts or overhead transparencies to record ideas during brainstorming.

The tempo of a meeting would vary. If I were conducting a focus group on a pretty emotionally charged subject, I might be very easy-paced, to reassure, to not cause undue concern, to build trust and confidence. If we were brainstorming, the pace would be faster. A focus group meeting will typically last an hour and a half to two hours, usually with about 8 to 12 people in a session.

Preparation for facilitation will vary depending on the group I'm working with, but there are some things I always do. First, I confirm my objectives. What kind of group is this? Why are we getting them together? What do we need to be getting out of it? If the objectives are not really crisp and clear, it will waste everybody's time. Second, I establish a clearly defined process, developing an agenda or the means of generating one. What is the starting point? What kinds of questions will I ask? What are the issues where I'll need to be particularly adept in terms of probing? In addition, I might do some research about the group I'll be meeting to get some background so that I do a better job. I might recommend that the organization add some additional people to the group if it appears to be incomplete, from my perception.

There are some skills essential to effective facilitation of groups. At the top of the list are listening and speaking skills—being able to express oneself, but also being able to quickly process what the participants are saying and distinguishing between the nuances and the intensity of emotion group members are feeling. Skill is also needed in building consensus. In emotional situations, we have to step back and find ways to get to common ground. Facilitators also need negotiating skills—an ability to deal with difficult people and personalities. As a facilitator, you don't have the power to tell a group what to do. You are trying to bring the group to consensus. If opinions are divergent, that may be just fine. But if the personalities are such that they are standing in the way of being able to accomplish the task, you need to very delicately work with that or the group process will break down. Another set of skills is interpersonal sensitivity. Some facilitators listen too quickly to the most outspoken group members without drawing out the perceptions of the people who are more quiet but may well be the majority. They may not sense a raised eyebrow that tells you there is some disagreement within the group. One person is saying something, and most of the group is nodding their heads, but "Joe" in the corner is ever so slightly rolling his eyes. And you think, "Wait a minute. Why did Joe roll his eyes?" If you can pick up on that and gently get him into the discussion, you may very well find that he has such a valid point to make that, upon his having made it, the people who were just nodding their heads are changing their minds. Those are the key skills I can identify.

I certainly didn't acquire the skills, especially at the level I work at now, overnight. My preparation goes all the way back to high school and college experiences in public speaking, competitive individual speaking events and debate. My academic preparation—an undergraduate degree from the University of Wisconsin at Eau Claire with a double major in speech and English and a master's degree in organizational communication from the University of Northern Iowa—was particularly helpful, given the work that I now do. In addition, I've had on-the-job training. In our firm, we often pair a very senior person with another staff person who can help serve as a notetaker and help in other ways in the discussion. That is excellent training. I've been able to watch other people and emulate some of the best of what I saw them do. I have also worked to develop technical skills relevant to a specific group with whom I might work. However, my academic training prepared me pretty quickly to lead focus groups and so on. My extensive experience in public speaking and the confidence that I developed in terms of standing up in front of groups and clearly articulating my position prepared me very, very well.

What I like best about my job is the creative problem solving it requires. That, and the opportunity to work at the strategic level of business. Organizations are realizing how critical effective communication is to their staff. Communicators are not just the newsletter writers anymore. Increasingly, communicators are the change agents. That's what's really exciting to me: that we are really making a difference.

If you have found that the study of small group communication is especially interesting, and perhaps even exciting, you may have wondered whether there are opportunities (beyond working as a skillful member of a group) to continue to develop your understanding of small groups and your ability to successfully influence their operations. One of the directions possible is that taken by Ruth Hunt: working with groups whose circumstances have led them to seek assistance from an expert facilitator.

Whether a group has existed for years or is developing in an organization with a new commitment to teaming, the group is not immune to problems. In an effort to enhance the work of the group, assistance from a facilitator may be sought. Frey (1995b) explains that "**group facilitation** can be defined as *any meeting technique, procedure, or practice that makes it easier for groups to interact and/or accomplish their goals*" (p. 4). The broad range of activities included within facilitation may make it difficult to pin down exactly what a facilitator does. The truth is, the specific tasks of a facilitator will vary. But they may include guiding a group through a meeting; focusing the group's attention on key issues; observing and interpreting member behavior, and then providing feedback to the group about these observations; identifying areas in which group members need skill development, and then training group members directly or indirectly (through modeling appropriate behaviors), and coaching members as the skills develop. Common to all of these behaviors is a **process focus,** for facilitators of small groups assist the members with the processes of their group. Because the process needs of groups differ from group to group and change over time, facilitators do not always perform the same tasks. Therefore, effective facilitators must be knowledgeable about small groups, enough so that they can diagnose the needs of groups and have a wide range of strategies useful to groups, and flexible enough to select appropriate strategies.

Types of Facilitation

In the narrative, Ruth Hunt described three types of group facilitation she performs in her job: internal, external, and focus group facilitation. Frequently, she functions as an *internal facilitator,* helping with the group processes in her own work group. Developing work teams often seek the assistance of a group of internal facilitators, and their organization usually provides training for them. A good training program gives these individuals a chance to practice their newly acquired skills before they actually have to facilitate a group of their colleagues at work (Kaeter, 1995). That is especially important because of the role change involved when a group member becomes a group facilitator. For some internal facilitators, it may be awkward to handle the power issues involved in leading meetings at which their superiors are a part of the group (Zimmerman & Evans, 1993). In Ruth Hunt's case, her leadership position within her organization gives her added authority as she facilitates internally. A group member with authority who becomes a facilitator may have another difficulty, however: a member who has spoken out on issues within a group may have difficulty reducing content-related contributions (or the perception of a content-related predisposition) as he or she focuses on the process within the group. Frequently it is impractical to use any facilitator except an internal one, whether because of costs involved in paying an outsider or the desire to keep information about the work of the group within the confines of the group (Clawson, Bostrum, & Anson, 1993).

Nevertheless, there are times when a group needs to turn for assistance to an outside facilitator who can provide a set of skills or a sense of objectivity not available within the group. When Ruth works as an *external facilitator,* she helps client groups in organizations of which she is not a member. Her meetings with members of the two organizations involved in a merger are examples of external facilitation. Because she has experience working with clients undergoing mergers, she has skills the groups themselves lack, along with a sense of objectivity as a third party to the merger. Other examples of external facilitation, all described by the contributors to Frey (1995a) include Broome's work (1995) with members of the Comanche tribe to identify ways of increasing participation in tribal government, Murphy's work (1995) on gender issues in a work group, Pearce's use (1995) of the principles of coordinated management of meaning to work with family and policy-making groups, and Keyton's work (1995) using SYMLOG to improve the teamwork in a group of medical residents.

While an internal facilitator is already known to group members, an external facilitator needs to build a credible image with the client group, both before and during the facilitation sessions. Not only is the group less familiar with an external facilitator, but he or she is also less familiar with the culture of the group being assisted. That may actually be an advantage for the facilitator who, freed from the group's culture, can see the patterns of group interaction more objectively. Both internal and external facilitators work on improving the functioning of a continuing group by improving members' skills and changing behaviors that impede effective group functioning.

The third type of facilitation involves *leading focus groups*. When Ruth leads a focus group, her immediate task does not involve improving a continuing group. Rather, her task is to lead an ad hoc group that has been formed to gather information for a client. This is an area in which work is available in varied contexts. For instance, developers of real estate are using focus groups to determine what features are desired by home buyers shopping for homes within a particular price range (Rose, 1997). Frey's edited book on *Innovations in Group Facilitation* (1995a) includes descriptions of focus group use by the *St. Louis Post Dispatch* (as it was planning to redesign its Sunday supplement); by a Chicago trial attorney who wanted to test the success of arguments in a civil case with a mock jury (Cragan & Shields, 1995); and by Northern Illinois University's student health services, which wanted to gather reactions to messages designed to reduce sexually transmitted diseases (Kreps, 1995). Health campaigns, as well as political and commercial campaigns, use focus groups to test proposed approaches on small groups representative of the larger population before committing financial resources to a broader, often national, campaign.

Even though focus group leaders are not working with continuing groups, they still need to have mastered communication skills within a small group in order to ask both primary and secondary questions that generate responses, to listen carefully to the responses, summarize comments and test for agreement, and draw all group members into the interaction.

Each type of facilitator has some special issues to consider, but common to all types of facilitation are steps that must be taken before, during, and after group meetings. We consider the activities involved at each of these stages.

Process of Facilitation

Prior to Facilitation

Just as a meeting is improved by careful planning, a facilitator must prepare for a meeting before it occurs. These preparations have particular importance for an external facilitator who must establish a connection with the group quickly and work efficiently to accomplish tasks during the time he or she is contracted to work with the group. But for all facilitators, whether internal or external, preparation of both content and the setting of the meeting are necessary.

Content Preparation.   The first step in content preparation is a discussion with the individual requesting facilitation to discover the goals for facilitation and some of the

Ethical Consideration

In a provocative essay, Cynthia Stohl (1995) raises several ethical issues for facilitators. One of those relates to the use that might be made of information gathered from contact between the facilitator and the organizational contact. Stohl asks how much of the information known to the facilitator should be shared with the participants. What do you think? Another ethical issue raised by Goldhaber (1986) relates to the information gathered prior to the actual facilitation: if your research uncovers the fact that the group hiring you is engaged in activity that is legally or morally questionable, what should you do?

issues the group seems to be facing. For Ruth Hunt, these conversations might reveal an executive's perception of the concerns employees might have when they are facing a merger. The conversations might also reveal what impact the executive anticipates the merger will have. Such information would allow Ruth to anticipate issues the group must consider. Further research (through surveys, face-to-face interviews with group members, reports of previous work with the group or on the topic, company publications, or relevant library sources) can uncover additional background information. The information may ground the facilitator on the content issues involved, help to anticipate the concerns of group members, and get a sense for the dynamics of the group and its decision-making processes. Such research has led Ruth Hunt, on occasion, to request that her contacts expand those invited to the meetings to include additional people with a key involvement in the issue.

In the case of a focus group, background information is useful, but an additional piece of information is also needed. Because the facilitator will probably be responsible for creating the focus group, the facilitator needs to discover the nature of the population whose opinions are being sought so that a group can be created that is representative of the broader population. To recruit focus group members, financial incentives may be necessary. Cragan and Shields (1995) say that $10 may be a sufficient enticement for a college student, while $150 or more may be necessary if the group is to be composed of professionals. In the focus groups Ruth Hunt facilitates, enticements are more psychological: the inducement to attend because it is part of the worker's job, curiosity, and pride at being asked to contribute. And, of course, a focus group meeting represents a break from the typical day's work, one at which refreshments are likely to be provided!

Background research allows each type of facilitator to be sure the group to be led is appropriately formed and to develop an agenda of questions to stimulate discussion in the meeting. So important is that agenda that Cragan and Shields (1995) describe it, along with the skills of the facilitator, as "the most important variables affecting the outcomes of a focus group interview" (p. 236). It has similar importance in other facilitation settings. A facilitator should have the skills described in Chapter 4 to formulate primary and secondary (probing) questions to lead a discussion. Time spent creating an agenda that can serve as a foundation for the discussion is time well spent. It need not restrict the group, because an effective facilitator can deviate from the prepared agenda when that seems best for the group.

Ethical Consideration

What responsibilities would you have as a facilitator to ensure that the information you give the group is current and accurate?

Setting Preparation

Preparing the setting for a facilitative meeting is as important as preparing to facilitate the meeting. Sometimes it is desirable to meet in an area away from the typical workplace of a continuing group, especially when preserving confidentiality of remarks is important. If you have been in classroom groups that have chosen to meet outside of the classroom, you have undoubtedly noticed how a change of setting can add to the comfort of the group. However, if changing the meeting place makes it difficult for group members to attend an important meeting, it would be ill-advised to do so. Ease of access to the meeting place is important. Zimmerman and Evans (1993) have identified a number of factors to consider in preparing the setting for a meeting. They include

- Having a room that is large enough to move around in, but not so large that the group is lost in the space
- Having a room arranged to minimize distance between members and to maximize interaction
- Selecting a room with movable furniture so that it can be arranged differently at different times
- Setting the temperature so that members are alert but still comfortable
- Making the room free from distractions (including ringing telephones and, perhaps, windows that bring outsiders into the view of the group and the group into the view of outsiders)
- Making light snacks available that could help the group to maintain its energy, without interfering with the involvement of group members in the discussion

If you are in a position to work as a facilitator, you might want to purchase some of the books prepared by the American Society for Training and Development (ASTD). The organization produces a series of trainers' sourcebooks on subjects ranging from facilitation skills and team building to leadership, strategic planning, and diversity. Included in the books are planning checklists that could help you remember to check each potential meeting room for the features you would need. For instance, if you plan to use transparencies during a meeting, you would need to be sure to check for the presence of an overhead projector and screen. If group members are going to be using computer equipment during a meeting, electrical outlets sufficient for your needs could be checked. Torres and Fairbanks (1996), authors of *Teambuilding: The ASTD Trainer's Sourcebook*, make the practical suggestion of getting the name of the technical support person for a meeting facility so that there is an emergency contact in case a fuse blows or a bulb burns out. Having a prepared checklist to be used with each new client or each new meeting makes your preparation more systematic and, thus, easier. Even if you do not purchase one of the ASTD books, you can prepare a standard checklist for yourself, suited to your needs. However, one of the other features of the ASTD series that may be attractive to you is that it includes plans, assessment tools, and materials for handouts and transparencies. Any individual who purchases a book is automatically granted copyright permission to reproduce the materials for use in training or facilitation sessions.

Work done prior to a facilitation session is important. The more that can be done ahead of time, the more likely it will be that a facilitator can be freed from unnecessary concerns during a facilitation session, thereby increasing the facilitator's ability to attend to what is happening in the meeting and adapt to it with flexibility and skill.

During Facilitation

There are some stock patterns that can be relied on to get a facilitation session off and running. The facilitator should begin with introductions. Facilitators should introduce themselves (and there often are two facilitators working with a group at any time), but they should also ask group members to introduce themselves. The facilitators can then identify the purpose of the meeting and establish any relevant ground rules. Then the session can begin to delve into the substantive issues, following the agenda established by the facilitators' questions.

It is useful to record ideas developed during a facilitation session. If the group is a focus group, the record is used to develop a report for the client. But even in ongoing groups, recording ideas is valuable. Rees (1991) presents a clear argument in favor of recording ideas while facilitating a group by mentioning several points. First, having an idea recorded shows the contributor that the idea was heard. Then the contributor can relax and listen to what others have to say. Second, others are less likely to repeat the ideas that have been recorded, making the meeting more efficient. Third, when it is time to move from generating ideas to evaluating them, there is a clear record of all suggestions, so the group does not have to spend time trying to recall the contributions. Fourth, evaluation can be more objective, since the recorded idea can be evaluated separately from the source who contributed it. Finally, the written record has value as a reminder of the group's progress, of group decisions, and even of issues of concern to the group. When two people work as a facilitation team, one person may serve to record ideas. The other is then more free to attend to the behaviors of group members, noting nonverbal behaviors—such as those that signal disagreement with others or the distancing of a member from the group—and then responding to these signals.

Both flexibility and skill are necessary to make a facilitation session effective. Flexibility is mentioned by practicing facilitators as an important skill that influences critical moments during facilitation sessions. The experienced facilitators who responded to Clawson, Bostrom, and Anson's (1993) study of the role of facilitators frequently mentioned the importance of being able to do more than one thing at a time and switching tasks easily. Flexibility is impossible if the facilitator lacks the varied skills needed in group work. Skill is necessary to create a comfortable climate for interaction, to manage the tempo of the meeting, to encourage participation, to

When Ruth Hunt (standing) facilitates group meetings, her knowledge of communication and her experience as a facilitator give her the flexibility to adapt to the needs of the group at the moment. (Photo compliments of PricewaterhouseCoopers LLP.)

Technology Note: Skills Needed by a Technology Facilitator

Facilitators who help groups in their efforts to integrate technological tools into the group's process need to have skill in using the tools themselves. Clawson, Bostrom, and Anson (1993) found that experienced facilitators described three role dimensions as being of particular importance when they were assisting groups with the use of technology: (1) having a conceptual understanding of the technology and its capabilities; (2) being able to select and prepare the appropriate technology; and (3) being able to help the group understand and feel comfortable with the technology and its capabilities. These skills do not substitute for those needed by other facilitators; they are expected in addition to the other skills.

reword contributions for clarity, to distinguish one issue from another so each can be handled separately, to summarize contributions of group members, to model desirable behaviors for handling conflict, to interpret group member behaviors, and to provide useful message feedback and behavior feedback that encourage member introspection and insight without creating defensiveness. Among the facilitator's tools of the trade may be such simple strategies as asking open-ended questions to encourage further discussion or knowing when to subdivide a large group, either so individuals will be more comfortable sharing ideas or to encourage diversity of expressed ideas.

Skill is essential, not just because of the variety of behaviors involved in facilitation, but also because those behaviors must be performed in such a way that the group

Ethical Consideration

In writing about facilitation, Stohl (1995) describes paradoxical features of facilitation. Facilitators are asked to empower groups by people whose control over a group may give them a vested interest in having the empowerment fail; facilitators empower groups whose newfound power may lead them to resist the recommendations of the facilitator; as facilitators attempt to rectify problems in the group, they may come to be seen as the cause of those problems. What are the ethical responsibilities of a facilitator who is dealing with these complexities?

being facilitated becomes empowered in the process. An effective facilitator, in essence, works him- or herself out of a job in the group being facilitated. In other words, if you were hired as an external facilitator for a group that is having trouble managing conflict, you will have earned your pay if you teach the group to handle its own conflict effectively, not if you simply handle the conflict for the group at a meeting you facilitate. It is unrealistic to expect that you can accomplish your full goal in the space of an hour's meeting. What is necessary is a sequence of behaviors: observing the difficulties the group is currently having, describing the behaviors to the group so that it can begin to recognize its own patterns, modeling and describing alternate approaches, getting the group to understand the advantages of change, helping the group members to practice new behaviors, and working with the group to adapt to the changes in the system when one element (in this case, the manner of dealing with conflict) changes. Only when the group has become able to manage its new behavior on its own has the facilitation been successful.

The more familiar a facilitator is with a variety of techniques for use in small groups, the more flexible he or she can be in adapting to the needs of a particular group. In the midst of a group meeting, when the group needs help with decision making, with understanding its patterns of leadership, or in changing its norms, the facilitator may need to act quickly, without time to review forgotten concepts or develop additional strategies. Although no two meetings are exactly alike, the ability to respond effectively in the midst of a meeting can be developed with experience.

Post-Meeting Facilitation

The task of the facilitator does not end when the focus group is over or when the meeting has adjourned. If a focus group has been conducted, the facilitator must report to the client the issues uncovered by the meeting. Cragan and Shields (1995) recommend a lengthy written report: about 7 pages in which the facilitator lays out the background, problem, objectives, and procedures; 15 to 18 pages of data analysis and recommendations, often relaying the comments of group members directly, so their voices are heard; finally, about 5 pages of summary. In addition to the written report, they recommend an oral presentation of about an hour (45 minutes of prepared presentation with 15 minutes for questions and answers). Ruth Hunt cautions that lengthy reports may be overlooked by a busy CEO who would prefer a distilled, executive summary. Only when the contracting agency wants considerable detail and the complexity of the situation warrants it would a lengthy report be in order.

In the case of an ongoing group, continued contact over some period of time is desirable after a facilitator has worked with a group. In the absence of the facilitator, a group may find its old, familiar behaviors too comfortable to abandon, despite the barriers they may pose for the group's effectiveness. Change is never easy for a group or for the individual members in the group. Change is more likely to occur if the facilitator has provided a written and oral summary of the decisions of the group, which will serve as reminders to the group; has forewarned the group of the temptations it will face to abandon the efforts to change, since to be forewarned is to be forearmed; and returns to the group to evaluate progress, make adjustments in recommendations, and continue the coaching process. Ruth Hunt mentioned in the opening narrative that she often makes a couple of return visits to a group that has received facilitation. The final success of facilitators in assisting ongoing groups may well depend on the facilitators' understanding of their role as change agents who are spreading an innovation throughout the group.

Innovation Diffusion: A Theoretical Perspective

Facilitation of continuing groups involves introducing change into the group. The study of how changes are introduced and adopted throughout society is the subject of a book first published in 1962 called *Diffusion of Innovations.* The author, Everett M. Rogers, has studied the spread of a number of innovations, from personal computers to family planning, among sociological groups. In a more recent edition of *Diffusion of Innovations,* Rogers (1995) reports on a number of the studies done in the field of innovation diffusion and identifies the general patterns followed when changes are introduced and adopted. Although his primary focus is on innovations of a technological nature, Rogers defines an **innovation** more broadly, as *"an idea, practice, or object that is perceived as new by an individual or other unit of adoption"* (p. 11). Thus, when facilitators introduce a new way of handling diversity issues, a new means of sharing power in the group, or a new strategy for enhancing cohesiveness, they are introducing innovations just as much as they are when they introduce electronic support systems to use in decision making. To understand the factors that assist the group in adopting the innovation, it is useful to understand some key concepts relevant to innovation diffusion.

Stages Leading to Adoption of an Innovation

Before a new idea or behavior is adopted by a small group, several stages have occurred. First, the facilitator teaches the group about the innovation and whatever skills are necessary to implement the new behaviors. These are the components of the first stage toward change, the *knowledge stage.*

The second stage involves *persuasion:* helping group members have a positive attitude toward the innovation. Discussing the new ideas or behaviors with others contributes to a positive attitude, as does support for the change from the larger system. When this stage is complete, group members not only understand the change, but they also accept its desirability.

Third, a *decision* stage occurs when group members plan to gather added information about the innovation and decide to try it. These decisions are followed up on in the fourth stage, *implementation,* when the group actually acquires the additional information about the innovation and actually uses it. By the fifth stage, the *confirmation* stage, the group members use the innovation regularly, acknowledge its utility for the group, and recommend it to others outside the group.

Although it appears that the process is quite simple, it is complicated by the fact that innovations introduce uncertainty into a group. When group members consider altering their patterns of behavior, they have questions about how the new behaviors will work. In addition, because the new behavior is performed within a system characterized by interdependence, one new behavior affects other behaviors in the system; and other elements in the system affect the ease with which the new behaviors are adopted. Even if, ultimately, the changes are all beneficial to the group, the uncertainties surrounding the changes create some discomfort in the group members, who may respond by rejecting the new ideas.

Factors Increasing the Chances of Adoption

Several factors can increase the chances of change being accepted by groups. The features of the change itself are of primary importance. If the change is understandable, clearly advantageous, compatible with other behaviors in the group, and can be used on a trial basis, it is more likely to be adopted by the group. Therefore, a facilitator who hopes a group will develop a new strategy should be sure to describe it clearly, identify its advantages for the group, allow the group to discuss the fit between the new strategy and other group behaviors and values, and have group members practice the behavior with facilitator assistance and encouragement. Groups that alter a facilitator-proposed behavior to suit their own needs are more likely to adopt the behavior over the long run.

Effective communication about the change within the group also increases its chances of being accepted. Communication about the change begins when the facilitator suggests doing something in a different way than it has been done before. A facilitator is a **change agent,** *someone who introduces change into the group.* A change agent is *different* (Rogers [1995] uses the term *heterophilous*) from the group, at least in terms of comfort with the change. Unfortunately, communication is more effective when individuals are *similar* (*homophilous*). Nonetheless, there are two ways to increase effectiveness. The first is that even heterophilous communicators can communicate effectively if they have a high degree of empathy. Therefore, a facilitator who can effectively take the role of the group members to understand their uncertainties about the change and their interests in resisting or supporting change will be able to communicate effectively with the group. The second strategy is for the facilitator to identify individuals who are more receptive to change and who wield some influence within the group. Diffusion theory calls these individuals "opinion leaders." Opinion leaders, who may be different from the official leaders of a group, will be sought after by group members for assurances about the position to take toward issues. If the facilitator can encourage the opinion leaders to accept the change, then informal channels of communication within the group will spread that acceptance in widening circles throughout the group. An effective facilitator builds in opportunities for the informal communication system to spread discussion about the proposed changes so that individuals' efforts to try the proposed changes are reinforced by comments from peers.

Adoption of an innovation by some members increases its chances of being adopted by others. A facilitator should not anticipate immediate adoption of a recommended change by all members of a group. Perhaps one or two group members will experiment with a change soon after it has been suggested. If it meets with failure, that may be all that is necessary to stop the change. If it is successful, then the change will spread, and more quickly than it had before. A few group members should be expected to lag behind the rest of the group. Continued contact with the group throughout this process increases the chances of the change being implemented. For instance, if a facilitator is trying to get the group to send electronic mail to one another to reduce the need for frequent, short meetings of limited utility, early users may be group members already used to sending E-mail for other purposes. A new user may become frustrated by the system and give up. A facilitator's return to the group can (1) identify such difficulties, (2) provide reinforcement for those who are trying to adopt the change, (3) encourage discussion of the advantages the group has seen so far, and (4) consider possible modifications of the procedure to better suit the group. When the facilitator performs those functions, then group members experimenting with the change will be more likely to continue, and the lagging resistors may be spurred to try the change at last.

By understanding the steps involved in the adoption of innovations and the factors influencing adoption, facilitators can be more effective at introducing change within the groups they are helping. Whether you become a facilitator yourself or are a member of a group that decides it needs the help of a facilitator, your understanding of the process involved in innovation diffusion and your understanding of the nature of facilitation should help make the facilitation process more effective.

Preparing to Become a Facilitator

It is probably obvious to you that a facilitator must be able to apply an understanding of small groups, such as the information discussed throughout this text, to actual groups. An individual who has been effective as a member of a small group may become an effective facilitator—assuming that the effectiveness stems from a thoughtful application of principles of small group communication to the group rather than from pure luck or the diligence of other group members. Consider the case of one student who worked as an intern at an insurance company during the summer after she completed a small group communication class (using this text as it was being developed). The company was about to undergo significant changes: it was adopting a teaming approach. The student intern was able to advise company management on the changes they would experience. She noted, for instance, that they would be appointing team leaders who might not have emerged naturally from group interaction. She warned them of the difficulties that might develop if the individuals were poorly suited to the leadership of the group. She suggested that they might pay particular attention to the roles other group members played in order to begin to identify other potential leaders. She described the stages the teams would be likely to go through in their development, so that expectations were reasonable. She also identified some strategies the groups could use to develop cohesiveness. In her role as an intern, this student was performing tasks related to group facilitation.

Other students have recognized the value of the techniques used in a small groups class in assisting groups of which they are members. They have been able to recommend brainstorming at a time when the groups needed to generate ideas. They have been able to institute strategies to avoid groupthink and thus increase the quality of decision making. They have developed an agenda to use in solving group problems. Like them, if you have understood the principles discussed in this text, retained them, and been able to apply them to groups, you may be on your way to being able to function as an internal facilitator.

In most situations, however, more experience and training are necessary to ensure that effective facilitation occurs. Some of that comes from experience, such as serving as an assistant during focus group facilitation. In addition, further education may be necessary. In Ruth Hunt's case, a master's degree in organizational communication complemented her undergraduate majors in English and speech and, along with her extensive speaking experience, gave her the confidence to serve as a facilitator.

Additional education is particularly important because a facilitator should have a solid understanding of relevant theoretical frameworks that form the basis for facilitation techniques. For instance, in leading focus groups, a facilitator may want to make use of symbolic convergence theory to stimulate the discussion of fantasy themes that group members hold about the subject under discussion. Bormann, Bormann, and Harty (1995) described three different themes that originated in focus group discussions of tobacco use by adolescents. In those focus groups, the planned questions stimulated interactions that revealed three distinct themes, each describing the kind of person likely to use tobacco as a teen: "the adventuresome jock in control of his world," "bored and drifting middle school males," and "family-oriented teenagers testing limits and searching for ties" (pp. 210–220). The discussions provided information that could be useful to public health groups in devising anti–tobacco-use campaigns. Cragan and Shields (1995) describe the leader of a symbolic-convergence-theory–based focus group as a "pyromaniac" who will "throw out a lit match (a fantasy theme) and see if it catches fire in the group" (p. 236). Both to effectively manage a focus group so that it will generate fantasy themes and to later analyze the discussion in order to discover the themes, some training in symbolic convergence theory that goes beyond the bounds of this text is necessary. Similarly, Keyton's (1995) work with medical residents used a SYMLOG approach. SYMLOG is described briefly in Chapter 11 of this book, but to use it in facilitation would require familiarity with that tool beyond the scope of this text.

Effective facilitation also requires ongoing attention to the research available on small group communication. Researchers may uncover a pattern that assists effective group functioning. For instance, ongoing research on cohesiveness in teams or on computer-assisted decision making may provide useful insights that can be applied by a facilitator to groups seeking improvement. Research in a given area may lead to changes in the recommendations a facilitator might give to a group. Keeping attuned to the work of small group researchers is, therefore, a continuing means of preparing to facilitate effectively.

Summary

Beyond your work in this class, there are opportunities to develop and use your understanding of small group communication. Facilitation requires your understanding of small group concepts and their application to groups. Small groups seeking improved functioning, as well as focus groups formed to serve as sources of information, require the services of trained facilitators.

With further experience and training, you might be capable of providing the process orientation common to all forms of group facilitation. Effective facilitation requires preparation prior to a group meeting, careful attention to group behaviors during the meeting, and follow-through after the facilitation has occurred. When a facilitator works to improve the functioning of an ongoing group, he or she needs to be aware of the connections between facilitation and the diffusion of innovations. In that way, the facilitator can anticipate the stages groups will go through on their way to adopting recommended changes and the factors that encourage or interfere with adopting the newly recommended behaviors.

Groups have undoubtedly been a part of your life from its very beginning. They will continue to play a large role in your life—in work and out. You may choose to make your understanding of groups an even larger part of your life by engaging in small group facilitation. But even if you do not, you will be likely to belong to a group that invites a facilitator to assist it. Understanding the way professionals function as they facilitate small groups should increase your appreciation of the strengths and limits of their work. In the long run, that should improve your ability to use their suggestions wisely and well.

QUESTIONS FOR DISCUSSION

1. Under what conditions would you hire an external facilitator rather than asking an inside group member to facilitate the group?

2. When two facilitators are working together, how can they distribute their activities so that both can have a positive influence on the group?

3. How can a facilitator find an appropriate balance in the degree of change asked from group members so that it is small enough to be viewed as manageable change but not so small that it is viewed as inconsequential?

4. How can a facilitator identify opinion leaders whose support for change might be solicited?

5. What recommendations would you give in these situations?

    a. As you enter the room where a group is meeting, you observe one member sitting, facing the other members who are seated in a line. As the group discusses an upcoming task, the member facing others talks most of the time. Then the group begins to get to work, but this member insists on completing most of the work herself, insisting that the others wait to start their tasks until she is done with hers. What problem(s) do you see in this group? What recommendations would you give the group?

b. A classroom group is asked to accomplish small tasks periodically. You notice that one of the group members always sits at a distance from the rest of the group and never volunteers an answer unless called upon. The other members of the group initially made some effort to involve this group member, but now they seem to have given up on that. You have been asked to meet with all of the group members and advise them. What will you recommend?

c. A work team has recently experienced personnel changes. The individual who has been functioning as an informal leader of the group has been transferred to a different plant. No one else in the group seems to be filling the leadership void. What will you recommend?

d. A task group has been having problems recently. Although the group was formed of individuals who described each other as good friends, most of the members are getting annoyed with the others. At any given meeting, at least one group member is absent. Part of the meeting is taken up with discussion of the frustration with the missing member and a decision to get tough with absentees. However, at the next meeting, someone different is missing; nothing gets said to the returned member about previous absences, but a new discussion about the frustration with the new absentees takes place. What will you recommend to this group?

e. You have been asked to facilitate groups at a company that is adopting a team approach to work. You observe one newly formed team that includes two individuals who have been among the company's most competent workers. You notice that both of them continue to work hard, but they are working independently, rather than together with each other or with the rest of the team members. How will you assist this group?

SUGGESTED ACTIVITIES

1. Identify an organization that could benefit from the information gained from a focus group. For instance, in a community, the library might learn from a focus group of library patrons how their new book selections are perceived; a group of citizens in a focus group could provide the city council with information about needed services. On a campus, departments may benefit from the information focus groups could provide about their majors. Once you have identified a need for a focus group, prepare to lead one by developing a set of appropriate questions to generate a relevant discussion and describing the location where the focus group could be held.

2. Solicit suggestions from qualified others about your focus group plans. When you have improved your plans based on the suggestions you have received, lead a focus group. Write a report to the organization to reflect the findings of the focus group.

3. Observe groups interacting. Identify the strengths of the group on which you can build. Identify areas of potential problems for the group. Present your recommendations to the group. Write a written report with your recommendations.

4. Interview someone who is working as a small group facilitator. Discover how the person came to be prepared to be a facilitator. Discuss whether you have the potential to make a career of facilitating.

SOURCES CITED

Bormann, E. G., Bormann, E., & Harty, K. C. (1995). Using symbolic convergence theory and focus group interviews to develop communication designed to stop teenage use of tobacco. In L. R. Frey (Ed.), *Innovations in group facilitation: Applications in natural settings*, pp. 200–232. Cresskill, NJ: Hampton Press.

Broome, B. J. (1995). The role of facilitated group process in community-based planning and design: Promoting greater participation in Comanche tribal governance. In L. R. Frey (Ed.), *Innovations in group facilitation: Applications in natural settings* (pp. 27–52). Cresskill, NJ: Hampton Press.

Clawson, V. K., Bostrom, R. P., & Anson, R. (1993). The role of the facilitator in computer-supported meetings. *Small Group Research, 24,* 547–565.

Cragan, J. F., & Shields, D. C. (1995). Using SCT-based focus group interviews to do applied communication research. In L. R. Frey (Ed.), *Innovations in group facilitation: Applications in natural settings* (pp. 233–256). Cresskill, NJ: Hampton Press.

Frey, L. R., Ed. (1995a). *Innovations in group facilitation: Applications in natural settings.* Cresskill, NJ: Hampton Press.

Frey, L. R. (1995b). Introduction: Applied communication research on group facilitation in natural settings. In L. R. Frey (Ed.), *Innovations in group facilitation: Applications in natural settings* (pp. 1–23). Cresskill, NJ: Hampton Press.

Goldhaber, G. M. (1986). *Organizational communication* (4th ed.). Dubuque, IA: Wm. C. Brown.

Kaeter, M. (1995, July). Facilitators: More than meeting leaders. *Training, 32,* 60–64.

Keyton, J. (1995). Using SYMLOG as a self-analytical group facilitation technique. In L. R. Frey (Ed.), *Innovations in group facilitation: Applications in natural settings* (pp. 148–174). Cresskill, NJ: Hampton Press.

Kreps, G. L. (1995). Using focus group discussions to promote organizational reflexivity: Two applied communication field studies. In L. R. Frey (Ed.), *Innovations in group facilitation: Applications in natural settings* (pp. 177–199). Cresskill, NJ: Hampton Press.

Murphy, B. O. (1995). Promoting dialogue in culturally diverse workplace environments. In L. R. Frey (Ed.), *Innovations in group facilitation: Applications in natural settings* (pp. 77–93). Cresskill, NJ: Hampton Press.

Pearce, W. B. (1995). Bringing news of difference: Participation in systematic social constructionist communication. In L. R. Frey (Ed.), *Innovations in group facilitation: Applications in natural settings* (pp. 94–115). Cresskill, NJ: Hampton Press.

Rees, F. (1991). *How to lead work teams: Facilitation skills.* San Diego: Pfeiffer & Company.

Rogers, E. M. (1995). *Diffusion of innovations* (4th ed.). New York: The Free Press.

Rose, J. (1997, September 7). The customer is always right: More developers are acting on what focus groups say they want in new homes. *Detroit Free Press,* pp. 1J, 14J.

Stohl, C. (1995). Facilitating bona fide groups: Practice and paradox. In L. R. Frey (Ed.), *Innovations in group facilitation: Applications in natural settings* (pp. 325–332). Cresskill, NJ: Hampton Press.

Stokes, J. P. (1983). Components of group cohesion: Intermember attraction, instrumental value, and risk taking. *Small Group Behavior, 14,* 163–173.

Torres, C., & Fairbanks, D. M. (1996). *Teambuilding: The ASTD trainer's sourcebook.* New York: McGraw-Hill.

Zimmerman, A. L., & Evans, C. J. (1993). *Facilitation . . . From discussion to decision.* East Brunswick, NJ: Nichols Publishing.

11 Researching Small Group Communication

CHAPTER OBJECTIVES

After reading this chapter, you should be able to

- Discuss the connection between practice and research of small groups
- Describe the steps used in each of five research approaches: participant observation, case study, message systems analysis, survey research, and experimental research
- Read a journal article reporting on previous research, describe the process used in the research, and report the results
- Raise questions about the process of research used to reach the findings reported throughout this book
- Identify a topic related to small group communication that you would like to research
- Design and conduct a simple research study of small group communication
- Use some research tools to informally study your own group or another you observe

The Narrative

Since January of 1998, **John Gastil,** 30, has been on the communication faculty at the University of Washington. While doing graduate work at the University of Wisconsin–Madison, he studied communication within a food co-op to identify obstacles to practicing democracy in small groups. That research became the basis of a book and two journal articles. For three years after graduate school, John worked at the Institute for Public Policy at the University of New Mexico in Albuquerque. Here he talks about small group communication research:

> *My interest in small group communication research comes from my background. I'm a Quaker, and the Quaker religion emphasizes group decision making, with the idea that everyone has access to the same basic information about what's right and wrong and what we should and shouldn't do, but that no one single individual quite understands it all. If we put our heads*

together, it is hoped, we'll do a little bit better—especially if we require that an affirmative deci-sion will only be made when we all agree. That early schooling in the philosophy of consensus and, to a lesser extent, the actual practice of it, really got me fascinated with the whole idea of groups and our inability to realize our whole human potential as individuals. It may make sense to make a lot of important decisions in your life collectively.

In graduate school, I lived in a housing co-op for two years, which had a big impact on me. Making every decision about every aspect of the house together in a group every week really made me appreciate just how difficult it is to get things done in groups, but how wonderful it can be when you really develop a strong group identity and can feel like you're part of some-thing much larger than yourself.

In graduate school, my long-standing interest in politics got me interested in democracy, something I'd never really studied formally. In my personal experience, as a 23-year-old at that point, I had no real grasp of how those large-scale systems worked. They were a little intimi-dating. My personal experience told me, though, that there's a lot of democracy, or the lack thereof, in our daily lives in the small groups we find ourselves a part of. I thought that some-where there ought to be written out what exactly democracy is at the level of the small group. But no one had really done this. There were a couple of books that touched on it. I actually wrote to the authors of those two books, both political theorists. And they both wrote back saying, "Go for it, kid. No one's done it. I'm busy doing something else. It sounds like a great idea." I was really inspired by that. I hung on to those two letters and cherished them. I had found a gap in the political science literature and found it easy to justify its study in a communication program. Democracy in a small group is about the way people communicate with one another. If you want to make decisions democratically, you need to be able to express your point of view, try to per-suade each other, and reach a decision collectively.

In my research lately I've been taking a good long look at whatever the concept is that I'm interested in to see what it means. In the case of democratic leadership, that has meant reading all the different unsatisfying definitions, each of which seemed to be missing part of a coherent definition of democratic leadership. Such a situation can cause problems for researchers who may discover that they have two totally different things in mind, and consequently have two totally different operational definitions. If they had started with a richer original defini-tion, they might have known what they were both talking about when they used the same term.

To date, I haven't done any experimental research on small groups, but I have used a case study approach. One problem for a researcher using case studies is choosing the wrong group. Let's say you want to demonstrate the ways in which humor can affect people's willingness to participate in group discussion. Well, it's very labor intensive to videotape and transcribe group discussions. You'd better find yourself a funny group before you start the cameras rolling. Another problem with case studies is that it's very hard to generalize from one.

I chose to study the food co-op after looking at about eight groups around Madison. I needed repeated observations of a group during several meetings. Only two of those eight groups had meetings frequently enough that I could get a master's degree done in a reasonable time. Everybody else was meeting only once a month or once every two months. Besides that, the food co-op appeared at first glance to be probably the most democratic, and for my case study, I needed a democratic group. I watched one meeting, and then I said, "Look, you guys seem to be what I'm looking for. I'm looking for a group that's making decisions in a relatively democratic man-ner. And you seem to be such a group." That interested them. But you know what the real catch was? They were willing to give me time and their resources in exchange for my publicizing whatever it was I found, for better or for worse.

Once I gained access to the group, I videotaped the group's meetings and transcribed them. In addition, I would sit down with each of them individually for about an hour or an hour and a half and ask a series of questions. They also filled out a written questionnaire. Also, when I met with them, I had a five-minute video clip that they each watched. It was of one of the most intense, painful parts of one of the meetings they'd been in. They watched the clip, and then I asked them, "All right, what was going through your head? Why did you say what you did?" or "Why didn't you say anything?" or "What did you think about what so-and-so said?" What was neat about it was that I could really assemble all the different perspectives on that particular sequence. I think others studying small groups might consider using that device— showing the group its own interaction at a very salient point so that people will recognize and remember it, and asking them what was happening.

I also had a lot of informal conversations with the staff members at the co-op. I shopped there. So I'd see someone, and they'd say, "Ya know, I was thinking about something the other day . . . ," and they'd go out on the porch with me while my ice cream melted and tell me something. I'd write notes about it later. Sometimes after a meeting, someone would say, "Boy, that must have been fun to videotape. What did you think of . . . ," and they would just spontaneously say things. At first, I didn't understand how important it was to write down notes immediately after hearing something. So some of that just slipped out of my conscious mind. But the bottom line is that I was constantly around them and was picking up on some themes and concepts I might not have recognized if I'd been less involved in gathering the data.

I think that my research has allowed me to help groups function more democratically. My study of the food co-op allowed me to offer some practical advice to a housing group. They were very grateful. My research has helped me behave relatively democratically in the groups I'm in. I alter my behavior if I catch myself talking too much, asserting myself too much, or withdrawing from the group. My mother ran for U.S. Congress in 1992 and had me come in and manage her campaign for the last two months. I think my understanding of small group democracy and my observation of other groups helped me guide us down a path toward a more democratic way of making decisions. We turned out to be a very unusual campaign staff, without any of the infighting or jealousies that so often develop in campaigns. I sometimes saw those things developing and cut them off before they happened.

In the future, I will do some experimental research on small groups. The important point is to have an appreciation for each of the different types of research, the benefits of each, and how they might fit into a research program. You can use a variety of approaches at different stages in a research program, instead of becoming infatuated with a particular approach to research. It is more appropriate to determine a topic for research, first, than to begin with a research method. The choice of topic should come because you care about it. If you really care about life and other people's lives, it will become apparent to you that there is more than one thing to which you can devote a research career. Everyone has experiences in their lives that lead them to care about things that are amenable to the research process. If you care about how groups come to have an identity, it might be because you felt that your family never really cohered as a family, or because you've never been able to sustain friendships in groups. Maybe you really care about that. Then go ahead and study it. So that's my recommendation: just do a little soul-searching. You might find that you can talk to other people and ask them, "What is your impression about what I am obsessed with?" They'll say, "Well, you're obsessed with relationships and how people fall in and out of them." And you'll say to yourself, "Well, I guess I am." Then go for it; that's what you should study.

Small group researchers have a tough row to hoe, as they say, because our sample sizes are at least three times larger, out of necessity, than they are for someone studying the communication patterns of single individuals. And we are also interested in studying groups in naturalistic settings, ultimately, which requires finding groups of people that have been around for a while. We really have some data-collection obstacles. I don't think they're unsolvable problems. But it's something to face honestly as you enter the field of small group research.

You do not have to be a Quaker to have, like John Gastil, an interest in continuing your study of small groups by initiating a program of research on group communication. But perhaps you have no desire to formally research small groups. You still may want—or need—to observe groups in a careful, thorough manner. Or perhaps you hope to better understand how our current knowledge of small groups has developed. Whatever the case, it will be important to discover how research relates to practice and what approaches to research are used by those studying small group communication. This chapter provides an introduction to the subject of small group communication research.

The Research Cycle
and Its Connection to Practice

Research in small group communication, like research in other areas, usually begins after observations of events in the practice of small group interaction raise questions in the mind of a researcher. For instance, after Owen (1986) observed that women in his classes often took the role of leader in small groups in a manner different from that described by Bormann's theory of emergent leadership described in Chapter 3 of this text, he wondered whether the communication patterns used by the women explained their leadership role. Therefore, Owen asked this question, "What are the rhetorical themes used by females who emerge as leaders of small task groups?" (p. 477). Nearly a decade later, Hawkins (1995) attempted to answer two questions closely related to the one Owen had asked: "Does communication content predict emerged leadership?" (p. 238), and "Are there gender differences in communication content areas that predict emerged leadership?" (p. 239). Questions about small group behavior of all types arise as observations identify patterns of communication behavior that are not yet explained or that appear to contradict the explanations provided by earlier research and theory.

As research results accumulate, they—along with the actual practices of groups—become the objects of observation. For instance, John Gastil (1994) noticed that, despite a number of studies comparing autocratic and democratic leaders, the nature of the differences in their outcomes and the reasons for those differences were far from clear. Therefore, he did a **meta-analysis**, *an analysis of an analysis*, of democratic and autocratic leadership. He compared the research procedures and results of 37 different studies and analyzed previous attempts to analyze the two styles of leadership. He found little consistency in the earlier studies' definitions of democratic leadership. Also, he discovered that when democratic leadership had occurred naturally in a group, it had enhanced group productivity; studies that found otherwise often involved a researcher appointing one group member to play the role of a democratic leader. Research such as this illustrates a key point about the research cycle: first, casual observations lead to initial research questions; then, research is designed to answer the questions (and functions as more sophisticated observation), which leads in turn to more sophisticated research questions.

Although it may seem that more sophisticated research is far removed from the actual practice of small groups, that is not the case. For instance, John Gastil (1994) saw the finding that democratic leadership enhances productivity as a promising one for democratic activists around the world. And in the opening narrative, he mentioned that the understandings he gained of democracy in small groups have positively influenced his performance as a group member, group leader, and advisor of small groups.

There are other communication researchers who agree with the notion that research and practice should be intimately connected. Notable examples are Mara Adelman and Lawrence Frey who together have been active in studying the small group communication occurring within Bonaventure House, a residential facility for individuals suffering from AIDS, which is located in the Chicago area. Their efforts (cited in Frey, 1994b) to discover how such a fragile group can develop and maintain a sense of community have included an analysis of the group members' use of metaphors to depict life at the house. They also have identified five underlying *dialectical tensions* in the group interactions. A **dialectical tension** exists *when there are two goals, both desired by the group, but inherently contradictory, such that achieving one automatically involves* not *achieving the other.* The dialectical tensions Adelman and Frey identified in the group at Bonaventure House are the tensions between individual identity versus group identity, illness versus wellness, attachment versus detachment, private life versus public life, and residents' autonomy versus staff control.

In addition to benefiting the research community with increased understanding of communication within a community, their program of research has benefited the community they researched. By telling the story of the House from the perspective of its residents, the researchers have given a voice to a marginalized community. In addition, there are other very direct connections between research and practice in their program of research. One study they completed is used in training new staff and volunteers at Bonaventure House. Frey (1994b) mentions that Adelman helped to develop a videotape about the House that is used in fund-raising and public education efforts; profits from the sale of the videotape go into a fund for the residents to use as they wish. Results of the studies have been used by administrators to improve practices within the House and to advise those establishing similar communities in other locations. Grant monies obtained by the researchers have compensated Bonaventure House residents for serving as interviewees in the research (Frey, 1994b). Although the connections between research and practice are more extensive and direct in this program of research than in most, the example serves to illustrate how closely intertwined with practice research can become.

The commitment of some researchers, such as Adelman and Frey, to social action enhances the connection between research and practice in small group communication. But the very nature of the research cycle ensures that some connections will exist. When researchers uncover a pattern that assists effective group functioning, the finding can be useful to group members or outside facilitators who are trying to help a group function more effectively. When practice reveals that the results researchers predict do not occur, then practitioners raise questions that encourage further and better research. To understand how both research and practice can be performed most effectively, it is necessary to consider the approaches involved in small group research.

Approaches to Research

There is no single approach to the study of small group communication. You could probably have predicted that if you have noticed the descriptions of some of the research highlighted in earlier chapters of this text. A useful categorization of research approaches is found in *Human Communication Theory*, where Sarah Trenholm (1991) identified five general approaches, all of which could be used to study small group communication. Although these approaches are not discussed in great detail here, a general description of the approaches should allow you to gain a sense of how each differs from the others. As you read about each approach, you may discover that while each has its advantages, it also has some limitations. Therefore, it is not uncommon for an issue to be studied using more than one research approach. **Triangulation** is *the process of using multiple research approaches to study a single research problem.*

The five approaches can be arranged on a continuum according to their *qualitative* or *quantitative* orientation. Approaches that are more **qualitative** in their orientation *gather a depth of information about a smaller number of groups.* Those that are more **quantitative** in their orientation *gather information from a greater number of groups and group members, but typically sacrifice the depth of information gathered about each in exchange for the breadth of groups studied.*

Case Studies and Participant Observation

Two *qualitative* approaches are **case studies** and **participant observation.** John Gastil's discussion of his research at the food co-op provides a thorough description of the steps involved in case study research: gaining access to a group for study; observing the group, typically over time; and using multiple sources of information, such as interviews and questionnaires, to add to the observations. When Irving Janis developed his groupthink concept described in Chapter 5 of this text, he, too, used case studies as the source of his data. In his case, historical documents were a primary source of the data he collected.

Like a case study, participant observation involves gaining access to a group to study. But a researcher engaged in participant observation functions both as a member of the group being studied and as a researcher. Data are gathered about a wide range of group activities: who is communicating with whom and with what frequency, the content of the messages and nature of responses, the setting of the group, the structure of the group, etc. If John Gastil had studied the housing co-op where he lived, rather than the food co-op (at which he was only a shopper, not a worker), he would have been a participant observer. His task as a researcher would have been complicated by the need to describe objectively processes in which he, himself, was involved. In his case study, John found it difficult to take thorough notes on comments made to him in passing; that difficulty would have increased if he had been collecting data on a group's decision-making activities at the same time that he participated in making the decisions.

In both participant observation and case studies, a researcher studies only a small number of groups. That makes it difficult to assume that what we know about those groups holds true for all or most other groups. Therefore, a researcher using case studies or participant observation is limited in his or her ability to generalize about the findings of the research.

Analysis of Message Systems

Moving toward the *quantitative* end of the continuum is a group of research approaches that Trenholm (1991) called **message systems analysis.** Although the approaches she described are more typically referred to by researchers as *content analysis, interaction analysis, and conversational analysis,* it is useful to consider them as a group because there are strong similarities in the way each of them gathers and analyzes data. A good example of this type of research is Randy Hirokawa's program of research described in Chapter 6. In several studies, Hirokawa recorded the interactions of group members as they made decisions on tasks assigned to the groups. The taped interactions, from which transcripts could be made, served as the data for the study. The data were first divided into units of analysis. A **unit of analysis** is *the size (or chunk) of the message to be analyzed.* A researcher could count each turn taken by a group member as one unit, but it would also be possible to use a smaller unit (each sentence completed by a group member) or a larger one (each decision made by a group)—depending on what is being studied. However, a turn is a typical unit of analysis for small group research. The data were then analyzed by a team of **coders,** *individuals who classified each unit of analysis according to a scheme (or code) that has been adopted by the researcher for the particular study.* The coding scheme used in at least some of Hirokawa's research is included in the Appendix, which follows this chapter. You could use this scheme, or any of the others included in the Appendix, in some informal research on groups or (even more informally) to describe the behaviors of a group you are observing.

To ensure that the coders can make sound decisions in coding, they are trained by the researcher, practicing on messages similar to those they will be responsible for coding after they have been trained. It is also typical to have two coders working independently on the same task, as an added way to check the accuracy of the coding decisions. When coders disagree, they are sometimes asked to discuss their differences until they can reach agreement; sometimes the data on which they disagree is submitted to another party (perhaps the primary researcher) to make a judgment; sometimes the data about which there is disagreement are eliminated and not analyzed any further. In Hirokawa's research program, the coded data were analyzed to discover which behavior categories were used by groups that made effective decisions and not used by those that made ineffective decisions, and vice versa. In other research, the data could be analyzed statistically to quantify patterns discovered from the data. This research approach has been commonly used in the studies that have attempted to analyze stages in group formation based on the kinds of comments typically made in each step of the group development process.

Hirokawa and his research associates have themselves identified some problems with this approach to research (Gouran, Hirokawa, Julian, & Leatham, 1992). For instance, they mention that they ask coders to classify each unit of analysis within one specific coding category, but many communication behaviors accomplish more than one function. Also, they say, an independent observer classifying a behavior may not recognize how the statement was intended to function or even the predominant function actually achieved by a comment in the eyes of the actual group members. Such factors complicate a coding process and may even reach a point of limiting the validity of research. Moreover, early research using such a coding system undoubtedly encountered even more problems. Before technology developed to allow capturing interactions on videotape, interactions were often analyzed as they occurred. An early coding scheme, the *interaction process analysis* developed by Bales (1970), is included in the Appendix. To code an interaction as it is occurring requires that coding decisions be made quickly and accurately, with no opportunity to reconsider at a later time. A simple coding scheme is a necessity in such a condition.

Survey Research

Survey research is located at the *quantitative* end of the continuum. *Questionnaires distributed to larger numbers of groups and their members can be used to gather information on a wide range of topics,* ranging from members' perceptions of the group's cohesiveness to a description of their own level of collaborativeness. In the Appendix, you will find four of the measures of cohesiveness that have been used in small group research and also a scale that has been developed to measure a group member's decision-making collaborativeness. You can compare the questions asked to measure cohesiveness to see which seems to be a more useful measure to you. You might analyze the collaborativeness scale to identify what factors the researchers thought contributed to collaborativeness. When researchers make an effort to use a questionnaire to measure a particular variable, such as "collaborativeness," they attempt to test the validity of the questionnaire itself. That is one reason that, rather than inventing new questionnaires, researchers often reuse one that someone else has developed and tested.

In some research, one set of surveys can be compared to another set to see what relationships exist between the two. For instance, a researcher could use one set of questions to discover whether the group was cohesive and another to discover how it handled conflict; then, using statistical analysis, relationships could be discovered between levels of cohesiveness and strategies for conflict management. If you suspect that groups composed of members who are more collaborative will be more cohesive than those groups whose members are less collaborative, you could ask members of groups to respond to both questionnaires and compare the results.

One of the difficulties facing small group researchers is a difficulty in the statistical analysis of data gathered from individual group members. It is easiest to treat the data as if they were gathered from independent individuals, but group members are, by definition, interdependent. The scales on cohesiveness raise a relevant question: if cohesiveness is something that describes a group as a whole, can it really be measured by surveying group members individually?

A tool that has been used quite frequently to describe whole groups is SYMLOG (system for the multiple level observation of groups). The tool was developed by Bales and Cohen and is available in their 1979 book *SYMLOG: A System for the Multiple Level Observation of Groups*. It is a more sophisticated tool for the analysis of small groups than Bales' (1970) earlier interaction process analysis coding scheme. Group members or observers of groups answer a series of questions about the verbal and nonverbal behaviors of each group member. The answers to the questions lead to the placement of circles representing each member on a diagram such the one shown in Figure 11.1.

In the diagram, the circle the farthest to the left represents an individual who is perceived as more unfriendly than friendly. That person is also depicted as some-what task oriented, although less so than the person represented by the circle the farthest to the right. The size of the circle represents its position in a third dimension, dominance/submissiveness, with the largest circle representing the most dominant of the three and the smallest representing the least dominant. If the diagram in Figure 11.1 represented an actual group, it would be analyzed as a group in difficulty, for each of the members seems to occupy a very different space. Groups that are both cohesive and productive would be likely to be found clustered in the upper-right quadrant (Keyton, 1992). Krôger, Drinkmann, Herzog, and Petzold (1991) reported on the use of SYMLOG in studying family groups in which there was a member with an eating disorder. Members of those families were represented as occupying distinctly different spaces, and the members typically saw themselves and others within the family quite differently, one from another. Also, placement of family members in the SYMLOG space changed as dynamics within the family changed during the process of family therapy. The SYMLOG survey technique and the visual representation of its results have been used by both researchers and facilitators of small groups (Keyton, 1995).

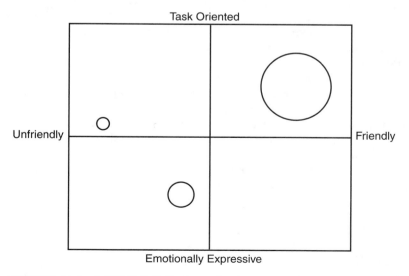

FIGURE 11.1 A SYMLOG diagram of a three-person group

Experimental Research

Experimental research differs from the other types of research in that it *involves an effort to discover relationships between two or more variables by* manipulating *at least one of the variables and* then observing and measuring *the effect on at least one different variable.* A **variable** is *something that varies,* such as the level of cohesiveness, the amount of talk, the quality of decisions, or the perception of leadership. Variables may exist in a causal relationship to one another. For instance, the level of cohesiveness in a group may cause the quality of decisions to be either better or worse; the amount of talk a person does may cause the person to be seen more (or less) as the leader of the group. The *variable that is thought to be the cause* is called the **independent variable;** the *one thought to be the effect, or the one to depend on the cause,* is called the **dependent variable.**

Researchers manipulate an independent variable by purposely altering the degree to which that factor exists within a group. Suppose, for instance, that a researcher wanted to discover whether increasing the amount of time a group member talked caused that person to be perceived as a group leader. The researcher could use **confederates,** *individuals who assist the researcher by playing the roles assigned to them as members of groups.* The confederates could be asked to speak at greater or lesser length, in whatever manner the researcher assigns them to participate. In some groups, the confederate member would speak frequently and at great length. In other groups, the confederate member would speak little. In this example, *amount of speaking* is the variable that is manipulated by the researcher. Then, after the group meetings had ended, all group members would be asked to evaluate the leadership in the group, perhaps by answering a questionnaire about the group members. The researcher pays particular attention to differences in perceptions about the confederate who spoke at length as opposed to the confederate who spoke little. Thus, in this example *perceived leadership* is the dependent variable, the variable that is observed and measured by the researcher.

In an effort to have the smallest number of unexpected factors affect their results, researchers typically perform experimental research in *laboratory* conditions. That is, rather than using groups that already exist and have been formed to achieve the goals of their members, researchers create ad hoc groups for the purpose of doing research. And, because a large portion of such research is done by faculty in departments of psychology, sociology, or communication at colleges and universities, a great number of the group members are college students enrolled in a class that requires them to participate as research subjects or that grants them extra credit for doing so. There may be many cases in which such groups operate in a manner very similar to a natural group, but that is not always the case. Therefore, you might anticipate that small group researchers have been criticized for the design of their research studies.

Criticisms of Small Group Research

The harshest critics of small group research have been the small group researchers themselves. They have identified three major problems: (1) too little study of groups formed for purposes other than those of the researchers, (2) a disproportionate emphasis on decision-making behaviors of groups, and (3) limited productivity.

The Nature of the Groups Studied

Although some researchers, such as John Gastil, have done case studies of real groups, many more researchers have created groups that they have studied in a more quantitative fashion. By increasing the number of groups studied, the researchers increase their opportunities to generalize from their data. However, there is the potential that a group manufactured for research purposes will bear little resemblance to groups that exist naturally. Frey (1995), whose own program of research is committed to the study of natural groups and who has actively supported such research by others, has identified the problems with research based on researcher-created groups of students:

> Students simply are not as invested in laboratory groups as those working and living in groups in the real world, where the consequences for success and failure are usually very high; the tasks groups are asked to perform in the laboratory hardly mirror the important tasks that real groups must solve; and groups meeting only once in a laboratory or in a classroom setting hardly develop the intricate relational bonds and a sense of shared history that characterize ongoing groups in the real world. (p. 14)

Consider, for instance, how much an ad hoc group created for research purposes and meeting for an hour or so can tell us about cohesiveness. Your own experiences in groups are likely to have convinced you that cohesiveness typically develops considerably later than one hour into the life of the group.

Studying actual, natural groups almost always increases the investment of time a researcher must make to complete the research. Consequently, it also almost always decreases the number of groups that can be examined in any study. Smaller sample sizes naturally limit the generalizations that can be made from the results. But it is also impossible to generalize about group processes after observing collections of individuals who do not actually resemble groups. It is no wonder that John Gastil closed his narrative by calling attention to the difficulty faced by small group researchers.

Ethical Considerations

College faculty and students doing research are generally required to submit their research plans to a committee that must approve their plans for the use of human subjects in their research. To understand why such review should be done, consider what might happen if researchers are trying to determine the impact of specific factors on a group's cohesiveness. What ethical responsibility does a researcher have if the research has negative effects on the cohesiveness of a natural group?

Emphasis on Decision-Making Behaviors

Spurred by an interest in the role of groups in a democratic society, early studies of small groups concentrated on their role in making decisions. Perhaps because researcher-created groups and natural groups are more alike in their decision making than they are in other dynamics, the study of decision making has continued to be the focus of much of the small group research. In fact, Frey searched the journals sponsored by the regional, national, and international communication associations and found that, of the small group research published between 1980 and 1988 in those journals, 80.8% of the studies focused on decision making in groups (cited in Frey, 1994a). This emphasis has been criticized, not because decision making is unimportant, but because the emphasis on this single task dimension of groups seems to have occurred at the expense of studying the relationship dimensions. Thus, Meyers and Brashers (1994) argue that studies of decision making should be balanced with the exploration of group survival mechanisms.

Productivity of Small Group Scholars

As Frey (1994a) reports, when he searched the communication journals from 1980 to 1988, he found that only 4.2% of the published research concerned small group communication. One of his explanations for the limits of the research was that small group research runs counter to the individualistic focus of our culture. More recently, he has noticed a sense of optimism among small group researchers that he attributes, in part, to an increased emphasis within the broader culture on teamwork and the empowerment of individuals within organizations. Others have suggested that there is no actual dearth of studies related to small group communication. By looking under several other "umbrella" terms, we could discover research related to groups in specific contexts, such as families or juries (Propp & Kreps, 1994).

Although Frey examined journals sponsored by communication associations, it would be a significant omission to overlook journals in which researchers from a variety of fields, including communication, publish group research. The key publication of that type is the international, interdisciplinary journal, *Small Group Research* (formerly called *Small Group Behavior*). It is an outlet for a significant amount of research on groups, including much that has been referred to throughout this text.

Of course, it is true that as the body of research in a given area is spread out among a variety of types of publication outlets, it becomes ever more difficult to engage in building theory about small groups. Theory building requires the integration of a body of previous research in order to identify research questions to be answered and hypotheses to be tested in future research. When parts of the puzzle are overlooked because they have not been found by a researcher, the task of developing theory is made more difficult.

An Agenda for Small Group Research

A priority on the agenda for future small group research is overcoming the problems observed in previous research: natural groups should be studied; relationship dimensions within groups should be analyzed; and research should continue in a manner that allows theory development. Several additional suggestions for the future of small group research were made throughout the spring 1994 issue of *Communication Studies.*

Keyton (1994) recommended the study of children's groups as a new direction for small group researchers. Her argument was based on observations that children are frequently placed in groups by others who may not understand group processes well, but children also choose to join a range of group activities, where their experiences are not always positive. As a virtually untapped source of research, then, children's groups are plentiful in number and provide opportunities to discover the nature of group influences on children as well as issues relevant to group members of all ages—such as the impact of individuals on the group and the nature of both environmental inhibitors and facilitators of group processes. Certainly there are other types of groups that are plentiful but as of yet have been given little attention by previous research programs. Some that come to mind are small musical ensembles that face the challenge of balancing a commitment to excellence with a commitment to each other; such semiformal groups as book clubs that blend task and learning purposes with a desire for social connection; and learning groups that are formed for students by teachers from elementary school to college or medical school. Research of such groups may require a more qualitative, case study approach, than a quantitative, experimental approach, but it would satisfy Frey's call for continued research of naturalistic groups (Frey, 1994b). He has argued that qualitative research succeeds in giving a voice to the members of groups and allows a partnership to develop between the researcher and the group members being studied.

An emphasis on the connection between organizational practices and communication research interests has been recommended by Barge (1994). His challenge to future researchers is to explore the areas in which the interests of the two fields converge. He has identified four such areas: concerns of language, the articulation of a common vision within groups; democracy, issues of shared power and influence; loyalty, maintaining cohesion within groups that operate in the face of changing structures; and learning, application of principles to practice.

Meyers and Brashers (1994) argue that new understandings of group processes could develop from a theoretical shift in research. Specifically, they recommend adopting a feminist perspective in small group research as a means of shifting the focus from issues of influence and competition to issues of connection and cooperation. They even describe a case in which shifting the theoretical lens drew attention to data previously unexamined by one of them. In a previous study on group argument, Meyers—working with Siebold—had noticed the use of narratives as argument. She found it to be an interesting, but not particularly significant, event. When she later reexamined the data, she realized that it was the women in groups who were likely to frame their arguments as stories; their strategy allowed the other group members to connect to the reasoning process as the argument developed, thereby achieving influence through connection, not at the expense of connection. It is the claim of Meyers and Brashers that accepting the legitimacy of a feminist perspective in small group research would enable researchers to see gender diversity as a resource for small groups rather than as a threat.

Certainly the field of small group communication research is one in which there is space for additional researchers interested in a wide range of issues. In an effort to increase communication between researchers, Marshall Scott Poole of Texas A & M University has developed a web page for those interested in small group communication to share information about grant opportunities, recent publications, and conferences relevant to the field. Its address is *http://scom.tamu.edu/group/group.html*. After being in existence for a few years, the site contains requests for individuals to report information about themselves and information they have gathered, but there is considerable room for the responses to those requests to grow. If individuals use that resource, the site could help to overcome the forces that hinder theory building in the area of small group communication by drawing together a community of scholars.

Summary

Beyond your work in this class, there are opportunities to develop your understanding of small group communication. Informal observation of groups requires your understanding of small group concepts; more formal research builds on that understanding and allows it to increase by generating new knowledge.

A variety of types of research can be done on small groups, ranging from participant observation and case studies to message systems analysis, survey, and experimental research. Because each type of research has both advantages and limitations, it is often desirable to study the same concept using varied research approaches (or to triangulate the research).

Knowing how research is done will give you greater understanding of the results of previous research that have been reported throughout this book. There is clearly more work to be done in the field of small group communication research, especially studying natural groups engaged not just in decision-making activities but in any of the many areas that affect the life of a group. You are invited to join in the process of extending the knowledge about small group communication.

Groups have undoubtedly been a part of your life from its very beginning. They will continue to play a large role in your life—in and out of work. You may choose to make your understanding of groups an even larger part of your life by engaging in small group research. But even if you do not, your life is likely to be influenced by findings of small group researchers, for their discoveries find their way into literature read by the general public, including people with whom you may end up working. Understanding the way professionals function as they research small groups should increase your appreciation of the strengths and limits of their work. In the long run, that should improve your ability to use their findings wisely and well.

QUESTIONS FOR DISCUSSION

1. What areas in small group communication seem to you to be worth researching further?

2. John Gastil recommended that rather than being committed to a particular research approach, you should select the approach best suited to the topic you want to discover. How can the appropriate research approach be selected?

3. Which of the measures of cohesiveness seems to you to be the most useful? Why?

SUGGESTED ACTIVITIES

1. Read a recent report of research that is published in a communication journal or in *Small Group Research*. Report to your class on the study.

2. Use one or more of the research tools that are found in the Appendix to analyze your own group in class or another that you observe.

3. Identify an area of interest to you, either independently or as a group. Determine the research approach you think would be best suited to studying that topic. Describe the steps that would be necessary to complete the study. Obtain whatever permission you need to protect the rights of anyone you would be observing in your study. Follow the steps you have decided to use, and then summarize your findings.

SOURCES CITED

Bales, R. F., & Cohen, S. P. (1979). *SYMLOG: A system for the multiple level observation of groups.* New York: The Free Press.

Barge, J. K. (1994). On interlinking language games: New opportunities for group communication research. *Communication Studies, 45,* 52–67.

Frey, L. R. (1994a). Introduction: Revitalizing the study of small group communication. *Communication Studies, 45,* 1–6.

Frey, L. R. (1994b). The naturalistic paradigm: Studying small groups in the postmodern era. *Small Group Research, 25,* 551–577.

Frey, L. R. (1995). Introduction: Applied communication research on group facilitation in natural settings. In L. R. Frey (Ed.), *Innovations in group facilitation: Applications in natural settings* (pp. 1–23). Cresskill, NJ: Hampton Press.

Gastil, J. (1994). A meta-analytic review of the productivity and satisfaction of democratic and autocratic leadership. *Small Group Research, 25,* 384–410.

Gouran, D. S., Hirokawa, R. Y., Julian, K. M., & Leatham, G. B. (1992). The evolution and current status of the functional perspective on communication in decision-making and problem-solving groups. *Communication Yearbook, 16,* 573–600.

Hawkins, K. W. (1995). Effects of gender and communication content on leadership emergence in small task-oriented groups. *Small Group Research, 26,* 234–249.

Keyton, J. (1992). Comment on Evans and Dion: Still more on group cohesion. *Small Group Research, 23,* 237–241.

Keyton, J. (1994). Going forward in group communication research may mean going back: Studying the groups of children. *Communication Studies, 45,* 40–51.

Keyton, J. (1995). Using SYMLOG as a self-analytical group facilitation technique. In L. R. Frey (Ed.), *Innovations in group facilitation: Applications in natural settings* (pp. 148–174). Cresskill, NJ: Hampton Press.

Krôger, F., Drinkmann, A., Herzog, W., & Petzold, E. (1991). Family diagnostics: Object representation in families with eating disorders. *Small Group Research, 22,* 99–114.

Meyers, R. A., & Brashers, D. E. (1994). Expanding the boundaries of small groups communication research: Exploring a feminist perspective. *Communication Studies, 45,* 68–85.

Owen, W. F. (1986). Rhetorical themes of emergent female leaders. *Small Group Behavior, 17,* 475–486.

Propp, K. M., & Kreps, G. L. (1994). A rose by any other name: The vitality of group communication research. *Communication Studies, 45,* 7–19.

Trenholm, S. (1991). *Human communication theory* (2nd ed.). Englewood Cliffs, NJ: Prentice-Hall.

APPENDIX

When researchers analyze small groups, they often use surveys or other research tools that have been developed and tested, sometimes over the course of years. This appendix includes seven such tools that have been used in programs of small group research. You might use any of the tools in informal observation of a group to which you belong, in a project involving research on small groups, or simply to better your understanding of the research reported in this text that has used these tools.

Function-Oriented Interaction Analysis System

From Hirokawa, R. Y. (1982). Group communication and problem-solving effectiveness I: A critical review of inconsistent findings. *Communication Quarterly, 30,* 134–141.

Trained coders categorized units from a taped 30-minute problem-solving group discussion. The unit of analysis was "functional utterance." If the message of a single speaker appeared to shift to a different function or if the speaker was interrupted by another, the utterance was deemed to have come to an end. The categories into which the message was coded involved two levels. The first level is the task function. The first of three digits in the code assigned to each utterance designated which of the four task functions it served. The second level in the coding was the utterance type. The second and third digits in the code designated the message as one of 12 types of utterance. The coding scheme is reproduced here, along with a brief segment of coded interaction to illustrate the nature of the coding scheme (p. 139).

1 Establish Operating Procedures
01 Introduction
02 Restatement
03 Development
04 Substantiation
05 Modification
06 Agreement
07 Disagreement
08 Summarization/synthesis
09 Asks for ideas
10 Asks for approval
11 Asks for clarification
12 Asks for summary/synthesis

2 Analysis of Problem
01 Introduction
02 Restatement
03 Development
04 Substantiation
05 Modification
06 Agreement
07 Disagreement
08 Summarization/synthesis
09 Asks for ideas
10 Asks for approval
11 Asks for clarification
12 Asks for summary/synthesis

3 Generation of Solutions
01 Introduction
02 Restatement

4 Evaluation of Solutions
01 Introduction
02 Restatement

03 Development	03 Development
04 Substantiation	04 Substantiation
05 Modification	05 Modification
06 Agreement	06 Agreement
07 Disagreement	07 Disagreement
08 Summarization/synthesis	08 Summarization/synthesis
09 Asks for ideas	09 Asks for ideas
10 Asks for approval	10 Asks for approval
11 Asks for clarification	11 Asks for clarification
12 Asks for summary/synthesis	12 Asks for summary/synthesis

Ron: OK, does everyone know what the problem is?   211

Group: Yeah . . . Yeah . . .   No code

Jack: I think they should, you know, like put those speed bumps on the road.   301

Dave: Yeah . . . that's a thought . . .   306

Ron: Yeah, but wouldn't that kinda' wreck the cars? I mean . . .   409

Jan: Yeah, I think they would really, you know, wreck the bottoms of the cars, the shocks and stuff like that . . .   401

Bales' Interaction Process Analysis

From Bales, R. F. (1970). *Personality and interpersonal behavior.* New York: Holt, Rinehart and Winston.

Bales' interaction process analysis (IPA) was designed to code "acts," defined as "a communication or an indication, either verbal or nonverbal, which in its context may be understood by another member as equivalent to a single simple sentence" (p. 68). Bales acknowledged that determining what is or is not a single act was highly dependent on the interpretation of the observer. To record the patterns of interaction within a group, an observer gives each group member a number and identifies the initiator and intended recipient of each act. Thus, the code 2-1 would indicate that the second group member had addressed a comment to the first group member. 0 is used to represent the group as a whole, so a comment made by the second group member, but addressed to the whole group, would be coded as 2-0; if the group as a whole responded, perhaps with laughter to the comment, that would be coded as 0-2. Bales explained that the coding scheme did not reflect much of the content of messages—just their role in the interaction. Thus, when an observer notes a 3-1 in the column for "disagrees," the record shows only that group member three disagreed with something group member one said; it does not reveal what the disagreement was or with what suggestion there was disagreement. Coders would use a chart on which the categories of interaction were reproduced, with space provided for indicating the group members performing the acts. Bales suggested a lot of practice with using the scoring sheets so that coders could find the appropriate spot quickly while still attending to the discussion. Videotaping capabilities (and the ability to pause and review) have

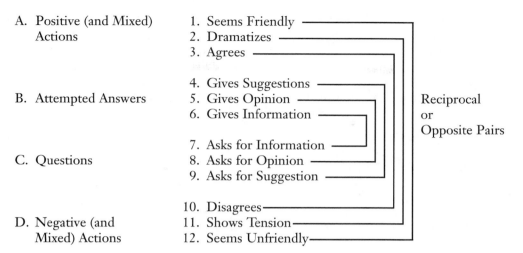

FIGURE A.1   Coding Scheme for Bales' interaction process analysis.

made the work of a coder less frantic—as long as the whole interaction is caught on camera. The categories in the coding scheme are found in Figure A.1, along with the labels and groupings that Bales used to show the relationships between categories (from p. 92).

Various Measures of Cohesiveness

As research has continued to consider the concept of cohesiveness, measurements of the concept have evolved. Some measures of cohesiveness consider only attraction to the other group members; others consider only attraction to the group task; while still others include both dimensions. Some measures assume that cohesiveness is connected to other behaviors, including the ability to express feelings openly, even when they might make others uncomfortable. Most of the measures of cohesiveness survey group members, asking them to fill out a Likert-type scale (one in which respondents read a question and then select one of five options from "strongly agree" to "strongly disagree," or a similar range of choices). Four different cohesiveness measures are provided so that you can see the differences among them.

Measures of Cohesiveness Used in a Study of Units in the Danish Military

From Langfred, C. W. (1998). Is group cohesiveness a double-edged sword? An investigation of the effects of cohesiveness on performance. *Small Group Research, 29,* 124–43. (p. 140) Reprinted by Permission of Sage Publications, Inc.

1. To what extent are other squad members prepared to give advice or help you with your own task?
2. How much do you need to rely on other group members to be able to complete your task?

3. To what degree can you rely or count on your fellow squad members to help you and support you if you are having difficulties?
4. To what extent do you agree with the following statement: "My fellow squad members don't help me when I have a problem"?
5. How willing would you be to switch to another squad?
6. How often does the squad do things together (like going to town) when off duty?

Adapted Gross Cohesion Questionnaire

From Stokes, J. P. (1983). Components of group cohesion: Intermember attraction, instrumental value, and risk taking. *Small Group Behavior, 14,* 163–173. (p. 167) Reprinted by Permission of Sage Publications, Inc.

1. How many of your group members fit what you feel to be the ideal of a good group member?
2. To what degree do you feel that you are included by the group in the group's activities?
3. How attractive do you find the activities in which you participate as a member of your group?
4. If most of the members of your group decided to dissolve the group by leaving, would you try to dissuade them?
5. If you were asked to participate in another project like this one, would you like to be with the same people who are in your present group?
6. How well do you like the group you are in?
7. How often do you think your group should meet?
8. I feel that working with the particular group will enable me to attain my personal goals for which I sought the group.
9. Compared to other groups like yours, how well would you imagine your group works together?

Three Factor Group Questionnaire

From Stokes, J. P. (1983). Components of group cohesion: Intermember attraction, instrumental value, and risk taking. *Small Group Behavior, 14,* 163–173. Reprinted by Permission of Sage Publications, Inc.

Risk Taking

There are certain topics which the group avoids talking about.

The group is honest and straight-forward with me.

Most people in this group are careful not to reveal too much of themselves to the group.

The group avoids saying anything which might upset someone.

Attraction to Group Members

Most of the people in the group are not the kind of people I would enjoy spending time with outside the group session.

If I were to participate in another group like this one, I would want it to include people who are very similar to the ones in this group.

There are not many people I like as individuals in this group.

Even if we stopped meeting as a group, I would still want to see the people in this group as often as I could.

I wish I had more time for socializing with other group members.

Instrumental Value

I haven't learned very much from participating in this group.

The group has influenced me in a lot of positive ways.

I don't think this group has been very helpful to me.

The group has helped me to meet the personal goals I had in mind when I joined it.

Measure of Group Cohesive Behavior

From Klein, S. M. (1996). Work pressure as a determinant of work group behavior. *Small Group Research*, 27, 299–315. Reprinted by Permission of Sage Publications, Inc.

How many people in your department do the following?

1. Stick up for each other on the job.
2. Are friendly toward each other.
3. Help each other out on the job.
4. Try to work faster than each other.

and

5. How well do your department members work together?
6. How much do you look forward to working with others in your department?

The Decision-Making Collaborativeness Scale

From Anderson, C. M., Martin, M. M., & Infante, D. A. (1999). Decision-making collaboration scale: Tests of validity. *Communication Research Reports*, 15, (245–255).

This survey is used by group members to describe themselves. It might be interesting to see whether another person using the scale to describe a group member would arrive at a description similar to the member's self-description. When you examine the specific questions asked by this survey, you will see that it is related to measures of argumentativeness and willingness to communicate.

These statements are about your communication behavior in general when it comes to decision making situations that involve others. Circle the number that best describes how true each of the statements is for you personally.

Almost always true = 5
Often true = 4
Occasionally true = 3
Rarely true = 2
Almost never true = 1

1. When others tell me I should do something, I insist on knowing why	5	4	3	2	1
2. I bargain with others when I think it's needed	5	4	3	2	1
3. When there are terms I don't understand, usually I won't bother to ask what they mean	5	4	3	2	1
4. Often I do not argue my point of view when conflicting views exist	5	4	3	2	1
5. I take charge when decisions have to be made	5	4	3	2	1
6. Often I do not explore alternative solutions	5	4	3	2	1
7. I enjoy participating in decision making	5	4	3	2	1
8. I tend to avoid offering suggestions for options	5	4	3	2	1
9. Most of the time I initiate suggestions	5	4	3	2	1
10. I do not ask about alternative solutions	5	4	3	2	1
11. Usually I speak frankly about how I feel	5	4	3	2	1
12. If I do not understand all the options, I keep quiet	5	4	3	2	1
13. I look others in the eyes when I disagree	5	4	3	2	1

Note: Reverse scoring for 3, 4, 6, 8, 10, and 12.

INDEX